"Project Censored's list of the top stories that get very little mainstream media traction should in fact drive the reporting agendas of every major news outlet. These 25 stories are clearly the most consequential of the year, and what is scary in looking at the list is how obvious it is that silencing reports of these themes protects corrupt governments and corporate gatekeepers. Project Censored is a lifeline to the world's most urgent and significant stories." —Naomi Wolf, bestselling author of the bestselling books *The Beauty Myth*; *The End of America*; and *Give Me Liberty*

"The systematic exposure of censored stories by Project Censored has been an important contribution." —Howard Zinn, author of *A People's History of the United States*

"Project Censored . . . has evolved into a deep, wide, and utterly engrossing exercise to unmask censorship, self-censorship, and propaganda in the mass media." —Ralph Nader, consumer advocate, lawyer, author

"[Project Censored] is a clarion call for truth telling."—Daniel Ellsberg, *The Pentagon Papers*

"[Project Censored] shows how the American public has been bamboozled, snookered, and dumbed down by the corporate media. It is chock-full of 'ah-ha' moments where we understand just how we've been fleeced by banksters, stripped of our civil liberties, and blindly led down a path of never-ending war." —Medea Benjamin, author of *Drone Warfare*, and cofounder of Global Exchange and CODEPINK

"Project Censored . . . not only shines a penetrating light on the American Empire and all its deadly, destructive, and deceitful actions, it does so at a time when the Obama administration is mounting a fierce effort to silence truth-tellers and whistleblowers. Project Censored provides the kind of fearless and honest journalism we so desperately need in these dangerous times."—Peter Kuznick, professor of history, American University, and coauthor, with Oliver Stone, of *The Untold History of the United States*

"The world needs more brave whistleblowers and independent journalists in the service of reclaiming democracy and challenging the abuse of power. Project Censored stands out for its commitment to such work." —Deepa Kumar, author of *Islamophobia and the Politics of Empire* and associate professor of media studies at Rutgers University

"Project Censored brings to light some of the most important stories of the year that you never saw or heard about. This is your chance to find out what got buried." —Diane Ravitch, author of *The Death and Life of the Great American School System*

"Most journalists in the United States believe the press here is free. That grand illusion only helps obscure the fact that, by and large, the US corporate press does not report what's really going on, while tuning out, or laughing off, all those who try to do just that. Americans—now more than ever—need those outlets that do labor to report some truth. Project Censored is not just among the bravest, smartest, and most rigorous of those outlets, but the only one that's wholly focused on those stories that the corporate press ignores, downplays, and/or distorts." —Mark Crispin Miller, author, professor of media ecology, New York University

"At a time when the need for independent journalism and for media outlets unaffiliated with and untainted by the government and corporate sponsors is greater than ever . . . we are fortunate to have an ally like Project Censored."—Dahr Jamail, independent journalist

"Those who read Project Censored are in the know." —Cynthia McKinney, former member of the US House of Representatives

"[Project Censored's] efforts to continue globalizing their reporting network could not be more timely or necessary."—Kristina Borjesson, award-winning freelance journalist

"Project Censored continues to do the work they've been persistently pursuing since 1976: Exposing the secrets that those in power would prefer to keep hidden and the corruption that should be scandalous, but isn't, cause the corporate media won't cover it." —David Rovics, musician and activist

"Project Censored is one of the organizations that we should listen to, to be assured that our newspapers and our broadcasting outlets are practicing thorough and ethical journalism."—Walter Cronkite, anchor, *CBS Evening News*, 1962-1981

"One of the most significant media research projects in the country." —I. F. Stone, American muckraker

"A terrific resource, especially for its directory of alternative media and organizations . . . Recommended for media collections." —*Library Journal*

"This book is evidence of Project Censored's profoundly important work in education readers on current events and the skills needed to be a critical thinker." —*Publishers Weekly*, on *Censored 2014*

"A distant early warning system for society's problems." —*American Journalism Review*

CENSORED 2016
MEDIA FREEDOM ON THE LINE

The Top Censored Stories and Media Analysis of 2014–15

Mickey Huff and Andy Lee Roth
with Project Censored

Foreword by
Nicholas Johnson
Cartoons by
Khalil Bendib

Seven Stories Press
New York • Oakland

Seven Stories Press
140 Watts Street
New York, NY 10013
www.sevenstories.com

ISBN 978-1-60980-645-3 (paperback)

ISBN 978-1-60980-646-0 (electronic)

ISSN 1074-5998

9 8 7 6 5 4 3 2 1

Book design by Jon Gilbert

Printed in the USA

Carl Jensen
Founder of Project Censored, 1976
(1929–2015)

A self-described "optimist by birth" and a tireless champion
for the bonds between freedom of expression and democracy,
Carl Jensen promoted critical media literacy and the training
of ethical journalists as ways to cultivate "more muckrakers
and fewer buckrakers." He taught investigative journalism
as a way to solve social problems and improve people's lives.

Contents

FOREWORD: Censorship: Its Causes and Cures by Nicholas Johnson 11

INTRODUCTION: by Mickey Huff and Andy Lee Roth 21

CHAPTER 1: The Top *Censored* Stories and Media Analysis of 2014–15
Compiled and edited by Andy Lee Roth 33
  Introduction 33
  Note on Research and Evaluation of *Censored* News Stories 37
  1. Half of Global Wealth Owned by the 1 Percent 39
  2. Oil Industry Illegally Dumps Fracking Wastewater 42
  3. 89 Percent of Pakistani Drone Victims Not Identifiable
     as Militants 45
  4. Popular Resistance to Corporate Water Grabbing 48
  5. Fukushima Nuclear Disaster Deepens 52
  6. Methane and Arctic Warming's Global Impacts 54
  7. Fear of Government Spying is "Chilling" Writers' Freedom
     of Expression 57
  8. Who Dies at the Hands of US Police—and How Often 58
  9. Millions in Poverty Get Less Media Coverage than
     Billionaires Do 61
  10. Costa Rica Setting the Standard on Renewable Energy 62
  11. Pesticide Manufacturers Spend Millions on PR Response
      to Declining Bee Populations 64
  12. Seeds of Doubt: USDA Ignores Popular Critiques of New
      Pesticide-Resistant Genetically Modified Crops 66
  13. Pentagon and NATO Encircle Russia and China 68
  14. Global Forced Displacement Tops Fifty Million 69
  15. Big Sugar Borrowing Tactics from Big Tobacco 71
  16. US Military Sexual Assault of Colombian Children 73
  17. Media "Whitewash" Senate's CIA Torture Report 75
  18. ICREACH: The NSA's Secret Search Engine 78
  19. "Most Comprehensive" Assessment Yet Warns against
      Geoengineering Risks 80
  20. FBI Seeks Backdoors in New Communications Technology 81
  21. The New Amazon of the North: Canadian Deforestation 83
  22. Global Killing of Environmentalists Rises Drastically 84
  23. Unprocessed Rape Kits 85
  24. NSA's AURORAGOLD Program Hacks Cell Phones
      around World 87
  25. Greenland's Meltwater Contributes to Rising Sea Levels 88

CHAPTER 2: Déjà Vu: What Happened to Previous *Censored* Stories?
by Susan Rahman, with research and writing from College of Marin
students Nathan Bowman, Isabelle Elias, Kayla Johnson, Katie Kolb, Nik
Kretzschmar, Quintton McCahey, Quiyarra McCahey, Caitlin McCoy, Miya
McHugh, Carl Nestler, Brande Neyhard, Molly Owens, Elizabeth Ramirez,
David Rodas, Karina Rodriguez, Ana Sanderson-Burglin, Joe Suzuki, and
Christian Vicente; with further research assistance by Diablo Valley College
students Darian Edelman and Ellie Kim.. 101

CHAPTER 3: A Vast Wasteland: The Ongoing Reign of Junk Food News
and News Abuse
by Nolan Higdon, Mickey Huff, and Ellie Kim, with contributions
by Brad Barna, Crystal Bedford, Emma Durkin, Darian Edelman,
Ariana Flotroy, Janet Hernandez, Daniel Park, Olivia Phillips, Rebecca
Rodriguez, Edwin Sevilla, Jaideep Singh, Jack Elliott Smith, Hajin
Lily Yi, and Mark Yolango.. 129

CHAPTER 4: Media Democracy in Action
compiled by Andy Lee Roth and Mickey Huff, with contributions
by Steven Wishnia (Dissent NewsWire), Alexander Reid Ross
(Earth First! Newswire), and Sue Udry (Defending Dissent Foundation);
Beatrice Edwards (Government Accountability Project); Adam Jonas
Horowitz (*Nuclear Savage*); Ian Thomas Ash (*A2-B-C*); Arlene Engelhardt
and Mary Glenney (*From a Woman's Point of View*); Crystal Bedford,
Lisa Davis, Darian Edelman, Lauren Freeman, and Ellie Kim (Project
Censored student interns); and Jyarland Daniels, and Rebekah Spicuglia
(Race Forward/*Colorlines*) 169

CHAPTER 5: A Vision for Transformative Civic Engagement:
The Global Critical Media Literacy Project
by Julie Frechette, Nolan Higdon, and Rob Williams................................. 199

CHAPTER 6: Modern Herlands: The Significance of Gilman's *Herland* for the
Next 100 Years
by Sheila Katz... 217

CHAPTER 7: "Dark Alliance": The Controversy and the Legacy, Twenty Years On
by Brian Covert... 227

CHAPTER 8: Twenty-First-Century Fascism: Private Military Companies in
Service to the Transnational Capitalist Class
by Peter Phillips, Ray McClintock, Melissa Carneiro, and Jacob Crabtree.. 255

CHAPTER 9: Existence Is Resistance: Women in Occupied
Palestine and Kashmir
by Tara Dorabji and Susan Rahman 277

CHAPTER 10: The Contours of Long-Term Systemic Crisis and the Need for Systemic Solutions
by Gar Alperovitz, James Gustave Speth, and Joe Guinan 301

Acknowledgments 317

Report from the Media Freedom Foundation President
by Peter Phillips 325

How to Support Project Censored 330

About the Editors 331

About the Cover Art 332

Index 333

Censorship
Its Causes and Cures

Nicholas Johnson

I had basic goals in mind and I haven't changed those goals and they're still not achieved. And they are, number one, to encourage professional journalists and editors to do more investigative journalism. . . . And the other goal was to get the information out about these [Project Censored-designated "censored stories"] to the general public so they are aware of them and can start looking for more information themselves.

—Carl Jensen (1989)[1]

This volume marks a landmark year for Project Censored—both the fortieth anniversary of its founding in 1976, and the first year without its founder, Carl Jensen,[2] to whom this foreword is dedicated.

Project Censored's annual story review process has been designed so that its evaluators select what they believe to be the best examples of stories of great significance that received little or no coverage by corporate media. These stories are subsequently highlighted in the Project's annual book, with this volume covering the most significant but underreported stories of 2014 and 2015.

Of course, those who nominate stories for Project Censored's consideration have learned of them somehow. Thus, the stories were not "censored" in the sense of being absolutely unavailable to all Americans.[3] Most often, they first appeared in print and in online publications of lesser circulation. Since the rise of the Internet, their "circulation" and impact may have been substantially enhanced by personal text messages, e-mails, website, blogs, YouTube videos, and Facebook, Twitter, and similar social media causing them to "go viral"—all of which makes their absence from corporate media the more remarkable.

Indeed, with the assistance of Google and other specialized searching tools, any skilled, serious journalist or researcher *who knows what she is looking for* has access to orders of magnitude more sources than were available forty years ago.[4]

Nonetheless, when it comes to media, most Americans, most of the time, are not doing research. To the extent they seek out "news" at all, they are still getting most of their information, and misinformation, from the remnants of ABC, CBS, Fox, and NBC, plus the twenty-four-hour news channels and local newspapers. And the bulk of what the cable channels bring into our homes is not even that close to journalism. As Barbara Kingsolver describes it, "The image that strikes me . . . is that of a faucet into the house that runs about 5 percent clear water and 95 percent raw sewage."[5]

MISSION: STORIES OR INFORMED CITIZENS?

At such times, it's often worthwhile to step back and ask ourselves, "What is it we're really trying to accomplish? How would we know if we'd ever been 'successful'?"

Is Project Censored's mission limited to the individual stories that lacked more general coverage? Or is the fundamental purpose or goal to enhance an informed and motivated population's participation in a vibrant, democratic, self-governing society? If the latter, then one of our first fundamental problems and challenges may be represented by the apocryphal story of the community pollster who asked a sampling of citizens, "What is the worst problem in our city, ignorance or apathy?" The plurality answer? "I don't know and I don't care."

Which is only to say that there are undoubtedly many related factors and forces that contribute to what we are calling "censorship" in a contemporary US context. Here are six examples:

Audience Lack of Education, Time, and Interest

Apparently the most circulation that a single national newspaper can hope for—print and online combined—is about 2.3 million (the

Sunday *New York Times* and the daily *Wall Street Journal*).[6]

Not too shabby, until one recognizes that those numbers are only 1 or 2 percent of the 320 million Americans, or their 130 million homes and/or offices.[7] Without commenting upon the possible relationship, those are percentages analogous to the division of America's wealth—with the top 0.1 percent of Americans worth as much as the bottom 90 percent.[8] Both are, in any event, percentages wholly inadequate to the maintenance of either a democratic society or its economy.

This is not to "blame the victim." Single mothers holding two jobs to raise three kids have little free time for quality journalism or public policy research. Apathy is not a totally irrational response for someone who repeatedly experiences the seemingly intractable control of local, state, and federal governments by the wealthy and powerful. And children with inadequate education, who have never had an adult—parent, guardian, or teacher—explain and involve them in the political process, are far less likely to inform themselves, and exercise their right to vote, than those who have.

Casting more investigative journalism upon those audiences will not have much more impact than casting seeds upon unprepared, baked clay soil with no fertilizer or water. If one wishes to alleviate the *consequences* of "censorship," efforts aimed at early audience preparation would be a promising place to start.

And everyone, regardless of education or political interests, has far more competition for their time now in the early twenty-first century than they did in the early twentieth, when media was largely limited to novels, phonograph records, live vaudeville, silent films, and the growing availability of radio.

We have now added television (broadcast, hundreds of cable channels, and streaming from the likes of Amazon, Google, and Netflix), texts and tweets, trillions of Web pages, video games, and millions of smartphone apps—among the many other sponges soaking up time from our twenty-four–hour days. Both lower quality and lower quantities of serious news and analysis must compete with ever more, and more attractive, distractions.

Ownership

But there is another need beyond a democracy's educated population with enough leisure to become informed. Project Censored focuses on this need with its underreported significant stories—and its implied suggestion (usually only whispered, and seldom proven by courtroom standards) of nefarious self-serving censorship by the media's corporate owners.

This risk can become reality—as I first discovered as a commissioner with the Federal Communications Commission (FCC) at the time of the proposed ABC–ITT merger in 1966–67.[9] In a book I wrote in 1970, I described potentially dozens of examples of "corporate censorship" with the comment, "Note what each of these items has in common: (1) human death, disease, dismemberment or degradation, (2) great profit for manufacturers, advertisers and broadcasters, and (3) the deliberate withholding of needed information from the public."[10]

But the self-serving greed that kills individual stories and gives placement to others—thereby putting the economic interests of owners, subsidiaries, and advertisers ahead of the needs of viewers and subscribers—is not the only source of "censorship."

Time and Space
Media owners decide the extent to which they will provide *any* meaningful news and opinion on air or in newspapers, and if so how much. Even the most civic-minded owner or journalist is unable to provide audiences all they need to know in the twenty minutes remaining after commercials in a "half-hour" newscast.

Junk Food News
Alas, few are so civic-minded as to try. They fill those precious minutes with what Carl Jensen called "junk food news"—Twinkies for the brain.[11] It's what Walter Lippmann once called "sideshows and three-legged calves."[12] There is a devastating opportunity cost to this waste of information channels, only made worse by efforts to scare and agitate the audience.

Randomly chosen consecutive *ABC Evening News* promos make the point with both the subject matter selected and the adrenaline-pumping nature of its presentation: "Coming up: Terror in Texas, the FBI on the scene tonight. We'll take you inside the deadly shootout.

The packed double-decker bus, the fire that erupts, the heroes that jump in. And a former student pilot that steals a plane. You will hear the audio trying to get him to land. Coming up." And the next evening, "Coming up: Our investigation, the hunt for a fugitive after that deadly attack in Texas, his secret messages. The oil tanker flipping on an American highway, the massive fireball. And a giant tree falling in a public park, landing on two children; the rescue. Coming up."[13]

This approach to "news" bears more similarity to what a televised version of Chuck Shepherd's "News of the Weird"[14] might look like than it does to anything Walter Cronkite ever put on the air. Ironically, one-time stand-up comics Jon Stewart (*The Daily Show*) and John Oliver (*Last Week Tonight*) have become, by default, among America's most popular mainstream sources of serious news and public affairs programming.[15]

Resources

The quantity and quality of reporting is impacted by available resources as well as available time: the number of news bureaus (especially overseas); the number, quality, and experience of reporters; time and expense account allowances for investigative reporting; and therefore, necessarily, the amount of money the media owner is willing to expend on informing the public.

Self-Censorship

As quoted at the outset of this foreword, Carl Jensen's first goal for Project Censored was "to encourage professional journalists and editors to do more investigative journalism." Not all, but perhaps most journalists and editors would need little encouragement to comply with that goal. The obstacles to their doing so do not lie within their characters or desires. Even if they are not self-driven workaholics who love the work, there are plenty of incentives including promotions and bonuses, public fame, the respect of colleagues, and the Pulitzer and other prizes.

Many of the restraints are beyond their control and are outlined above, such as lack of resources, time on TV or space in a newspaper, plus advertisers' and shareholders' preferences for the ratings and profits of junk news over those for investigative reporting. Other restraints are self-imposed—though often, sadly, not irrational.

Depending on the media company's culture, critical ("investigative") reports and opinion pieces may be known to be the reason for other employees' demotions, firing, inability to get work elsewhere—or even death, the ultimate censorship.[16]

A cautious (or sensible) journalist might find that reason enough to decline assignments or explorations of stories capable of being interpreted as contrary to the interests of their company (or its parent corporation and subsidiaries), major advertisers, a pro-corporate elected official (or political party), or a US president's efforts to build support for something like our "preemptive war" in Iraq.[17] Journalists' concerns about the recent prevalence of government surveillance have contributed to the increase in self-censorship in journalists' use of phones and e-mail as well as selection of topics.[18]

Others, sometimes perhaps irrationally timid, may choose to avoid *any* "controversial" topics.

Censorship may be the result of pressure from a corporate owner, or the frustration and timidity of an idealistic young reporter. Regardless of the cause, because it most often leaves no trail, it is difficult to spot and almost impossible to prove. This can make it, in some ways, more insidious than even a government censor.

CONCLUSION: "WHAT THE AMERICAN PEOPLE DON'T KNOW CAN KILL THEM"[19]

This has been, in part, an effort to distinguish "ends" (the fully informed, active participation by the citizens of a self-governing democracy) from "means" (the publicizing of "censored" stories and other approaches)—while acknowledging what can be the substantial contribution of the latter to the former.

Either, or both, requires that the corporate media contribute substantially more than they have to the American people's information and understanding of their challenges and opportunities. It's not easy, but they simply must present a greater range of information and opinion as fully, fairly, and accurately as possible.

What we don't know *can* kill us—whether in wars better avoided, unsafe working conditions neither reported nor repaired, or drugs inadequately tested.

But that's not all.

Engineers refer to the "signal-to-noise ratio" of electronic communications in order to explain. Censorship eliminates the signal entirely. But as the old saying has it, "It's not what we don't know that's the problem, it's what we know that ain't so."[20] "Misperceptions" are another way of confusing noise with signal. And both can as easily come from a reporter's self-censorship as from a global media conglomerate's pushing its owner's ideology or stock price.

Both ignorance or misperception can or occasionally does kill one of us—along with our hopes for democracy. This volume, like those that preceded it, is our modest effort to at least slightly reduce that risk.

NICHOLAS JOHNSON, one of Project Censored's judges since its founding, served as commissioner of the Federal Communications Commission from 1966 to 1973, and as chair of the National Citizens Committee for Broadcasting from 1974 to 1978. See his full biography at www.nicholasjohnson.org and follow his blog at FromDC2Iowa .blogspot.com.

Notes

1. "Project Censored Over the Years: The View From Its Founder," interview, *Utne Reader*, September/October 1990, 110–11; excerpted from Craig McLaughlin's interview, *San Francisco Bay Guardian*, May 24, 1989.
2. Peter Phillips, "Close to Home: A Life Shedding Light on Areas Left Dark by Corporate Media," *Press Democrat*, May 1, 2015, http://www.pressdemocrat.com/opinion/3873399-181/ close-to-home-a-life.
3. Nor do many involve First Amendment issues. The Supreme Court has expanded the word "Congress" (in the Constitutional prohibition that "Congress shall make no law . . . abridging the freedom of speech," US Constitution, Amendment I) into a restriction on all governmental bodies, including local and state, not just the Congress. But its prohibition does not extend to abridgments by corporate and individual media owners. Journalists, as such, have no "First Amendment rights" vis-à-vis their editors and owners.
4. The Internet is an information blessing in many ways, with its overwhelming volume and diversity of sources. Google searches over thirty trillion Web pages, one hundred billion times a month. John Koetsier, "How Google Searches 30 Trillion Web Pages, 100 Billion Times a Month," VentureBeat News, March 1, 2013, http://venturebeat.com/2013/03/01/how-google-searches-30-trillion-web-pages-100-billion-times-a-month. However, precisely because of that diversity, the Internet limits, rather than enhances, the kind of 1960s-style evolving national political consensus resulting from a three-major-network information economy.
5. Barbara Kingsolver, "The One-Eyed Monster and Why I Don't Let Him In," *Small Wonder* (New York: HarperCollins, 2002), 137.
6. Christine Haughney, "Newspapers Post Gains in Digital Circulation," *New York Times*, May 1, 2013, B5; http://www.nytimes.com/2013/05/01/business/media/digital-subscribers-buoy-newspaper-circulation.html.

7. US Census Bureau, "Quick Facts," 2015; http://quickfacts.census.gov/qfd/states/00000. html.

8. Angela Monaghan, "US Wealth Inequality—Top 0.1% Worth As Much As the Bottom 90%," *Guardian*, November 13, 2014, http://www.theguardian.com/business/2014/nov/13/us-wealth-inequality-top-01-worth-as-much-as-the-bottom-90.

9. Nicholas Johnson, "The Media Barons and the Public Interest: An FCC Commissioner's Warning," *Atlantic*, June 1968; https://www.theatlantic.com/past/docs/unbound/flashbks/media/johnsonf.htm. *The Atlantic* summarized the conflicts over media ownership identified in my article in these terms: "Local monopolies, regional baronies, nationwide empires, and corporate conglomerates are more and more in control of the nation's communications media—newspapers, TV, radio, magazines, books, the electronic 'knowledge industry.'" Descriptions of the ABC–ITT proposed merger, characteristics of both companies, and the author's opinions dissenting from the FCC majority's willingness to approve the merger—including the risks of self-serving corporate censorship—can be found in ABC-ITT Merger, 7 F.C.C. 2d 245, 278, 9 Rad. Reg. 2d (P & F) 12, 46 (1966) (dissenting opinion) [Dkt. No. 16828, December 21, 1966, 74]; http://myweb.uiowa.edu/johnson/FCCOps/1966/7F2-245. html; ABC-ITT Merger, 7 F.C.C. 2d 336, 343, 9 Rad. Reg. 2d (P & F) 87, 94 (1967) (concurring statement) [Dkt. No. 16828, February 1, 1967, 4] (the FCC's permission for the intervention in the proceeding by the U.S. Department of Justice, Antitrust Division); http://myweb. uiowa.edu/johnson/FCCOps/1967/7F2-336.html; and ABC-ITT Merger, 9 F.C.C. 2d 546, 581,10 Rad. Reg. 2d (P & F) 289, 329 (1967) (dissenting opinion of Commissioners Bartley, Cox and Johnson) [Dkt. No. 16828, June 22, 1967, 62], http://myweb.uiowa.edu/johnson/FCCOps/1967/9F2-546.html. And see, Karen Beth Possner, An Historical Analysis of the ABC-ITT Merger Proceeding Before the Federal Communications Commission, 1966–67, University of Iowa, Doctoral Dissertation, 1975; http://www.nicholasjohnson.org/about/kpabcitt.html (with links to portions of dissertation).

10. Nicholas Johnson, *How to Talk Back to Your Television Set* (1970; 3rd ed.: Lulu, 2013), 53, 59, 66.

11. See, for example, Carl Jensen, "Junk Food News 1877-2000," in *Censored 2001*, ed. Peter Phillips and Project Censored, (New York: Seven Stories Press, 2001), 251–64.

12. "It is because they [the people] are compelled to act without a reliable picture of the world, that governments, schools, newspapers and churches make such small headway against the more obvious failings of democracy, against violent prejudice, apathy, preference for the curious trivial as against the dull important, and the hunger for sideshows and three legged calves. This is the primary defect of popular government . . . and all its other defects can, I believe, be traced to this one." Walter Lippmann, *Public Opinion* (New York: Free Press, 1997[1922]), 230. And see Nicholas Johnson, "Three Legged Calves, Wolves, Sheep and Democracy's Media," December 1, 2014; http://fromdc2iowa.blogspot.com/2014/12/three-legged-calves-wolves-sheep-and.html.

13. As recorded by the author from KCRG-TV9, ABC, Cedar Rapids, Iowa, May 4 and 5, 2015, about 5:28 p.m.

14. Chuck Shepherd's "News of the Weird," http://www.newsoftheweird.com/index.html.

15. Johnson, "Three Legged Calves." Oliver's commentaries can be seen on YouTube (https://www.youtube.com/user/LastWeekTonight) where many of them receive six or seven million views. Randomly selected recent subjects—serious presentations interlaced with humor—have included standardized testing; the death penalty; government surveillance (with Edward Snowden); Ferguson, Missouri, and police militarization; civil forfeiture; drones; net neutrality; wealth gap; prison; nutritional supplements; predatory lending; and the price of fashion. Of course, their efforts are supplemented by the more somber programming and approach of public television and National Public Radio—the latter aided by its substantial carriage of what the author views as the world's best journalism, that of the BBC.

16. "1125 Journalists Killed Since 1992," Committee to Protect Journalists, https://cpj.org/killed; of whom 188 were murdered, https://cpj.org/killed/murdered.php. "2015: Journalists Killed," Reporters Without Borders," https://en.rsf.org/press-freedom-barometer-journalists-killed.html?annee=2015.

17. "I sometimes tell the (apocryphal) story of a young reporter who starts out with enthusiasm. She works very hard investigating, interviewing, researching, writing, and editing an 'investigative journalism' article exposing the corruption of one of the major advertisers in the paper. The story is so good it may win for her a journalism prize. She proudly gives it to her editor. She never hears about it again, and it never appears in the paper. The next time she has an idea about an investigative journalism piece, about an incompetent local official, she decides to check with her editor first. He discourages her from doing the story, and she drops the idea. The third time she thinks of an investigative journalism topic (different property tax rates paid by local citizens) she not only doesn't research and write it, she doesn't even bother talking to her editor about it. The fourth time? The fourth time the idea doesn't even cross her mind." Nicholas Johnson, *Your Second Priority: A Former FCC Commissioner Speaks Out* (3rd ed.: Lulu, 2008), 1, 24 n. 39.

18. The PEN survey findings demonstrate that "increasing levels of surveillance in democracies are seriously damaging freedom of expression and thought, the free flow of information, and creative freedom around the world. Perhaps most remarkably, the levels of self-censorship reported by writers in Free countries [34-42%] are beginning to approach the levels reported by writers in Partly Free or Not Free countries (as classified by Freedom House) [44-61%]." Journalists' self-censorship has increased in the context of topics chosen for writing or speaking, participation in social media, phone calls, e-mails, Internet searches, and Web page visits. "Global Chilling: The Impact of Mass Surveillance on International Writers," PEN America, January 5, 2015, 9–12, http://www.pen.org/sites/default/files/globalchilling_2015.pdf. See *Censored* story #7, "Fear of Government Spying is 'Chilling' Writers' Speech Worldwide," in this volume.

19. One of three quotes with which Fred Friendly began his book, *Due to Circumstances Beyond Our Control* (New York: Random House, 1967), unnumbered page (credited to Dorothy Greene Friendly, 1958). The quote is an obvious play on the old saying, "What you don't know can't hurt you." *A Dictionary of Proverbs*, ed. Jennifer Speake, (Oxford and New York: Oxford University Press, 2008), 174.

20. The quote, in a variety of forms, is variously attributed to Mark Twain, Will Rogers, and others. *The Dictionary of Modern Humorous Quotations* (New York and London: Penguin, 1987) attributes it to Josh Billings.

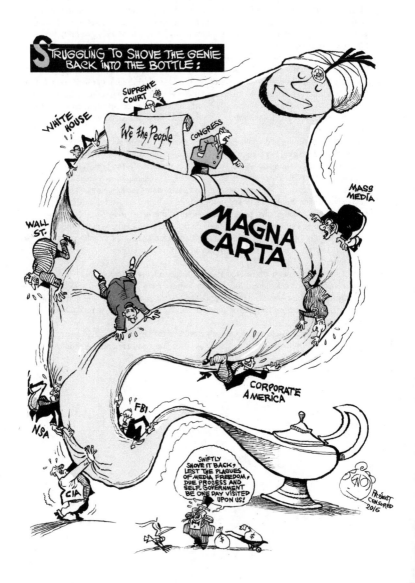

Introduction

Mickey Huff and Andy Lee Roth

When I started Project Censored in 1976, I developed an alternative definition of censorship. Rather than starting with the source of censorship as traditionally defined—with the obligation of an elite to protect the masses (the classic "we know what's best for the people and they're better off without this information" syndrome)—my definition starts at the other end—with the failure of information to reach the people. . . . [F]or the purposes of this project, censorship is defined as the suppression of information, whether purposeful or not, by any method—including bias, omission, underreporting, or self-censorship—which prevents the public from fully knowing what is happening in the world.

—Carl Jensen, founder of Project Censored[1]

CENTERING CENSORSHIP

In 1976, Dr. Carl Jensen's perception of a developing crisis in journalism prompted him to launch Project Censored. The combination of his past professional experience—as a daily newspaper reporter, a weekly newspaper publisher, and a public relations and advertising executive—and his scholarly understanding of the history of investigative journalism helped define the Project's goals and approach.

Jensen celebrated the United States' best investigative journalism of the twentieth century. However, much earlier than many of his colleagues, he also recognized that newly developing social factors

21

within journalism itself and in the broader society threatened to undermine the conditions for contemporary journalists to continue practicing what he called "good old-fashioned muckraking."[2]

Analyzing increasingly sophisticated political propaganda and consolidated ownership patterns, he and his students set out to investigate corporate news as the product of an "information industry" that censored "anything contradictory, any dissonant messages that might come in from the outside." Jensen explained:

> Since 1976, I have been conducting a national media research project which seeks to locate and publicize those dissonant messages, messages the media elite don't want the rest of us to know about.[3]

Two components that were original to Jensen's project then remain central to it today.

First, as noted, Jensen involved students directly in his research project, providing them with hands-on experience in both critical media literacy education and engaging the public beyond the confines of their university campus.[4] Today, taking advantage of electronic networking made possible by the Internet, faculty and students at dozens of college and university campuses across the nation and around the world continue the Project that Carl Jensen first launched at Sonoma State University forty years ago, through the Project's campus affiliates program.

Second, Jensen's distinctive definition of censorship continues to guide Project Censored's work. Thus, compare Jensen's definition in the epigraph above with one offered in *Censored 2013: Dispatches from the Media Revolution*, which defined "modern media censorship" to include not only "overt, intentional omission," but also "anything that interferes with the free flow of information in a society that purports to have a free press system."[5] Consistent with Jensen's original definition of censorship, the Project continues to advocate that an accurate understanding of US news media requires a broader definition of censorship—one that goes beyond the conventional focus on either direct government control or simple editorial "gate keeping" of news content; in this view, censorship should be understood more subtly as "a form of propaganda."[6]

For this reason, Project Censored rejects the "mainstream" versus "alternative" labels that many media pundits and some activists employ. Because six big corporations control over 90 percent of US news media, often providing a megaphone for the plutocracy, the corporate media hardly represent the mainstream.[7]

By contrast, the independent journalists and news reporting organizations that Project Censored has celebrated since its inception, along with Project Censored itself, are now best understood as vital components of what experts have identified as a newly developing "networked fourth estate," characterized by its diversity and decentralized organization.[8] As Joel Simon of the Committee to Protect Journalists has written:

> As technology makes it easier for individuals and smaller outlets to gather and distribute information, power will continue to shift away from the larger media organizations that were once dominant.[9]

Although "legacy media" will continue to reach mass audiences, the networked fourth estate—much in evidence throughout *Censored 2016*—offers an affirmative way forward as the crisis of corporate news continues. The networked fourth estate also provides one basis for believing that we may be witness to a new era of networked muckraking.

That possibility would undoubtedly have pleased Carl Jensen, who died on April 23, 2015.[10] As Nicholas Johnson, a Project Censored judge since 1976, writes in this book's foreword, *Censored 2016* is the first volume published without the Project's founder. Johnson's foreword reminds us that one of Carl Jensen's original goals for the project was to inform the public. The Project, Johnson writes, aims to inform and engage the public with the goal of contributing to "a vibrant, democratic, self-governing society." This ultimately is why we should value media freedom and oppose censorship.

Over a decade ago, media scholar Robert W. McChesney recalled a pointed insight of Johnson's regarding why the state of journalism ought be everyone's concern. Noting that corporate news media are "set up to maximize profit for a relative handful of large companies," McChesney wrote:

The system works well for them, but it is a disaster for the communication needs of a healthy and self-governing society. So if we want to change the content and logic of the media, we have to change the system. . . . As former Federal Communications Commission member Nicholas Johnson likes to put it . . . whatever your first issue of concern, media had better be your second, because without change in the media, progress in your primary area is far less likely.[11]

Johnson's point, paraphrased by McChesney, explains the crucial role of a free press in maintaining all of our liberties, and why censorship—broadly defined—must be a central domain of shared concern. A free press that is resistant to censorship in all its diverse forms is necessary if, as McChesney wrote, "we are going to have a viable self-governing society and transform this country for the better."[12]

MEDIA FREEDOM ON THE LINE

Censored 2016's subtitle, "Media Freedom on the Line," is both a warning and a call to action. As a warning, it points to the ongoing crisis of journalism, in which the future of a free press is now at stake. As a call to action, it suggests runners at the start of a footrace, toeing the line, ready to run with determination, endurance, and skill. (A footrace need not pit its participants against one another; the Latin root for "competition" means "to seek, with others."[13])

Artist Hilary Allison's cover image provides for additional interpretations of the phrase "on the line." From the perspective of crisis, we might see newspapers and broadsheets, the Magna Carta and the US Constitution, hung out to dry—that is, abandoned to danger, left without support.[14] Certainly some of the Top 25 stories reported in this and previous *Censored* volumes provide compelling evidence for this critical interpretation. See, for example, "No Habeas Corpus for 'Any Person'" (story #1 in *Censored 2008*), "Fear of Government Spying is 'Chilling' Writers' Freedom of Expression" (story #7 in this volume); and increasing threats to our commons (including water rights, as featured in story #4, "Popular Resistance to Corporate Water Grabbing," also in this volume).

But an entirely negative interpretation of this year's book cover is not warranted. An affirmative interpretation of it challenges us to consider a robust free press as one of the pillars that provides crucial support for other vital social institutions and values. In this view, a free press is one of the pillars that holds up and supports what's "on the line"—including the US Constitution and the venerable Magna Carta. This affirmative view aligns with the understanding championed by Carl Jensen, Project Censored, and others that media freedom is most valuable in support of broader rights, including especially the fundamental right to freedom of expression.

As noted already, Jensen was clear about the ultimate importance of a free press: the role it plays in making democratic government possible. Along with the principles ensconced in other pillars of our society—including due process and specifically habeas corpus in the Magna Carta, and the rights to free speech, assembly, the redress of grievances, as well as privacy, in the US Constitution—these do not stand alone. They support one another, or they crumble and fall. Twenty years ago, Jensen stressed the mutual dependence among these pillars when he wrote:

> The press has the power to stimulate people to clean up the environment; to prevent nuclear proliferation; to force corrupt politicians out of office; to reduce poverty; to provide quality health care for all people; to create a truly equitable society; and, as we have seen, to literally save the lives of millions of human beings.
>
> And this is why we must look to, prod, and support a free, open, and aggressive press. We have a free press in the United States guaranteed by the First Amendment and we have the best communications technology in the world. Now let us see a more responsible and responsive press—a press that truly earns its First Amendment rights. Indeed, a press not afraid to do a little muckraking. Then, and only then, will we all have the information we need to build a more enlightened and responsive society.[15]

INSIDE *CENSORED 2016*

Each chapter in *Censored 2016* reflects the Project's efforts to continue to build the "more enlightened and responsive society" to which Carl Jensen dedicated his life work.

Chapter 1 presents Project Censored's listing and analysis of the Top 25 underreported news stories of 2014–15. Once again we call attention to the truth telling of independent journalists, celebrating not only their individual contributions, but also the independent news organizations and constitutional protections that make their reporting possible. Chapter 1 also pays tribute to another champion of free expression who passed away in 2015, journalist and historian Eduardo Galeano (1940–2015). Galeano's understanding of censorship and lifelong advocacy of free expression resonate strongly with Jensen's views and commitments, and these provide the framework for our presentation of this year's Top *Censored* stories and analysis.

In Chapter 2, it's "Déjà Vu" all over again as we track what happened to some of the top stories from *Censored 2015*. Researched by students of Susan Rahman at the College of Marin, with assistance from students at Diablo Valley College, this year's chapter updates Project Censored's coverage of independent and corporate news reporting on the ongoing crisis in the Ukraine; the practice of restorative justice; the latest in the battle over net neutrality; the situation in Gaza, including Israel's threats to its perilous water supply; and the record number of US prison inmates serving life sentences. This year's chapter features some pleasant surprises—a few of these stories have finally garnered (better) coverage in the corporate press. Unfortunately, others continue to languish in obscurity despite their continued significance.

Carl Jensen coined the term "junk food news" in 1983, and in doing so he laid the foundation for a form of media criticism that is now pervasive.[16] Chapter 3, titled "A Vast Wasteland," provides analysis of this year's offering of corporate junk food news and news abuse stories. As Nicholas Johnson states in his foreword, "The bulk of what the cable channels bring into our homes is not even that close to journalism. . . . As Barbara Kingsolver describes it, 'the image that strikes me . . . is that of a faucet into the house that runs about 5 percent clear water and 95 percent raw sewage.'" This year, Nolan Higdon, Mickey Huff, and Ellie Kim, along with students from Diablo Valley College, Las Positas College, Ohlone College, College of Alameda, and California State University East Bay provide snapshots of the bilge, inanity, and 24/7 propaganda that dominate the so-called "public" airwaves under the private custody of the corporate overlords. The chapter calls out the past year's most odiferous distractions and distortions, while providing a clear view of important news stories whose coverage would have better served the public interest.

Chapter 4, "Media Democracy in Action," highlights individuals and organizations that work to support a truly free press, to inform the public, and to protect additional cherished liberties when those are under attack. This year's chapter includes good news on independent media's efficacy in supporting activism, from Steven Wishnia, of Dissent NewsWire, Alexander Reid Ross, of Earth First! Newswire, and Sue Udry, with the Defending Dissent Foundation. Beatrice Edwards provides an introduction to the crucial role of the Government Accountability Project in supporting whistleblowers and advocating for their rights and protection. Adam Jonas Horowitz, director of the documentary *Nuclear Savage*, tells a cautionary tale of censorship at PBS, while documentary filmmaker Ian Thomas Ash describes a similar, ongoing battle in securing distribution and public screenings for his Fukushima documentary, *A2-B-C*. Pacifica radio hosts Arlene Engelhardt and Mary Glenney describe their twenty years of experience presenting *From a Woman's Point of View*, a weekly public affairs program. And Project Censored student interns Crystal Bedford, Lisa Davis, Darian Edelman, Lauren Freeman, and Ellie Kim provide an overview of their new report on women in media. Finally, Jyarland Daniels, and Rebekah Spicuglia provide an insider's view on the work of Race Forward and *Colorlines*, two online outlets for news and activism that readers of previous *Censored* volumes will recall as sources for some of past years' Top 25 stories. We are honored to be able to include contributions from this illustrious group of truth tellers in this year's Media Democracy in Action, and we are inspired by their work.

Chapter 5, by Julie Frechette, Nolan Higdon, and Rob Williams, announces and describes a new partnership between Project Censored and the Action Coalition for Media Education (ACME). The authors unveil a new Global Critical Media Literacy Project (GCMLP) that will expand and enhance each organization's current mission and programs by establishing service-learning courses based on media literacy curricula and outreach. This chapter builds on contributions to previous *Censored* volumes by Michael I. Niman, on service learning, and Elliot D. Cohen, on critical thinking as applied to news media coverage, all of which inform this exciting new collaboration in twenty-first–century media education.[17]

In Chapter 6, sociologist Sheila Katz reflects on the one hundredth anniversary of *Herland*, a novel by one of the pioneering women in US sociology, Charlotte Perkins Gilman. *Herland* portrayed an all-female utopia as a means to express ideas about gender, sexuality, and social relations that a woman—even one as courageous and dedicated as Gilman—probably could not have published in the professional sociology journals of her time. Though much has improved for women (and women sociologists) since Gilman wrote, Katz demonstrates the continued relevance of Gilman's marginalized classic.

As Brian Covert writes, 2016 marks the twentieth anniversary of Gary Webb's "Dark Alliance" investigation, "one of the most compelling US news stories in the latter half of the twentieth century." Longtime *Censored* readers will recall that Webb wrote the introduction to *Censored 1999* and that Seven Stories Press published his book, *Dark Alliance: The CIA, the Contras, and the Crack Cocaine Explosion* (1998). In Chapter 7, Covert provides what we believe will come to be recognized as the definitive account of Gary Webb's "Dark Alliance" reporting and its legacy. A Hollywood film, *Kill the Messenger* (2014), rekindled interest in Webb's work, but Covert retrieves forgotten pieces of the puzzle, documenting in careful detail not only the failure of the corporate media to support Webb's stellar muckraking journalism, but also how they ostracized Webb for it. As Covert's chapter reminds us, the key claims in Webb's coverage have never been disproven, and it stands "the test of time as a classic, high-quality work of investigative journalism."

In Chapter 8, Peter Phillips, Ray McClintock, Melissa Carneiro, and Jacob Crabtree examine "Twenty-First–Century Fascism: Private Military Companies in Service to the Transnational Capitalist

Class." They note that globalization of trade and central banking have empowered private corporations to positions of power and control never before seen in human history. New private military companies (PMCs) have emerged in the past few decades to protect transnational capitalist class interests and global capitalism. In this chapter, the authors evaluate six of the largest PMCs in terms of their history, growth, and stability, and evaluate the potential global consequences. They also suggest a novel approach to confronting this twenty-first–century form of fascism.

Tara Dorabji and Susan Rahman explore commonalities in experience and forms of resistance shared by women in Kashmir and Palestine, in Chapter 9, "Existence is Resistance: Women in Occupied Palestine and Kashmir." Noting that, "as storytellers, mothers, and organizers, women make up the backbone of these movements for sovereignty and independence," Dorabji and Rahman detail the realities of life for women living under military occupation and explore how they have been instrumental in sustaining two independence movements that have suffered from grossly inadequate and/or distorted coverage in the corporate media.

In *Censored 2016*'s concluding chapter, "The Contours of Long-Term Systemic Crisis and the Need for Systemic Solutions," Gar Alperovitz, James Gustave Speth, and Joe Guinan discuss the Next System Project, launched in March 2015. They describe it as a "concerted effort to break through the national media silence and to radically shift the national dialogue about the future." The chapter provides an introductory overview of a robust set of "system-building answers to system-threatening challenges." The Next System Project's goal of moving the US public in a new direction characterized by "sustainable, lasting and more democratic social, economic, and ecological outcomes" provides a positive, fitting conclusion to *Censored 2016: Media Freedom on the Line.*

A LIVING LEGACY

After Carl Jensen's passing, former Project Censored director Peter Phillips published a tribute in the *Santa Rosa Press Democrat.* Noting that "Jensen's published works include five *Censored* yearbooks, his definitive *Stories that Changed America*, all published by Seven Stories Press, and a three-volume encyclopedia, titled simply *Censorship*," Phillips pointed out that Jensen's "legacy is not fully encompassed by his published work."[18] It also includes the generations of students, in college and university classrooms across the nation and around the world, who each year research the stories that comprise the Project's list of the Top 25 *Censored* stories, its Déjà Vu review of past years' top stories, and the analysis of corporate junk food news and news abuse. By extension, Carl Jensen's legacy includes all of the contributors to this book, who each in their own way carry on his lifework, publicizing dissonant and dissident messages that the media elite marginalize or seek to suppress, in service of creating a more enlightened society for all.

Notes

1. Carl Jensen and Project Censored, *Censored 1995: The News that Didn't Make the News—and Why* (New York: Four Walls Eight Windows, 1995), 15–16.
2. Jensen later published systematic analyses on these topics. See, e.g., Carl Jensen, *Stories That Changed America: Muckrakers of the 20th Century* (New York: Seven Stories Press, 2000), and Carl Jensen, "What Happened to Good Old-Fashioned Muckraking?" in *Into the Buzzsaw: Leading Journalists Expose the Myth of a Free Press*, ed. Kristina Borjesson (Amherst NY: Prometheus Books, 2002), 333–50.
3. Carl Jensen and Project Censored, *Censored: The News That Didn't Make the News—and Why* (New York: Four Walls Eight Windows, 1994), 23.
4. The first *Censored* annual report published in book form specifically noted that students— "Project Censored researchers participating in a seminar in news media censorship offered by the Communications Department at Sonoma State University"—produced the Project's synopses of the Top 25 stories. Ibid., 8.
5. Mickey Huff and Andy Lee Roth, eds., *Censored 2013: Dispatches from the Media Revolution* (New York: Seven Stories Press, 2012), 30.
6. Ibid.
7. See, for example, Bridget Thornton, Britt Walters, and Lori Rouse, "Corporate Media is Corporate America," in *Censored 2006: Media Democracy in Action*, eds. Peter Phillips and Project Censored (New York: Seven Stories Press, 2005), 245–62. The authors conclude, "In corporate-dominated capitalism wealth concentration is the goal and corporate media are the cheerleaders," 246. See story #9 in Chapter 1 of this volume, "Millions in Poverty Get Less Media Coverage than 482 Billionaires," as further evidence in support of this perspective.
8. See both Yochai Benkler, "WikiLeaks and the Networked Fourth Estate," in *Beyond WikiLeaks: Implications for the Future of Communications, Journalism and Society*, eds. Benedetta Reveni, Arne Hints, and Patrick McCurdy (New York: Palgrave Macmillan, 2013), 11–34; and the introduction to Chapter 1 in this volume.
9. Joel Simon, *The New Censorship: Inside the Global Battle for Media Freedom* (New York: Columbia University Press, 2015), 173.
10. See Peter Phillips, "A Life Shedding Light on Areas Left Dark by Corporate Media," *Press Democrat* (Santa Rosa CA), May 1, 2015, http://www.pressdemocrat.com/opinion/closeto-home/3873399-181/close-to-home-a-life.

11. Robert W. McChesney, "Waging the Media Battle," *American Prospect*, June 17, 2004, http://prospect.org/article/waging-media-battle. Also see Nicholas Johnson, *Your Second Priority* (Lulu, 2008).

12. McChesney, "Waging the Media Battle."

13. See, e.g., Sally Jackson and Mihaly Czikszentmihalyi, *Flow in Sports* (Champaign IL: Human Kinetics, 1999), 80.

14. For example, on the 800th anniversary of the Magna Carta, and its continued relevance to contemporary global issues, including especially our relationship to the environment, see both Noam Chomsky, "Magna Carta Messed up the World, Here's How to Fix it," *Nation*, March 23, 2015, http://www.thenation.com/article/198513/killing-commons; and Peter Linebaugh, "Wake up the Earth!," *Counterpunch*, May 18, 2015, http://www.counterpunch.org/2015/05/18/wake-up-the-earth.

15. Carl Jensen, "20 Years of Raking Muck, Raising Hell," in *Censored: The News That Didn't Make the News—and Why*, 20th ann. ed., eds. Carl Jensen and Project Censored (New York: Seven Stories Press, 1996), 19.

16. Carl Jensen, "Junk Food News 1877–2000," in *Censored 2001*, ed. Peter Phillips and Project Censored (New York: Seven Stories Press, 2001), 251–64.

17. Michael I. Niman, "Service Learning: The SUNY—Buffalo State and Project Censored Partnership," in Roth and Huff, *Censored 2015*, 193–98; and Elliot D. Cohen, "Digging Deeper: Politico-Corporate Media Manipulation, Critical Thinking, and Democracy," in Huff and Roth, *Censored 2014*, 251–69.

18. Phillips, "A Life Shedding Light."

CHAPTER 1

The Top *Censored* Stories and Media Analysis of 2014–15

Compiled and edited by Andy Lee Roth

INTRODUCTION

What is the use of writing if not to defy the blockade which the system places round the dissident message? . . . By writing it is possible to offer, despite persecution and censorship, the testimony of our time and our people—for now and for posterity.

—Eduardo Galeano (September 3, 1940–April 13, 2015)[1]

Journalist and historian Eduardo Galeano (1940–2015) experienced state censorship repeatedly in his life. In 1973, after a military dictatorship took power in Uruguay, Galeano left his home country to live in exile in Argentina, where he founded the journal *Crisis*, which gave voice to the poor. The Argentinean military censored and confiscated *Crisis* for "unprofessional opinions." In 1976, he moved to Spain, where he wrote *The Open Veins of Latin America* and *Memory of Fire*, both of which the governments of Argentina, Chile, and Uruguay censored. Censorship did not silence Galeano, who continued to write and speak on behalf of the poor and socialism, and against censorship and neoliberalism, for the rest of a long, distinguished career.[2]

In a 1977 essay, "In Defence of the Word," Galeano distinguished between direct and indirect censorship. Noting that "much has been said" about direct forms of censorship—including "the prohibition of inconvenient or dangerous books or periodicals and the destiny

of exile, prison or death dealt out to some writers and journalists"—
Galeano wrote that indirect censorship "operates more subtly." He
continued:

> That it is less obvious does not make it less real . . . it is what
> defines most profoundly the oppressive and prohibitory
> nature of the system from which the majority of our coun-
> tries suffer. . . . It means that the ship doesn't sail because
> there's no water in the sea.[3]

By writing despite "persecution and censorship," Galeano concluded his essay, we "offer testimony of our time and our people—for
now and for posterity."

Project Censored's Top 25 stories for 2014–15 offer the kind of testimony Galeano advocated, and they do so despite the indirect censorship of the United States' corporate media.

Independent journalists and news organizations bring to the
public important news stories that the corporate media either will not
cover at all—for example, *Censored* story #9, "Millions in Poverty Get
Less Media Coverage than 482 Billionaires"—or that they only cover
in an incomplete or slanted manner (e.g., #17, "Media 'Whitewash'
Senate's CIA Torture Report"). These stories give voice to people
whom the corporate media seldom feature (e.g., #23, "Unprocessed
Rape Kits") due to establishment journalism's well-documented preference for official sources.

Independent news reporting also provides an alternative frame for
understanding "our time." We live in an era characterized by both
(1) increasing corporate control and government erosion of civil liberties, as well as (2) some of the most well-organized and effective
popular movements in history. Too often marginalized or ignored
altogether by corporate news outlets, stories covering communities
that have organized to resist corporate control and environmental
degradation (as in #4, "Popular Resistance to Corporate Water Grabbing") are regular features in the "solutions journalism" practiced by
an increasing number of committed independent journalists.[4] Community organizing—and independent press accounts of it—make
good on Galeano's observation that "the act of creation is an act of

solidarity."[5]

The production of Project Censored's annual list of Top *Censored* stories is a collective effort organized through the Project's campus affiliates program. This year's list reflects the combined efforts of 191 students and thirty-one faculty members from eighteen college and university campuses across the US and Canada, plus the expertise of an additional nine community experts. Together this networked team identified, reviewed, and summarized 203 Validated Independent News stories, from which the 2014–15 top *Censored* stories are drawn. Our panel of twenty-eight esteemed judges voted to determine the rank order of the Top 25 list. (See the "Note on Research and Evaluation of *Censored* Stories," below, for more on the review process and determination of the Top 25 list.)

Project Censored's work can be understood as part of what Yochai Benkler has described as the newly emerging "networked fourth estate."[6] Diverse and organizationally decentralized, the networked fourth estate challenges the previous dominance of an elite-controlled, centralized, top-down mass media. As Benkler wrote, the networked fourth estate has "an agility, scope, and diversity of sources and pathways" that allows it to "collect and capture information on a global scale that would be impossible for any single traditional organization to replicate by itself."[7] Each year, Project Censored's campus affiliates program coordinates the efforts of hundreds of college and university students and professors from campuses across the country and around the world in an electronically networked, collective effort to raise public awareness of the limits of corporate news coverage and public appreciation for the importance of free expression and a truly independent press.[8]

For each of the following *Censored* story synopses, we identify not only the names and publication sources of the original news stories, but also the names and campus affiliations of the students and faculty members who both investigated whether the story received any coverage in the corporate media and wrote the original synopsis of it. We identify the student researchers and faculty evaluators, not only to give credit where credit is due—the independent press is so diverse and extensive today that no single small group of people can keep track of it—but also to inspire other students and teachers who might want to do this kind of work themselves to join us. Those interested can learn more about how to do so in this volume or on the Project Censored website.[9] The brief synopses that follow are not meant to replace the original news reports on which they are based. Instead, they summarize the stories' key points, hopefully in ways that lead interested readers back to the original reports themselves.

"One writes," Galeano tells us, "to denounce pain and share joy."[10] At its best, journalism serves as an expression of our aspirations—*newsworthiness* defined not only by what's most troubled in our society, but also what's most excellent. In this view, journalism is a means of communicating and inspiring engaged action. In the spirit of Galeano's lifework, we present this year's Top *Censored* stories as Project Censored's contribution to the developing global press freedom movement.

ACKNOWLEDGMENT: Special thanks to Sierra Shidner, Miya McHugh, Ellie Kim, Tereese Abuhamdeh, and Austin Heidt for crucial assistance in the final review of this year's *Censored* stories.

A NOTE ON RESEARCH AND EVALUATION OF
CENSORED NEWS STORIES

How do we at Project Censored identify and evaluate independent news stories, and how do we know that the Top 25 stories that we bring forward each year are not only relevant and significant, but also trustworthy? The answer is that each candidate news story undergoes rigorous review, which takes place in multiple stages during each annual cycle. Although adapted to take advantage of both the Project's expanding affiliates program and current technologies, the vetting process is quite similar to the one Project Censored founder Carl Jensen established thirty-nine years ago.

Candidate stories are initially identified by Project Censored professors and students, or are nominated by members of the general public, who bring them to the Project's attention through our website.[11] Together, faculty and students vet each candidate story in terms of its importance, timeliness, quality of sources, and corporate news coverage. If it fails on any one of these criteria, the story does not go forward.

Once Project Censored receives the candidate story, we undertake a second round of judgment, using the same criteria and updating the review of any competing corporate coverage. Stories that pass this round of review get posted on our website as Validated Independent News stories (VINs).[12]

In early spring, we present all VINs in the current cycle to the faculty and students at all of our affiliate campuses, and to our national and international panel of judges, who cast votes to winnow the candidate stories from nearly 300 down to twenty-five.

Once the Top 25 list has been determined, Project Censored student interns begin another intensive review of each story using LexisNexis and ProQuest databases. Additional faculty and students contribute to this final stage of review.

The Top 25 finalists are then sent to our panel of judges, who vote to rank them in numerical order. At the same time, these experts—including media studies professors, professional journalists, and a former commissioner of the Federal Communications Commission, among others—offer their insights on the stories' strengths and weaknesses.[13]

Thus, by the time a story appears in the pages of *Censored*, it has undergone at least five distinct rounds of review and evaluation.

Although the stories that Project Censored brings forward may be socially and politically controversial—and sometimes even psychologically challenging—we are confident that each is the result of serious journalistic effort and, so, deserves greater public attention.

THE TOP CENSORED STORIES AND
MEDIA ANALYSIS OF 2014–15

1

Half of Global Wealth Owned by the 1 Percent

Larry Elliott and Ed Pilkington, "New Oxfam Report Says Half of Global Wealth Held by the 1%," *Guardian*, January 19, 2015, http://www.theguardian.com/business/2015/jan/19/global-wealth-oxfam-inequality-davos-economic-summit-switzerland.

Sarah Dransfield, "Number of Billionaires Doubled Since Financial Crisis as Inequality Spirals Out of Control–Oxfam," Oxfam, October 29, 2014, http://www.oxfam.org.uk/blogs/2014/10/number-of-billionaires-doubled-since-financial-crisis-as-inequality-spirals-out-of-control.

Samantha Cowan, "Every Kid on Earth Could Go to School If the World's 1,646 Richest People Gave 1.5 Percent," TakePart, November 3, 2014, http://www.takepart.com/article/2014/11/03/worlds-wealthiest.

Student Researchers: Izzy Michaelson (Pitzer College) and Inna Tounkel (Scripps College)

Faculty Evaluator: Andy Lee Roth (Pomona College)

In January 2015, Oxfam, an international nonprofit organization that aims to eliminate poverty, published a report stating that 1 percent of the global population will own more wealth than the rest of the 99 percent combined by 2016.[14] The Oxfam report provided evidence that extreme inequality is not inevitable, but is, in fact, the result of political choices and economic policies established and maintained by the power elite, wealthy individuals whose strong influence keeps the status quo rigged in their own favor. In addition to reporting the latest figures on global economic inequality and its consequences, the Oxfam study outlined a nine-point plan that governments could adopt in creating new policies to address poverty and economic inequality.

According to the Oxfam report, the proportion of global wealth owned by the 1 percent has increased from 44 percent in 2009 to 48 percent in 2014 and is projected to reach 50 percent in 2016. In October 2014, a prior Oxfam report, "Even It Up: Time to End Extreme Poverty," revealed that the number of billionaires worldwide had more than doubled since the 2009 financial crisis, showing that, although those at the top have recovered quickly, the vast majority of the world's population are far from reaping the benefits of any recent economic recovery.[15] Even more staggering, the world's richest eighty-five people now hold the same amount of wealth as half the world's poorest population. "Failure to tackle inequality will leave hundreds of millions trapped in poverty unnecessarily," the report's authors warned.

Through its reports and the "Even It Up" campaign, Oxfam described how to address economic inequality, identifying nine specific actions:

1. Make governments work for citizens and tackle extreme inequality.
2. Promote women's economic equality and women's rights.
3. Pay workers a living wage and close the gap created by skyrocketing executive rewards.
4. Share the tax burden fairly to level the playing field.
5. Close international tax loopholes and fill holes in tax governance.
6. Achieve universal free public services by 2020.
7. Change the global system for research and development and pricing of medicines so everyone has access to appropriate and affordable medicines.
8. Implement a universal social protection floor.
9. Target development finance at reducing inequality and poverty, and strengthening the compact between citizens and their government.[16]

Oxfam calculated that taxing billionaires just 1.5 percent of their wealth "could raise $74 billion a year, enough to fill the annual gaps in funding needed to get every child into school and to deliver health services in the world's poorest countries."

Corporate coverage of the two Oxfam reports has been minimal in quantity and problematic in quality. A few corporate television networks, including CNN, CBS, MSNBC, ABC, FOX, and C-SPAN covered Oxfam's January report, according to the TV News Archive.[17] CNN had the most coverage with approximately seven broadcast segments from January 19 to 25, 2015. However, these stories aired between 2:00 and 3:00 a.m., far from primetime. Other coverage focused on Obama's push for tax reform.[18] CBS and MSNBC ran segments with this focus four times between 1:00 and 4:00 a.m., January 20–21, 2015, with the exception of one MSNBC story, broadcast

on February 2, 2015, at 12:00 p.m. ABC covered the story once on January 19, 2015. FOX also covered the story once on January 19, 2015, questioning Oxfam's motives for releasing the report just before the World Economic Forum in Davos, Switzerland.

Forbes was consistently critical in its coverage of the two Oxfam reports. For instance, *Forbes* columnist Tim Worstall summarized his response to the October 2014 Oxfam report in these terms: "The last 40 years of market fundamentalism have led to the largest reduction in absolute poverty in the history of the human race. Oxfam, a charity that claims to be concerned about absolute poverty, therefore insists that we must reverse market fundamentalism."[19] Subsequent *Forbes* coverage of the January report was, if anything, more dismissive.[20] *USA Today* covered the January Oxfam report, but mentioned none of the organization's proposed solutions to spiraling inequality.[21]

In sum, much of the corporate news coverage was brief, broadcast at odd hours (either late at night or early in the morning when not that many people were watching), questioned the report, and/or focused on Obama's tax reforms rather than the Oxfam reports' contents. In contrast with independent news coverage, none of the televised stories addressed details of the Oxfam reports, such as the organization's nine-point plan. The Oxfam studies received better coverage in the international press.[22]

2
Oil Industry Illegally Dumps Fracking Wastewater

Dan Bacher, "Massive Dumping of Wastewater into Aquifers Shows Big Oil's Power in California," IndyBay, October 11, 2014, http://www.indybay.org/newsitems/2014/10/11/18762739.php.

"California Aquifers Contaminated with Billions of Gallons of Fracking Wastewater," Russia Today, October 11, 2014, http://rt.com/usa/194620-california-aquifers-fracking-contamination/.

Donny Shaw, "CA Senators Voting NO on Fracking Moratorium Received 14x More from Oil & Gas Industry," MapLight, June 3, 2014, http://maplight.org/content/ca-senators-voting-no-on-fracking-moratorium-received-14x-more-from-oil-and-gas-industry.

Dan Bacher, "Senators Opposing Fracking Moratorium Received 14x More Money from Big Oil," IndyBay, June 7, 2014, http://www.indybay.org/newsitems/2014/06/07/18757051.php.

Student Researchers: Carolina de Mello (College of Marin) and Steven Feher (San Francisco State University)

Faculty Evaluators: Susan Rahman (College of Marin) and Kenn Burrows (San Francisco State University)

California state documents obtained by the Center for Biological Diversity in October 2014 revealed that the oil industry had illegally dumped almost three billion gallons of wastewater from fracking (hydraulic fracturing to extract oil and gas) into central California aquifers.[23] According to the Center for Biological Diversity report, the leaking occurred through at least nine injection disposal wells used by the oil industry to dispose of contaminated waste.

The affected aquifers supply water for human consumption and for irrigation of crops for human consumption. The documents also revealed that water supply wells located close to wastewater injection sites were tested and found to have high levels of arsenic, thallium, and nitrates, all toxic chemicals linked to the oil industry's wastewater.

According to the documents obtained by the Center, the California State Water Resources Control Board admitted that an additional nineteen wells could have been leaking wastewater into protected aquifers. One state agency official claimed that errors in the permitting process for wastewater injection could have occurred in multiple places. Adding to the magnitude of the danger, toxic chemicals such as benzene can migrate into water sources over a period of years, making accurate risk assessment difficult.

A previous study by the Center for Biological Diversity showed that "54 percent of California's 1,553 active and new wastewater injection wells are within 10 miles of a recently active fault (active in the past 200 years)."[24] The findings "raise significant concerns," this report's authors wrote, "because the distance from a wastewater injection well to a fault is a key risk factor influencing whether a well may induce an earthquake." Microseismic activity as a result of underground injection wells has been well documented in other states such as Oklahoma and Texas.

The Center for Biological Diversity report's revelations about water contamination came amidst legislative deliberation to regulate fracking in California. As both Donny Shaw of MapLight and Dan Bacher for IndyBay reported in May 2014, over the past five years, the oil industry has lobbied powerfully in the California state legislature, spending over sixty-three million dollars in efforts to persuade state policymakers to permit the continuation and expansion of fracking. In May 2014, state senators rejected a fracking moratorium bill, SB 1132. The senators who voted against the moratorium received fourteen times more money in campaign contributions from the oil industry

than those who voted for it. Shaw quoted MapLight figures: senators voting "No" on the moratorium bill received, on average, $24,981 from the oil and gas industry, while those who voted "Yes" received just $1,772 on average. "If the five active senators who abstained from voting—all Democrats—voted in favor, the moratorium would have passed." The Democrats who abstained received, on average, 4.5 times as much money as those who voted "Yes."

Although corporate media have covered debate over fracking regulations, the Center for Biological Diversity study regarding the dumping of wastewater into California's aquifers went all but ignored at first. There appears to have been a lag of more than three months between the initial independent news coverage of the Center for Biological Diversity revelations and corporate coverage.[25] In May 2015, the *Los Angeles Times* ran a front-page feature on Central Valley crops irrigated with treated oil field water; however, the *Los Angeles Times* report made no mention of the Center for Biological Diversity's findings regarding fracking wastewater contamination.[26]

In June 2015, the Environmental Protection Agency (EPA) released its study of the impacts of fracking on drinking water supplies. Although the EPA's assessment identified "important vulnerabilities to drinking water resources," it concluded that "hydraulic fracturing activities have not led to widespread, systemic impacts to drinking water resources."[27] In response, Food & Water Watch issued a press release by Executive Director Wenonah Hunter, who wrote: "Sadly, the EPA study released today falls far short of the level of scrutiny and government oversight needed to protect the health and safety of the millions of American people affected by drilling and fracking for oil and gas." Noting that the oil and gas industry refused to cooperate with the EPA on a single "prospective case study" of fracking's impacts, Hunter concluded, "This reveals the undue influence the industry has over the government and shows that the industry is afraid to allow careful monitoring of their operations."[28]

3

89 Percent of Pakistani Drone Victims Not Identifiable as Militants

Jack Serle, "Almost 2,500 Now Killed by Covert US Drone Strikes Since Obama Inauguration Six Years Ago," Bureau of Investigative Journalism, February 2, 2015, http://www.thebureauinvestigates .com/2015/02/02/almost-2500-killed-covert-us-drone-strikes-obama-inauguration/.

Jack Serle, "Get the Data: A List of US Air and Drone Strikes, Afghanistan 2015," Bureau of Investigative Journalism, February 12, 2015, http://www.thebureauinvestigates.com/2015/02/12/ us-drone-war-afghanistan-list-american-air-strikes-2015/#AFG009.

Steve Coll, "The Unblinking Stare: The Drone War in Pakistan," New Yorker, November 24, 2014, http://www.newyorker.com/magazine/2014/11/24/unblinking-stare.

Abigail Fielding-Smith, "John Kerry Says All those Fired at by Drones in Pakistan are 'Confirmed Terrorist Targets'—But with 1,675 Unnamed Dead How Do We Know?" Bureau of Investigative Journalism, October 23, 2014, http://www.thebureauinvestigates.com/2014/10/23/ john-kerry-says-all-those-fired-at-by-drones-in-pakistan-are-confirmed-terrorist-targets-but-with-1675-unnamed-dead-how-do-we-know/.

Jack Serle, "Only 4% of Drone Victims in Pakistan Named as al Qaeda Members," Bureau of Investigative Journalism, October 16, 2014, http://www.thebureauinvestigates.com/namingthedead/only-4-of-drone-victims-in-pakistan-named-as-al-qaeda-members/?lang=en.

Jeremy Scahill, "Germany is the Tell-Tale Heart of America's Drone War," Intercept, April 17, 2015, https://firstlook.org/theintercept/2015/04/17/ramstein/.

Student Researchers: Jordan Nakamoto (College of Marin) and Dylan Morrissey (Claremont McKenna College)

Faculty Evaluators: Susan Rahman (College of Marin) and Andy Lee Roth (Pomona College)

Since President Barack Obama's inauguration in 2009, an estimated 2,464 people have been killed by drone strikes targeted outside of the United States' declared war zones; this figure was posted in February 2015 by Jack Serle and the team at the Bureau of Investigative Journalism, who maintain a database of all known strikes—based on fieldwork, media reports, and leaked documents—which provides a clearer picture of the scale and impact of the US drone program than the episodic reporting provided by corporate media.

According to Bureau data, al-Qaeda members comprise only 4 percent of the total 2,379 people killed by US drone strikes in Pakistan as of October 2014, just over ten years after the first such strikes. Of the total killed, about 30 percent could be identified and 11 percent were defined as militants. Little is known about the remaining 1,675 unnamed victims. The Bureau of Investigative Journalism reported these numbers after conducting a yearlong investigation that compiled information from various sources to provide an overview of drone strike casualties.

US drone missions are flown mainly over Pakistan, where the CIA aims to weaken al-Qaeda and limit its movement into neighboring Afghanistan. The use of unmanned drones is seen as a way to mini-

mize involvement and resentment in a country that is characterized by the *New Yorker* as "unstable" and that is known to possess over a hundred nuclear weapons. While the unofficial drone war for control over the Pakistan–Afghan border ended in mid-2013, the drone campaign continued with five strikes recorded in January 2015, the most since July of 2014. In the month of January, additional strikes were reported to kill at least forty-five in Somalia and three in Yemen, where a twelve-year-old child was among the casualties.

The Bureau of Investigative Journalism's findings undermine the validity of US Secretary of State John Kerry's claim that "the only people we fire a drone at are confirmed terrorist targets at the highest level." Regardless of whether or not those killed were in fact dangerous, the inability to account for their identities invites skepticism toward US military operations and raises moral concerns about basic respect for human dignity.

In April 2015, Jeremy Scahill reported that a US military base in Ramstein, Germany, is the "the high-tech heart of America's drone program." Top-secret US documents obtained by the *Intercept*, Scahill reported, provide "the most detailed blueprint seen to date of the technical architecture used to conduct strikes with Predator and Reaper drones." Most drone pilots operate in the US, but depend on Ramstein to control their aircraft.

Corporate news coverage of US drone strikes tends to rely heavily on official government sources, many of whom are not authorized to know about those strikes, much less to discuss them publicly.[29] Exceptional occasions sometimes force government officials to reveal more about the killing programs. For instance, in April 2015, President Obama publicly apologized for a January drone strike in Pakistan that had accidentally killed two al-Qaeda hostages, including an American aid worker, Warren Weinstein. *The New York Times'* coverage included front-page news analysis by Scott Shane that included criticism of the drone strike program. For example, the article quoted Micah Zenko, a scholar at the Council on Foreign Relations, on how Obama's statement "highlights what we've sort of known: that most individuals killed are not on a kill list, and the government does not know their names." Notably, Shane's analysis made use of the Bureau of Investigative Journalism's research to show the scope of US drone strikes in Pakistan's tribal areas since 2004.[30]

New York Times reporters Mark Mazzetti and Matt Apuzzo also deserve credit for their April 2015 report, "Deep Support in Washington for C.I.A.'s Drone Missions," which made waves in Washington and among the establishment press for publicly identifying three high-ranking CIA officials with key roles in secret drone operations.[31] Consistent with usual practice, the CIA had asked the *Times* to withhold the names.[32] Among the three CIA officials revealed by Mazzetti and Apuzzo was Michael D'Andrea, whom they identified as "chief of operations during the birth of the agency's detention and interrogation program," and who subsequently, as head of the CIA Counterterrorism Center, "became an architect of the targeted killing program." D'Andrea, they revealed, "presided over the growth of C.I.A. drone operations and hundreds of strikes in Pakistan and Yemen during nine years in the position."

However, the reports by Shane, Mazzetti, and Apuzzo prove exceptional in corporate news coverage of the US drone programs. More typical in this regard is the treatment offered by *Newsweek* in an April 2015 cover story, "Can America Win a War?"[33] This piece identified drone strikes as one of the "twin prongs of U.S. strategy abroad" that are "often unreliable, discredited or unsavory." The article went on to balance Alexander Cockburn's critique—that drone strikes against alleged high-value targets increase violence against US and allied troops—with the perspective of former National Security Agency (NSA) and CIA director and retired Air Force general Michael V. Hayden—who, *Newsweek* reported, "insists that drone strikes on Al-Qaeda were crucial in preventing another big attack on the United States." The *Newsweek* coverage quoted Hayden at least nine separate times, more than any other source. It made no mention of the Bureau of Investigative Journalism's findings about drone strikes' civilian death toll.

4

Popular Resistance to Corporate Water Grabbing

Ellen Brown, "California Water Wars: Another Form of Asset Stripping?," Nation of Change, March 25, 2015, www.nationofchange.org/2015/03/25/california-water-wars-another-form-of-asset-stripping.

Victoria Collier, "Citizens Mobilize Against Corporate Water Grabs," *CounterPunch*, February 11, 2015, www.counterpunch.org/2015/02/11/citizens-mobilize-against-corporate-water-grabs.

Larry Gabriel, "When the City Turned Off Their Water, Detroit Residents and Groups Delivered Help," *YES! Magazine*, November 24, 2014, http://www.yesmagazine.org/issues/cities-are-now/when-detroit-s-citizens-fought-for-their-right-to-water.

Madeline Ostrander, "LA Imports Nearly 85 Percent of Its Water—Can It Change That by Gathering Rain?," *YES! Magazine*, January 5, 2015, http://www.yesmagazine.org/issues/cities-are-now/los-angeles-imports-nearly-85-percent-of-its-water.

Student Researchers: Antonio Arenas and Nguyet (Kelley) Thi Luu (San Francisco State University)

Faculty Evaluator: Kenn Burrows (San Francisco State University)

In January 2000, the people of Cochabamba, Bolivia, shut down the city in protest against the privatization of their municipal water system, which had resulted in rate hikes that doubled or tripled their water bills. In February of that year, Pacific News Service correspondent Jim Shultz broke the story in the Western press with "A War Over Water," his firsthand report of clashes between riot police and protesters.[34] On the fifteenth anniversary of the Cochabamba protests, popular resistance to corporate water control continues to expand around the world, encompassing remunicipalization of privatized water utilities, direct action against unjust water shutoffs, and rainwater harvesting. A common theme—access to water as a fundamental human right—unites these three issues.

As Ellen Brown reported, today's "water wars" not only pit local farmers against ranchers or urbanites, but also involve new corporate "water barons," including Goldman Sachs, JPMorgan Chase, Citigroup, the Carlyle Group, and other investment firms that are purchasing water rights from around the world at an unprecedented pace.[35] A 2014 report on water grabbing defined it in these terms:

> Water grabbing refers to situations where powerful actors are able to take control of or reallocate to their own benefit water resources at the expense of previous (un)registered local users or the ecosystems on which those users' livelihoods are based. It involves the capturing of the decision-making power around water, including the power to decide how and for what purposes water resources are used now and in the future.[36]

The authors of this report identified five "interlinked" drivers of the current "new wave of water grabbing":

1. Changing patterns in global food markets have triggered a renewed interest in acquiring land and water resources for agricultural production.
2. Rising oil prices and concerns that a "peak oil" period has been reached have led to the rise of agrofuels that use large amounts of water throughout the production cycle.
3. Growing global demand for raw materials underpins the continued expansion of the extractive industries and large-scale mining projects—including, in particular, hydraulic fracturing or "fracking."
4. The market-based management of water resources, especially the privatization of water systems and services, which jeopardizes water access for poor and marginalized groups in many developing countries.
5. The financialization of water utilities, infrastructures, and the resource itself.[37]

Much corporate news coverage of water shortages—including California's highly publicized drought—and their potential remedies fails to take into account these five drivers of water grabbing and how they intertwine.

Corporate efforts to privatize water rights are meeting robust grass-roots resistance as communities around the world assert their rights to decide how water resources are used. Over the past fifteen years, Victoria Collier reported for *CounterPunch*, there have been 180 cases across thirty-five countries of water "remunicipalization," with water control returned from private ownership to the public. "From Spain to Buenos Aires, Cochabamba to Kazakhstan, Berlin to Malaysia, water privatization is being aggressively rejected," she reported.

In opposition to the fast-growing private-public-partnership (PPP) model, which she described as "a marketing euphemism for privatization," communities in Japan, the Netherlands, India, Costa Rica, Brazil, and other countries are now pursuing public-public partnerships (PUPs) to forestall corporate water takeovers and to develop "non-profit, public-driven solutions for water infrastructure needs."

While the remunicipalization movement grows, protests in US cities, including Detroit and Baltimore, show how some forms of ostensibly public water remain deeply problematic. As Collier reported, since the summer of 2014, Detroit residents have engaged in direct action to resist city water shutoffs that disproportionately affected low-income, mostly African-American residents. In Detroit, water rates had increased by 119 percent over the past decade and the poverty level was roughly 40 percent. In consequence, many residents could not afford to pay their water bills, and the city's Water and Sewerage Department began shutting off residential water services, sometimes without providing households any advance notice. Food & Water Watch reported, "The extensive service disconnections are closely tied to Emergency Manager Kevyn Orr's plan to privatize or corporatize the water and sewer system."[38] Notably, the city exempted from shutoffs many businesses that also had past-due water bills. Some forty businesses owed approximately $9.5 million in past bills, but were not subject to shutoffs.

As of October 2014, Detroit's Water and Sewerage Department had shut off water service for some 27,000 Detroit residents. However, as *YES! Magazine*'s Larry Gabriel reported, "Grassroots progressive action has backed down aggressive action by the city and its contractors."

Residents of Baltimore faced similar challenges in spring 2015, as their city threatened to shut off water service for some 250,000 households, affecting approximately 750,000 residents. An April 2015 Food & Water Watch press release asserted that "Baltimore is repeating Detroit's mistakes," and that disconnecting water services posed "a very real public health threat."[39] In May 2015, the *Baltimore Sun* reported that the city's enforcement of "long-unpaid" water bills was "starkly uneven," with businesses that owed the greatest amounts exempted, while residents faced summary shutoffs. The *Sun* quoted Charly Carter, director of the advocacy group Maryland Working Families: "If the city can shut off 1,600 working families from their water, but hasn't shut off even one commercial account, I think that speaks volumes about where their priorities are."[40] According to the *Sun*, over 350 large commercial accounts—a category that includes businesses, nonprofits, and government offices—account for a total of $15 million in unpaid water bills.

Direct action and other community efforts were ongoing in Detroit and Baltimore as this volume went to press.

The practice of rainwater harvesting is becoming increasingly widespread and sophisticated, showing another way that ordinary people and local communities can reclaim control of their water. In light of a growing population, climate change, and projected long-term water shortages, many cities and their residents are rethinking water use. As Madeline Ostrander reported for *YES! Magazine*, the city of Los Angeles currently imports more than 85 percent of its water, yet every year Los Angeles drains billions of gallons of rainwater into the ocean. New leaders are stepping forward to offer time-proven techniques to meet urgent local needs, including TreePeople, which is partnering with the city of Los Angeles to rewrite its storm water management plan, to develop distributed rainwater harvesting, and to transform the city's landscape. TreePeople and other organizations, including The River Project, are showing how restoring the landscape's natural capacity to slow, filter, and store water could solve many problems and vastly reduce Los Angeles's reliance on external water sources.[41] The River Project is a pioneer in the "urban acupuncture" approach to water sustainability along the Los Angeles River watershed. In partnership with the Los Angeles Department of Water and Power and the California Coastal Commission, the Project's "Water LA" program empowers communities to design and install home gray-water systems. Due to these efforts, Los Angeles property owners can now obtain low-cost, over-the-counter permits for gravity flow systems running from their laundries, tubs, or lavatory sinks.[42]

Rainwater harvesting and its positive impacts are not limited to big cities like Los Angeles. In fall 2015, Rajendra Singh, an Indian activist, will be awarded the esteemed Stockholm Water Prize for his work empowering poor farmers by reviving traditional knowledge and guiding people to build small rainwater ponds. Over the past thirty years, he has helped local communities revive five rivers and a thousand villages using these techniques. Where the World Bank asserts that countries like India need to continue building large dams, Singh's life provides evidence of robust, sustainable alternatives.[43]

5

Fukushima Nuclear Disaster Deepens

"TEPCO Drops Bombshell About Sea Releases; 8 Billion Bq Per Day," Simply Info: The Fukushima Project, August 26, 2014, http://www.fukuleaks.org/web/?p=13700.

Sarah Lazare, "Fukushima Meltdown Worse Than Previous Estimates: TEPCO," Common Dreams, August 7, 2014, http://www.commondreams.org/news/2014/08/07/fukushima-meltdown-worse-previous-estimates-tepco.

Michel Chossudovsky, "The Fukushima Endgame: The Radioactive Contamination of the Pacific Ocean," Global Research, December 17, 2014, http://www.globalresearch.ca/the-fukushima-endgame/5420188.

Student Researcher: Cassie Kahant (Florida Atlantic University)

Faculty Evaluator: James F. Tracy (Florida Atlantic University)

The 2011 nuclear reactor meltdown in Fukushima, Japan, continues unresolved, despite both assurances by government authorities and major news media that the situation has been contained and the assessment of the United Nations' International Atomic Energy Agency that Japan has made "significant progress" in cleaning up the site.[44]

The continued dumping of extremely radioactive cooling water into the Pacific Ocean from the destroyed nuclear plant, already being detected along the Japanese coastline, has the potential to impact

entire portions of the Pacific Ocean and North America's western shoreline. Aside from the potential release of plutonium into the Pacific Ocean, Tokyo Electric Power Company (TEPCO) recently admitted that the facility is releasing large quantities of water contaminated with tritium, cesium, and strontium into the ocean every day.

While acknowledging that the water in remaining tanks at the Fukushima facility is heavily "tainted," a December 2014 statement from the Japanese government's Nuclear Radiation Authority affirmed a decision to dump it into the Pacific. Aside from the potential release of plutonium into the Pacific Ocean, TEPCO admitted that the facility is releasing a whopping 150 billion becquerels of tritium and seven billion becquerels of cesium- and strontium-contaminated water into the ocean every day. By contrast, the Japanese government does not allow over 100 becquerels per kilogram to be sold to its citizenry. "This water contains plutonium 239 and its release into the ocean has both local as well as global repercussions," wrote Michel Chossudovsky at Global Research.

In August 2014, TEPCO acknowledged that nearly every fuel rod at Reactor 3 in the No. 1 plant had melted as a result of the earthquake and tsunami, Sarah Lazare reported, drawing on Japanese press sources. Previously, TEPCO had estimated that only 63 percent of the reactor's nuclear fuel had melted. The TEPCO statement also noted that the fuel began melting six hours earlier than previously believed. Both factors, Lazare wrote, would make the extraction and disposal of melted fuel more difficult.

More than four years since the tsunami and earthquake devastated Fukushima, corporate media do not treat the ongoing disaster itself as significantly newsworthy. Instead, most developing corporate coverage focuses on whether other countries, including the US, are adequately prepared if a similar type of nuclear disaster were to occur elsewhere. Certainly this is an important consideration, but the plight of the Japanese people displaced by the disaster, not to mention its long-term, potentially global environmental consequences, remain dramatically underreported in the corporate press.

In May 2015, the Japanese Nuclear Regulation Authority gave final clearance to the Sendai Nuclear Power Plant, which is owned and operated by the Kyushu Electric Power Company, to restart operations. It is the nation's first nuclear power plant to resume operations, under new government regulations, since the 2011 Fukushima disaster. Russia Today reported that "despite objections from almost two thirds of the public," Japanese Prime Minister Shinzo Abe "wants nuclear plants to supply about 20–22 percent of Japan's energy needs by 2030."[45]

6
Methane and Arctic Warming's Global Impacts

Dahr Jamail, "The Methane Monster Roars," *Truthout*, January 13, 2015, http://truth-out.org/news/item/28490-the-methane-monster-roars.

Student Researcher: Michael Brannon (Sonoma State University)

Faculty Evaluator: Peter Phillips (Sonoma State University)

In recent years, atmospheric methane levels have reached an all-time high. A greenhouse gas that is a leading contributor to global warming, methane is far more destructive than carbon dioxide. In his report for *Truthout*, Dahr Jamail quoted Paul Beckwith, a professor of climatology and meteorology at the University of Ottawa: "Our climate system is in early stages of abrupt climate change that, unchecked, will lead to a temperature rise of 5 to 6 degrees Celsius within a decade or two." Such changes would have "unprecedented effects" for life on Earth.

The melting of arctic ice releases previously trapped methane into the atmosphere. "What happens in the Arctic," Beckwith observed, "does not stay in the Arctic." The loss of arctic ice affects the Earth as a whole. For example, as the temperature difference between the Arctic and the equator decreases, the jet stream increases. This in turn speeds the melting of arctic ice.

Leonid Yurganov, a senior research scientist at the University of Maryland, stated that "increased methane would influence air temperature near the surface. This would accelerate the Arctic warming and change the climate everywhere in the world."

The East Siberian Arctic Shelf (ESAS) is one area of particular concern. Some million square kilometers in size, the ESAS releases seventeen million tons of methane into the atmosphere each year, according to a recent study. Natalia Shakhova, a researcher with the University of Alaska Fairbanks' International Arctic Research Center, reported that ESAS emissions "are prone to be non-gradual (massive, abrupt)."

A 2013 study, published in *Nature*, reported that a fifty-gigaton "burp" of methane is "highly possible at any time." As Jamail clarified, "That would be the equivalent of at least 1,000 gigatons of carbon dioxide," noting that, since 1850, humans have released a total of approximately 1,475 gigatons in carbon dioxide. A massive, sudden change in methane levels could, in turn, lead to temperature increases of four to six degrees Celsius in just one or two decades—a rapid rate of climate change to which human agriculture, and ecosystems more generally, could not readily adapt.

In April 2015, US Secretary of State John Kerry became chair of the eight-nation Arctic Council. On this occasion, he spoke about methane emissions, saying, "These pollutants are a threat to everybody." Kerry's remarks and the Council's meeting received coverage in corporate outlets such as the *New York Times* and the *Los Angeles Times*. The *New York Times*' coverage did not elaborate at all on

methane threats, much less raise scientists' concerns about the East Siberian Arctic Shelf, but it did focus on the Arctic Council's biennial gathering as another arena in which Western nations saber-rattled with Russia over the Ukraine.[46] The *Los Angeles Times*' coverage also emphasized Russia–US relations: for example, it reported that "the Kremlin has underscored its role in the Arctic with massive military exercises, including a readiness drill last month that sent 40,000 troops, 50 warships and more than 100 combat aircraft into and over the Barents Sea." The only quoted source to mention methane in the *Los Angeles Times*' coverage was Whit Sheard of the Ocean Conservancy, who represents a consortium of environmental groups at the council. Sheard said, "Considering the challenges facing the Arctic, it's easy to dwell on the negative. But I think today's proceedings give us some optimism that these incredibly complex issues can be resolved." However, noting that some 30 percent of the world's untapped natural gas rests beneath the Arctic seafloor, the *Los Angeles Times* reported that opportunities to access these resources has "set off a scramble among energy giants of the council member states, as well as other countries that claim a share of the region's bounty or an existential stake in how the demands of development and environmental protection are managed."[47]

7
Fear of Government Spying is "Chilling" Writers' Freedom of Expression

Lauren McCauley, "Fear of Government Spying 'Chilling' Writers' Speech Worldwide," Common Dreams, January 5, 2015, http://commondreams.org/news/2015/01/05/fear-government-spying-chilling-writers-speech-worldwide.
Lauren McCauley, "Government Surveillance Threatens Journalism, Law and Thus Democracy: Report," Common Dreams, July 28, 2014, http://commondreams.org/news/2014/07/28/government-surveillance-threatens-journalism-law-and-thus-democracy-report.

Student Researcher: Shelby Meyers (Diablo Valley College)
Faculty Evaluator: Mickey Huff (Diablo Valley College)

Mass surveillance has "badly shaken writers' faith that democratic governments will respect their rights to privacy and freedom of expression," according to a January 2015 PEN America report based on the responses of 772 writers from fifty countries.[48] Reporting for Common Dreams, Lauren McCauley covered not only the PEN America report, but also a July 2014 report by the American Civil Liberties Union and Human Rights Watch indicating that US journalists and lawyers increasingly avoid work on potentially controversial topics due to fear of government spying.[49]

McCauley's January 2015 Common Dreams story quoted one of the conclusions from the PEN America report: "If writers avoid exploring topics for fear of possible retribution, the material available to readers—particularly those seeking to understand the most controversial and challenging issues facing the world today—may be greatly impoverished."

According to the PEN America survey, 34 percent of writers in liberal democracies reported some degree of self-censorship (compared with 61 percent of writers living in authoritarian countries, and 44 percent in semi-democratic countries). Nearly 60 percent of the writers from Western Europe, the US, and the latter's "Five Eyes" surveillance partners (Australia, the United Kingdom, Canada, and New Zealand) indicated that US credibility "has been significantly damaged for the long term" by revelations of the US government surveillance programs.

In the few instances when corporate news media covered the PEN America report, that coverage downplayed the scope of the report's implications. For instance, while the *New York Times'* Jennifer Schuessler filed a substantive story on the PEN America report, the *Times* ran her article in its arts section.[50] A second *Times* article based on the PEN America report focused specifically on press freedom in Hong Kong, effectively ignoring the forty-nine other countries that the report addressed.[51]

8

Who Dies at the Hands of US Police—and How Often

Richard Becker, "U.S. Cops Kill at 100 Times Rate of Other Capitalist Countries," *Liberation*, January 4, 2015, http://www.liberationnews.org/u-s-cops-kill-100-times-rate-capitalist-countries/.

Jon Swaine, Oliver Laughland, and Jamiles Lartey, "Black Americans Killed by Police Twice as Likely to be Unarmed as White People," *Guardian*, June 1, 2015, http://www.theguardian.com/us-news/2015/jun/01/black-americans-killed-by-police-analysis.

Student Researcher: Brooks Brorsen (Sonoma State University)

Faculty Evaluator: Peter Phillips (Sonoma State University)

Compared with other capitalist countries, the US is unquestionably different when it comes to the level of state violence directed against minorities, Richard Becker reported in January 2015 for *Liberation*. Using 2011 figures, Becker wrote that, on a per capita basis, "the rate of killing by U.S. police was about 100 times that of English cops in 2011." Similarly, US police were forty times as likely to kill as German police officers, and twenty times as likely to kill as their Canadian counterparts. This, Becker noted, is probably not the kind of "American exceptionalism" that President Obama had in mind when he addressed graduating West Point cadets in May 2014.

It is not clear how many people police in the US kill each year, since there is no federal agency that accurately keeps track of such information. The Federal Bureau of Investigation (FBI) compiles annual statistics for "justified homicides" by police, and all reported police killings are registered as "justified" killings by the FBI. Since participation in reporting homicides to the FBI by police and sheriff's departments is voluntary, only about 800 police agencies—out of 18,000—provide statistics.

According to FBI statistics, there were 461 "justified homicides" by police in 2013, but the website KilledByPolice.net, reported that US police killed around 748 people in just the last eight months of 2013, and 1,100 in 2014. The Killed By Police figures were compiled using establishment media sources; because not every police killing is reported, and checking all news sources across the country is virtually impossible, these figures likely underestimate the number of police killings of civilians.

In England, which Becker characterized as "a capitalist country with a long history of racism," police do not carry guns on patrol. Official records indicate that British police only used guns three times while on duty in all of 2013, with zero reported fatalities.

In recent months, there has been an outpouring of opposition to police murder in the United States. Hundreds of thousands of people have taken to the streets in hundreds of cities, towns, and campuses. "As in all other progressive struggles throughout history," Becker wrote, "it is the movement of the people in the streets, schools and workplaces that is the key to real change."

In June 2015, a team of reporters at the *Guardian* filed a major new report on police killings in the US.[52] Summarizing findings from the *Guardian* study, Jon Swaine, Oliver Laughland, and Jamiles Lartey reported that 102 unarmed people were killed by US police through the first five months of 2015, and that agencies are killing people at twice the rate calculated by the US government.[53] Furthermore, they wrote, "black Americans are more than twice as likely to be unarmed when killed during encounters with police as white people." Based on analysis of public records and local news reports, and the *Guardian*'s own reporting, they reported that "32% of black people killed by police in 2015 were unarmed, as were 25% of Hispanic and Latino people, compared with 15% of white people killed."

Over the five-month period covered in the study, *Guardian* researchers identified twenty-seven people killed by police use of Tasers. All but one of these victims were unarmed. The study also documented fourteen officer-involved deaths following altercations in custody, including that of Freddie Gray, whose death from a broken neck sustained in a Baltimore police van led to public protests and the indictment of six city police officers.

Twenty-six percent of people killed by police exhibited some sort of mental illness, with at least twenty-nine cases involving a victim who was suicidal.

To its credit, the *Washington Post* also published a significant investigation of US police killings, around the same time as the *Guardian* study.[54] *The Post* analysis corroborated many of the findings from the *Guardian* investigation.[55] Both studies found that police fatally shot approximately 2.5 people per day across the first five months of 2015. Both studies found significant racial disparities among the dead, especially in cases of unarmed suspects. In the 385 cases that the *Post* identified, only three officers have faced charges. *The Post* study found that, "for the vast majority of departments, a fatal shooting is a rare event." Of some 18,000 law enforcement agencies, only 306 have recorded a fatal shooting in the first five months of 2015. *The Post* found that nineteen state and local agencies were involved in three or more fatal shootings each, including departments in Los Angeles, Oklahoma City, and Bakersfield, California.

Among many sources quoted in the *Post*'s significant report was

Jim Bueermann, a former police chief and president of the Police Foundation, a nonprofit dedicated to improving law enforcement. Bueermann spoke for many when he said, "These shootings are grossly underreported. . . . We have to understand the phenomena behind these fatal encounters. . . . There is a compelling social need for this, but a lack of political will to make it happen."

9
Millions in Poverty Get Less Media Coverage Than Billionaires Do

Steve Rendall, Emily Kaufmann, and Sara Qureshi, "Even GOP Attention Can't Make Media Care about Poor," *Extra!*, Fairness and Accuracy in Reporting, June 1, 2014, http://fair.org/extra-online-articles/even-gop-attention-cant-make-media-care-about-poor/.

"Millions in Poverty Get Less Coverage Than 482 Billionaires," Fairness and Accuracy in Reporting, June 26, 2014, http://fair.org/press-release/millions-in-poverty-get-less-coverage-than-482-billionaires/?utm_source=rss&utm_medium=rss&utm_campaign=millions-in-poverty-get-less-coverage-than-482-billionaires.

Frederick Reese, "Billionaires Get More Media Attention Than The Poor," MintPress News, June 30, 2014, http://www.mintpressnews.com/billionaires-get-media-attention-poor/193174/.

Tavis Smiley, "Poverty Less Than .02 Percent of Lead Media Coverage," *Huffington Post*, March 7, 2014, http://www.huffingtonpost.com/tavis-smiley/-poverty-less-than-02-of_b_4921119.html.

Student Researchers: Feather Flores and Susanne Boden (Pomona College)

Faculty Evaluator: Andy Lee Roth (Pomona College)

In June 2014, Fairness and Accuracy in Reporting (FAIR) published a study showing that *ABC World News, CBS Evening News*, and *NBC Nightly News* give more media coverage to the 482 billionaires in the US than to the fifty million people in poverty, airing almost four times as many stories that included the term "billionaire" as stories including terms such as "homeless" or "welfare."

"The notion that the wealthiest nation on Earth has one in every six of its citizens living at or below the poverty threshold reflects not a lack of resources, but a lack of policy focus and attention—and this is due to a lack of public awareness to the issue," Frederick Reese of MintPress News wrote.

The FAIR study showed that between January 2013 and February 2014, an average of only 2.7 seconds per every twenty-two-minute episode discussed poverty in some format. During the fourteen-month study, FAIR found just twenty-three news segments that addressed poverty. Those segments featured fifty-four sources, only twenty-two of which were people personally affected by poverty. "That means, on average, someone affected by poverty appeared on any nightly news show only once every 20 days," FAIR reported.

Television news coverage of the rich was not only four times more frequent, but also "painted them in a favorable light," according to the study. For instance, during an August 2013 segment of *NBC Nightly News*, anchor Brian Williams explained that billionaires such as Warren Buffett and Jeff Bezos were purchasing newspapers "because they believe in quality work and a robust press." (As questionable as it may have been at the time, Williams's assessment becomes rather ironic in light of his own travails in journalistic credibility.)

In March 2014, Tavis Smiley reported that "poverty represents less than 0.02 percent of lead media coverage." His article focused on how the media could increase the "quantity and quality of coverage of this crucial issue." Smiley's recommendations included calling on media to "promote our collective appreciation of the inherent values we all share in alleviating domestic poverty." He asked, "Are we really telling the diversity of stories among the 50 million people impacted by poverty?"

"There is no legitimate justification for ignoring a story affecting tens of millions of our most vulnerable, under any circumstances," said FAIR's Steve Rendall. Nevertheless, the disproportionate amount of airtime corporate media have allotted to covering billionaires has—perhaps not surprisingly—not been covered by the corporate press.

10

Costa Rica Setting the Standard on Renewable Energy

Myles Gough, "Costa Rica Powered with 100% Renewable Energy for 75 Straight Days," Science Alert, March 20, 2015, http://www.sciencealert.com/costa-rica-powered-with-100-renewable-energy-for-75-days.

Adam Epstein, "Costa Rica is Now Running Completely on Renewable Energy," Quartz, March 23, 2015, http://qz.com/367985/costa-rica-is-now-running-completely-on-renewable-energy/.

Student Researcher: Lauren Kemmeter (College of Marin)

Faculty Evaluator: Susan Rahman (College of Marin)

For seventy-five days straight during the first months of 2015, the nation of Costa Rica did not burn any fossil fuels to generate electricity. Instead, as a result of heavy rainfall, hydropower plants generated almost all of the country's electricity. The country's geothermal, wind, and solar energy sources made reliance on coal and petroleum sources unnecessary.

As Myles Gough reported, Costa Rica's primary industries are tourism and agriculture, which require little energy, compared with industries such as mining or manufacturing. The nation also has topographical features (including volcanoes) that are conducive to producing renewable energy.

Both Lizzie Wade, writing for *Wired*, and Lindsay Fendt, of the *Guardian*, noted that the heavy rainfall that allowed Costa Rica to generate all its electricity from renewable sources in early 2015 is likely the result of climate change.[56] (Most years, Costa Rica generates approximately 90 percent of its electricity without burning fossil fuels.) Drought would seriously disrupt Costa Rica's ability to generate electricity with hydropower. As Wade reported, in 2014, Costa Rica "declared a state of emergency in the country's northwest because of an El Niño-fueled drought," which forced utilities to switch on some diesel generators. Nevertheless, as Gough noted, "100 percent renewable energy generation, for any extended period of time, is an enviable achievement."

Other communities, cities, and countries aim to follow in Costa Rica's footsteps, Adam Epstein reported. Bonaire, a Dutch island territory off Venezuela's coast operates on nearly all renewable energy sources; Iceland already produces 100 percent of its electricity from renewable energy sources, with about 85 percent of all its energy from geothermal and hydropower source; and Denmark obtains 40 percent of its energy from wind, with plans to cease all fossil fuel use by 2050.

In the US, Samantha Page reported, "Hawaii is on its way to having the greenest grid in the nation."[57] In May 2015, the state legislature sent a bill (HB 623) to the governor's office that requires all electricity provided by electric companies to come from renewable sources by 2045. Around the world, over fifty cities, including Vancouver, Canada; San Diego and San Francisco, in California; and Sydney, Australia, have announced their progress towards 100 percent renewable energy. Some are aiming for 2020, others by 2030 or 2035.[58]

11

Pesticide Manufacturers Spend Millions on PR Response to Declining Bee Populations

Michele Simon, "Follow the Honey: 7 Ways Pesticide Companies Are Spinning the Bee Crisis to Protect Profits," Friends of the Earth, April 28, 2014, http://www.foe.org/news/blog/2014-04-follow-the-honey-7-ways-pesticide-companies-are-spinning-bee-crisis.

Rebekah Wilce, "Pesticide Firms Use Tobacco Playbook to Spin Bee Crisis," PR Watch, Center for Media and Democracy, May 12, 2014, http://www.prwatch.org/news/2014/05/12468/pesticide-industry-uses-big-tobacco-playbook-spin-bee-crisis#sthash.gy3guWE9.dpuf.

Timothy Brown et al., "Gardeners Beware 2014: Bee-Toxic Pesticides Found in 'Bee-Friendly' Plants Sold at Garden Centers across the U.S. and Canada," Friends of the Earth, June 2014, http://www.foe.org/projects/food-and-technology/beeaction.

Brandon Keim, "How Your Bee-Friendly Garden May Actually Be Killing Bees," *Wired*, June 25, 2014, http://www.wired.com/2014/06/garden-center-neonicotinoids.

Student Researcher: Stephanie Armendariz (San Francisco State University)

Faculty Evaluator: Kenn Burrows (San Francisco State University)

A May 2014 study from the Harvard School of Public Health showed that two widely used neonicotinoids appear to significantly harm honeybee colonies.[59] In April 2015, *Science* magazine published two additional studies whose findings corroborated and extended those of the Harvard study.[60] Neonicotinoids are used as seed treatments in more than 140 crops. They are systemic pesticides, meaning they are absorbed through roots and leaves and distributed throughout an entire plant, including its pollen and nectar. For pollinators, low-level exposure can lead to sublethal effects such as altered learning, impaired foraging, and immune suppression; at higher levels, exposure can be deadly.

In response to scientific evidence like this, three of the leading corporations that produce neonicotinoid pesticides—Bayer, Syngenta, and Monsanto—have engaged in massive public relations campaigns, costing more than $100 million and employing tactics similar to those that Big Tobacco used for decades to deny public health findings.

As Michele Simon reported in a study for Friends of the Earth, these tactics include creating distractions by blaming anything but the pesticides for documented collapses in honeybee populations—including, for example, blaming farmers for misuse of the pesticides. These companies also attack scientists and journalists to discredit their findings. At the same time, Bayer, Syngenta, and Monsanto attempt to buy credibility by cultivating alliances and strategic partnerships with farmers, beekeepers, and agricultural organizations in hopes of representing themselves as "friends of the bees." Thus, for example, Monsanto announced the formation of a Honey Bee Advisory Council, a strategic alliance of Monsanto executives and others. The British Bee-Keepers Association received significant funding from Bayer, Syngenta, and other pesticide companies. In return, they endorsed the insecticides as "bee-friendly."[61]

As Rebekah Wilce reported for PR Watch, "Rather than taking action on a problem that threatens food production worldwide, pesticide companies have taken a leaf from the tobacco industry playbook, ramping up efforts to sow doubt about the extent of the problem and their own potential role in the crisis." By contrast, she noted, the European Union has implemented a two-year ban on use of the three most common neonicotinoids, imidacloprid, clothianidin, and thiamethoxam.

In June 2014, Brandon Keim, writing for *Wired*, reported on another Friends of the Earth study showing that big-box garden centers in North America—including Home Depot, Lowe's and Walmart—sell ostensibly bee-friendly plants that actually contain high levels of neonicotinoids. The study found that thirty-six out of seventy-one (51 percent) garden plant samples purchased at top garden retailers in eighteen cities across the US and Canada contained neonicotinoid pesticides. Forty percent of the positive samples contained two or more types of neonicotinoids. "Unfortunately," the report's authors wrote, "home gardeners have no idea they may actually be poisoning pollinators through their efforts to plant bee-friendly gardens."

Although major news outlets—including, for example, the *New York Times*, the *Washington Post*, and National Public Radio—covered *Nature*'s two reports about neonicotinoids' negative effects on bees, they did not report the public relations campaigns by Bayer, Syngenta, and Monsanto, which aimed to undermine the scientific studies' findings and deflect blame from pesticides.[62] Similarly, the establishment press covered Lowes' announcement that it would no longer sell products containing neonicotinoids,[63] but did not report that "bee-friendly" plants sold by home garden centers across the US may actually be tricking well-intentioned customers into exposing pollinators to neonicotinoids in their own home gardens.

12

Seeds of Doubt: USDA Ignores Popular Critiques of New Pesticide-Resistant Genetically Modified Crops

Anastasia Pantsios, "USDA Approves Controversial GMO Corn and Soy," EcoWatch, September 18, 2014, http://ecowatch.com/2014/09/18/usda-dow-gmo-corn-soy-glyphosate.

Mary Ellen Kustin and Soren Rundquist, "Elementary School Students at Increased Pesticide Risk," Environmental Working Group, August 14, 2014, http://www.ewg.org/agmag/2014/08/elementary-school-students-increased-pesticide-risk.

Student Researcher: Stephanie Santiago (Indian River State College)

Faculty Evaluator: Elliot D. Cohen (Indian River State College)

Despite nearly 400,000 petition signatures from citizens, health professionals, and farmers expressing public opposition, in September 2014 the US Department of Agriculture (USDA) approved a new generation of genetically engineered corn and soybeans, created by the biotech company Dow AgroSciences.[64] The new Enlist brand seeds will tolerate a new weed killer also engineered by Dow, called Enlist Duo, which combines for the first time two common herbicides: 2,4-Dichlorophenoxyacetic acid, a component of the toxic Agent Orange herbicide used during the Vietnam War,

and glyphosate, the key element in Monsanto's Roundup herbicide. Since some weeds have developed resistance to either 2,4-D or glyphosate, Dow's Enlist Duo aimed to combine the two into a single, more effective herbicide.

The USDA approved the new Enlist Duo–resistant seeds even though it acknowledged that this approval "could increase use of 2,4-D by as much as 600 percent and possibly affect nearby crops such as tomatoes and grapes not engineered to resist the chemical," according to Anastasia Pantsios's reporting. Her report continued:

> As farmers have been encouraged to devote more and more acres to single crops (aka "monocropping") and use huge doses of glyphosate-based herbicides to deal with weeds, so-called "superweeds" have cropped up that are resistant to the herbicides. But many farmers and food safety advocates fear that increased applications of more powerful herbicides will only cause more resistant weeds to appear.

2,4-D not only threatens crop integrity, but is also associated with public safety risks, including various forms of cancer, Parkinson's disease, hormone disruption, and birth defects.

Spokespersons for numerous organizations, including the Center for Food Safety and the Organic Consumers Association, condemned the USDA decision, Pantsios reported. "The USDA ignored public opposition and its responsibility to protect public health and agriculture," said Wenonah Hauter, executive director of Food & Water Watch. She called the approval of 2,4-D–ready crops "one of the most negligent decisions that the USDA has made in the nearly twenty years since genetically engineered crops have been on the market."

As Mary Ellen Kustin and Soren Rundquist reported, research shows that almost 500 elementary schools are located within 200 feet of soybean and corn fields. "This finding is alarming," they wrote, "because young children are especially vulnerable to the toxic herbicide 2,4-D in Dow AgroSciences' Enlist Duo." Kustin and Rundquist noted that although Dow claims that Enlist Duo would not drift more than 202 feet if applied properly, the EPA's own risk assessment found that other formulations of 2,4-D have drifted more than 1,000 feet. They concluded that "the EPA needs to pay considerably more attention to the additional exposure risks borne by young children who live or study near corn and soybean fields than it did in its risk assessment."

Corporate news coverage of this story has been limited. For instance, CNBC's coverage of the USDA decision emphasized the "controversy" over so-called superweeds and their billion-dollar cost to farmers, but did not address the human health affects of glyphosate or 2,4-D.[65] the *Los Angeles Times* relegated the topic to its editorial pages—where, to its credit, it did take a strong position regarding a loophole in the federal regulatory process: noting that the USDA assesses whether genetically engineered crops threaten other crops, while the EPA is charged with overseeing the safety of herbicides, the *Los Angeles Times* pointed out that "no agency looks at the bigger policy question of whether the nation is embarking on a potentially dangerous path toward creating ever-more-resistant weeds and spraying them and crops with larger and larger doses of stronger herbicides." That question, the *Los Angeles Times* editors wrote, "should be answered before the country escalates the war out in the fields."[66]

13
Pentagon and NATO Encircle Russia and China

Bruce K. Gagnon, "The Pentagon's Strategy for World Domination: Full Spectrum Dominance, from Asia to Africa," Plymouth Institute for Peace Research, August 20, 2014, http://www.pipr.co.uk/all/the-pentagons-strategy-for-world-domination-full-spectrum-dominance-from-asia-to-africa/.

Student Researcher: Jacob Crabtree (Sonoma State University)

Faculty Evaluator: Peter Phillips (Sonoma State University)

In service of corporate capital and with vested interests in the regions' natural resources, the Pentagon and the North Atlantic Treaty Organization (NATO) have been encircling Russia and China with military bases and missile defense systems, Bruce K. Gagnon reported.

The US has established military bases in Romania and Bulgaria with plans for another in Albania, in an attempt to surround Russia. Bases with missile defense systems are located in Turkey, Poland, and Romania, while US Navy destroyers with comparable capabilities operate in the Black Sea. Similarly, NATO has expanded into Latvia, Lithuania, and

Estonia on Russia's border, with talk of Georgia, Sweden, Ukraine, and Finland joining NATO and thus adding to the potential for encirclement. US and NATO deployment is designed to "safeguard oil and gas fields in the [Caspian Sea] region," according to General James Jones in 2006 when he was NATO's Supreme Allied Commander.

The US Navy is also preparing to increase its presence in the Arctic, officially to "protect shipping." However, Senator Angus King (Independent-ME) has observed that previously inaccessible fossil fuels in the Arctic will now be accessible, suggesting that, as in the Caspian Sea region, protection of sea lanes is linked to the potential for increased oil extraction in the Arctic.

In encircling China, the US Navy has Aegis destroyers with missile capabilities patrolling the region. In addition to the naval presence, there are thirty ground-based missile defense systems in South Korea as well as at bases located in Hawaii, South Korea, Japan, Guam, Okinawa, Taiwan, Australia, and the Philippines. Author Noam Chomsky has described US foreign and military policy regarding oil supplies as a "lever of world domination." Control over natural resources keeps competing markets dependent on the US as well as in line with its interests.

14
Global Forced Displacement Tops Fifty Million

"World Refugee Day: Global Forced Displacement Tops 50 Million for First Time in Post-World War II Era," United Nations High Commissioner for Refugees (UNHCR), June 20, 2014, http://www.unhcr.org/53a155bc6.html.

War's Human Cost, UNHCR Global Trends 2013, June 20, 2014, http://www.unhcr.org/5399a14f9.html.

Student Researchers: Stephanie Sun and Chinasa T. Okolo (Pomona College)

Faculty Evaluator: Andy Lee Roth (Pomona College)

On World Refugee Day 2014, the global total of people who had undergone forced displacement was the highest on record since World War II. A Global Trends report compiled by the UNHCR (United Nations High Commissioner for Refugees) established a figure of 51.2 million globally displaced people at the end of 2013, an increase of six million from 45.2 million in 2012. The globally displaced population consists of refugees, asylum seekers, and internally displaced people—those who have fled their homes to other parts of their home countries.

Refugees account for 16.7 million people worldwide—including over six million who had been in exile for more than five years by the end of 2013. Over half (53 percent) of the 11.7 million refugees under the UNHCR's mandate came from three countries—Afghanistan (2.56 million), the Syrian Arab Republic (2.47 million), and Somalia (1.12 million). (The remaining five million Palestinian refugees are registered under the United Nations Reliefs Works Agency, UNRWA.) In a span of just five years, Syria has gone from being the world's second largest refugee-hosting county to being its second largest refugee-producing country.

The report documented nearly 1.2 million asylum seekers, including a record 25,300 asylum applications from children who had been separated from or were unaccompanied by their parents. Internally displaced people amounted to a record 33.3 million people, the largest increase of any group in the Global Trends report. The UNHCR noted that "helping these people represents a special challenge as many are in conflict zones."

Further, the report noted that the figure of 51.2 million forcibly displaced people does not include the worldwide population of stateless people. Noting that statelessness "remains hard to quantify with precision," the UNHCR reported a figure of 3.5 million stateless people based on data reported by the governments of seventy-five countries. However, recognizing limits in that data, the UNHCR estimated that statelessness affected closer to ten million people in 2013.

"We are seeing here the immense costs of not ending wars, of failing to resolve or prevent conflict," said UN High Commissioner for Refugees António Guterres. "Peace is today dangerously in deficit. Humanitarians can help as a palliative, but political solutions are vitally needed. Without this, the alarming levels of conflict and the mass suffering that is reflected in these figures will continue."

15

Big Sugar Borrowing Tactics from Big Tobacco

"Added Sugar, Subtracted Science: How Industry Obscures Science and Undermines Public
    Health Policy on Sugar," Union of Concerned Scientists, June 2014, http://www.ucsusa.org/
    center-for-science-and-democracy/sugar-industry-undermines-public-health-policy.html#.
    VRdgIoK3BUQ.
Kristen Bole, "'Sugar Papers' Reveal Industry Role in 1970s Dental Program," University of Cali-
    fornia, San Francisco, March 10, 2015, https://www.ucsf.edu/news/2015/03/123636/"sugar-
    papers"-reveal-industry-role-1970s-dental-program.

Student Researcher: Kaitlin Allerton (College of Marin)

Faculty Evaluator: Susan Rahman (College of Marin)

The Union of Concerned Scientists (UCS) reported in June 2014 that "food and beverage manufacturers along with industry-supported organizations such as trade associations, front groups, and public relations firms" have actively sought to ensure that Americans continue to consume sugar at high levels. The sugar industry has adopted many of the same tactics previously developed and employed by the tobacco industry, including attacking scientific evidence; spreading misinformation through industry websites, research institutes, and trade associations to deceive the public; deploying industry scientists; influencing academia; and undermining policy.

For example, in 2003 the World Health Organization (WHO) was to publish its *Global Health Strategies on Diet and Health* (GHSDH), which included a report that recommended lowering sugar consumption. In response, the Sugar Association—which represents sugar cane and sugar beet producers and refiners—threatened to "exercise every avenue available . . . including asking congressional appropriators to challenge future [WHO] funding." When the GHSDH was released the following year, it did not include the recommendation on reduced sugar consumption. In 2009, Coca-Cola, Pepsi Co., and the American Beverage Association spent over $37 million to lobby against a proposed federal sugar-sweetened beverage tax. And in 2010, food and beverage companies, along with related trade associations, made "substantial political contributions" to members of the US Senate Committee on Agriculture, Nutrition, and Forestry, which had responsibility for the Healthy, Hunger-Free Kids Act of 2010 (HHFKA). Among other goals, the HHFKA sought to implement healthier school lunches, for example by eliminating sugary drinks.

The UCS report recommended greater accountability and trans-

parency combined with science-based policy to counter the sugar industry's aims.

In March 2015, researchers at University of California, San Francisco, published a report based on sugar industry documents that reveal how the industry "worked closely with the National Institutes of Health in the 1960s and '70s to develop a federal research program focused on approaches other than sugar reduction to prevent tooth decay in American children."[67] The authors analyzed 319 internal sugar industry documents from 1959 to 1971 and National Institute of Dental Research (NIDR) documents to show how the sugar industry's interaction with the NIDR altered the research priorities of the institute's National Caries (Tooth Decay) Program (NCP).

The UCSF study showed that the sugar industry could not deny the scientific evidence regarding the role of sucrose in tooth decay. Instead, the industry adopted a strategy "to deflect attention to public health interventions that would reduce the harms of sugar consumption rather than restricting intake." Industry tactics included funding a vaccine against tooth decay, even though the vaccine had questionable potential for widespread use; cultivation of relationships with NIDR leadership; and submission of a report to the NIDR that became the foundation of the first request for proposals issued for the NCP. The 1971 NCP first request for research proposals from scientists directly incorporated 78 percent of the trade organization's own research priorities.

"These tactics are strikingly similar to what we saw in the tobacco industry in the same era," said Stanton A. Glantz, one of the study's coauthors and a pioneer in exposing tobacco industry tactics. "Our findings are a wake-up call for government officials charged with protecting the public health, as well as public health advocates, to understand that the sugar industry, like the tobacco industry, seeks to protect profits over public health."

Tooth decay, though largely preventable, remains the leading chronic disease among children, according to the Centers for Disease Control. "The dental community has always known that preventing tooth decay required restricting sugar intake," said the UCSF study's first author Cristin Kearns. "It was disappointing to learn that the policies we are debating today could have been addressed more than 40 years ago."

16
US Military Sexual Assault of Colombian Children

Adriaan Alsema, "At Least 54 Colombian Girls Sexually Abused by Immune US Military: Report," Colombia Reports, March 23, 2015, http://colombiareports.co/more-than-54-colombian-girls-sexually-abuses-by-us-military-report/.

Adam Johnson, "Colombian Report on US Military's Child Rapes Not Newsworthy to US News Outlets," Fairness and Accuracy in Reporting, March 26, 2015, http://fair.org/blog/2015/03/26/colombian-report-on-us-militarys-child-rapes-not-newsworthy-to-us-news-outlets/.

Student Researcher: Madeline Pajerowski (Burlington College)

Faculty Evaluator: Rob Williams (Burlington College)

According to an 800-page report commissioned by the Colombian government and the Revolutionary Armed Forces of Colombia (FARC), US military personnel raped at least fifty-four children in Colombia between 2003 and 2007.[68] Adriaan Alsema, writing for Colombia Reports, was first to report the story in the English-language press on March 23, 2015.

Alsema's article highlighted the subsection of the report authored by scholar Renan Vega, who documented that US military contractors sexually abused more than fifty underage girls in the town of Melgar in 2004. Vega reported "abundant information about the sexual violence" as well as the US contractors' "absolute impunity" due to "bilateral agreements and the diplomatic immunity of United States officials." According to Vega, the US military contractors also "filmed [the abuse] and sold the films as pornographic material."

His report documented additional instances of sexual abuse, including the drugging and rape of a twelve-year-old girl by Sergeant Michael Coen and defense contractor César Ruiz in 2007.[69] Despite warrants issued for the arrest of Coen and Ruiz by Colombian prosecutors, the warrants were not executed due to diplomatic immunity granted to US military personnel and civilian contractors. In fact, Alsema reported, no arrests have been made in any of the cases regarding children raped by US military contractors.

Three days after Columbia Reports published Alsema's article, Adam Johnson of Fairness and Accuracy in Reporting quoted exten-sively from it and noted the lack of coverage in major US outlets, including CNN, MSNBC, and the *New York Times*, among others. Johnson concluded, "There's a virtual media blackout in America over the case." Noting that these "aren't fringe claims, nor can the government of American ally Colombia be dismissed as a peddler of Bolivarian propaganda," Johnson wrote, "a blistering report about systemic US military child rape of a civilian population should be of note—if for no other reason than, as the report lays out, it under-mined American military efforts to stop drug trafficking and fight leftist rebels."[70]

Johnson's assessment of a virtual media blackout in the US remains accurate, with a small handful of telling exceptions. For example, in mid-April 2015, *Time* and National Public Radio each ran stories that questioned the allegations. *Time* reported: "There's no dispute that thousands of Colombians were sexually abused during the country's 51-year-old conflict. The perpetrators were usually Colombian soldiers, paramilitaries or guerrillas. But a Colombian truth commission report claims that U.S. troops and foreign mili-tary contractors were part of the problem."[71] The article subsequently characterized Vega as "a left-wing university professor," and "a FARC appointee," who "is fiercely critical of U.S. troops and foreign contractors in Colombia." John Otis, the *Time* reporter, wrote that Vega "does not cite criminal complaints or other sources to back up his claim of 53 sexual assaults," and that he "could not be reached for comment." Otis did quote a spokesman for the Colombian attorney general's office and Keith Sparks, who during the 2000s was country manager for DynCorp, one of the largest US military contractors in Columbia. Both the Colombian official and Sparks denied any record of sexual abuse or rape by US troops or military contractors. NPR's coverage featured a four-minute interview with John Otis in which he previewed most of the points from his *Time* article.[72]

17
Media "Whitewash" Senate's CIA Torture Report

Nafeez Ahmed, "America Is Committing Brutal Acts of Torture Right Now," December 11, 2014, AlterNet, http://www.alternet.org/civil-liberties/america-committing-brutal-acts-torture-right-now.
Crofton Black, "Revealed: Only 29 Detainees from Secret CIA Torture Program Remain in Guantánamo Bay," Bureau of Investigative Journalism, January 15, 2015, http://www.thebureauinvestigates. com/2015/01/15/28-detainees-secret-cia-torture-program-guantanamo-bay/.

Student Researchers: Brooks Brorsen (Sonoma State University) and Alison Gorrell (Florida Atlantic University)

Faculty Evaluators: Peter Phillips (Sonoma State University) and James F. Tracy (Florida Atlantic University)

Although the corporate and progressive press alike focused public attention on the Senate Intelligence Committee's December 2014 report on the CIA's secret program of abductions, "brutal" interrogations, and torture of terrorism suspects, Nafeez Ahmed reported that this coverage has "whitewashed the extent to which torture has always been an integral and systematic intelligence practice since the second World War." Despite President Barack Obama's claims that he officially banned torture in 2009, these practices continue today, "under the careful recalibration of Obama and his senior military intelligence officials," serving to legitimize the existence and expansion of the national security apparatus, Ahmed wrote.

President Obama did not ban torture in 2009, Ahmed reported, and now his administration is "exploiting the new Senate report to convince the world that the intelligence community's systematic embroilment in torture was merely a Bush-era aberration that is now safely in the past."

In fact, Obama's 2009 executive order rehabilitated torture. That order required that interrogation techniques fit the US Army Field Manual, which complies with the Geneva Convention prohibitions against torture that date back to 1956. However, in 2006, revisions to the manual added nineteen different methods of interrogation that "went far beyond the original Geneva-inspired restrictions" of the original field manual. At the time, Obama's director of national intelligence, Admiral Dennis Blair, advised the Senate Intelligence Committee that the Army Field Manual revisions allowing new forms of harsh interrogation would remain classified.

"What we are seeing now," Ahmed wrote, "is not the Obama administration putting an end to torture, but rather putting an end to the open acknowledgement of the use of torture as a routine intelligence practice."

The Senate's complete report ran to 6,700 pages, yet after White House objections only a 499-page summary was published in December 2014, with significant details redacted. As the Bureau of Investigative Journalism reported, less than one quarter of the 119 detainees named in the Senate report on the CIA's secret torture pro-

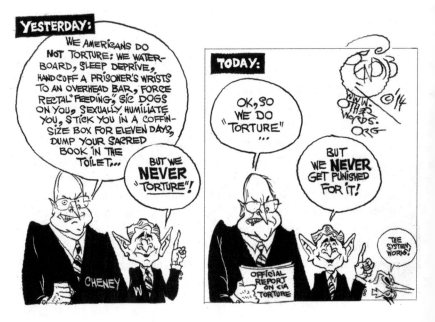

gram are actually housed at the Guantánamo Bay military prison. The Bureau's investigation has produced a database providing details of what occurred to each of the 119 individuals.

Research by the Bureau of Investigative Journalism documented that only thirty-six individuals of the 119 were sent to Guantánamo after CIA interrogation. Of these, twenty-nine remained as of January 2015. Seven of the thirty-six were released between March 2007 and January 2010, with six moved abroad and one sent to a maximum-security prison on the US mainland.

As Crofton Black reported, the Bureau's research "opens fresh possibilities" for accountability and legal redress, according to lawyers who have worked on some of these cases.

"This project to restore information blacked out in the Senate report reveals important data about former detainees' time in the CIA's detention system," said Meg Satterthwaite, director of the Global Justice Clinic at New York University School of Law. "This kind of careful analysis is crucially important for those working to understand the US extraordinary rendition and torture program."

Steven Watt, senior staff attorney at the American Civil Liberties Union, similarly remarked, "This research, confirming the dates and duration of the men's confinement, is important not just for transparency purposes but also for the men themselves."

In April 2015, Amnesty International issued a report criticizing the Obama administration's lack of action in response to the Senate's report.[73] "Four months after the declassification of the report summary, the U.S. administration has yet to take any meaningful steps toward ending the impunity associated with this secret detention program. Instead, they have effectively buried the Senate report, leaving the door open for similar programs in the future." The Amnesty International report characterized the lack of government response to the Senate torture report as amounting to "de facto amnesty" for those responsible for CIA torture.

18
ICREACH: The NSA's Secret Search Engine

Ryan Gallagher, "The Surveillance Engine: How the NSA Built Its Own Secret Google," *Intercept*, August 25, 2014, https://firstlook.org/theintercept/2014/08/25/icreach-nsa-cia-secret-google-crisscross-proton/.

Jack Crone, "NSA Builds Its Own Google: Spy Agency Secretly Providing Data to Dozens of Government Agencies with Search Engine that Shares 850 Billion Phone and Email Records," *Daily Mail* (UK), August 26, 2014, http://www.dailymail.co.uk/news/article-2734498/NSA-builds-Google-Spy-agency-secretly-providing-data-dozens-government-agencies-search-engine-shares-850-BILLION-phone-email-records.html.

Student Researcher: Kori Williams (Sonoma State University)

Community Evaluator: Nick Sedenquist

Based on documents leaked by Edward Snowden, Ryan Gallagher reported for the *Intercept* that the National Security Agency (NSA) has developed a "Google-like" search engine called ICREACH, which has the capacity to gather personal information. This search engine can access over 850 million personal records, including private e-mails, chats, and some phone locations. The NSA is sharing the data collected through its ICREACH program with nearly two dozen US government agencies. "The documents provide the first definitive evidence," Gallagher wrote, "that the NSA has for years made massive amounts of surveillance data directly accessible to domestic law enforcement agencies." Planning documents specifically identify the Federal Bureau of Investigation (FBI), the Central Intelligence Agency (CIA), and the Drug Enforcement Agency (DEA) as "core participants," Gallagher reported.

According to a December 2007 NSA secret document, "The ICREACH team delivered the first-ever wholesale sharing of communications metadata within the U.S. Intelligence Community." *The Intercept* reported that one key issue raised by the ICREACH program is whether domestic law enforcement agencies, such as the FBI or the DEA, have used ICREACH to trigger secret investigations of US citizens through a controversial process known as "parallel construction." As Gallagher explained, parallel construction involves information gathered covertly by law enforcement agents, who subsequently create a new evidence trail that excludes the original, covert one. "This hides the true origin of the investigation from defense lawyers and, on occasion, prosecutors and judges—which means the legality of the evidence that triggered the investigation cannot be challenged in court."

Spurred by Gallagher's *Intercept* report, a few establishment news organizations covered this story. For instance, Fox News reported that ICREACH has put NSA "snooping back in the spotlight," which is accurate, but the Fox coverage also reported that an e-mail from the Office of the Director of National Intelligence neither confirmed nor denied the program's existence, but did assert that "data sharing is crucial to U.S. national security."[74] The *PBS NewsHour* ran a story based on Gallagher's article for the *Intercept*.[75]

19

"Most Comprehensive" Assessment Yet Warns against Geoengineering Risks

Tim McDonnell, "Scientists Are Pretty Terrified about These Last-Minute Fixes to Global Warming," *Mother Jones*, February 10, 2015, http://www.motherjones.com/environment/2015/02/scientists-geoengineering-climate-bad-idea.

Robinson Meyer, "The Best Technology for Fighting Climate Change? Trees," *Atlantic*, February 9, 2015, http://www.theatlantic.com/technology/archive/2015/02/the-best-technology-for-fighting-climate-change-trees/385304/.

Jeremy Schulman, "We Could Stop Global Warming With This Fix—But It's Probably a Terrible Idea," *Mother Jones*, March 27, 2015, http://www.motherjones.com/environment/2015/03/geoengineering-caldeira-climate-change.

Student Researcher: Elora West (Burlington College)

Faculty and Community Evaluators: Rob Williams (Burlington College) and Ian Baldwin (Chelsea Green Publishing)

A comprehensive pair of reports by dozens of researchers convened by the National Academy of Sciences (NAS) offered "a damning critique of geoengineering," according to Tim McDonnell of *Mother Jones*. Highly controversial, geoengineering refers to technological efforts to counteract global warming by altering the atmosphere's chemical composition.

The first of the two NAS reports found that most proposals to remove carbon dioxide from the atmosphere—through processes such as fertilizing the ocean with iron to dissolve carbon dioxide—are too expensive to be widely implemented.[76] However, as Robinson Meyer reported in *Atlantic*, a February 2015 University of Oxford study found that reforestation—planting trees—is among the "most promising" short-term responses to climate change.[77]

The Academy's second report evaluated proposals to seed the atmosphere with particles to reflect sunlight back into space, a process known as albedo modification. According to the NAS study, albedo modification is inexpensive, compared with carbon dixode removal proposals, but involves unknown risks.[78] Implementing technologies to block solar radiation would entail "significant potential for unanticipated, unmanageable, and regrettable consequences in multiple human dimensions . . . including political, social, legal, economic, and ethical dimensions," according to the authors of the NAS study.

As Jeremy Schulman reported in a subsequent *Mother Jones* article, one of the climate scientists who first ran models to test potential geoengineering solutions, Ken Caldeira, continues to advocate geoengineering research—but not as an immediate or best response. As Schulman reported, Caldeira would "much rather stave off global warming by drastically cutting carbon emissions." Caldeira's stance aligns with the conclusions of the National Academy of Sciences: "There is no substitute for dramatic reductions in greenhouse gas emissions to mitigate the negative consequences of climate change, together with adaptation of human and natural systems to make them more resilient to changing climate."

The corporate media have covered geoengineering as a potential but divisive silver bullet to climate change. For example, a December 2014 issue of *Newsweek* featured "Science to the Rescue: Rebooting the Planet" as its cover story and included an article on geoengineering.[79] Both *USA Today* and the *Washington Post* ran editorials on the reports, but neither outlet covered them as hard news.[80] *The New York Times* did cover the reports as hard news, but that coverage was neither prominent nor accurate: the *Times'* story, titled "Geoengineering Research is Urged before Climate Crisis," appeared on page five of the February 12, 2015, edition and summarized the National Academy of Sciences as concluding that, "with proper oversight, experiments of climate intervention technologies should pose no significant risk."

20

FBI Seeks Backdoors in New Communications Technology

"FBI Wants Congress to Mandate Backdoors in Tech Devices to Facilitate Surveillance," Homeland Security News Wire, October 20, 2014, http://www.homelandsecuritynewswire.com/dr20141020-fbi-wants-congress-to-mandate-backdoors-in-tech-devices-to-facilitate-surveillance.

Cindy Cohn, Jeremy Gillula, and Seth Schoen, "What Default Phone Encryption Really Means For Law Enforcement," Vice News, October 8, 2014, https://news.vice.com/article/what-default-phone-encryption-really-means-for-law-enforcement.

Ed Pilkington, "FBI Demands New Powers to Hack into Computers and Carry out Surveillance," *Guardian*, October 29, 2014, http://www.theguardian.com/us-news/2014/oct/29/fbi-powers-hacking-computers-surveillance.

Student Researcher: Chelsea McCampbell (Indian River State College)

Faculty Evaluator: Elliot D. Cohen (Indian River State College)

Responding to announcements by Apple and Google that they would make customers' smartphone and computer data more secure, in October 2014 the Federal Bureau of Investigation's director James Comey announced that the Bureau was seeking to enlarge its data collection capabilities to include direct access to cell phones, tablets, and computers through an expansion of the 1994 Communications Assistance for Law Enforcement Act (CALEA). Comey told an audience at the Brookings Institution that expanding surveillance was in the interest of "public safety" to protect the nation against "potential terrorist threats."

According to the FBI director, "Unfortunately, the law hasn't kept pace with technology, and this disconnect has created a significant public-safety problem." Specifically, Comey called on Congress to update CALEA to mandate all software and hardware providers to build interception methods into their products and services.

The debate hinges on this language in CALEA: "A telecommunications carrier shall not be responsible for decrypting, or ensuring the government's ability to decrypt, any communication encrypted by a subscriber or customer, unless the encryption was provided by the carrier and the carrier possesses the information necessary to decrypt the communication." Commenting on CALEA and Comey's appeal, Cindy Cohn of the Electronic Frontier Foundation wrote, "Nothing in the bill is intended to limit or otherwise prevent the use of any type of encryption within the United States. Nor does the Committee intend this bill to be in any way a precursor to any kind of ban or limitation on encryption technology."[81]

In a Vice News article, published after the Apple and Google announcements, Cohn, Jeremy Gillula, and Seth Schoen anticipated FBI director Comey's well-rehearsed arguments against encryption: "The common misconception among the hysteria is that this decision will put vital evidence outside the reach of law enforcement. But nothing in this encryption change will stop law enforcement from seeking a warrant for the contents of a phone, just as they seek warrants for the contents of a laptop or desktop computer."

In late October, Ed Pilkington of the *Guardian* reported that the FBI also sought to expand its powers by proposing "operating changes related to rule 41 of the federal rules of criminal procedure, the terms under which the FBI is allowed to conduct searches under court-approved warrants." Under existing wording, Pilkington wrote, warrants have to be highly focused on specific locations where suspected criminal activity is occurring and approved by judges located in that same district. The FBI proposed changing this rule so that a judge could issue a warrant permitting the FBI to hack any computer, no matter where it is located. The proposed change, Pilkington reported, would allow federal investigators to target computers that have been "anonymized," meaning that their location has been hidden using tools such as Tor, which hide IP addresses and prevent browser fingerprinting to protect online users against tracking and surveillance.

21

The New Amazon of the North: Canadian Deforestation

Stephen Leahy, "World's Last Remaining Forest Wilderness at Risk," Inter Press Service, September 5, 2014, http://www.ipsnews.net/2014/09/worlds-last-remaining-forest-wilderness-at-risk.

Student Researcher: Chinasa T. Okolo (Pomona College)

Faculty Evaluator: Andy Lee Roth (Pomona College)

Since 2000, Canada has led the world in deforestation, despite being overshadowed by reports of the forests in Brazil and Indonesia. With only 10 percent of the world's forests, Canada now accounts for 21 percent of all deforestation in the world. Surges in oil sands and shale gas development, logging, and road expansion have been the major contributors to the destruction of Canada's forests. According to Stephen Leahy, writing for the Inter Press Service, deforestation by Canada and other countries deposits more carbon dioxide into the atmosphere than does all of the world's transportation machinery.

Canada's large wild forests are crucial to the survival of many animal species such as the whooping crane, black-footed ferret, and woodland caribou. The benefits of these large areas of wilderness are not limited to habitat for animals. These places also serve as reservoirs of water, producers of oxygen, absorbers of carbon dioxide, and sources of food and wood. "While forests can re-grow, this takes many decades, and in northern forests more than 100 years," Leahy reported. "However, if species go extinct or there are too few individuals left, it will take longer for a full forest ecosystem to recover—if ever."

Corporate media coverage of Canada's increasing deforestation has been lacking. When the story has been covered in the Canadian press, headlines often diminish the significance of the issue. For example, the *Calgary Herald* reported that "Size Does Matter" (January 20, 2014); while the *Vancouver Province* reported "Campaign Splits Ken from Barbie" (June 8, 2011), humorously addressing issues related to the problem of deforestation in ways that divert readers from completely understanding its impact on the world. A December 11, 2014, article in the *Los Angeles Times*, titled "In Global Climate Talks, Some Major Polluters Drag Their Feet," briefly describes Canada's gas and oil industries but makes no mention of their roles in deforestation.

22

Global Killing of Environmentalists Rises Drastically

Will Potter, "When an Activist Falls in the Rain Forest Does It Make A Sound?" *Foreign Policy*, April 23, 2014, http://www.foreignpolicy.com/articles/2014/04/23/activist_falls_rain_forest_sound_brazil_murder_environmentalist.

Student Researchers: Rachel Song and Inga Van Buren (Pomona College)

Faculty Evaluator: Andy Lee Roth (Pomona College)

Deadly Environment, a report by the nongovernmental organization (NGO) Global Witness, revealed that, from 2002 to 2013, at least 908 people were killed globally due to their environmental advocacy, with the rate of murder doubling in the last four years. Latin America and Asia show the highest rates of violence as tensions over limited natural resources in these regions escalate. Will Potter wrote for *Foreign Policy* that, today, "Brazil remains overwhelmingly more dangerous for environmentalists than other countries"; twice as many environmentalists were killed in Brazil as in any other country. However, Brazil is just one especially striking case in what is a global trend.

In a growing global economy, competition for resources is intensifying, pitting local communities against powerful business industries such as mining and logging. Problems arise when indigenous people are unaware of, or unacknowledged by, business deals that violate their land rights. Without more widespread attention on this growing problem, rural communities whose livelihood depend on the land will continue to be threatened by powerful businesses.

Political and economic elites benefit from silencing environmental defenders. In one case, gunmen shot a man, José Cláudio Ribeiro da Silva, and his wife, Maria do Espírito Santo, both of whom had worked in the Amazon forests for twenty-four years and served as members of an NGO founded to preserve the forests. The two assassins "were convicted in 2013—a rare victory in these kinds of cases—but the landowner accused of hiring the assassins walked free," Potter reported. This case is typical, he wrote. "Only 34 people worldwide are currently facing charges for violence against environmentalists, and only 10 killers were convicted between 2002 and 2013." Lack of prosecution sends the message that environmentalists can be "killed with impunity."

Though the Global Witness report is significant, it has limitations of its own, Potter noted. "The research is confined to 74 countries in Africa, Asia, and Central and South America, and it only includes murders," he observes. "Nonlethal violence and intimidation, which is much more pervasive, are left out." Further, the Global Witness report does not address the "well-documented history of violence against environmentalists in Western countries."

23
Unprocessed Rape Kits

Emily Homrok, "How Often Do Rape Kits Go Unprocessed?," *Truthout*, October 3, 2014, http://www.truth-out.org/news/item/26561-how-often-do-rape-kits-go-unprocessed.

Nora Caplan-Bricker, "The Backlog of 400,000 Unprocessed Rape Kits Is A Disgrace," *New Republic*, March 9, 2014, http://www.newrepublic.com/article/116945/rape-kits-backlog-joe-biden-announces-35-million-reopen-cases.

Taylor Kate Brown, "New Hope for Rape Kit Testing Advocates," BBC, January 5, 2015, http://www.bbc.com/news/magazine-30554719.

Student Researchers: Jessika Bales (Indian River State College) and Nathan Bowman (College of Marin)

Faculty Evaluators: Jared Kinggard (Indian River State College) and Susan Rahman (College of Marin)

Rape and Sexual Assault: A Renewed Call to Action, a report by the White House Council on Women and Girls issued in January 2014, revealed that nearly one in five US women have experienced rape or attempted rape in their lifetimes. Furthermore, the report indicated that, although the testing of rape kits—forensic exams that collect evidence of rape or sexual assault, including the perpetrator's DNA—can be "vital for the prosecution of cases," a backlog of untested rape kits may factor into low rape prosecution rates.

The White House report cited a 2011 study of more than 2,000 law enforcement agencies, which found that 44 percent of the agencies did not send forensic evidence to a laboratory because the suspect had not been identified; another 15 percent said they did not submit the evidence because the prosecutor did not request it; and 11 percent cited the lab's inability to produce timely results.[82] The White House report described a DNA Backlog Reduction Program, administered through the National Institute of Justice, which would fund 120 state and local crime labs to conduct DNA testing.[83]

Writing for *Truthout*, Emily Homrok reported that a five-month study conducted by CBS News in 2009 had found a minimum of at least 20,000 unprocessed rape kits across the US.[84] Homrok's article detailed Jessica Ripley's case. In February 2012, Ripley was raped in a parking garage in Salt Lake City, Utah. When the responding officer interviewed Ripley, he alluded several times to the fact that she was intoxicated and should not have been somewhere the officer "would never allow his daughter to go." At the hospital, a rape kit was used and police were contacted—yet despite evidence produced by the kit, no investigative advances have been made in Ripley's case. Ripley's kit never even made it to the lab for testing; it was one of 788 that got destroyed or was left untouched by the Salt Lake City Police Department over an eight-year period, Homrok wrote. Rape tests are often not taken seriously by police officers because the victims are seen as "dumb drunk girls."

In March 2014, the White House announced that its fiscal year 2015 budget would provide thirty-five million dollars for a new grant program to "inventory and test rape kits, develop 'cold case' units to pursue new investigative leads, and support victims throughout the process."[85] As Nora Caplan-Bricker reported for the *New Republic*, the Department of Justice estimated that as many as 400,000 rape kits were currently going unexamined because local authorities could not afford to analyze them. Testing a rape kit costs between $500 and $1,500, so, Caplan-Bricker wrote, "the administration's proposed investment is only enough to make a moderate-sized dent in the issue."

Less than a year later, in January 2015, the BBC's Taylor Kate Brown reported significant progress in processing the backlog of untested rape kits. Using funds from a National Institute of Justice grant, Detroit police had tested some 2,000 unprocessed rape kits and were in the process of testing another 8,000. In Cleveland, Brown reported, police had submitted all of its 4,300 backlogged kits for testing. Cleveland police opened more than 1,800 investigations, and local prosecutors had "indicted 231 people, a third of whom had at least one previous rape conviction." As Brown wrote, "Amid a reinvigorated call to test the estimated hundreds of thousands of rape kits in police storage across America, other US cities are also seeing dramatic results—a high number of previously unidentified serial rapists and dozens of unsolved cases going to prosecution."

According to the Rape, Abuse & Incest National Network (RAINN), approximately 68 percent of sexual assault cases go unreported.[86]

24
NSA's AURORAGOLD Program Hacks Cell Phones around World

Ryan Gallagher, "Operation Auroragold: How the NSA Hacks Cellphone Networks Worldwide," *Intercept*, December 4, 2014, https://firstlook.org/theintercept/2014/12/04/nsa-auroragold-hack-cellphones/.

Student Researcher: Michael Brannon (Sonoma State University)

Faculty Evaluator: Peter Phillips (Sonoma State University)

The National Security Agency (NSA) has hacked cell phone networks worldwide for many years, according to a report in the *Intercept* based on documents provided by Edward Snowden. Ryan Gallagher's article analyzed the contents of at least nine NSA documents that show how the NSA has spied on hundreds of companies, as well as other countries that are close to the US. As Gallagher reported, through a secret program codenamed AURORAGOLD, the NSA sought security weaknesses in cell phone technology to exploit for surveillance. Furthermore, Gallagher wrote, the documents also revealed NSA plans "to secretly introduce new flaws into communication systems," which would make those systems easier for the NSA to access—a "controversial tactic," Gallagher wrote, because doing so could expose "the general population to criminal hackers."

AUROAGOLD monitored the contents of messages sent and received by over 1,200 e-mail accounts associated with major cell phone service providers. In some cases, this allowed the NSA to intercept "confidential company planning papers" that would help it "hack into phone networks," Gallagher wrote.

"Even if you love the NSA and you say you have nothing to hide, you should be against a policy that introduces security vulnerabilities," according to Karsten Nohl, a leading cell phone security expert and cryptographer. "Once NSA introduces a weakness, a vulnerability, it's not only the NSA that can exploit it."

The existence of the NSA surveillance units that conducted AURORA-GOLD has not been publicly disclosed. But the NSA documents revealed that as of May 2012, the agency had technical information on "about 70 percent of cellphone networks worldwide—701 of an estimated 985—and was maintaining a list of 1,201 email 'selectors' used to intercept internal company details from employees." (Selector is an NSA term for a unique identifier, such as an e-mail address or a telephone number.) AURORA-GOLD appears to have been active since 2010, according to the documents.

As Gallagher summarized, "The operation appears aimed at ensuring virtually every cellphone network in the world is NSA accessible."

The corporate media did not cover AURORAGOLD when the *Intercept* broke the story in December 2014. News archive searches indicate no coverage, for example, in the *New York Times*, the *Washington Post*, the *Los Angeles Times*, or on any of the major television and cable news stations. Among independent media, *Der Spiegel* (December 4, 2014), TechTimes (December 9, 2014), and the *Christian Science Monitor* (December 24, 2014) ran stories on it, while *Democracy Now!* featured AURORAGOLD among its December 5, 2014, headlines.

25

Greenland's Meltwater Contributes to Rising Sea Levels

Tim Radford, "Greenland's Hidden Meltwater Lakes Store Up Trouble," Climate News Network, February 5, 2015, http://www.climatenewsnetwork.net/greenlands-hidden-meltwater-lakes-store-trouble/.

Student Researcher: Elora West (Burlington College)

Faculty Evaluator: Rob Williams (Burlington College)

In February 2015, Tim Radford reported for the Climate News Network that atmospheric warming is capable of reaching thousands of meters below Greenland's massive ice sheet, potentially increasing the glaciers' rate of flow and creating pools of "meltwater" trapped below the ice. Two separate but related studies confirmed that surface melt can drain down to fill concealed lakes under the ice, ultimately contributing to rising sea levels.

A team led by Ian Howat of Ohio State University found "the

first direct evidence for concentrated, long-term storage, and sudden release, of meltwater" at the bed of the Greenland ice sheet.[87] The team observed and measured a depression, two kilometers (approximately 1.25 mile) wide and seventy meters (over seventy-five yards) deep in the icecap of southwest Greenland. "The fact that our lake appears to have been stable for at least several decades, and then drained in a matter of weeks—or less—after a few very hot summers, may signal a fundamental change happening to the ice sheet," Howat said. As Radford reported, the slumped crater suggested a holding capacity of more than thirty million cubic meters of water, which had suddenly drained away.

A second team of researchers, led by Cornell University's Michael Willis, also studied the crater, which they discovered in 2011. Their report estimated a rate of flow of 215 cubic meters (over 56,000 gallons) per second from the subglacial lake.[88] The researchers also reported that, "As the lake beneath the ice fills with surface meltwater, the heat released by this trapped meltwater can soften surrounding ice, which may eventually cause an increase in ice flow."

Together, the studies indicated that the effects of atmospheric warming can reach far below the ice sheet, warming the glacial base and potentially increasing its rate of flow. As Radford wrote, "Were all Greenland's ice to melt, sea levels would rise catastrophically. At least one billion people live on coasts and estuaries vulnerable to a mere one metre rise."

Although corporate news media have frequently and prominently covered aspects of climate change—and debates over its reality—coverage of the melting Greenland ice sheet has been limited.[89] In March 2015, a *Washington Post* article—focused on research indicating that global warming is slowing the circulation of the world's oceans—mentioned the melting of Greenland's ice sheet only in passing, as one factor contributing to the slowing circulation.[90] By contrast, a January 2015 *Los Angeles Times* article provided substantive coverage of the role played by a University of California, Los Angeles, team of researchers in documenting the massive melt of the Greenland ice sheet.[91]

Readers concerned with this topic should see Jeff Orlowski's 2012 documentary film, *Chasing Ice*, which depicts environmental photographer James Balog and his Extreme Ice Survey's ongoing efforts to document disappearing arctic ice.[92]

TOP 25 STORY ANALYSES: RIGHTS, RESPONSIBILITIES, AND BREAKING NEWS

In *The New Censorship*, Joel Simon, executive director of the Committee to Protect Journalists, asked, "Are the rights of journalists distinct from others who provide information and commentary?"[93] Put another way, is it possible—or necessary—to draw a line between journalism, activism, and other kinds of speech? The answer, Simon and others contend, is extremely significant.

Simon argued that journalists' rights—"freedom of the press" in the US, for example—must be understood in broader context, as part of the new, developing "global information ecosystem," within which journalists, activists, and others all operate. Given increasingly blurred boundaries between journalists and non-journalists, Simon wrote, "Journalists have to recognize that their rights are best protected not by the special realm of 'press freedom,' but rather by ensuring that guarantees of freedom of expression are extended to all." Thus, "Respect for freedom of expression is the enabling environment for global journalism." This ultimately leads Simon to call for a "a grand coalition to advance the shared goal of expanding global freedom of expression."[94]

Simon's insightful interpretation of journalists' rights also suggests their responsibilities. Of course, it is journalists' vocational duty to document facts and events, to provide context and analysis, and to disseminate those to the public—especially when authorities seek to suppress access to or understanding of those facts and events. But, beyond that, Simon specifically charges journalists with protecting not only their own press freedoms but also freedom of expression more generally.

This understanding of rights and responsibilities contrasts dramatically with how rights are conventionally understood in contemporary US society. As numerous commentators have noted, in the US, legal rights are now defined more extensively, for a greater number of people, than ever before. The United States' strong rights tradition is admirable in many ways—and we at Project Censored often invoke and celebrate it.

However, the emphasis on rights in the US context often reflects an individual perspective that can be problematic. Responsibility—and especially the moral bonds of community—tends to be secondary to individual rights. From this individual perspective, our responsibilities consist primarily of not violating other peoples' rights.

We could benefit from stronger connections, conceptually and behaviorally, between rights and responsibilities.[95]

In *Censored 2015*, we suggested that readers might play with how "different stories connect to one another, advocating for different groupings, imagining different categories" as a way to encourage "critical thinking about the underlying dynamics—the social institutions, the cultural values, and the otherwise taken-for-granted assumptions—that link groups of stories."[96] We recommend that active, imaginative exercise to readers again this year—with the additional recommendation, based on the preceding discussion, that readers consider the top *Censored* stories in terms of rights and responsibilities.

For a given story, or collection of stories, what rights are involved? How does the story entail conflicting rights? Does the tension in the story arise from conflicts between individual rights and shared responsibilities? For the issues that story raises, how could the connection between rights and responsibilities be strengthened? Does the story inform you, the reader, in ways that help you to understand your rights and energize you to act on your responsibilities?

Similar to the activity of creating story categories from the top *Censored* story list, analyzing the stories in terms of rights and responsibilities, examining the balance between what is individual and what is shared, will transform the reader from a passive recipient of information into an active, engaged interpreter.

As an example of this approach, consider this brief treatment of stories #18, "ICREACH: The NSA's Secret Search Engine," #20, "FBI Seeks Backdoors in New Communications Technology," and #24, "NSA's AURORAGOLD Program Hacks Cell Phones around World." The common theme of government surveillance of the US public—without its permission or knowledge—links the three stories. As Joel Simon has written, surveillance may constitute one of the new forms of censorship.[97] He quotes from a 2013 report by the United Nations Special Rapporteur for Freedom of Expression: "Privacy and freedom of expression are interlinked and mutually dependent; an infringement upon one can be both the cause and consequence of an infringement upon the other."[98] Story #7, "Fear of Government Spying is "Chilling" Writers' Freedom of Expression," exemplifies the links among surveillance, privacy, and freedom of expression.

How, then, do rights and responsibilities come into play in the three stories on government surveillance? The following discussion illustrates three potential levels of analysis.

First, and perhaps most obviously in terms of Project Censored's mission, the inclusion of these three stories among this year's top *Censored* stories is evidence of the corporate news media's failure to inform the public about NSA and FBI programs whose importance is undeniable. On these crucial topics, corporate news media have defaulted on their responsibilities to the public. Fortunately, independent journalists and outlets—including Ryan Gallagher of the *Intercept*; Jack Crone at the *Daily Mail*; Cindy Cohn, Jeremy Gillula, and Seth Schoen, writing for Vice News; and Ed Pilkington of the *Guardian*—have reported these stories. In doing so, they live up to our best expectations of journalists as watchdogs who warn against abuses of power.

This first point focuses attention on rights and responsibilities to *tell* the story. A second level of analysis involves the play of rights and responsibilities *within* the frame of the story, including specifically how the protagonists in the story position themselves and the issues. Thus, for example, in planning—and defending—surveillance programs, government agencies invoke their responsibilities to protect the public and the nation. Thus FBI Director James Comey told his audience at the Brookings Institute, "The people of the FBI are sworn to protect both security and liberty."[99] A "disconnect" between the law and technology has created "a significant public-safety problem," Comey explained. Here, then, the FBI director invokes an institutional responsibility to the US public to provide for its safety. Aware that critics saw the FBI and other government agencies emphasizing security at the cost of citizens' rights to privacy and other civil liberties, Comey told his audience that a commitment to rule of law and civil liberties is "at the core of the FBI. It is the organization's spine."

By contrast, critics of government surveillance programs, such as the Electronic Frontier Foundation, contested Comey's rationale. As Cohn, Gillula, and Schoen wrote in Vice News, Apple's decision to encrypt more data is "about protecting the security of its customers." Furthermore, addressing the contention of public safety, the authors noted, "Nothing in this encryption change will stop law enforcement from seeking a warrant for the contents of a phone." In this view, the FBI can fulfill its institutional responsibilities without violating citizens' rights to privacy or companies' needs to remain competitive in a global market place. (Other critics of government agencies' efforts to establish backdoors in new technology had noted that few foreign customers would want to buy devices manufactured in the US under these requirements.)

Within the framing of these stories, we find government agencies emphasizing institutional responsibilities, while acknowledging civil liberties, and critics of surveillance programs invoking individual rights, while downplaying claimed threats to public safety and national security. This sort of analysis goes beyond the issue of journalistic balance—the responsibility to report "both sides" of a story—so often invoked as a keystone of objectivity.[100] Instead, the perspective illustrated here highlights how the protagonists of the story position themselves and the issues at stake, in terms of rights and responsibilities.

A third level of analysis explicitly brings the story's audience into focus. Does the public have a right to know this information? The NSA did not freely share any information about its ICREACH and AURORAGOLD programs. The documents used by independent reporters to inform the public about these programs were secret and unknown until Edward Snowden revealed them. As previous volumes of *Censored* have documented, government officials and many segments of the press viciously attacked Snowden and the reporters most closely connected to his revelations.[101] Calling Snowden a traitor and questioning whether the figures who reported on the leaked documents—including, most prominently, Glenn Greenwald—were "real" journalists, these critics took the secrecy of the government programs as both necessary to national security and as an unquestionable premise of public debate. Others—including, of course, the whistleblowers and journalists whose efforts Project Censored highlights—contended that, in a nation that purports to be a democracy, the public has a right to know how government programs affect citizens' daily lives and enhance or undermine their participation in self-government.

Once a story informs its audience, what responsibilities do we—as members of the public—have to act on this understanding? As Ralph Nader wrote in the foreword to *Censored 2015*, "If citizens and civic organizations do not use readily available information, there is less pressure to report important news stories. . . . [T]oo often, we as a society fail to follow up."[102] A full discussion of this point goes beyond the scope of this brief section, but at least one fundamental question can be instructively applied to any news report, including those featured in this volume, and those produced by corporate news outlets: does the story provide its audience with information they need in order to take action?

A final point ties together the three levels of rights and responsibilities sketched in this discussion that concludes this chapter. On June 1, 2015, the big news of the day was that the US Senate had allowed the portion of the 2006 USA PATRIOT Act amendments that provided legal authority to engage in bulk collection of phone data to expire. This story was highly anticipated and widely covered, in both the corporate and independent news media. (In early May 2015, the Second District US Court of Appeals had ruled that the NSA's bulk collection program exceeded "the scope of what Congress has authorized.") Some of this coverage gave credit to whistleblower Edward Snowden for helping to make public the secret NSA documents that led to increased public awareness—and criticism—of the program. But little of the corporate news coverage acknowledged the crucial roles played by the independent journalists and news organizations, which first broke the story and often provided the most comprehensive coverage in terms of context and analysis. Even as the corporate media caught up on covering NSA surveillance, they failed to provide the public with the independent news reporting that provided a context for, and in all likelihood contributed crucially to, this historic change in government surveillance.

In producing this year's list of the top *Censored* stories, we at Project Censored pay tribute to independent journalists and news organizations. To adapt Galeano's insight about the importance of writing: the independent journalists and news organizations whose work we celebrate here bring forward dissident messages—denouncing pain, sometimes sharing joy—in defiance of an ongoing corporate media blockade. These independent journalists and news organizations deserve your support, and the otherwise censored stories they report demand your engagement.

Notes

1. Eduardo Galeano, "In Defence of the Word," *Index on Censorship* 6, no. 4 (July 1977): 20.
2. See "Eduardo Galeano: Anti-censorship Activist and Historian," File Room, National Coalition Against Censorship, http://www.thefileroom.org/documents/dyn/DisplayCase.cfm/id/1144. In July 2013, *Guardian* columnist Gary Younge described Galeano as "the poet laureate of the anti-globalisation movement."
3. Galeano, "In Defence," 16.
4. On solutions journalism, see Sarah van Gelder, "Solutions in a Time of Climate Meltdown: The Most Censored (and Indispensable) Story," *Censored 2014: Fearless Speech in Fateful Times*, eds. Mickey Huff and Andy Lee Roth (New York: Seven Stories Press, 2013), 13–23.
5. Galeano, "In Defence," 19.
6. Yochai Benkler, "WikiLeaks and the Networked Fourth Estate," in *Beyond WikiLeaks: Implications for the Future of Communications, Journalism and Society*, eds. Benedetta Reveni, Arne Hints, and Patrick McCurdy (New York: Palgrave Macmillan, 2013), 11–34.
7. Ibid., 29–30.
8. This paragraph draws on Andy Lee Roth and Project Censored, "Breaking the Corporate News Frame: Project Censored's Networked News Commons," forthcoming in *Media Education for a Digital Generation*, eds. Julie Frechette and Rob Williams (New York and London: Routledge, 2016).
9. See "How to Support Project Censored" in this volume's back matter, and "Project Censored in the Classroom," http://www.projectcensored.org/project-censoreds-commitment-to-independent-news-in-the-classroom.
10. Galeano, "In Defence," 15.
11. For information on how to nominate a story, see "How To Support Project Censored," at the back of this volume.
12. Validated Independent News stories are archived on the Project Censored website at http://www.projectcensored.org/category/validated-independent-news.
13. For a complete list of the national and international judges and their brief biographies, see the acknowledgments section of this book.
14. Deborah Hardoon, "Wealth: Having It All and Wanting More," Oxfam Policy & Practice, January 19, 2015, http://policy-practice.oxfam.org.uk/publications/wealth-having-it-all-and-wanting-more-338125.
15. Emma Seery and Ana Caistor Arendar, "Even It Up: Time to End Extreme Inequality," Oxfam Policy & Practice, October 29, 2014, http://policy-practice.oxfam.org.uk/publications/even-it-up-time-to-end-extreme-inequality-333012.
16. For detailed descriptions of each, see Seery and Arendar, "Even It Up."
17. Launched in September 2012, TV News Archive is an online research library service "intended to enhance the capabilities of journalists, scholars, teachers, librarians, civic organizations and other engaged citizens." See https://archive.org/details/tv.
18. For example, Sally Kohn, "GOP, Support Obama on Taxing the Wealthy," CNN, January 20, 2015, http://www.cnn.com/2015/01/19/opinion/kohn-obama-sotu.

19. Tim Worstall, "Oxfam's New Report: Number of Billionaires Has Doubled Since the Crash," *Forbes*, October 30, 2014, http://www.forbes.com/sites/timworstall/2014/10/30/oxfams-new-report-number-of-billionaires-has-doubled-since-the-crash/2.

20. Tim Worstall, "There's Probably More One Percenters Working for Oxfam than There are Billionaires," *Forbes*, January 22, 2015, http://www.forbes.com/sites/timworstall/2015/01/22/theres-probably-more-one-percenters-working-for-oxfam-than-there-are-billionaires; also see John Tamny, "With '1 Percenter' Wealth Set To Surge, '99 Percenters' Should Rejoice," *Forbes*, January 25, 2015, http://www.forbes.com/sites/johntamny/2015/01/25/with-1-percenter-wealth-set-to-surge-we-99-percenters-should-all-rejoice.

21. Kim Hjelmgaard, "Oxfam: Richest 1% Own Nearly Half of World's Wealth," *USA Today*, January 20, 2014, http://www.usatoday.com/story/news/world/2014/01/20/davos-2014-oxfam-85-richest-people-half-world/4655337.

22. See, for example, "Richest 1% to Own More Than Rest of World, Oxfam Says," BBC, January 19, 2015, http://www.bbc.com/news/business-30875633.

23. "Documents Reveal Billions of Gallons of Oil Industry Wastewater Illegally Injected Into Central California Aquifers: Tests Find Elevated Arsenic, Thallium Levels in Nearby Water Wells," Center for Biological Diversity, October 26, 2014, http://www.biologicaldiversity.org/news/press_releases/2014/fracking-10-06-2014.html.

24. Jhon Arbelaez, Shaye Wolf, and Andrew Grinberg, "On Shaky Ground: Fracking, Acidizing, and Increased Earthquake Risk In California," Center For Biological Diversity, March 2014, http://www.biologicaldiversity.org/campaigns/california_fracking/pdfs/ShakyGroundReport-March2014.pdf.

25. See, for example, "Hundreds of Illicit Oil Wastewater Pits Found in Kern County," *Washington Times*, Associated Press, February 27, 2015, http://www.washingtontimes.com/news/2015/feb/27/hundreds-of-illicit-oil-wastewater-pits-found-in-k.

26. Julie Cart, "Central Valley's Growing Concern: Crops Raised with Oil Field Water," *Los Angeles Times*, May 2, 2015, http://www.latimes.com/local/california/la-me-drought-oil-water-20150503-story.html#page=1.

27. "EPA Releases Draft Assessment on the Potential Impacts to Drinking Water Resources from Hydraulic Fracturing Activities," United States Environmental Protection Agency, June 4, 2015, http://yosemite.epa.gov/opa/admpress.nsf/21b8983ffa5d0e4685257dd4006b85e2/b54 2d827055a839585257e5a005a796b!OpenDocument.

28. Wenonah Hauter, "EPA's Fracking Study Has Industry's Oily Fingerprints All Over It," Food & Water Watch, June 4, 2015, http://www.foodandwaterwatch.org/pressreleases/epas-fracking-study-has-industrys-oily-fingerprints-all-over-it.

29. "Congress members have been muzzled by executive claims of secrecy to protect national security and/or co-opted by lobbyists representing drone manufacturers." Andy Lee Roth, "Framing Al-Awlaki: How Government Officials and Corporate Media Legitimized a Targeted Killing," *Censored 2013: Dispatches from the Media Revolution*, eds. Mickey Huff and Andy Lee Roth (New York: Seven Stories Press, 2012), 353–54.

30. Scott Shane, "Drone Strikes Reveal Uncomfortable Truth: U.S. Is Often Unsure about Who Will Die," *New York Times*, April 23, 2015, http://www.nytimes.com/2015/04/24/world/asia/drone-strikes-reveal-uncomfortable-truth-us-is-often-unsure-about-who-will-die.html.

31. Mark Mazzetti and Matt Apuzzo, "Deep Support in Washington for C.I.A.'s Drone Mission," *New York Times*, April 25, 2015, http://www.nytimes.com/2015/04/26/us/politics/deep-support-in-washington-for-cias-drone-missions.html.

32. Ibid. See also Michael Calderone, "Why the New York Times Is Naming Names in CIA Drone Story," *Huffington Post*, April 27, 2015, http://www.huffingtonpost.com/2015/04/27/new-york-times-drone-security_n_7155844.html.

33. Jeff Stein and Jonathan Broder, "Can America Win a War?," *Newsweek*, April 30, 2015, http://www.newsweek.com/2015/05/08/can-america-win-war-326812.html.

34. Jim Schultz, "A War over Water," Democracy Center, February 4, 2000; and Pacific News Service, February 8, 2000. This article and the complete series of Schultz's reports have been archived at http://democracyctr.org/bolivia/investigations/bolivia-investigations-the-water-

revolt/bolivia%E2%80%99s-war-over-water-%E2%80%93-the-dispatches-in-full. On the fifteenth anniversary of the Cochabamba protests, see Aldo Orellana López, "Bolivia, 15 Years on from the Water War," *Narco News Bulletin*, April 23, 2015, http://www.narconews.com/ Issue67/article4799.html.

35. See also Jo-Shing Yang, "The New 'Water Barons': Wall Street Mega-Banks and the Tycoons Are Buying up Water at Unprecedented Pace," Market Oracle, December 21, 2012, http://www.marketoracle.co.uk/Article38167.html.

36. "The Global Water Grab: A Primer," Transnational Institute of Policy Studies and Hands Off the Land Alliance, March 2014, 3, www.tni.org/files/download/the_global_water_grab.pdf.

37. Ibid., 10.

38. "Massive Water Shutoffs Leading Up to Secret Deals," Food & Water Watch, http://www.foodandwaterwatch.org/studies/detroit-mi.

39. "Baltimore Water Shut-Offs Violate Human Right to Water," Food & Water Watch, April 7, 2015, http://www.foodandwaterwatch.org/pressreleases/baltimore-water-shut-offs-violate-human-right-to-water.

40. Luke Broadwater, "City Shuts Off Water to Delinquent Residents; Hits Baltimore Co. Homes Hardest," *Baltimore Sun*, May 15, 2015, http://www.baltimoresun.com/news/maryland/baltimore-city/bs-md-ci-water-shutoffs-20150515-story.html.

41. See, for example, Andy Lipkis, "Reimagining California's Water Infrastructure," TreePeople, November 26, 2014, http://blog.treepeople.org/treepeople-news/2014/11/parched-lawns-wasted-water-reimagining-californias-infrastructure#.VRc7z-Fz_IU.

42. "Water LA," The River Project, http://www.theriverproject.org/projects/water-la. On urban acupuncture more generally, see Jaime Lerner, *Urban Acupuncture* (Washington DC: Island Press, 2014).

43. Peter Bosshard, "Rainwater Harvesting Pioneer Wins International Water Prize," *Huffington Post*, March 20, 2015, http://www.huffingtonpost.com/peter-bosshard/rainwater-harvesting-pion_b_6911280.html.

44. On "significant progress": Miwa Suzuki, "Fukushima Decommissioning Made 'Significant Progress': IAEA," Phys.org, February 17, 2015, http://phys.org/news/2015-02-fukushima-decommissioning-significant-iaea.html.

45. "Japan Gives Final Clearance for 1st Nuclear Plant Restart Since Fukushima," Russia Today, May 27, 2015, http://rt.com/news/262521-fukushima-japan-nuclear-restart.

46. "Despite Tensions, US, Russia Vow Cooperation in the Arctic," *New York Times*, Associated Press, April 24, 2015, http://mobile.nytimes.com/aponline/2015/04/24/world/europe/ap-cn-arctic-council.html.

47. Carol J. Williams, "U.S. Takes Helm of Arctic Council, Aims to Focus on Climate Change," *Los Angeles Times*, April 24, 2015, http://www.latimes.com/world/la-fg-us-arctic-council-20150425-story.html.

48. "Global Chilling: The Impact of Mass Surveillance on International Writers," PEN America, January 5, 2015, http://www.pen.org/sites/default/files/globalchilling_2015.pdf.

49. "With Liberty to Monitor All," American Civil Liberties Union and Human Rights Watch, July 28, 2014, http://www.hrw.org/print/reports/2014/07/28/liberty-monitor-all.

50. Jennifer Schuessler, "Writers Say They Feel Censored by Surveillance," *New York Times*, January 15, 2015, C3, http://www.nytimes.com/2015/01/05/arts/writers-say-they-feel-censored-by-surveillance.html. Similarly, National Public Radio covered a previous PEN America report on the same topic as part of its "Book News" section. See Annalisa Quinn, "Book News: Spying Concerns Driving Writers To Self-Censor, Study Finds," November 12, 2013, http://www.npr.org/sections/thetwo-way/2013/11/12/244744204/book-news-spying-concerns-driving-writers-to-self-censor-study-finds.

51. Chris Buckley and Michael Forsythe, "Press Freedom in Hong Kong Under Threat, Report Says," *New York Times*, January 16, 2015, http://www.nytimes.com/2015/01/17/world/asia/press-freedom-in-hong-kong-under-threat-report-says.html.

52. "The Counted," the study on which Swaine, Laughland, and Lartey's report is based, is a comprehensive interactive database that aims to keep records on all police killings in the US.

For each such death, it tracks data points including age, location, gender, ethnicity, whether the person killed was armed, and which policing agency was responsible. See "The Counted: People Killed by the Police in the US," *Guardian*, June 1, 2015, http://www.theguardian.com/us-news/ng-interactive/2015/jun/01/the-counted-police-killings-us-database#.

53. On problems with the official US figures, see Peter Phillips, Diana Grant, and Greg Sewell, "Law Enforcement-Related Deaths in the US: 'Justified Homicides' and Their Impacts on Victims' Families," *Censored 2015: Inspiring We the People*, eds. Andy Lee Roth and Mickey Huff (New York: Seven Stories Press, 2014), 243–68, and at http://www.projectcensored.org/law-enforcement-related-deaths-us.

54. Kimberly Kindy et al., "Fatal Police Shootings in 2015 Approaching 400 Nationwide," *Washington Post*, May 30, 2015, http://www.washingtonpost.com/national/fatal-police-shootings-in-2015-approaching-400-nationwide/2015/05/30/d322256a-058e-11e5-a428-c984eb077d4e_story.html.

55. For a concise summary of the *Guardian* and *Post* studies, see Jaeah Lee, "What 2 Big New Reports on Police Killings Tell Us," *Mother Jones*, June 2, 2015, http://www.motherjones.com/politics/2015/06/data-police-shootings-washington-post-guardian.

56. Lizzie Wade, "Water, Fire, and Costa Rica's Carbon-Zero Year So Far," *Wired*, March 27, 2015, http://www.wired.com/2015/03/water-fire-costa-ricas-carbon-zero-year-far; and Lindsay Fendt, "The Truth behind Costa Rica's Renewable Energy," *Guardian*, March 30, 2015, http://www.theguardian.com/commentisfree/2015/mar/30/truth-behind-costa-rica-renewable-energy-reservoirs-climate-change. Fendt concludes, "While the world may not be able to tailor its energy programmes to Costa Rica's geography-specific model, the lesson here is not about science and infrastructure, but about volition and ideals."

57. Samantha Page, "Hawaii Will Soon Get All of Its Electricity from Renewable Sources," *Think-Progress*, May 7, 2015, http://thinkprogress.org/climate/2015/05/07/3656346/hawaiis-green-grid-plans.

58. "Over fifty cities": see Stephen Leahy, "Vancouver Commits to Run on 100% Renewable Energy," *Guardian*, April 10, 2015, http://www.theguardian.com/environment/2015/apr/10/vancouver-commits-to-run-on-100-renewable-energy.

59. See Marge Dwyer, "Study Strengthens Link between Neonicotinoids and Collapse of Honey Bee Colonies," Harvard T.H. Chan School of Public Health, May 9, 2014, http://www.hsph.harvard.edu/news/press-releases/study-strengthens-link-between-neonicotinoids-and-collapse-of-honey-bee-colonies.

60. Maj Rundlöf et al., "Seed Coating with a Neonicotinoid Insecticide Negatively Affects Wild Bees," *Nature*, April 22, 2015, http://www.nature.com/nature/journal/vaop/ncurrent/full/nature14420.html; and Sébastien C. Kessler et al., "Bees Prefer Foods Containing Neonicotinoid Pesticides," *Nature*, April 22, 2015, http://www.nature.com/nature/journal/v521/n7550/full/nature14414.html.

61. The complete "Follow the Honey" report is available online at http://libcloud.s3.amazonaws.com/93/f0/f/4656/FollowTheHoneyReport.pdf.

62. See, for example, Rachel Feltman, "New Studies Find that Bees Actually Want to Eat the Pesticides that Hurt Them," *Washington Post*, April 22, 2015, http://www.washingtonpost.com/news/speaking-of-science/wp/2015/04/22/new-studies-find-that-bees-actually-want-to-eat-the-pesticides-that-hurt-them/; Michael Wines, "Research Suggests Pesticide Is Alluring and Harmful to Bees," *New York Times*, April 22, 2015, http://www.nytimes.com/2015/04/23/us/research-suggests-pesticide-is-alluring-and-harmful-to-bees.html; and Allison Aubrey, "Buzz over Bee Health: New Pesticide Studies Rev Up Controversy," National Public Radio, April 22, 2015, http://www.npr.org/blogs/thesalt/2015/04/22/401536105/buzz-over-bee-health-new-pesticide-studies-rev-up-controversy.

63. See, for example, "Lowe's to Stop Selling Neonicotinoid Pesticides That May Be Harmful to Bees," *Huffington Post*, Reuters, April 9, 2015, http://www.huffingtonpost.com/2015/04/09/lowes-pesticides-bees_n_7035208.html; and "Lowe's to Stop Selling Neonic Pesticides Linked to Bee Deaths," NBC News, April 9, 2015, http://www.nbcnews.com/science/environment/lowes-announces-ban-bee-killing-pesticides-n338631.

64. On public opposition prior to the USDA decision, see John Deike, "GMO Pesticide-Resistant Crops Prompt Widespread Backlash Due to Environmental and Health Risks," EcoWatch, March 11, 2014, http://ecowatch.com/2014/03/11/gmo-pesticide-resistant-crops.
65. Mark Koba, "A Farmland Controversy Sprouts over 'Superweeds,'" CNBC, September 30, 2014, http://www.cnbc.com/id/102041464.
66. "Escalating the Seed Wars," Los Angeles Times, September 29, 2014, http://www.latimes.com/opinion/editorials/la-ed-gmo-food-20140930-story.html.
67. Cristin E. Kearns, Stanton A. Glantz, and Laura A. Schmidt, "Sugar Industry Influence on the Scientific Agenda of the National Institute of Dental Research's 1971 National Caries Program: A Historical Analysis of Internal Documents," PLOS Medicine, March 10, 2015, http://journals.plos.org/plosmedicine/article?id=10.1371/journal.pmed.1001798.
68. Comisión Histórica del Conflicto y sus Víctimas, "Contribución al entendimiento del conflicto armado en Colombia," February 2015, https://www.mesadeconversaciones.com.co/sites/default/files/Informe%20Comisi_n%20Hist_rica%20del%20Conflicto%20y%20sus%20V_ctimas.%20La%20Habana%2C%20Febrero%20de%202015.pdf.
69. Gerardo Reyes and Gonzalo Guillen, "U.S. Soldier's Immunity Clouds 2007 Colombian Rape Case," El Nuevo Herald, September 3, 2009, http://www.mcclatchydc.com/2009/09/03/74828/us-soldiers-immunity-clouds-2007.html.
70. Also see a later Al Jazeera opinion piece by Jonathan Levinson, who wrote: "The United States has little interest in drawing more attention to its controversial assistance to Colombia, much of it covert, and its support for a regime that has almost entirely disregarded human rights and accountability. But in turning a blind eye to crimes committed by its troops, the U.S. is essentially validating corruption and indifference in the Colombian military and ensuring Plan Colombia's failure." Jonathan Levinson, "How the US Enables Human Rights Abuses in Colombia," Al Jazeera, May 4, 2015, http://america.aljazeera.com/opinions/2015/5/how-the-us-enables-human-rights-abuses-in-colombia.html.
71. John Otis, "Colombians Accuse US Soldiers and Officials of Sexual Assault and Rape," Time, April 15, 2015, http://time.com/3823044/colombia-us-soldiers-rape.
72. John Otis, "Army Reviewing Rape Charges against U.S. Troops In Colombia," Morning Edition, National Public Radio, April 11, 2015, http://www.npr.org/2015/04/11/398948800/army-reviewing-rape-charges-against-u-s-troops-in-colombia.
73. "USA Crimes and Impunity: Full Senate Committee Report on CIA Secret Detentions Must Be Released, and Accountability for Crimes under International Law Ensured," Amnesty International, April 2015, http://www.amnestyusa.org/sites/default/files/cia_torture_report_amr_5114322015.pdf.
74. James Rogers, "'Google-Like' Search Engine Puts NSA Snooping Back in the Spotlight," Fox News, August 26, 2014, http://www.foxnews.com/tech/2014/08/26/google-like-search-engine-puts-nsa-snooping-back-in-spotlight.
75. Charles Pulliam-Moore, "Google-Like NSA Search Engine Implemented to Learn about Civilians," PBS NewsHour, August 25, 2014, http://www.pbs.org/newshour/rundown/google-like-nsa-search-engine-icreach-used-learn-civilians.
76. Committee on Geoengineering Climate, "Climate Intervention: Carbon Dioxide Removal and Reliable Sequestration," National Academy of Sciences, 2015, see http://nas-sites.org/americasclimatechoices/public-release-event-climate-intervention-reports.
77. Ben Caldecott, Guy Lomax, and Mark Workman, "Stranded Carbon Assets and Negative Emissions Technologies," Smith School of Enterprise and the Environment Working Paper, University of Oxford, February 2015, http://www.smithschool.ox.ac.uk/research-programmes/stranded-assets/Stranded%20Carbon%20Assets%20and%20NETs%20-%2006.02.15.pdf.
78. Committee on Geoengineering Climate, "Climate Intervention: Reflecting Sunlight to Cool Earth," National Academy of Sciences, 2015, see http://nas-sites.org/americasclimatechoices/public-release-event-climate-intervention-reports.
79. Erin Biba, "Planet Reboot: Fighting Climate Change with Geoengineering," Newsweek, December 4, 2014 (print ed., December 12, 2014), http://www.newsweek.com/2014/12/12/can-geoengineering-save-earth-289124.html.

80. "Geoengineering Won't Solve Climate Change," *USA Today*, February 15, 2015, http://www.usatoday.com/story/opinion/2015/02/15/climate-change-solar-geoengineering-greenhouse-gases-editorials-debates/23465849; and "Can Science Solve Climate Change?," *Washington Post*, February 16, 2015, http://www.washingtonpost.com/opinions/can-science-solve-climate-change/2015/02/16/8b921ea4-b308-11e4-886b-c22184f27c35_story.html.

81. For both quotations, see Cindy Cohn, "EFF Response to FBI Director Comey's Speech on Encryption," Electronic Frontier Foundation, October 17, 2014, https://www.eff.org/deeplinks/2014/10/eff-response-fbi-director-comeys-speech-encryption#footnoteref1_ur5l5sh.

82. "Rape and Sexual Assault: A Renewed Call to Action," White House Council on Women and Girls, January 2014, https://www.whitehouse.gov/sites/default/files/docs/sexual_assault_report_1-21-14.pdf, 18.

83. Ibid., 24.

84. Laura Strickler, "Rape Kits Data, by the Numbers," CBS News, November 9, 2009, http://www.cbsnews.com/news/rape-kits-data-by-the-numbers.

85. "Fact Sheet: Combatting Violence against Women," White House, Office of the Press Secretary, March 5, 2014, https://www.whitehouse.gov/the-press-office/2014/03/05/fact-sheet-combatting-violence-against-women.

86. "Statistics," Rape, Abuse & Incest National Network, https://www.rainn.org/statistics.

87. I. M. Howat et al., "Sudden Drainage of a Subglacial Lake beneath the Greenland Ice Sheet," *Cryosphere* 9 (January 15, 2015): 103–08, http://www.the-cryosphere.net/9/103/2015/tc-9-103-2015.html.

88. Michael J. Willis et al., "Recharge of a Subglacial Lake by Surface Meltwater in Northeast Greenland," *Nature* 518 (January 21, 2015): 223–27.

89. Corporate media coverage of climate change is often problematic. For one example, see "Corporate News Ignores Connections between Extreme Weather and Climate Change," *Censored 2015*, 50–52.

90. Chris Mooney, "Global Warming Is Now Slowing Down the Circulation of the Oceans—With Potentially Dire Consequences," *Washington Post*, March 23, 2015, http://www.washingtonpost.com/news/energy-environment/wp/2015/03/23/global-warming-is-now-slowing-down-the-circulation-of-the-oceans-with-potentially-dire-consequences.

91. Geoffrey Mohan, "Ice Researchers Capture Catastrophic Greenland Melt," *Los Angeles Times*, January 12, 2015, http://touch.latimes.com/#section/-1/article/p2p-82518875/.

92. "Chasing Ice," https://chasingice.com/about-the-film/synopsis. See also Balog's Extreme Ice Survey, http://extremeicesurvey.org.

93. Joel Simon, *The New Censorship: Inside the Global Battle for Media Freedom* (New York: Columbia University Press, 2015), 153.

94. Ibid., quotes at 164, 171, 167, and 191.

95. See, for example, Arthur J. Dyck, *Rethinking Rights and Responsibilities: The Moral Bonds of Community* (Washington DC: Georgetown University Press, 2005), 115.

96. Roth and Huff, *Censored 2015*, 90.

97. Simon, *The New Censorship*, 112–24, 181–83,

98. Ibid., 113.

99. For the full text of Comey's speech, see "Going Dark: Are Technology, Privacy, and Public Safety on a Collision Course?," Federal Bureau of Investigation, http://www.fbi.gov/news/speeches/going-dark-are-technology-privacy-and-public-safety-on-a-collision-course.

100. For a concise, compelling critique of journalistic "balance," see Robert M. Entman, *Democracy Without Citizens: Media and the Decay of American Politics* (New York: Oxford University Press, 1989), 30–38.

101. See, e.g., *Censored 2014*, 65–84, and *Censored 2015*, 99–110 and 148–50. The "war on whistleblowers" includes, but is by no means limited to, Edward Snowden's case, though it has received the greatest amount of attention in corporate news.

102. Ralph Nader, "Foreword," *Censored 2015*, 11.

CHAPTER 2

Déjà Vu
What Happened to Previous *Censored* Stories?

Susan Rahman, with research and writing from College of Marin
students Nathan Bowman, Isabelle Elias, Kayla Johnson, Katie
Kolb, Nik Kretzschmar, Quintton McCahey, Quiyarra McCahey,
Caitlin McCoy, Miya McHugh, Carl Nestler, Brande Neyhard, Molly
Owens, Elizabeth Ramirez, David Rodas, Karina Rodriguez, Ana
Sanderson-Burglin, Joe Suzuki, and Christian Vicente; with further
research assistance by Diablo Valley College students Darian
Edelman and Ellie Kim

*The only way to make sense out of change is to plunge
into it, move with it, and join the dance.*

—Alan Watts

The Déjà Vu chapter has become a mainstay in *Censored* annual volumes. Here, censored and underreported stories featured in the previous year's Top 25 are reexamined for coverage. What has happened since these stories were first reported and highlighted by Project Censored? Did the corporate media join the dance?

Typically, stories featured in *Censored*'s Top 25 either never end up getting corporate media coverage or, if they do, there is usually an eighteen- to twenty-four-month lag time. Further, that coverage is oft accompanied by a certain amount of spin associated with that new coverage.

Were it not for the work of intrepid independent journalists, Project Censored would have nothing to report. Fortunately, there have been thousands of independent news stories submitted to us by students, faculty, and community members over the past thirty-nine years. They have provided readers with an opportunity to learn about the news that didn't make the news. These under covered stories are sourced transparently and vetted by a panel of media scholars and professors from across the US that work with Project Censored. These stories often challenge the official, establishment narratives found in corporate media, which partially explains their absence from so-called mainstream discourse. Project Censored continues to highlight the work of independent journalists in hopes that the public will become more aware of alternatives to the corporate news and not only become more media literate, but more aware about key issues taking place around the world. This year's "Déjà Vu" stories include the corporate media propaganda and hypocrisy surrounding the Ukraine, restorative justice programs that are turning around violent schools, preserving and protecting net neutrality, the depletion of drinking water for residents of Gaza, and a drop in US prisoners serving life sentences.

Like with many of the previous Top 25 *Censored* stories, we find that they languish in obscurity, and the ones regarding Gaza and the Ukraine are such examples. But, in other instances, there is more expansive coverage. There was also "good news" to report concerning the restorative justice programs used in troubled schools, protections for net neutrality, as well as a softening in mandatory sentencing for nonviolent crimes to help reduce those serving life terms in prison.

In the capsule summaries and highlights that follow, Project Censored provides updates on some of the most important developments concerning these stories over the past year.

Censored 2015 #9

US Media Hypocrisy in Covering Ukraine Crisis
(with research assistance by political analyst Eric Draitser of StopImperialism.org)

SUMMARY: Russia's annexation of Crimea has caused US corporate media and government officials to call for a stern US response. Secretary of State John Kerry declaimed the Russian intervention as "a nineteenth-century act in the twenty-first century." What Russia's US critics seem to forget, Robert Parry reported, is the United States' own history of overthrowing democratic governments, including the illegal invasion of Iraq, which Kerry supported.

Corporate media also failed to acknowledge that Vladimir Putin ordered Russian troops to secure Crimea and the Russian Black Sea fleet stationed there after a coup led at least partly by neo-Nazis—conditions arguably less criminal than the US invasion of Iraq, which the US legitimized with false claims. "If Putin is violating international law by sending Russian troops into the Crimea after a violent coup spearheaded by neo-Nazi militias ousted Ukraine's democratically elected president," wrote Robert Parry, "then why hasn't the US government turned over George W. Bush, Dick Cheney and indeed John Kerry to the International Criminal Court for their far more criminal invasion of Iraq?"

At the very same time that Russia was moving to secure its navy, based for more than two centuries in the Crimean port of Sevastopol, the US and its NATO allies were moving significant naval assets into the Black Sea, quite literally to the borders of Russian territorial waters. As political analyst and commentator Eric Draitser explained, "It is interesting to note that Russia's moves in Crimea in 2014 came within a matter of days of the entrance into the Black Sea of . . . US naval assets. Anyone who doubts that Moscow's decision to support Crimea's vote for reunification with the Russian Federation was motivated by something other than military and strategic pragmatism would do well to examine this timeline of events."

The resurgence of Cold War rhetoric correlates in part to increased geopolitical oil interests. Nafeez Ahmed reported that Ukraine finds itself between the two superpowers and their ongoing struggle for influence in the Eurasian oil market. Russia's Gazprom Company already controls roughly one-fifth of the world's oil supply and provides about one third of Europe's gas. The Obama administration has since spent over five billion dollars to "ensure a secure and prosperous and democratic Ukraine." For those who are pondering whether we face the prospect of a New Cold War," Ahmed concluded, "a better question might be—did the Cold War ever really end?"

UPDATE: In the lead up to, and aftermath of, Russia's annexation of Crimea in March of 2014, the United States corporate media negatively covered Russian President Putin for acting, as he saw it, to protect Russia's national interests and those of the Russian-speaking population of Eastern Ukraine. The corporate media in the US either distorted or completely failed to report that Ukraine's corrupt, but democratically elected, president Viktor Yanukovich, was ousted unconstitutionally with the help of neo-Nazis during a violent coup. *The Wall Street Journal* published an article called "Putin the Improviser," stating "the Ukraine showdown is even scarier and more dangerous than you think," framing the situation as evil dictator Putin and the "just" West trying to liberate oppressed Ukraine—a familiar and convenient narrative used in so many past US aggressions. The reality is far more complicated than America = good, Russia = bad, but one has to dig far outside the corporate media to notice.

Among the main events catalyzing a volley of propaganda between the US and Russia was the downing of Malaysian passenger airliner MH-17 on July 17, 2014, killing all 298 aboard. The US immediately blamed Russia, who denied involvement. After months of trading barbs, Robert Parry writes that according to detailed German intelligence reports, it appears at the very least the Russians did not attack, and it may be that a Ukrainian jetfighter was involved, possibly to create a false flag event, even possibly designed to shoot down Putin who was supposed to be flying in a similar plane and trajectory as MH-17, or that it was Ukrainian rebels. However, to date, there is no definitive accounting outside that the Germans seemed to have cleared Russia on the matter, a point further underscored by relative silence from Washington since the intel report was made pubic.

The blame game is a big part of the propaganda war surrounding Ukraine. Secretary of State John Kerry criticized Russia, pointing out the illegality of any country acquiring "part or all of another state's territory through coercion or force." Yet Kerry stated it is "unrealistic" for Israel to relinquish territories they have acquired in the same way. Furthermore, spokesperson for US Department of State Jen Psaki went so far as to remark, "As a matter of longstanding policy, the United States does not support political transitions by unconstitutional means. Political transitions must be democratic, constitutional, peaceful and legal." Associated Press correspondent Matt Lee, in a rare show of courage from a major media outlet, asked Psaki, "How longstanding is that?"

Keep in mind Psaki stated this in response to questions from the press regarding a failed coup attempt in Venezuela that took place a day earlier, and on the heels of Kerry's remarks about Russia's use of coercion or force the previous summer. To believe Psaki, one must also overlook US backing of the Ukrainian coup itself (which was illegal). Lee directly called out Psaki in the exchange, she replied that any claim about the US supporting a coup in Venezuela, or elsewhere for that matter, was "ludicrous." Lee was right to call Psaki on such a bogus claim, whether Afghanistan or Iraq, Honduras or the Ukraine, just in the past decade, the US has overthrown and occupied several foreign countries and tried to in other places. Indeed, irony is not dead and the hypocrisy in official statements as well as US media coverage regarding Ukraine continued into 2015.

According to John Chipman, director-general of the International Institute for Strategic Studies, "a growing body of opinion in the US Congress considers that the US has a moral obligation and a strategic duty to provide Ukraine with increased means to defend itself." However, the conflict is not as black and white as the corporate news would like people to think, and the United States has a stake in any conflict between Ukraine and Russia. The crisis is causing shifts in power in the region and these changes are reshaping the international landscape.

On energy politics in the region, an article in the *Hill* reported leaked policy papers which noted that Ukraine gets much of its coal from within its own borders, yet Russia has been the highest recipient of Ukraine's coal export in recent months. Russia and US companies have other competing energy interests in the region as well, considering the large deposit of natural gas. It ought be noted that in May 2014, shortly after the coup, US vice president Joe Biden's son Hunter Biden was hired on to the board of directors of the largest natural gas company in Ukraine, Burisma Holdings. Though most US media outlets that covered the story said it was not illegal nor did it present any conflict of interests, it raised eyebrows in the international community. While Russia and Putin are highly criticized and held suspect by the US for their interests in Ukraine, the US seems to apply a different standard to itself.

Since last year, the United States has provided what Obama deemed "nonlethal" aid to Ukraine in the form of over three billion dollars in Humvees, drones, and equipment. Fox News reports that the US has sent 600 paratroopers to the National Guard in Ukraine to teach the troops how to "defend" themselves from Russian rockets. The US has also deployed fighter jets in Europe in order to "protect" European NATO members from Russian attacks. What should stand out is that many neo-Nazis are members of the National Guard and are receiving US training and support. One such group is Azov Battalion. Their training was to begin on April 20, 2015, the birthday of Adolf Hitler.

Despite such brazen actions by the US, on May 6, 2015, US Ambassador to Ukraine Geoffrey Pyatt, interviewed on Radio Free Europe/ Radio Liberty, called on Russia to "change its approach" in eastern Ukraine in order to achieve peace. Decrying what he called "a manufactured war" built upon supplies of weapons from Russia to Russian separatists and a "very effective" information warfare campaign, Pyatt made clear that the US and its allies are doing everything possible to achieve peace. Pyatt further stated that the United States has knowledge of Russian training programs for fighters and the movement of Russian surface-to-air missile systems "very close to the contact line inside the Ukrainian territory." However, Pyatt omitted the fact that US military advisors were on the ground in Ukraine providing training and support to both regular Ukrainian military and neo-Nazi paramilitary organizations, such as the aforementioned Azov Battalion. The Ukraine claims that some 8,000 people have died in the conflict that began April of 2014, while the United Nations says the number is 6,400.

On top of the human costs, there are also economic costs. The Ukrainian currency is losing value, which is one reason the US pumps in money, to help create anti-Russian sentiment. The World Bank and the International Monetary Fund issued a loan to Ukraine to the tune of seventeen billion dollars, yet written into the loan was a catch: Ukraine had to agree to grow and sell genetically modified organisms (GMOs). US mega-corporation and GMO producer Monsanto immediately began doing business in the country which boasts some of the world's most fertile and financially lucrative agricultural land—the famed "Black Earth" belt of Ukraine has been prized by European and global powers for centuries.

The Ukrainian economy continues to teeter on the verge of collapse. Having lost roughly 70 percent of its value since 2014, the currency is in free fall. According to Johns Hopkins professor and researcher at the Cato Institute, Steve Hanke, "the official inflation rate has consistently and massively understated Ukraine's brutal inflation. At present, Ukraine's implied annual inflation rate is 272 percent." In addition, Ukraine's GDP decreased by 17.6 percent in the first quarter of 2015. These economic woes have led to a financial crisis in which workers remain unpaid, pensioners without income, and a social emergency becoming ever more impossible to ignore or suppress.

Yet, in the midst of a fiscal and humanitarian crisis in Ukraine, the US-backed regime in Kiev continues to funnel its financial aid into its ongoing war against the self-proclaimed Donetsk and Lugansk People's Republics. Essentially, it is US and European taxpayers now financing Kiev's war against the East while the people of Ukraine proper pay a heavy price. And the reporting on what's happening in Ukraine remains as murky and propaganda laden as when the coup took place in 2014. Many of the independent and some foreign press try to show how complicated matters have become, with varying perspectives, while most all corporate sources take the US State Department hard line against Russia. It harkens to another time when propaganda ran high between the US and Russia during the latter half of the twentieth century. Nafeez Ahmed's question from last year's #9 *Censored* Story still lingers—did the Cold War ever really end?

SOURCES:

Martin Kirk and Frederic Mousseau, "The Hidden Hands Behind East-West Tug of War in Ukraine," Common Dreams, August 1, 2014, http://www.commondreams.org/views/2014/08/01/hidden-hands-behind-ea.

Stephen F. Cohen, "The New Cold War and the Necessity of Patriotic Heresy," *Nation*, August 12, 2014, http://www.thenation.com/article/180942/new-cold-war-and-necessity-patriotic-heresy#.

Stephen Zunes, "US Leadership against Russia Crippled by its Own Hypocrisy," *Foreign Policy in Focus*, September 15, 2014, http://fpif.org/u-s-leadership-russia-crippled-hypocrisy.

Christina Sarich, "What They're Not Telling You About Monsanto's Role in Ukraine," *Natural Society*, January 11, 2015, http://naturalsociety.com/theyre-not-telling-monsantos-role-ukraine/#ixzz3cafNsDzC.

Frank Jacobs, "Why China Will Reclaim Siberia," *New York Times*, January 13, 2015, http://www.nytimes.com/roomfordebate/2014/07/03/where-do-borders-need-to-be-redrawn/why-china-will-reclaim-siberia.

Andrew Weiss, "Putin the Improviser," *Wall Street Journal*, February 20, 2015, http://www.wsj.com/articles/putin-the-improviser-1424473405.

Ben Wolfgang, "John McCain 'Ashamed' over Lack of US Aid to Ukraine," *Washington Times*, February 22, 2015, http://www.washingtontimes.com/news/2015/feb/22/john-mccain-ashamed-over-lack-of-us-aid-to-ukraine.

Steven H. Hanke, "Ukraine Hyperinflates," Cato Institute, February 24, 2015, http://www.cato.org/blog/ukraine-hyperinflates.

Matt O'Brien, "Ukraine Unofficially Has 272% Inflation," *Washington Post*, Wonkblog, March 1, 2015, http://www.washingtonpost.com/blogs/wonkblog/wp/2015/03/01/ukraine-unofficially-has-272-percent-inflation.

Barbara Starr, "US Sending Humvees, Non-Lethal Aid to Ukraine," CNN, March 11, 2015. http://www.cnn.com/2015/03/11/politics/ukraine-us-sends-money-humvees-non-lethal-aid.

Robert Parry, "US Intel Stands Pat on MH-17 Shoot Down," *Consortium News*, March 14, 2015, https://consortiumnews.com/2015/03/14/us-intel-stands-pat-on-mh-17-shoot-down.

Eli Stephens, "Did You Hear the One about How the U.S. Doesn't Support Coups?" *Liberation*, March 15, 2015, http://www.liberationnews.org/did-you-hear-the-one-about-how-the-u-s-doesnt-support-coups.

Agnia Grigas, "One Year Since Crimea's Annexation: Russia's Interests in Ukraine Run Deep," *The Hill*, March 23, 2015, http://thehill.com/blogs/congress-blog/foreign-policy/236487-one-year-since-crimeas-annexation-russias-interests-in.

Paul Craig Roberts, "Russia Under Attack" *CounterPunch*, March 23, 2015, http://www.counterpunch.org/2015/03/23/russia-under-attack.

Hayley Richardson, "Chechnya Threatens to Arm Mexico if US Sends Weapons to Ukraine," *Newsweek*, March 26, 2015, http://www.newsweek.com/chechnya-threatens-arm-mexico-if-us-sends-weapons-ukraine-316959.

Adam Johnson, "On Hitler's Birthday, US Will Begin Training Ukraine's Far-Right National Guard," AlterNet, April 2, 2015, http://www.alternet.org/world/hitlers-birthday-us-will-begin-training-ukraines-far-right-national-guard.

"A Geopolitical Game Changer," *US News*, April 17, 2015, http://www.usnews.com/opinion/blogs/world-report/2015/04/17/ukraine-crisis-is-a-geopolitical-game-changer-that-weakens-russia.

"US Ambassador to Ukraine Says 'Russia Has to Change its Approach,'" Radio Free Europe/Radio Liberty, May 7, 2015, http://www.rferl.org/content/ukraine-us-ambassador-pyatt-russian-approach/26999887.html.

"Merkel Urges Russia to Pressure Ukraine Rebels to Abide by Ceasefire," *Guardian*, May 10, 2015, http://www.theguardian.com/world/2015/may/10/merkel-urges-russia-to-pressure-ukraine-rebels-to-abide-by-ceasefire.

Eric Draitser, "Battlefield: Black Sea," *New Eastern Outlook*, May 14, 2015, http://journal-neo.org/2015/05/14/battlefield-black-sea.

Tyler Durden, "US Taxpayer on the Hook as Ukraine Prepares Moratorium on Debt Repayments, Increases Military Spending," *Zero Hedge*, May 19, 2015, http://www.zerohedge.com/news/2015-05-19/us-taxpayer-hook-ukraine-prepares-moratorium-debt-repayments-increases-military-spen.

Censored 2015 #24

Restorative Justice Turns Violent Schools Around

SUMMARY: In 2007, Restorative Justice for Oakland Youth (RJOY) spearheaded an initiative to reduce suspensions, expulsions, and violence in the Oakland Unified School District in California, the public school district in one of the most violent cities in the nation. In 2012, American Paradigm Schools (APS) took over Philadelphia's John Paul Jones Middle School and collaborated with Alternatives to

Violence Project (AVP). Like RJOY in Oakland, the two organizations radically changed what was known as "Jones Jail" by implementing a non-coercive, nonviolent conflict resolution program in order to emphasize student empowerment, relationship building, and anger management skills. Under these programs, schools removed metal detectors and replaced their security guards with veterans trained in mediation and conflict resolution.

This approach, used at John Paul Jones Middle School and throughout public schools in Oakland is called restorative justice. Restorative justice originally developed for use in prison settings, but has since been adapted to violent schools thanks to the work of organizations like APS and RJOY. Under the restorative justice model, engagement coaches "help mediate disputes rather than dole out punishment." As cofounder and executive director of RJOY Fania Davis reported for *YES! Magazine*, everyone has a chance for their voice to be heard, conflicts are resolved, and students are engaged in a process that promotes "dialogue, accountability, a deeper sense of community, and healing" instead of resorting to violence.

Restorative justice programs seem to be working. As reported in *Censored 2015*, the number of serious incidents in John Paul Jones Middle School fell by 90 percent in its first year and a University of California, Berkeley, study found that RJOY's middle school program reduced suspensions by 87 percent and violent incidents by 77 percent.

UPDATE: There has been success in schools that have implemented restorative justice. American Paradigm Schools in Philadelphia has continued to see improvement in student achievement and a reduction in behavior issues over the past year. In Oakland, California, restorative justice has been so successful that over thirty schools in the area now practice restorative justice and are seeing similar results. The continued success of these schools has not gone unnoticed. Numerous other schools across the country are applying for charter licenses and implementing restorative justice practices into their curriculum, to the immense benefit of students.

Since American Paradigm Schools (APS) took over John Paul Jones Middle School, it has been renamed as Memphis Street Academy Charter School. As reported by Kevin McCorry writing for Newsworks.org, Memphis Street Academy gained twenty points on its SPP rating, earning a 52.9 compared to its district's average of 56.8. SPP, or School Performance Profile, is a school evaluation system based largely on student test scores but considers other factors, such as student involvement and graduation rates. McCorry notes that this jump in score is mostly due to an increase in enrollment, however the drastic improvement is still significant.

In November 2014, APS announced that they would be submitting applications to open two new charter schools in the northeastern part of Philadelphia. If their applications are approved, APS will run a total of five charter schools in Philadelphia, although it is unclear at the time of writing this whether APS will implement a restorative justice program in these new schools as well.

Restorative Justice for Oakland Youth (RJOY) has expanded and now has a presence in almost thirty schools in Oakland, California. Focusing on Edna Brewer Middle School in Oakland, a December 2014 National Public Radio report explained what restorative justice aimed to do in Oakland schools. "The hope of restorative justice is that dialogue builds trust and community and reduces the need for suspensions and expulsions." As Fania Davis, cofounder and executive director of RJOY, reported in the *San Jose Mercury News* that same month, "suspensions of African-American students for defiance decreased by 40 percent [and] harm was repaired in 70 percent of conflict circles," for the 2011–14 academic years.

The *Mercury News* continued reporting in January 2015 by stating, "In schools that have the programs, suspensions dropped by more than half over three years starting in 2011, from 34 percent to 14 percent, according to a new school district report. Graduation rates increased 60 percent at high schools with the programs, compared to 7 percent at schools without them, and chronic absenteeism dropped 24 percent at middle schools with the programs, compared to a 62 percent increase at those middle schools that didn't have them."

Due to success during test trials in Oakland, restorative justice has built a positive reputation and gained attention nationwide. What started as an experimental study has now taken root in public and charter schools in cities such as New York City, Los Angeles, Denver, Boston, and Cambridge.

Restorative justice is not limited to RJOY. The International Institute for Restorative Practices Graduate School (IIRP) is a private, accredited graduate school in Bethlehem, Pennsylvania, dedicated to research to develop the growing field of restorative practices. The IIRP helps individual schools develop a customized plan based on their own needs and goals. Everyone on the school staff has a say and a role in implementation, and there are professional development instructors assigned to ensure program sustainability.[1]

Restorative justice holds promise as a solution to the negative impacts of the high incarceration rate in the US. It is well known that "the United States has the highest rate of incarceration in the world, but several factors indicate that this response is ineffective—particularly with respect to juveniles." There is a strong correlation between zero-tolerance policies in our school systems and later increased prison recidivism. Studies have found the existence and prevalence of the school-to-prison pipeline (particularly for African-American boys), and the negative impact of zero-tolerance policies in schools that target minority students.

"In recent decades suspensions increased from 1.7 million in 1974 to more than 3.3 million in 2006." The more a student is excluded by being suspended or expelled, the higher the possibility that they will struggle in academics and fail to graduate as these policies give no access to alternative educational opportunities. "The CSG report found that 23 percent of students who experienced exclusionary disciplinary actions in school had subsequent contact with the juvenile justice system."[2] Implementing programs like APS and RJOY in low-income, high-crime communities where students are not expected to succeed based on their ethnic, economic, and educational background will make a difference.

SOURCES:

Mary Schmid Mergler, Karla M. Vargas, and Caroline Caldwell, "Alternative Discipline Can Benefit Learning," *Phi Delta Kappan* 96, no. 2 (October 2014): 25; http://evansimpsonportfolio. weebly.com/uploads/3/0/6/0/30600261/phi_delta_kappan-2014-mergler-25-30.pdf.

Kevin McCorry, "How Philly's Charter Schools Stack Up On PA's Performance Measure," *Newsworks*, November 10, 2014, http://www.newsworks.org/index.php/local/education/74985-how-do-phillys-charter-schools-stack-up-on-pas-performance-measure.

Dale Mezzacappa, "With Days Until Deadline, 46 New Charter Applications," *Notebook*, November 11, 2014, http://thenotebook.org/blog/147912/days-until-deadline-46-new-charter-applications.

Judy C. Tsui, "Breaking Free of the Prison Paradigm: Integrating Restorative Justice Techniques into Chicago's Juvenile Justice System," *Journal of Criminal Law & Criminology* 104, no. 3

(Fall 2014): 634–66, http://scholarlycommons.law.northwestern.edu/cgi/viewcontent.
cgi?article=7486&context=jclc.

Fania Davis, "Guest Commentary: 'Restorative Justice' Program Has Become a Vital Tool
for Public," *San Jose Mercury News*, December 10, 2014, http://www.mercurynews.com/
ci_27112472/guest-commentary-restorative-justice-program-has-become-vital.

Eric Westervelt, "An Alternative to Suspension and Expulsion: 'Circle Up!'" NPR, December 17,
2014, accessed June 2, 2015, http://www.npr.org/sections/ed/2014/12/17/347383068/an-
alternative-to-suspension-and-expulsion-circle-up.

Doug Oakley, "Oakland: School District to Expand Restorative Justice Programs to All 86
Schools," *San Jose Mercury News*, January 14, 2015, http://www.mercurynews.com/education/
ci_27320766/school-district-expand-restorative-justice-programs-all-86.

Carly Berwick, "Zeroing Out Zero-Tolerance," *Atlantic*, March 17, 2015, http://www.theatlantic.
com/education/archive/2015/03/zeroing-out-zero-tolerance/388003/.

"Public Policy Points of Intervention Along the School-to-Prison Pipeline," *American Mosaic: The
African-American Experience* (2014).

Censored 2015 #4

Corporate Internet Providers Threaten Net Neutrality

SUMMARY: In May of 2014, A 3–2 vote by the FCC opened a four-month window for formal public comments on the severity of proposed Internet rules. The decision galvanized corporate media attention on the issue of net neutrality. By contrast, for months leading up to this development, independent journalists, including Paul Ausick, Cole Stangler, and Jennifer Yeh, had been informing the public about the anticipated showdown over net neutrality and the stakes in that battle.

This was the eventual result of a federal appeals court of Washington DC, which began a crucial case brought by Verizon Communications Inc., challenging the authority of the Federal Communications Commission (FCC) to regulate Internet service providers in September of 2013. Under the FCC's current Open Internet Order, service providers such as Verizon, cannot charge varying prices or give priority to users that access certain websites or may be able to pay more for faster speeds compared to competitors. Verizon claimed the FCC violated their First Amendment right and they should have the ability to manage and promote the content they see fit. The FCC has continually ruled that controlling communications is not in the best interest of the public. If the court decides in favor of Verizon and revokes the Open Internet Order, the FCC will have no way to regulate unbiased data access, changing the future for everyday Internet users in the twenty-first century.

Verizon v. FCC has been well covered by both corporate and independent media. However, corporate outlets such as the *New York Times* and *Forbes* tend to highlight the business aspects of the case, skimming over vital particulars affecting the public and the Internet's future.

UPDATE: Last year's report on net neutrality foresaw a bleak future in the fight to maintain a free and open Internet. But by February of 2015 the FCC ruled in favor of preserving net neutrality. While many conservative politicians are already drafting legislation and telecommunications corporations are filing suits against the ruling, the public has been largely ecstatic about the decision, and the continued support of individuals working collectively bodes well for the future of Internet freedom. Several factors lead to this historic decision.

In June 2014, comedian John Oliver, host of HBO's *Last Week Tonight*, gave a thirteen-minute monologue about the imminent threat to a free Internet. He asked the "monsters" who leave Internet comments to go to the FCC's website during the public commenting period, and express their support for net neutrality. Public response was so immense that it crashed the FCC website. FCC.gov received over 22,000 comments in two days, and about 40,000 more in the next month. In September a number of popular websites, including Reddit, Etsy, and Upworthy, displayed a loading symbol on their webpages to illustrate the effect tiered levels of service might have on the web. The event, called "Internet Slow Down Day," raised public awareness and drummed up more support for net neutrality.

Perhaps this is why, in November of last year, President Barack Obama posted a video to WhiteHouse.gov, in which he expressed his support for net neutrality and a "free and open Internet," saying it could only be preserved by classifying broadband providers as "common carriers" under Title II of the Telecommunications Act. Corporate media began covering the net neutrality debate at this point, with Fox News identifying net neutrality as a threat to innovation, to quality, and to consumer pricing, claiming net neutrality would inevitably lead to higher taxes.

In independent media, various outlets discussed the consequences of an Internet controlled by corporate interests, while *Wired* firmly held that the lack of competition between ISPs was the real problem in the net neutrality debate. Growing public support for an open Internet seemed to be turning the debate around.

The White House stated on January 15, 2015, that legislation was not necessary to settle net neutrality rules as the FCC possessed the authority to write said rules—thus supporting the FCC's legal ability regarding net neutrality. On February 4, FCC Chairman Tom Wheeler made an announcement in *Wired* "proposing that the FCC use its Title II authority to implement and enforce open Internet protections." This was the first indication that the FCC would treat the Internet—both fixed and mobile broadband—as a public utility and regulate it accordingly, and corporate media had decided it was finally worth reporting about. On February 26, the FCC reclassified broadband access as a utilities service. Now classified as "common carriers," Internet Service Providers are under the regulation of the FCC. Republican lawmakers wasted no time responding to the FCC's new regulations; Speaker John Boehner called the Open Internet Order "a secret plan to put the federal government in control of the Internet."

In March 2015, the FCC released a 300-page document regarding the regulations voted upon in the prior month. Opponents of net neutrality used this page count to claim that the regulations were too complex; however, out of those 200 pages only eight were dedicated to regulatory speech. USTelecom and Alamo Broadband filed lawsuits against the FCC's Open Internet Order on March 23. According to John Ribeiro of IDG News Service, the broadband industry believes that they function "in conformance with the open Internet principles" and thus do not require further regulation. The lawsuit requested that the Open Internet Order be recognized as unlawful, stating that its terms were in excess of the FCC's authority.

On April 10, 2015, the Federal Register placed the Open Internet Order out on "public inspection," setting its publishing date to April 13. Once published to the Federal Register, the daily record of rules and regulations set forth by the United States government, the Open Internet Order goes into effect June 12, 2015. Now that the regulations are being made public, the door opens for opponents of net neutrality to file more lawsuits against the Federal Communications Commission.

While the FCC has ruled in favor of net neutrality with its Open Internet Order, corporate Internet providers are unlikely to allow the ruling to go into effect without a lengthy legal fight. Net neutrality does not work in favor of the bottom line, after all. More lawsuits are predicted by news sources both corporate and independent, but either way net neutrality remains an important issue worthy of public attention and scrutiny. Some hold to the claim that the FCC's interests in net neutrality are purely political as the federal government is more interested in taxation. However, in spring of 2015, FCC chair Tom Wheeler stated his opposition to a $45 billion merger between Comcast and Time Warner, and Comcast withdrew its proposal. Wheeler explained that "the decisions to create new net neutrality rules and to block Comcast's merger with Time Warner Cable were driven by a common factor: the transition of cable TV firms into businesses that primarily supply high-speed Internet." One thing is for sure, the battle over a free and open Internet is not over, but the developments through early 2015 are clear victories for the public interest. Net neutrality and the Open Internet Order are an example of how grassroots movements can change the rules on a federal level and pressure the government into working toward the greater good of society and its people.

SOURCES:

Andrew Leonard, "The FCC Just Sold Out the Internet," *Salon*, April 23, 2014, http://www.salon.com/2014/04/23/the_fcc_just_sold_out_the_internet/.

Klint Finley, "Google Backs Netflix in Epic Battle with Comcast," *Wired*, May 22, 2014, http://www.wired.com/2014/05/google-fiber-netflix/.

Sarah Gray, "FCC Passes Proposal to Create Rules on Net Neutrality, Further Threatening an Open Internet," *Salon*, May 15, 2014, http://www.salon.com/2014/05/15/fcc_passes_proposal_to_create_rules_on_net_neutrality_in_a_3_2_vote/.

Sarah Gray, "Following John Oliver Net Neutrality Rant, FCC Site Completely Overloaded With 22,000 Comments," *Salon*, June 4, 2014, http://www.salon.com/2014/06/04/post_john_oliver_net_neutrality_rant_fcc_site_completely_overloaded_with_22000_comments/.

Brent Skorup, "The FCC Has More Important Things to Worry About Than Netflix," *Wired*, June 18, 2014, http://www.wired.com/2014/06/fcc-netflix-is-a-goose-chase/.

Robert McMillan, "What Everyone Gets Wrong in the Debate Over Net Neutrality," *Wired*, June 23, 2014, http://www.wired.com/2014/06/net_neutrality_missing/.

Reed Hastings, "How to Save the Net: Don't Give In to Big ISPs," *Wired*, August 18, 2014, http://www.wired.com/2014/08/save-the-net-reed-hastings/.

Sarah Gray, "Why Your Internet Could Be Slowing Down Today," *Salon*, September 10, 2014, http://www.salon.com/2014/09/10/internet_slowdown_day_net_neutrality_and_the_battle_for_the_internet/.

Matt Stoller, "The Plot To Maim Google: How AT&T and Comcast Plan to Upend the Internet," *Salon*, October 17, 2014, http://www.salon.com/2014/10/17/the_plot_to_maim_google_how_att_and_comcast_plan_to_upend_the_internet/.

Alex Fitzpatrick, "Comcast Just Trolled Us All on Net Neutrality," *Time*, November 11, 2014, http://time.com/3579332/comcast-obama-net-neutrality/.

Simon Maloy, "Ted Cruz Gets Even More Annoying: Why He Wants to Make the Internet Worse," *Salon*, November 11, 2014, http://www.salon.com/2014/11/11/ted_cruz_gets_even_more_annoying_why_he_wants_to_make_the_internet_worse/.

Jim Hightower, "Why Corporations Are Desperate to Destroy Net Neutrality," *Salon*, November 13, 2014, http://www.salon.com/2014/11/13/why_corporations_are_desperate_to_destroy_net_neutrality_partner/.

Steve Tobak, "Why Comcast vs. Netflix Is Not About Net Neutrality," *Fox Business*, November 13, 2014, http://www.foxbusiness.com/2014/11/13/why-comcast-vs-netflix-is-not-about-net-neutrality/.

Robert McMillan, "The Simple Question Nobody's Asking about Net Neutrality," *Wired*, November 14, 2014, http://www.wired.com/2014/11/net_neutrality/.

Josh Peterson, "Perry: Obama Net Neutrality Internet Regulations Are From 'Era of the Great Depression,'" Fox News, November 14, 2014, http://www.foxnews.com/politics/2014/11/14/perry-obama-net-neutrality-internet-regulations-are-from-era-great-depression/.

"FCC Official Warns Obama-Backed Net Neutrality Plan Would Bring 'Immediate' Internet Tax," Fox News, November 17, 2014 http://www.foxnews.com/politics/2014/11/17/fcc-official-warns-obama-backed-net-neutrality-plan-will-bring-backdoor-tax-on/.

Alina Selyukh and Roberta Rampton, "Exclusive: White House Says Net Neutrality Legislation Not Needed," Reuters, January 15, 2015, http://www.reuters.com/article/2015/01/15/us-usa-internet-neutrality-exclusive-idUSKBN0KO2JO20150115.

Liz Claman, "Claman on Call: FCC to Propose Strong Net Neutrality Rules," *Fox Business*, February 2, 2015, http://www.foxbusiness.com/markets/2015/02/02/claman-on-call/.

Simon Maloy, "Obama's Open Internet Win: The FCC's Plan to Upend US Internet Policy," *Salon*, February 5, 2015, http://www.salon.com/2015/02/05/obamas_open_internet_win_the_fccs_plan_to_upend_u_s_internet_policy/.

Sam Gustin, "How Net Neutrality Came Back from the Dead," *Vice*, February 26, 2015, http://motherboard.vice.com/read/the-fight-for-an-open-internet-and-how-david-beat-goliath.

John Zangas, "How Net Neutrality Activists Won the Fight for the Internet," *Popular Resistance*, March 5, 2015, https://www.popularresistance.org/how-net-neutrality-activists-won-the-fight-for-the-internet/.

Kit Walsh, "Net Neutrality: Are We There Yet?," Electronic Frontier Foundation, March 11, 2015, https://www.eff.org/deeplinks/2015/03/net-neutrality-are-we-there-yet.

Russell Berman, "Having Lost on Net Neutrality, Republicans Offer a Deal," *Atlantic*, March 23, 2015, http://www.theatlantic.com/politics/archive/2015/03/surrender-now-in-our-moment-of-triumph-i-think-you-overestimate-their-chances/388357/.

"Net Neutrality and the FCC's Overreach Are Political," *Wall Street Journal*, March 23, 2015, http://www.wsj.com/articles/net-neutrality-and-the-fccs-overreach-are-political-letters-to-the-editor-1427036252.

John Ribeiro, "US FCC Faces Lawsuits Against Proposed Net Neutrality Order," *PC World*, March 23, 2015, http://www.pcworld.com/article/2901092/us-fcc-faces-lawsuits-against-proposed-net-neutrality-order.html.

Brian Fung, "Net Neutrality Will Be Fair Game For Lawsuits Starting Next Week," *Washington Post*, April 10, 2015, http://www.washingtonpost.com/blogs/the-switch/wp/2015/04/10/net-neutrality-is-about-to-land-in-the-official-record-making-it-fair-game-for-lawsuits/.

John Ribeiro, "FCC Net Neutrality Rules Published To Federal Register," *PC World*, April 12, 2015, http://www.pcworld.com/article/2909132/fcc-net-neutrality-rules-published-to-federal-register.html.

Cecilia Kang, "FCC Chair Defends Net Neutrality, Blocking Comcast," *Washington Post*, May 6, 2015, http://www.washingtonpost.com/blogs/the-switch/wp/2015/05/06/fcc-chair-defends-net-neutrality-blocking-comcast.

Censored 2015 #17

2016 Will Find Gaza out of Drinking Water

SUMMARY: In Gaza, 1.7 million Palestinians currently live without clean drinking water. With no perennial streams and low rainfall, Gaza relies on a single aquifer for all of its fresh water. The coastal aquifer, Zander Swinburne reported, is contaminated with sewage, chemicals, and seawater. The Palestinian Water Authority recently determined that 95 percent of the water in Gaza does not meet World Health Organization (WHO) standards for human consumption. The polluted water causes chronic health problems and contributes to high rates of child mortality. One study estimated that 26 percent of disease in Gaza results from contaminated water supplies. "A crippling Egyptian-Israeli blockade on Gaza has exacerbated the problem," Al Jazeera reported.

A recent United Nations report warned that the water situation for Palestinians in Gaza was "critical." According to that report, "the aquifer could become unusable as early as 2016, with the damage irreversible by 2020." Even with immediate remedial action, the 2012 report stated the aquifer would take decades to recover; otherwise it would "take centuries for the aquifer to recover."

As a result of the contaminated water supply, Al Jazeera reported the Palestinian Ministry of Health recommend that residents boil water before using it for drinking. However, residents contend that even with boiling, the tap water "is not fit to drink," and, in many cases, is simply unavailable. According to people in the territory, Zander Swinburne reported, "during the summer months, water might spurt out of their taps every other day . . . pressure is often so low that those living on upper floors might see just a trickle."

Instead, according to United Nations estimates, over 80 percent of Gazans buy their drinking water with some families paying as much as a third of their household income, according to June Kunugi (UNICEF). Palestinians purchase more than a quarter of their water from Israel's national water company, Mekorot, Al Jazeera reported. Mekorot sells Gaza 4.2 million cubic meters of water annually.

UPDATE: Several factors make the depletion of Gaza's water complicated, such as the atmosphere of political unrest and greed, along with the crippling poverty, overcrowding, and large-scale environmental degradation in the Gaza Strip. The over-exhaustion of the lone aquifer has significantly outpaced its annual recharging through annual precipitation. The high permeability of the aquifer also allows hazardous levels of seawater, coastal pollutants, and contaminants from one of the most industrialized shorelines in the world to creep their way into the water supply. These toxins have caused child mortality rates in Gaza to skyrocket and the increasing contaminants in the irrigation water continue to negatively affect crops.

The residents of Gaza continue to face the reality of depleted drinking water. This is compounded by the restrictions of movements for the residents of Gaza. Its residents live in what has been compared to an open-air prison.[3] They may not come and go as they please. The borders both into Israel and Egypt are heavily guarded and most of the time completely closed to movement of people. Goods are often

restricted by the occupying Israeli military from entering and exiting, thus making international trade and access to necessary supplies nearly impossible for Gazans who are then often forced to purchase Israeli-made products.[4]

Further, the Gaza Strip is currently under Israeli military control and has been since 1948. In 2005–06, after much international pressure, Israel moved its illegal settlers out of the region, some back into Israel, with others, in continued violation of international law settling in the West Bank.[5] In 2008 the citizens of Gaza, previously governed by the Fatah party, voted in Hamas. This was not well received by Israel because despite initially helping establish Hamas in the hopes of creating infighting with Fatah,[6] Hamas has been critical of the policies of expansion into the occupied West Bank and expulsion of Palestinians both within Israel and in the West Bank. Since 2008 there have been three massive offensives on Gaza by Israel, and as of this writing there were thirteen additional Israeli air attacks the last week of May, 2015.[7]

The results of these attacks have killed many civilians and destroyed infrastructure. This endless cycle of destruction and rebuilding has been a part of the daily lives of Palestinians, but since the 2014 assault on Gaza, no rebuilding has taken place. Currently many Gazans remain without homes, schools, hospitals, and other necessary institutions. Rebuilding without necessary supplies is highly problematic. Cement and other building materials are highly restricted goods and, when allowed entry, come at an exorbitant cost which is often too high for many Gazans.[8]

With Gaza on the verge of collapse due to this summer onslaught in 2014, unemployment is as high as 44 percent, and access to drinking water is now just one of the many imminent dangers the people of Gaza face.[9] While the sustainability of the aquifers remains a major issue, it is not the only one. Most of these historical details have been ignored by the corporate media in the US and continue to be as of this writing. Much of what was discussed above is context for the actual Gaza water story, which gives the reader a deeper understanding of how dire the situation has become for residents there. It is important to note not only what the corporate media include in their reporting on the matter, but what they frame out all together.

The only accessible aquifer in Gaza is polluted and maintains its current trajectory of irreversible damage. The denizens of Gaza are still suffering immeasurably, especially because of the raging battle between Israel and Gaza that took place in July and August 2014.[10] The Gaza Strip, is a very small and densely populated Palestinian exclave roughly double the size of Washington DC, yet is home to more than 1.8 million people. It consists of semi-arid coastal steppe, has a warm desert climate with mild winters and dry summers, comparable to that of Tijuana, Mexico. Similar to California, sufficient fresh water and desertification from climate change have long been some of the most pressing concerns of Gaza's citizens, who depend on their lone aquifer as their source of fresh water for drinking, irrigating their food, domestic uses and industrial production.

The latest Israeli assaults on Gaza resulted in devastating consequences to the already fragile water supply. Before the latest assaults, 25 percent of households in Gaza had daily access to water, 40 percent every other day, 20 percent once every three days, and 15 percent one in every four days. The head of the ICRC delegation Israel, Jacques de Maio, said, "Water and electrical services are also affected as a result of the current hostilities. If they do not stop, the question is not if but when an already beleaguered population will face an acute water crisis."

Israeli bombings in Gaza on July 29, 2014, took out Gaza's only functional power plant and destroyed many of Gaza's water wells. The power shortage has slowed the pumping capacity of Gaza's water supply systems, and eighty million tons of raw sewage continues to drain into the Mediterranean Sea on a daily basis. One-third of Gaza's water wells are not working and remain unusable because it is too dangerous for technicians to access them, while the remaining operating wells only function between six and eight hours a day due to the lack of electricity.

There have been efforts to relieve this inevitable water crisis. Emirates Red Crescent Authority (ERC) has been working on projects to send clean water tanks to the Palestinians living in this severe water crisis. This operation has already delivered food aid, shelter and clothes, and medicine as part of the relief. Unfortunately, the Egyptian-Israeli blockade of Gaza makes it impossible for architectural resources and water to be imported.

One news outlet covered a possible solution to Gaza's water woes. Yahoo! News picked up an Agence France-Presse (AFP) story on a Palestinian engineer Diaa Abu Assi is seeking to desalinate water from the Mediterranean. "In five years, there will be no drinkable water in Gaza," Abu Assi said. "Water shortages are a real threat to life in Gaza. The only solution is to filter water from the Mediterranean." With the support of Gaza's Islamic University, Abu Assi hopes a solution will materialize using nanotechnology to desalinate sea water, though worries about the possibility that another Israeli bombardment could wreck havoc on any possible developments. A March AFP article claimed the Israeli government was going to double the water piped into Gaza, but as of this writing, no evidence of that had occurred.

The constant bouts of war through the years have ruined any semblance of infrastructure in Gaza, and the water story is only one of many that if readers want to learn more about, they have to look far beyond the corporate media in the US to find.

SOURCES:

Jen Marlowe, "Parting the Brown Sea: Sewage Crisis Threatens Gaza's Access to Water," Al Jazeera, April 18, 2014, http://america.aljazeera.com/articles/2015/4/18/sewage-crisis-threatens-gazas-access-to-water.html.
Shalom Bear, "IDF's Operation 'Protective Edge' Begins Against Gaza" *Jewish Press*, July 8, 2014, http://www.jewishpress.com/news/breaking-news/idfs-operation-protective-edge-begins-against-gaza/2014/07/08/.
Ala Qandil, "Gaza Faces Imminent Water Crisis," Al Jazeera, July 17, 2014, http://www.aljazeera.com/news/middleeast/2014/07/gaza-faces-imminent-water-crisis-201471755035576420.html.
Neal Sandler and Debra K. Rubin, "Israeli-Palestinian Tension Takes Toll on Regional Infrastructure and Construction Sectors," *ENR: Engineering News-Record*, July 28, 2014, "ERC to Send 10 Drinking Water Tanks into Gaza Strip," Emirate News Agency, August 4, 2014, https://www.wam.ae/en/news/emirates-arab/1395268355231.html.
Amira Hass, "Gaza Severely Short of Water for Drinking and Bathing," *Haaretz*, August 21, 2014, http://www.haaretz.com/news/diplomacy-defense/.premium-1.611677.
"Ministry: Death Toll from Gaza Offensive Topped 2,310," Ma'an News Agency, January 3, 2015, http://www.maannews.com/eng/ViewDetails.aspx?id=751290.
Adel Zaanoun, "Gaza Engineer Seeks Solution to Water Woes," Agence France-Presse, May 12, 2015, accessed June 2, 2015, http://news.yahoo.com/gaza-engineer-seeks-solution-water-woes-062317446.html.

Censored 2015 #23

Number of US Prison Inmates Serving Life Sentences Hits New Record

SUMMARY: A report released by the Sentencing Project, a Washington DC–based nonprofit criminal justice advocacy group, revealed that the number of prisoners serving life sentences in the US state and federal prisons reached a new record of close to 160,000 in 2012. Of these, 49,000 are serving life without possibility of parole, an increase of 22.2 percent since 2008. The study's findings place in striking context the figures promoted by the federal government, which indicate a reduction in the overall number of prisoners in federal and state facilities, from 1.62 million to 1.57 million between 2009 and 2012.

Ashley Nellis, senior research analyst with the Sentencing Project, argued that the rise in prisoners serving life sentences has to do with political posturing over "tough on crime" measures. "Unfortunately, lifers are typically excluded from most sentencing reform conversations because there's this sense that it's not going to sell, politically or with the public," Nellis said. "Legislators are saying, 'We have to throw somebody under the bus.'"

California is the leader in lifers, with one-quarter of the country's life-sentenced population (40,362), followed by Florida (12,549) and New York (10,245), Texas (9,031), Georgia (7,938), Ohio (6,075), Michigan (5,137), Pennsylvania (5,104), and Louisiana (4,657). There are currently 3,281 prisoners in the US serving a life sentence—with no chance of parole—for minor, nonviolent crimes, according to a November 2013 report by the American Civil Liberties Union (ACLU). Louisiana, one of nine states where inmates currently serve life sentences for nonviolent crimes, has the nation's strictest three-strike law, which states that after three offenses the guilty person is imprisoned for life without parole. As Ed Pilkington reported in the *Guardian*, the ACLU study documented "thousands of lives ruined and families destroyed" by this practice. Among those is Timothy Jackson, now fifty-three, who in 1996 was caught stealing a jacket from a New Orleans department store. "It has been very hard for me," Jackson wrote the ACLU. "I know that for my crime I had to do some time, but a life sentence for a jacket valued at $159."

The ACLU study reported that keeping these prisoners locked up for life costs taxpayers around $1.8 billion annually. The study stated that the US is "virtually alone in its willingness to sentence non-violent offenders to die behind bars." Life without parole for nonviolent sentences has been ruled a violation of human rights by the European

Court of Human Rights. With 2.3 million people imprisoned in the US today, Felicia Gustin of *War Times* has asked, is locking people away the answer to creating safer communities? She reported on the work of the Restorative Community Conferencing Program, based in Oakland, California. According to the program's coordinator, Denise Curtis, "restorative justice is a different approach to crime. Our current justice system asks: What law was broken? Who broke it? How should they be punished? Restorative justice asks: Who has been harmed? What needs have arisen because of the harm? Whose responsibility is it to make things as right as they can?"

As Gustin reported, the program works with youth cases referred by the district attorney. Some involve felonies such as assault, robbery, and burglary. The Oakland Unified School District has also successfully incorporated restorative justice practices as an alternative to expelling and suspending youth which, according to Curtis, "impact Black and Brown youth disproportionately much more than white youth." Variations of restorative justice programs currently operate in Baltimore, Minneapolis, New York, Chicago and New Orleans, among other cities, and at least one study has shown such programs have been effective in reducing recidivism. Nevertheless, few are aware of restorative justice as a real alternative to mass incarceration and this positive development deserves more news coverage.

UPDATE: Although the number of incarcerated US citizens remains staggering, there have been several developments in the last year. In November of 2014, Proposition 47 was passed in the state of California. This proposition softens the mandatory sentencing of many nonviolent crimes and has already led to the parole of hundreds of prisoners statewide. As time passes it should also lead to fewer nonviolent offenders being jailed for extended periods. The goal of these acts and actions is to give people a chance to reclaim their lives after they have served reasonable, appropriate sentences for their crimes—a much-needed alternative to the current system.

According to the California Department of Corrections of Rehabilitation (CDCR) weekly report of population the total number of people in custody as of March 18, 2015, stands at 130,632 inmates in prison. Compared to the population in February 2015, the population has gone down 1,289 inmates. Keep in mind that is barely 0.01 percent in decrease from February to March. The slight decrease in California's inmate numbers may be the result of the work of Prop 47.

On November 4, 2014, California voters passed the proposition, which states that nonviolent offenses are now reduced from felonies to misdemeanors. This does not mean anyone can get released from prison automatically; prisoners must petition the court for re-sentencing, followed by parole. A prison guard at San Quentin State Prison, who asked to remain anonymous, stated that prior to the passing of Prop 47, "not every inmate had a cell, we had to lay blankets out in the basketball courts. Overpopulation of the prisoners is dangerous to both the prisoners and the guards. More fights break out and as for the guards, each officer is assigned to one tier in the prison containing about 180 inmates, making it even more challenging to maintain order. Many good things would come from lessening the prison population; less overcrowding means for inmates a better quality of life, for guards a safer work environment, and for taxpayers less money."

Although positive effects can be seen within the prisons themselves, corporate media work diligently to create a sense of fear in the average media consumer. This is used as a tool by media outlets as a way of supporting the status quo against reforms in maintenance of state authority and control. In the article "County Jail Populations Across California Dip After Prop 47," Christine Ward argued that while prison populations will lower, this may mean unsafe communities. She explained, "It just means more people are out in our communities that perhaps shouldn't be there."

Despite backlash of the state's proposition, efforts to reduce inmate populations on the national scale continue to be pursued and are beginning to take effect. On March 9, 2015, Senators Cory Booker and Rand Paul reintroduced the REDEEM Act. As stated by the Sentencing Project, the REDEEM Act, "would repeal the felony drug ban for some people convicted of non-violent drug offenses . . . allow the sealing of criminal records and improve the accuracy of FBI background checks. It would also make necessary improvements to the treatment of young people who encounter the juvenile justice system." The REDEEM Act shows that the nation is beginning to take small steps toward addressing these staggeringly high numbers of inmates. A similar bill, the Smarter Sentencing Act, was also introduced in Congress where both bills sat in committee as of this writing.

While actions are being taken, the priorities of funding in California and the United States as a whole toward fixing this issue appear to be misplaced. According to the Public Policy Institute of California, it is stated that California has made available $2.2 billion in bond revenue to build county jails, which is estimated to add more than 14,000 beds across the state. The American Legislative Exchange Council (ALEC) posted that the California Department of Corrections of Rehabilitation average annual cost per inmate is $45,006. But according to Scott Graves in his article, "Bending the Prison Cost Curves," "under the governor's proposed spending plan for 2014-15, California is expected to spend more than $62,000 on each prison inmate": meanwhile, "our state is expected to spend slightly less than $9,200 for each K-12 student in 2014-15."

While prisons do serve a purpose in the justice system of the United States, the disproportionate amount of money toward punishment rather than efforts to solve the problem at the root seems to be a Band-Aid solution. Imagine a nation where the numbers were reversed and $62,000 was spent on a child's chance at a better future rather than building another cement structure as a rug to sweep our country's problems under.

A *New York Times* article from May 2015 addressed reforms along the lines of the REDEEM Act. The article stated that in order to end mass incarceration, sentences for violent crimes must be cut in half and it noted that drug courts had been able to reduce substance abuse without incarceration. "We need to lock up fewer people on the front end as well as enhance reintegration and reduce collateral consequences that impede rehabilitation on the back end." Hopefully these developments will not only continue, but the news media will report on them more as a way to build public awareness and support for such reforms in the interests of social justice.

SOURCES:

Scott Graves, "Bending the Prison Cost Curve," California Budget & Policy Center, March 26, 2014, accessed April 10, 2015, http://calbudgetcenter.org/blog/bending-the-prison-cost-curve.
Brandon Martin, "Corrections Infrastructure Spending in California," PPIC Publication, March 1, 2015, accessed April 10, 2015, http://www.ppic.org/main/publication_show.asp?i=1142.

"Senators Booker and Paul Reintroduce REDEEM Act to Protect and Restore Lives," Sentencing Project, March 10, 2015, http://www.sentencingproject.org/detail/news.cfm?news_id=1914&id=107.

Don Thompson, "County Jail Populations across California Dip after Prop 47," Southern California Public Radio, February 2, 2015, accessed April 10, 2015, http://www.scpr.org/news/2015/02/02/49608/county-jail-populations-across-california-dip-afte.

Anonymous interview, San Quentin State Prison guard, conducted April 5, 2015, interview by Amanda Jones.

"Prison Overcrowding: California," American Legislative Exchange Council (ALEC), no date, accessed April 10, 2015, http://www.alec.org/initiatives/prison-overcrowding/prison-over-crowding-California.

"Public and Employee Communication," no date, accessed April 10, 2015, http://www.cdcr.ca.gov/news/Proposition_47.html.

"Weekly Report of Population," March 18, 2015, accessed April 10, 2015, http://cdcr.ca.gov/Reports_Research/Offender_Information_Services_Branch/WeeklyWed/TPOP1A/TPOP1Ad150408.pdf.

Cory Booker, "Our Criminal-Legal System: Justice Doesn't Have to be Missing from the Equation," *Huffington Post*, April 15, 2015, http://www.huffingtonpost.com/cory-booker/our-criminal-legal-system_b_7071792.html.

Marc Mauer and David Cole, "How to Lock Fewer People Up," *New York Times*, May 23, 2015, http://mobile.nytimes.com/2015/05/24/opinion/sunday/how-to-lock-up-fewer-people.html?referrer=&_r=0.

CONCLUSION

In the last year, there was a continuation of troubling patterns in Gaza and Ukraine, but there were also positive developments regarding the success of restorative justice programs, a more inclusive discussion concerning the future of the Internet, and a reduction in the numbers of prison inmates for nonviolent offenses. While corporate media picked up on a few of these, they especially continued to neglect details of the foreign policy stories.

In a world that is increasingly complicated, where transnational corporations work diligently with governments to maintain and build upon the current power structure against the public interest, we the people are wise to remember the words of the late historian Howard Zinn: "You can't be neutral on a moving train." We are all in motion, and we must arm ourselves with the power knowledge gives. We should read and support the grassroots, independent media outlets and journalists that help us understand the many changes going on around us. As Alan Watts said, "The only way to make sense out of change is to plunge into it, move with it, and join the dance."

Thanks to Mickey Huff and Nolan Higdon of Project Censored for additional editing and updating of stories in this chapter.

SUSAN RAHMAN teaches sociology and behavioral sciences at the College of Marin. She loves using Project Censored as part of her classroom curriculum to teach media literacy and to raise awareness about issues both locally and globally. She lives in Sonoma County with her partner, Carlos, her daughter Jordan and two dogs Rosie and Phoebi.

Notes

1. International Institute for Restorative Practices, http://www.iirp.edu.
2. Studies further show correlations with statistics and data of the exclusionary policies of those that students experience, and later may determine their future in the justice system. See Mary Schmid Mergler, Karla M. Vargas, and Caroline Caldwell, "Alternative Discipline Can Benefit Learning," *Phi Delta Kappan* 96, no. 2 (October 2014): 25.
3. Ali Abunimah, *One Country: A Bold Proposal to End the Israeli-Palestinian Impasse* (New York: Henry Holt, 2006).
4. Phyllis Bennis, *Understanding the Palestinian-Israeli Conflict* (Lowell MA: TARI, 2003).
5. Francis Boyle, *Palestine, Palestinians, and International Law* (Atlanta: Clarity Press, 2003).
6. Ishaan Tharoor, "How Israel Helped Create Hamas," *Washington Post*, July 30, 2014, http://www.washingtonpost.com/blogs/worldviews/wp/2014/07/30/how-israel-helped-create-hamas.
7. "Press TV Israeli Air Force Launches Multiple Attacks on Gaza Strip," PressTV, May 27, 2015, http://www.presstv.com/Detail/2015/05/27/413018/gaza-israel-attack-hamas-islamic-jihad. These include Operation Cast Lead in 2008–09, Operation Pillar of Cloud in 2012, and Operation Protective Edge in 2014. To truly understand the scope of the social issues occurring in this region of the world, one must look back on its recent history.
    In 2008, Israel launched a major air attack, "Operation Cast Lead," on Hamas, the democratically elected ruling Palestinian party in Gaza. Israel attacked Hamas political and military targets suspected of smuggling illegal arms into Gaza. Hamas responded to these attacks by launching rockets into Israel. In January 2009, Israel launched the "second stage of Operation Cast Lead" through a ground invasion. After fourteen days of fighting, both sides agreed to end the fighting and enacted a unilateral ceasefire in order to restore what very little stability they have back into the region.
    On July 8, 2014, Israel launched "Operation Protective Edge" in response to rocket attacks organized by Hamas. Hamas claimed to have fired the rockets in retaliation to the Israeli-blockade and to put pressure on Israel to release Palestinian political prisoners. After nearly two months of fighting, on August 26, 2014, a ceasefire was negotiated between the two sides. During this assault over 2,200 people were killed, nearly 1,600 of them being civilians, 7 Israeli, and the remaining Palestinians.
8. Jonathan Cook, "Israel's Starvation Diet Formula in Gaza and the Expansion of the 'Dahiya Doctrine,'" *Mondoweiss*, October 24, 2012, http://mondoweiss.net/2012/10/israels-starvation-diet-formula-in-gaza-and-the-expansion-of-the-dahiya-doctrine.html; Ana Nogueira and Eron Davidson, director/producer, *Roadmap to Apartheid* [documentary], United States: Ubuntu Films, 2012.
9. Diaa Hadid, "Gaza Strip Economy on 'Verge of Collapse,' World Bank Says," *Washington Post*, May 22, 2015, http://www.nytimes.com/2015/05/23/world/middleeast/gaza-strip-economy-on-verge-of-collapse-world-bank-says.html.
10. See Deepa Kumar, "Play it Again (Uncle) Sam," in Andy Lee Roth and Mickey Huff, eds., *Censored 2015: Inspiring We the People* (New York: Seven Stories Press, 2014), 295–314.

CHAPTER 3

A Vast Wasteland
The Ongoing Reign of Junk Food News and News Abuse

Nolan Higdon, Mickey Huff, and Ellie Kim, with contributions by
Brad Barna, Crystal Bedford, Emma Durkin, Darian Edelman,
Ariana Flotroy, Janet Hernandez, Daniel Park, Olivia Phillips,
Rebecca Rodriguez, Edwin Sevilla, Jaideep Singh,
Jack Elliott Smith, Hajin Lily Yi, and Mark Yolango

When television is good, nothing—not the theater, not the magazines or newspapers—nothing is better. But when television is bad, nothing is worse. I invite each of you to sit down in front of your own television set when your station goes on the air and stay there, for a day, without a book, without a magazine, without a newspaper, without a profit and loss sheet or a rating book to distract you. Keep your eyes glued to that set until the station signs off. I can assure you that what you will observe is a vast wasteland.

—Newton Minow, chairman, Federal Communications Commission, 1961

INTRODUCTION

Project Censored founder Dr. Carl Jensen was a pioneer in education. He not only constructively criticized the corporate news media, he educated students in how to help them hold it accountable. As a result, Project Censored has left an indelible mark on thousands of individuals since 1976. Jensen inspired educators, students, and activists to not only unearth problems in the way news is consumed, but to look for solutions in creating a more democratic media. The collaboration resulted in an annual list of news stories underreported or censored by the corporate press, and much more. His work drew the attention of news insiders who accused him of overstating the problem of censorship. They claimed that they were not censoring information, but simply had a limited amount of television time and print space to cover every story. They called it news judgment. Jensen, again demonstrating his commitment to the importance of a free press, refuted those claims, stating that, if it was news judgment, it had gone terribly awry. He called much of what the news media covered Junk Food News, another product of the vast wasteland of media that extended well beyond television.

Junk Food News analysis highlights how the corporate media peddle irrelevant, sensationalist, and entertaining tales in place of actual newsworthy stories, like those covered by the independent press (showcased in Chapter 1). Each year, when students compile Junk Food News stories, they provide a context for how corporate and independent media decide to use their news judgment. Unfortunately, Junk Food News is like Kanye West at an awards ceremony. It keeps popping up everywhere to interrupt and distract viewers' focus.[1] This chapter of our annual book illuminates the important work of independent news outlets that could be further covered if the corporate media were not hell-bent on peddling Junk Food News.

When Peter Phillips became the director of Project Censored, he created an offshoot of Junk Food News known as News Abuse. Like his predecessor, Phillips provided students with an opportunity to learn about the news while holding the corporate media accountable. A News Abuse story *is* a newsworthy story that is covered by the corporate press in a manner that makes it less newsworthy. This is because the spin or perspective on the particular story acts as a mechanism to distort information while distracting viewers and readers from other significant perspectives (or other stories entirely). One example was the extensive coverage of Ebola, which was a potentially important health story, but it was over-covered by corporate media and the threat wildly over-exaggerated. Further, this sensational deluge came in lieu of 2014 midterm election coverage in the US, something that actually affected Americans, unlike Ebola.

A News Abuse story dupes viewers like Holly Fischer duped family values conservatives in 2015. Fischer was known as a flag-waving, gun-toting, Bible-reading, pro-life Tea Partier. She caught her fifteen minutes of Internet fame as pictures emerged of her brandishing an assault rifle and Bible in front of a US flag on Facebook after supporting Chick-fil-A's and Hobby Lobby's stance against gay marriage. But then the online darling was caught having sex at a family values convention with a Tea Party cameraman while her husband was overseas serving in the US military.[2] Some things aren't what they seem. News Abuse stories have a tendency to leave people feeling they've been played by the media, and indeed, in the examples we bring forward, they often have.

Illusions of Objectivity: Ongoing Challenges Behind the News

One way that audiences are played or duped by the corporate news media is by their acceptance of the media's claims of objectivity. However, the conflicts of interest between the political elite and corporate media act to shape public opinion to serve the interests of the powerful over the public. This conflict is derived from the coveted ratings and subsequent profits garnered by journalists for big media because of their access to those in power. The corporate news outlets believe that an interview or segment on the economic or political elites will result in a larger audience than those stories that focus on common people, or those who challenge the status quo. However, in order to maintain access to those in power, corporate media journalists are pressured to provide favorable, or at the very least noncritical, coverage of those in power or risk their access to those individuals and their careers as journalists. This is a serious blight on any pretensions toward objectivity.

The corporate media's acquiescence to those in power is not actually a secret to those paying attention. For example, in 2014, MSNBC's Chuck Todd of *Meet the Press* admitted that his career goals prevented him from asking tough questions. Todd explained that if he asked his guests tough questions, they would not return to his program. He believes if he cannot get high-profile guests, his ratings will drop and his show could be cancelled.[3] In fact, journalists' dependency on high-profile figures fosters friendships to the point where the reporting is done to serve rather than challenge those in power (what Edward S. Herman and Noam Chomsky call the "sourcing" filter in their 1988 groundbreaking book, *Manufacturing Consent*).

In another example, in 2015, Hillary Clinton held a dinner with journalists before announcing her candidacy for president of the United States, presumably trading friendly reporting for the inside scoop on her announcement.[4] Similarly, President Barack Obama held a private meeting with journalists in 2015 to garner favorable news coverage of his proposed nuclear deal with Iran. It resulted in Obama's favor as the corporate media discussion over the Iran deal was largely complimentary, with the White House controlling the dialogue on the topic and the perspectives of the people of Iran rarely sought.[5]

The close relationship between those in power and the corporate media is quite visible in the well-publicized White House Correspondents' Association (WHCA) dinner. The annual event is attended by politicians, celebrities, and journalists for a night of laughs, drinks, food, and friendship. The WHCA is a collection of journalists who report on the president and national political affairs. The event includes ritualized mocking of the president and the press as they revel in their close relationship between laughs. In 2007, the *New York Times* columnist Frank Rich argued that the dinner is "a crystallization of the press's failures in the post-9/11 era" as it "illustrates how easily a propaganda-driven White House can enlist the Washington news media in its shows."[6]

While the real story of the event is the dangerously close relationship between those in power and the supposed watchdog corporate press, the corporate journalists distract the public with coverage of the First Lady's dress or the top ten jokes of the evening.[7] Similarly, the corporate press lauds President Obama for making jokes at the expense of former vice president Dick Cheney, but ignores that the jokes do nothing to undo the Bush/Cheney–era policies, some of which Obama has kept in place and even expanded.[8] This is what Noam Chomsky called maintaining necessary illusions—in this case, that the press is free and challenges and holds those in power to account in the public interest. If only that were the case.

New Technology, Same Censorship: An Issue of Media Literacy

While the work of Project Censored has increased students' knowledge and awareness about censorship, the larger population lacks basic critical media literacy skills. The US education system does not provide the citizenry with the skills to access, analyze, evaluate, create, reflect, and act in the digital world.[9] Without these skills, Americans are unaware of and susceptible to the dangers of corporate media reporting. Since the start of the twenty-first century Americans have celebrated the invention of digital technologies as a form of liberation from the problematic corporate media. However, the technology has not always lived up to the hype as Americans are unaware of how to use these technologies to position themselves as equitable democratic participants in the twenty-first century. This is an issue of media literacy.

Since the 1990s, critics have argued that the problems with corporate media would be ameliorated by the advent of the Internet and digital technologies. This vision seemed to be coming to fruition as the millennial generation (those born between 1982 and 2004) developed different news consumption habits than previous generations. According to a 2015 Pew Research Center study on media consumption, roughly 60 percent of the millennial generation relies on Facebook as their main source of political news. In contrast, baby boomers (ages fifty to sixty-eight) get 60 percent of their news from local television.[10]

Despite the advent of the Internet and the work of groups like Project Censored, the previous three generations differ little in their trust and mistrust of news sources. Pew found that fourteen out of thirty-six sources were trusted by all three generations, while only four out of ten are mistrusted. The three sources that millennials trust more so than the other generations are *The Daily Show*, *The Colbert Report*, and Al Jazeera America. Two of these are not news programs (one no longer airs), and the other is a foreign source.

Digital technologies have not made US citizens more media literate or interested in the political process. Almost a quarter of millennials on social networking sites report that over half of the content they are exposed to is related to politics, yet they express less interest in political news than baby boomers and Generation Xers (aged thirty-three to fifty). While the baby boomers have more of an interest in political news, they are more likely to read articles on social media that confirm rather than challenge their views.[11] The Pew study implies that if millennials maintain their news consumption habits, they will mirror previous generations who use news to confirm rather than challenge their views.[12] Project Censored remarked upon this very trend in Censored 2011, Chapter 3, "Manufacturing Distraction: Junk Food News and News Abuse on a Feed to Know Basis." It seems that with the rise of social media this pattern has continued with self-selection biases simply taking place on smaller screens.

When former FCC Chairman Newton Minow used the phrase "vast wasteland," he was referring to a wasteland in terms of potential for a mass medium squandered and a TV world where news was only fifteen minutes a day. Now, we have news 24/7, which has created what Carl Jensen called news inflation. While there is now more time spent on news programming, it seems to be worth less and less when one critically assesses content. Despite the existence of digital technologies and the vast troves of information they hold, it remains up to the public to acquire critical media literacy skills as users of digital technology. These skills enable citizens to use digital tools to find factual information paramount for equitable democratic participation in the twenty-first century (see Chapter 5). Otherwise, the close relationship between corporate news outlets and the political elite will continue to obfuscate stories in maintenance of the plutocracy (News Abuse) or report on stories that are outright nonsensical distractions (Junk Food News). Both act to divert attention away from the real scandals and issues that matter to citizens and keep the public anemic on factual stories while offering an all-you-can-eat buffet of bread and circuses. In this regard, the 2014–15 year does not disappoint, unless one values intellect, integrity, and a civic-minded news frame.

JUNK FOOD NEWS FROM 2014–15

If, however, the public does not receive all the information it needs to make informed decisions . . . then some form of news blackout is taking place . . . some issues are overlooked (what we call "censored") and other issues are over-covered (what we call "junk food news").

—Carl Jensen[13]

The 2014–15 year was jam-packed with more junk than Courtney Love's veins. In a year that saw important issues raised such as race in Ferguson, Missouri, imperialism in Palestine, human rights over the US drone strikes, and democracy with the protests in Hong Kong, the corporate media continued to peddle junk. Their coverage was obsessed with deflated balls and the Oscars as corporate pundits freaked the public out over Ebola in between speculative coverage of the presidential campaigns and the death of Mrs. Doubtfire.

Liberally Snubbing a Celebrated Sniper

The Academy Awards come around once a year providing those in the film industry with an opportunity to laud each other. It is an ego-fueled spectacle of lavish waste from a community of profit-driven entertainers. Despite much of the triviality of the Oscars, the corporate media give it extensive coverage every year.

After the coverage of the outfits worn by the guests and the speculation over who would win, the corporate media focused on the politics behind the awards. Fox News, clinging to its conservative image, attacked "liberal Hollywood" for not awarding the film *American Sniper* with the Oscar for Best Picture.[14] *American Sniper* is the work of the Republican director (and frequent empty chair whisperer) Clint Eastwood, who based the film on the autobiography of US Navy SEAL Chris Kyle (played by Bradley Cooper) concerning his time in Iraq. Kyle, like Christopher Columbus centuries earlier, used superior military technology to occupy, subdue, and murder people in a foreign land. In 2013, Kyle was accidentally killed at a shooting range while a controversy over the unsubstantiated claims in his book emerged.[15] Nonetheless, Sean Hannity and others at Fox News were enraged that this nationalistically charged film about an American sniper killing people from a distance did not win the coveted Award for Best Picture. Hannity tweeted, "AMERICAN Sniper snubbed by liberal hwood Predictable. #CluelessOscars."[16] Fox's morning talk show *Fox and Friends* ran a discussion segment asking if *American Sniper* got snubbed. The online entertainment publication *Mediaite* summed up the segment as "Hollywood bad, Oscars bad, Sniper good."[17]

The same morning that *Fox and Friends* hosts gossiped about who should have won Best Picture, *Democracy Now!* reported that in the five months prior to February 2015, the US had killed 1,600 people in Syria. The Syrian Observatory for Human Rights concluded that most of those killed had been ISIS fighters, a group deemed to be an enemy by the US government. However, at least sixty-two civilians were also killed in those attacks by the US.[18] Thus, while Fox went on a diatribe demanding that the factious portrayal of Kyle's actions be celebrated, more innocent people were dying at the hands of the US for reasons not provided to the American people nor condoned by a war resolution in Congress.

Corporate Media Has Deflated Balls

Every year when the National Football League (NFL) Super Bowl concludes, sports fans face the reality that they have to wait almost seven months for the next season to begin. However, by the time the 2015 Super Bowl ended, the corporate press was still blue over the balls from the American Football Conference (AFC) Championship Game, a game that saw the New England Patriots defeat the Indianapolis Colts to earn a chance to play for the NFL Championship at Super Bowl XLIX. The Colts then accused the Patriots of cheating in the game by intentionally using underinflated footballs to improve their passing game. The NFL has rules on the inflation weight of balls and determined that, indeed, eleven of the twelve game balls in the AFC Championship Game were underinflated.[19] The corporate media fixated on an elderly man who was seen on camera entering a restroom with twelve footballs, where he stayed for "98 seconds," before exiting the restroom and returning the balls to the field.[20] What this elderly man did with the balls in the restroom remains a mystery. The corporate press covered the league fallout as NFL Hall of Famers Joe Montana and Jerry Rice blamed Brady for the underinflated balls and called the act "cheating."[21] The Deflategate or Ballghazi scandal was featured on the corporate news channels heavily through February 2015.[22]

While the corporate media ran up the middle to cover the deflated ball scandal, the independent press went deep for the long bombs—those involving US drone strikes in Yemen.[23] By the start of 2015, the Yemeni government collapsed.[24] The US did not seek government clearance to carry out drone strikes in the region, which meant there was no mechanism to warn or help the citizens impacted by drone strikes. In fact, drone strikes in Yemen are not uncommon. Between 2001 and 2015, there were 90 to 109 confirmed strikes in Yemen, which left up to 639 dead. At least ninety-six of the dead were confirmed as civilians not targeted by the US and eight others were children.[25] Presumably, this will lead to anti-American sentiment among individuals who have had loved ones unjustly killed by the US, which could result in future attacks on US soil. When much of the nation's attention was spent on getting down and dirty on the Patriots' deflated balls, the US was busy creating potential enemies for tomorrow in the end zone of the Middle East as the war on terror goes into sudden death overtime for many in the region.

Mrs. Hamas-Fire

It can be tough to lose someone and everyone copes in their own way. The corporate press copes by using death as a sensationalistic story to distract from more relevant stories. In summer 2014, their grief porn parade hit full stride with the suicide of comedian and actor Robin Williams. Almost immediately, Williams, the star of such great films as *Mrs. Doubtfire*, *Dead Poets Society*, and *Good Will Hunting*, became a staple story of the twenty-four-hour news cycle. In fact, President Obama and Secretary of Defense Chuck Hagel paid tribute to Williams for his contribution to the armed forces.[26] CNN provided coverage of the celebrities who paid tribute on social media to the fallen star.[27] However, the coverage went beyond parroting the comments of

Williams's fans. ABC News streamed a live video of Robin Williams's home. They later apologized because Williams's family had asked for privacy.[28] Yahoo! published an article on its webpage that had a picture of Robin Williams with the headline "HANGED" among other sensationalist phrases.[29] The coverage dragged out over weeks as the media morbidly awaited the coroner's report, which, given how Williams had died, was merely the final phase of this mourning sickness saga.

The coverage of Williams's death distracted from the US involvement in Israeli and Palestinian relations. While the corporate press tried to outdo one another for best grief porn POV, independent journalists found that the US had knowledge of and allowed Israel to target citizens in Gaza.[30] Israel had a blockade against Gaza, even "restrict[ing] food imports to levels below those necessary to maintain a minimum caloric intake."[31] These restrictions were put in place in order to target the group Hamas, which Israel views as a terrorist organization.[32] However, it is likely that the treatment of people in Gaza is not to remove Hamas. In fact, in 2006, the levels of poverty and malnutrition were so severe that Hamas sent a letter to then President George W. Bush stating that they would recognize Israel as a state and cease hostilities to end the blockade.[33] These were two key demands that the US and Israel had, but the offer was ignored.[34] Thus, the US allowed the targeting of citizens in the region by Israel while denouncing the Palestinians for violence. It occurred while thousands of people watched *One Hour Photo* and reruns of *Mork and Mindy* to cope with losing Williams. Meanwhile, 2,139 Palestinians were killed as a result of Israel's Operation Protective Edge. Most were civilians, including 490 children, and the onslaught destroyed twenty thousand homes in Gaza, creating half a million refugees. While the loss of Robin Williams is tragic, what happened in Gaza is something that truly deserves collective grief and far more attention from the news media.[35]

Will They? Won't They?

Americans love a great *Will they? Won't they?* story, like the sexual tension between Ross and Rachel on *Friends* or LeBron James choosing between Miami and Cleveland. The US presidential elections are the biggest *Will they? Won't they?* for the corporate media. What makes this upcoming presidential cycle extra junky is that in 2014–15, the corporate press was not even covering an election; they were covering people who *might* run in the election. Much of their focus was on the dynastic implications of a 1992 rematch involving the Bushes and Clintons in the 2016 election.

The corporate media was fixated on the prospect of a Bush dynasty, with Jeb as the third potential president from the family. In late 2014, CNN mused openly about a possible 2016 presidential run from the former Florida governor and the son and brother of former presidents.[36] A month later, the corporate press questioned if 2012 presidential candidate Mitt Romney would make another run at the White House. He quickly claimed he would not be running, which led the corporate media to muse on whether Romney dropping out improved Jeb's chances of becoming president.[37] While the corporate media covered Bush not announcing anything, the independent outlet *ThinkProgress* noted that David and Charles Koch, a.k.a. the Koch brothers, a pair of wealthy conservative donors, were spending $889 million of their wealth on candidates in the 2016 elections. That is more than double the amount the Kochs spent on the 2012 election.[38] The Kochs are known for using their funds to create and disseminate disinformation about numerous issues such as climate change. In fact, in 2012, they surpassed companies such as ExxonMobil in funding climate change denial research.[39] Thus, the implications of their campaign donations are a much more newsworthy story than the fodder surrounding Bush and his potential competitors.

Bush was not the only former president surname to be agonizingly followed with the question: *Will you run?* Former US senator, secretary of state, and first lady Hillary Clinton garnered much of the corporate media's speculative 2016 election coverage. In February 2015, a full two months before Clinton announced her campaign for the presidency, the *New York Times* and Fox News were already criticizing her for not giving a clear answer on issues of wealth inequality.[40] Then Fox went after Hillary's donors, noting that many of them are the most hated companies in America.[41] The coverage of Hillary was very extensive, so much so that the corporate media covered her meal at Chipotle—a chicken burrito bowl—instead of covering that another candidate had entered the race: US Senator Marco Rubio.[42]

Hillary's Chipotle visit did not just distract from the Rubio campaign, it was deemed more newsworthy than national workers' mass protests. On April 15, 2015, while Hillary was eating at Chipotle, thousands of fast food workers around the nation went on strike, demanding fifteen dollars an hour.[43] The protest was referred to as the "largest low-wage worker protest" in US history.[44] In two hundred US cities, tens of thousands of working-class men and women in the "fast food, laundry, home care, child care, retail, and education" fields protested for better wages. Solidarity strikes were held in thirty-five countries on six continents.[45] Rather than cover the people in the streets fighting for equality, fair treatment, and workers' rights, including fast food workers, the corporate media covered the trivial and meaningless fast food order of a powerful woman running for president. That photo op is likely as close to standing with the working poor that Hillary, merely ordering from them at Chipotle, will get all year.

While the coverage of the potential presidential candidates may be newsworthy, their fast food purchases are the essence of Junk Food News. One can witness how journalists become enamored by their proximity to those in power as they follow and get close to potential candidates, cataloging their every irrelevant move, while ignoring other more significant stories. The *Will they? Won't they?* horse-race approach to elections is another type of coverage used to keep the voters uninformed yet at the edge of their seats.

NEWS ABUSE AS PROPAGANDA

More than a half century ago Hitler said the masses take a long time to understand and remember, thus it is necessary to repeat the message time and time and time again. The public must be conditioned to accept the claims that are made . . . no matter how outrageous or false those claims might be.

—Carl Jensen[46]

News Abuse is a subtle form of censorship; it relies on news coverage as a mechanism of manipulating public opinion. The reason for the manipulation is not always clear, but often its goal is to further the economic and political interests of those in power. By manipulating public opinion, the corporate press can influence voters to support or defeat legislation regardless of how well it addresses the voters' interests. That awesome amount of power holds extreme potential to improve the larger society. However, it is often used at the expense of the majority of people.

Viewers often know they are watching Junk Food News and have lamented its increase over the years. But News Abuse is a different calamity because while viewers believe they are being well informed about important matters, the actual coverage of the stories acts to manipulate, misinform, and even disinform—i.e., News Abuse is a form of propaganda. This past year, once again the corporate press strived to introduce important stories on police killings, ISIS, and sexual assault, only to skew coverage of these issues to such an extent that potential meaningful discussions of these stories were squashed under bad puns, false and biased data, and celebrity-focused coverage. While corporate media battled over the question of who was the bigger liar—Bill O'Reilly of Fox News or Brian Williams, then at *NBC Nightly News*—there was no clear winner declared. However, there was a clear loser: the American public.

The News Is the News

Journalists, pundits, and reporters are supposed to provide information and perspective about important issues of the day. However, in the era of homogenized, for-profit infotainment, the corporate news media has birthed news celebrities such as Bill O'Reilly, Brian Williams, Rachel Maddow, and Anderson Cooper, among others. The intersection of corporate media personality and celebrity status with a news outlet's dedication to covering entertainment-based stories has resulted in the news *becoming* the news in its own distracting way. Throughout the previous year, the networks, journalists, reporters, and pundits who frequently mislead the public in various ways turned on each other by accusing each other of misleading the public. This hypocritical attempt at retribution for the sins of a deceitful past made for a never-ending cycle of News Abuse, which falsified the past to manipulate the present and almost certainly destroy the future.

This past year, Fox News remained the most watched twenty-four-hour news station.[47] Their ratings undermine CNN's claim that CNN is the "most trusted" news channel. Despite its popularity and significant global exposure, Fox claimed it was the victim of "censorship." Fox, a network that has censored various news stories and perspectives—particularly left-of-center ones—since 1996, claimed that DISH Network, a television service provider, was censoring Fox programming. DISH refused to broadcast Fox programming until they agreed to DISH's financial demands.[48]

Fox's commitment to anticensorship could hardly be considered genuine given that they ignore issues of censorship unless they decrease their profits. For example, when journalist Jeremy Scahill argued that the White House intimidation and judicial decisions to force journalists to turn over their sources was an assault on press freedoms, Fox did not cover it.[49] In fact, Fox has intimidated reporters into self-censorship. In 2015, a *Daily Caller* journalist was told that he could not criticize Fox News because Tucker Carlson, who also works for the *Daily Caller*, is a Fox News contributor.[50] Fox apparently warned Carlson that if he criticizes Fox he could lose his job, and that the same could happen if he is associated with someone who criticizes the network.

BILL O'LIELY VS. B.S. WILLIAMS

In February 2015, Americans were exposed to a series of developments that implicated top journalists in the corporate news media lie. Despite there being tomes written on the matter over the decades, this drew major attention in the corporate media. The controversy initially swirled around Brian Williams, host of *NBC Nightly News*. Stars and Stripes, a military news organization, exposed Williams for lying in a news report about having been in a helicopter that had been hit by rocket-propelled grenades (RPGs) in Iraq.[51] Rather than reflect on how Williams's behavior is part of a widespread structural problem in the industry, the corporate media created its own tangled tale, turning a story about false statements in journalism into a distracting and misleading celebrity sideshow. In fact, when NBC publicly noted that they were investigating Williams's claims (while he received six months unpaid leave), pundits pondered the meaning for his career as a celebrity anchorman.[52] Would he be fired? Would he still get invites to *The Late Show* with David Letterman and *The Daily Show*?[53] Could NBC manage without the easy recognition that Williams's celebrity offered? Further, how might they deal with the real fallout from the fact that Williams lied during his reporting?[54]

In the weeks following the revelations about Williams's initial fraudulent tale, the corporate media began to report on other misleading statements and outright lies from Williams. The false stories included Williams's hotel in New Orleans allegedly being attacked by gangs shortly after Hurricane Katrina in 2005 and the falsification of the number of puppies rescued from a fire.[55] A report in *New York* magazine revealed that, among other systemic issues, celebrity treatment of news personalities was part of the problem. In fact, Williams's career goal was to take over *The Tonight Show*.[56] In the midst of the illumination of Williams's lies, many in the corporate news industry defended Williams as simply conflating his role as a journalist with his role as an entertainer.[57] However, by late spring 2015, more reports of Williams's deceptions appeared to end any chance of Williams returning to television.[58]

Fox News personality Bill O'Reilly responded to the Williams story by encouraging greater scrutiny of journalists, all while excusing Williams's lies.[59] The independent news outlet *Mother Jones* responded to O'Reilly's comments by doing what Project Censored has done for thirty-nine years: documenting the lies of corporate media. *Mother Jones* noted that O'Reilly had his own history of lying, including falsified claims about his war coverage.[60] *Mother Jones*'s coverage of an already well-documented story—that Fox News pundits lie—explained that O'Reilly had lied about rescuing a cameraman from an approaching army during the Falklands War in Argentina. In fact, O'Reilly was not even in the Falkland Islands during that time,[61] and even the cameraman claimed the event never happened.[62] In response, O'Reilly changed his story, claiming he had been talking about the riots on the mainland. Even if that is true, O'Reilly is being quite liberal, for once, in interpreting what constitutes a "war zone."[63] Journalists dug deeper into O'Reilly's claims and, similar to Williams's case, numerous other lies were unearthed. For example, O'Reilly had lied about seeing nuns murdered in El Salvador and being outside the door of George de Mohrenschildt as he shot himself. Mohrenschildt was a friend of Lee Harvey Oswald, the alleged assassin of President John F. Kennedy.[64] In April 2015, Media Matters found so many O'Reilly lies they were able to create an e-book about them.[65] And back in 2003, Seven Stories Press (publisher of the *Censored* yearbooks) published *The Oh Really? Factor*, written by Peter Hart of Fairness and Accuracy in Reporting (FAIR), filled with the false statements and reports of O'Reilly, so there is long-standing precedent on the matter.

While the O'Reilly versus Williams coverage had the flare of Junk Food News, it qualifies as News Abuse because it was obfuscated into a liberal versus conservative debate rather than proof of the institutional obfuscation, disinformation, and manipulation of the corporate news industry. In fact, the only area where Williams and O'Reilly differed was in their apology. Williams admitted fault while O'Reilly did not; instead the latter continuously amended his statements while claiming to be the victim of the liberal media.[66] This contributed to the false corporate news media narrative that the claims against O'Reilly were not factually based, but an ideological attack by the "liberal left."[67]

If the corporate media were dedicated to holding themselves accountable, not only should they have removed Williams *and* O'Reilly from the air, but they should have also covered the various manipulations of truth in corporate reporting during the 2014–15 year. For example, NBC's Richard Engel was reportedly kidnapped in 2012 by the Syrian government. His kidnapping was used to support the call for the US invasion and overthrow of the Syrian government. However, *Democracy Now!* and First Look Media, among others, reported that Engel appeared to have been captured by rebels in Syria, not the Syrian government.[68] Yet NBC did not retract the false story.

Furthermore, if the corporate media wanted to report on factors that contribute to deceitful news coverage, they could have covered the *New York Times* for failing to disclose that their pro-oil policy op-ed was funded by the oil companies, or the clear conflict of interest concerning the *Washington Post*'s frequent publication of climate change denial pieces by Ed Rogers, a former member of the Reagan and Bush I administrations, who is also a Chevron lobbyist.[69]

Lastly, if the corporate media were interested in unearthing the truth, they could illuminate their own coverage of staged events. For example, in 2015, when a Florida district considered taking land from large sugar companies in order to expand access to water for residents, a massive Tea Party rally in opposition emerged at the water plant, garnering a lot of corporate media coverage. However, *Raw Story* reported that the protesters were actually actors hired by the Tea Party of Miami and US Sugar, a major sugar company.[70] These stories and the others like them demonstrate that the corporate news media is not only uninterested in reporting truthfully, but also that—considering the Williams versus O'Reilly debacle—they seem to be less committed to honest reporting as a whole.

JUDITH THE DUPLICITOUS

While the corporate media put up a divisive front against contemporary celebrity journalists' lies, a ghost of the deceptive past reemerged. In 2015, former *New York Times* reporter and current Fox News contributor Judith Miller, whose 2002–03 inaccurate articles on Iraq's chemical weapons program were integral in shifting US public opinion toward a war in Iraq, released the book *No Apologies*.[71] In a series of television appearances promoting the book, Miller argued that the invasion of Iraq was not her fault because her sources, mostly from Bush administration connections and insiders, had lied to her and her editors published them.[72] Of course a journalist's job is not only to find evidence but to verify it, but that did not happen in this case. Miller acted unfamiliar with that elementary rule of journalism.

MSNBC and the *New York Times* took Miller's rewriting of history as an opportunity to rewrite their own. MSNBC allowed *New York*

Times reporter Nick Confessore to lambaste Miller over her excuses for the false reporting that led to the Iraq invasion. While Miller deserves a tongue lashing at the very least, Confessore's diatribe was a bait and switch on the matter, serving to obfuscate the history of the affair.[73] First, it positioned the *New York Times* as a paper of record, concerned with the truth, despite over a decade earlier publishing Miller's false tales. Furthermore, MSNBC, by providing the interview for Confessore, positioned itself as the antiwar, pro-truth, corporate network. However, it was MSNBC that sacked antiwar programmers such as Phil Donahue and Jesse Ventura from their network to make space for more pro-war voices in the year leading up to the 2003 Iraq invasion. In fact, according to MSNBC's own internal memos, they let go of their antiwar voices to increase ratings.[74] Thus, while the corporate press lambasted Judith Miller for rewriting history, they were rewriting their own, excluding the role they played in the calamitous 2003 invasion of Iraq, which by 2015 had cost US taxpayers over three trillion dollars, the lives of thousands of Americans, and over a million dead Iraqis.[75]

Ebola: The Outbreak that Wasn't

In the 2014–15 news cycle, the corporate media used the Ebola "crisis" as a Trojan horse to instill fear in Americans while inciting anti-immigrant sentiments. Ebola is a virus largely found in West Africa. It starts with flu-like symptoms and can be fatal. However, Ebola patients are extremely rare in the US.[76] The first case of Ebola in the US came from a medical assistant working with Doctors Without Borders. The patient recovered twenty days later.[77] There would only be three other cases of Ebola diagnosed in the US after the medical assistant, but the corporate media saw an opportunity to turn this non-health emergency into a sensationalistic issue.[78]

The corporate media quickly politicized Ebola. ABC and Fox contributor Laura Ingraham claimed that the Obama administration does not understand the importance of "our nation-state" and has an obsession with "open borders."[79] Ingraham's statement ignored that in Obama's first term he removed more than one million undocumented immigrants.[80] Conservative radio host Rush

146

Limbaugh echoed Ingraham, arguing that the US purposely "had somebody come across the border carrying Ebola with them."[81] A Fox News guest further perpetuated public fear by stating, "It's not that they're undocumented, it's that they're uninspected."[82] However, the Centers for Disease Control (CDC) reported that there was "zero evidence" to state that immigrants are carrying Ebola into the country.[83] In fact, US Naval Medical Researcher Daniel G. Bausch said, "The likelihood of an illegal migrant getting infected and introducing the disease to the US is probably less than that of a 'legal' traveler." Meanwhile, Fox's Bill O'Reilly accused the CDC director of being a "propagandist" and demanded that he "should resign."[84]

The hysteria over Ebola symbolizes the corporate media's xenophobic and racist perspective on other contemporary issues as well. Corporate media frequently emphasize the use of non-Western medicine in Africa in order to create more fear in the US.[85] For example, Fox News's Andrea Tantaros stated, "In these countries, they do not believe in traditional medical care. So someone could get off a flight and seek treatment from a witch doctor that would practice Santeria."[86] Fox News contributor Stacy Hooks suggested that each state needs an Ebola quarantined hospital.[87] Instead of providing more medical assistance to the region actually in need, Hooks argued to throw millions of dollars to assist the nonexistent Ebola "epidemic" in the US. CNN went a step farther, bringing the war on terror into the mix by airing the headline, "Ebola: The ISIS of Biological Agents?"[88]

However, there was no proof for CNN's claim. The corporate media criticized health care professional Kaci Hickox, who returned from overseas with no sign of symptoms but was asked by Maine Governor Paul LePage to be quarantined. When she refused, she was called "selfish" on *Hannity* and *The O'Reilly Factor*.[89] More fear was generated by *CNN Tonight*, which interviewed the author of a fiction book, *Outbreak*, that portrayed an Ebola outbreak in the US.[90] The author's lack of official medical credentials did not make him unfit to scare people. In fact, the only thing about Ebola going viral in the US was the media's meme of fear. The corporate media did not once touch on the correlation between the deforestation in West Africa and its impact on the surrounding ecosystem.[91] Bats, most likely the primary carriers of the Ebola virus, came in contact with people more often as their habitats were compromised.

The timing of the Ebola story is also suspect. It ran in the months before the 2014 midterm election, causing fear that was so powerful it distracted from coverage of the candidates. Nearly a thousand news segments regarding Ebola ran from October 7 through the day before the November 4 election. Once the election was over, only forty-nine segments were aired in the two weeks after November 4, also downplaying the hysteria and confirming there was no widespread outbreak.[92] Thus, the corporate media played the American public like a fiddle, spreading fear, if not Ebola, in an effort to distract the public from the substantive issues of the election and candidate positions.

Ongoing Islamophobic Narratives

Islamophobia has largely been accepted by the establishment culture of the US in the post-9/11 era. The corporate media and US government have sensationalized these fears by legitimizing ethnocentric and xenophobic policies and practices domestically, as well as military intervention internationally. For example, corporate news outlets have unanimously sided with Israel by slanting their coverage to justify or mitigate the realities of its human rights abuses against Muslims in Palestine.[93] Critics in the independent media have noted that terms such as *genocide* are applied elsewhere in the world such as in Guatemala, but not for the Palestinians in Gaza, despite the conflict entering its eighth decade.[94] Thus, the corporate press maintains public support for US foreign policy in the Middle East by promoting domestic Islamophobia.

US foreign policy in the Middle East is largely shaped by US dependence on natural resources from the region and on the resulting geopolitical alliances. US dependence specifically on foreign oil has increased since the twentieth century, making it the world's largest consumer of foreign oil.[95] Currently, the US imports 44 percent of its oil to maintain its consumer economy.[96] Because several Middle Eastern economies depend on oil consumption levels, the US is vulnerable to the will of oil-producing nations.[97] The largest oil deposits in the world are in the Middle East, which has 55 percent of the

world's oil reserves.[98] To maintain affordable access to the Middle East oil supply, the US keeps a large military presence in the region; the US has a military base in every Persian Gulf nation except Iran.[99] This strong military presence has resulted in military conflicts with thirteen Middle Eastern nations since 1980.[100] In the 1990s, when the US imposed sanctions on Iraq, it still imported 9 percent of its oil from the country.[101] Though US foreign policy is largely dependent upon support from the American public, much of this domestic support is not tied to the overt need for resources in the region, but rather to the fear engendered in a post-9/11 world coupled with irrational xenophobia of Islam.

In February 2015, the Obama administration hosted a three-day "Summit on Countering Violent Extremism" to address violent episodes around the globe. The White House released a statement in January that focused on recent attacks carried out by Muslim groups in Paris, Ottawa, Sydney, and elsewhere. Following the press release, many high-profile Muslim organizations, non-Muslim religious groups, and civil rights advocates criticized the administration's tendency to "single out American Muslim communities" in its anti-extremist strategies.[102] Obama and other world leaders tried to quell the controversy by insisting that the US and its allies were not "at war with Islam."[103]

Despite claiming to support multiculturalism and inclusion, the corporate news reinforces the public perception that Muslims are inherently violent and brutal savages through inequitable coverage of Muslim and white American violence.[104] For example, in February 2015, three Muslim American students were shot and killed by Craig Stephen Hicks, a white neighbor in Chapel Hill, North Carolina.[105] Major corporate news outlets such as CNN, the *New York Times*, and Fox News initially remained silent on the attack and President Obama waited two days to issue an official statement.[106] No corporate coverage labeled the triple homicide as an act of domestic terrorism—rather, Hicks was referred to as a lone loon.[107] The corporate coverage of white shooters such as Hicks differs from the coverage of Muslim shooters. Muslim attacks are often portrayed as part of some larger act of terrorism while whites are "lone loons." A month before the shooting in Chapel Hill, the satirical French magazine *Charlie Hebdo* was attacked in Paris by three radical Muslims for its portrayal of Muhammad. The response around the world was a massive march condemning jihadist violence and terrorism, which have almost universally become conflated.[108] Protester signs and social media hashtags trended the phrase "Je Suis Charlie" (I am Charlie), and marchers chanted for liberty, tolerance, and coexistence.[109] Nothing similar happened for the Chapel Hill or other Muslim victims when they experienced attacks at the hands of whites. In fact, a father of two of the North Carolina victims remarked that "if a Muslim commits a crime, it's on the news 24/7 for two months. When we are executed in numbers, it's on the news for seconds."[110]

The inequitable points of view in corporate news outlets spread Islamophobia and absolve whites for similar behavior. For example, on February 27, 2015, Pooja Podugu from the *Harvard Political Review* published a media analysis of international terrorist attacks (executed by Islamic groups). The report found that the corporate media gave less coverage, if any, when Muslims were the victims of violent episodes.[111] For example, in December 2014, nine Taliban members killed 145 Muslims, 132 of which were children, but the story was covered only for a few days.[112] Similarly, and weeks before the *Charlie Hebdo* media frenzy, the Baga Massacre of January 3, 2015, saw 2,000 Muslims murdered, but the story garnered little to no corporate news attention.[113] The corporate media's decision to ignore white violence and Muslim deaths but sensationalize and cover Muslim murder ad nauseam is especially egregious considering that from 1970 to 2012, only 60 of 2,400 terrorist attacks in America were carried out by Muslims—approximately 2.5 percent of all attacks.[114]

Despite the lack of evidence of logical fears of Islamic terrorism, the corporate media spew Islamophobic coverage to garner support for US military interventions. For example, in June 2014, a group of Islamists, formerly known as "al-Qaeda in Iraq," called for the formation of ISIS, the Islamic State of Iraq and Syria, to be ruled by a single, absolute religious and political leader.[115] ISIS was initially a faction of al-Qaeda, some of whose members were trained and funded by the US.[116] However, by 2014, they were challenging US interests and power in the Middle East. The talk of war in the corporate news increased especially after the release of ISIS videos that documented journalists' beheadings.[117] The corporate media framed the discussion of using airstrikes against ISIS as an absolute rather than a debate. From September 7 to 21, 2014, the media research group FAIR examined the corporate news outlets and *PBS News Hour* discussions concerning the US response to ISIS. Only six people out of 205 opposed US military interventions and 125 directly stated that they favor intervention.[118]

The corporate coverage of ISIS and the question of intervention demonstrate that the media act as a megaphone for US leaders' foreign policy. They use their dominance over the airwaves and digital technologies to spread Islamophobia, which engenders public support for intervention. Although the focus on radical Muslims is overstated and sensationalized by the corporate press, it does have real implications. It has created an environment in which Muslims, and those mistaken for Muslims, have to live in fear of aggressive assault or death at the hands of the paranoid American populace.

The Race to Racism in Post-Racial America

In the previous year, Americans were glued to their television screens as images of race, police violence, poverty, crime, protests, and rioting converged in cities across the US. The "justifiable homicides" of Michael Brown in Ferguson, Missouri, and Freddie Gray in Baltimore, Maryland, erupted in politically charged protests and public debates across the country. The corporate coverage of these killings and their aftermaths blamed African-Americans for their own deaths while justifying police behavior and excusing whites for the same crime.

This coverage distracts from the racism built into the legal system and results in public sympathy for state violence. Bill O'Reilly of Fox News and former New York City mayor and Fox News contributor Rudolph Giuliani sustained this narrative, arguing that the true victims of these protests are the police. Giuliani went so far as to say, in defense of police, "It is untrue. It's like Soviet propaganda. The police are not racist. There is not a systemic problem with police racism."[119] The statistics say otherwise: white Americans who engage in similar

behaviors as people of color are twenty-one times less likely to be shot by police.[120] Annually, 1,500 people die from law enforcement–related deaths and not all are guilty.[121] Many of these victims tend to be people of color. Furthermore, Americans are nine times more likely to be killed by a police officer than a terrorist.[122]

While there are numerous examples of police killings of unarmed men and women of color in 2014–15, two stand out in terms of media coverage. In August 2014, Michael Brown, a young unarmed African-American man, was shot dead in Ferguson, Missouri, by police officer Darren Wilson following an alleged convenience store robbery.[123] In November 2014, Wilson was acquitted by a grand jury of any wrongdoing. In Baltimore, Maryland, on April 12, 2015, police stopped Freddie Gray, an African-American male, for looking at them and then running. After being apprehended "without force or incident," police removed a switchblade knife from him and put him in the back of a police van.[124] Amid numerous stops by the van, Gray's head was beaten into the van, causing his neck to break and leading to his death.[125] Immediately thereafter, community members, likely inspired by the outcome of the investigation in Ferguson, took to the streets to demand justice.

DOUBLE STANDARDS

Corporate media tend to blame victims of color for their own deaths while justifying police behavior and excusing whites for similar actions. For example, Fox News and the *New York Times* degraded Brown with phrases such as "bad guy" and "no angel."[126] Weeks after the Brown shooting, the *New York Times* asked citizens to give police the benefit of the doubt.[127] More broadly, Fox News host Bill O'Reilly blamed "family culture," not police, for the death.[128] He further argued that "blacks commit more murders than whites . . . which is why juries give police the benefit of the doubt when there is an incident in the black community."[129] However, O'Reilly did not mention that between the years 1991 and 2008, crimes committed by African-Americans declined by over half. In cities such as New York and Chicago, where African-American crime is most prominent, the rate has fallen by close to 80 percent since the 1960s.[130] In fact, 87 percent of mass shootings in the US are committed by whites aged thirteen to fifty-six.[131]

Other voices at Fox News, like psychiatrist Dr. Keith Ablow, went as far as to accuse Michael Brown's stepfather of being the kind of man who would have "influenced Michael Brown to lose his life."[132] Giuliani argued that black people should take responsibility for the police killings because "white police officers wouldn't be there if you weren't killing each other."[133] Geraldo Rivera justified the Brown shooting because Brown was suspected of robbing a convenience store—a crime not punishable by death.[134] Eventually, Fox News coverage relied on manufactured justifications for Brown's killing, including a fictitious report that Brown broke Wilson's eye socket.[135]

In fact, the trend seems to be that the corporate media take the word of the police over their African-American victims without researching the claims. Another clear example of this took place in South Carolina on April 4, 2015, after the shooting of Walter Scott, an unarmed African-American man. The media bought the narrative of the police officer who shot him; he fully justified his own actions until a video surfaced proving that the police totally fabricated the story, and in fact likely murdered Scott, shooting him in the back as he fled.[136] The existence of this later video evidence proves why it is necessary that it be lawful for citizens to film police in the line of duty, as accountability cannot be assured simply through the word of the state.

In contrast, when whites commit crimes, even shootings, they receive more sympathetic coverage by corporate media than African-Americans who are the victims of police shootings. For example, news outlets ran headlines claiming that Michael Brown had "struggled with police" in his past.[137] Yet James Egan Holmes, a twenty-four-year-old white doctoral student was referred to as a "brilliant science student" after his 2012 mass shooting at a Colorado movie theater.[138] Similarly, in 2014, Elliot Rodger, who was the son of a Hollywood director, killed six people and injured fourteen others with his car before committing suicide in Isla Vista, California.[139] The corporate media dug deep into the killer's history, but unlike the coverage of Brown, the corporate media did not make a racial, cultural, or regional generality for what caused Rodger's behavior. Instead they relied on soft language, naming him the "kissless virgin" and "isolated son" coming from a "twisted world."[140] Similarly, sympathetic coverage was given to Amy Bishop. Bishop, a white female, was a former college professor of biology who killed three and wounded three others in a 2010 shooting.[141] The corporate media covered her backstory as "tragic" because she had been denied tenure at her college a year earlier.[142] They pondered her motives and wondered what could have gone wrong. This reflective approach is rarely afforded to nonwhite people who commit similar or even far lesser crimes, if any at all.[143]

UNEQUAL COVERAGE OF "RIOTS" AND "CELEBRATIONS"

Rather than address the roots of police violence against minority communities, the corporate media focused on the portion of protesters who turned violent. Citizens protested peacefully, and in a few cases violently, throughout the world in the wake of last year's police killings of African-Americans.[144] The nature of these protests was often exaggerated by outlets such as CNN, which tended to justify violent police response without noting the role police play in creating that violence.[145] However, in reality, the police have been complicit in creating public violence. For example, in December 2014, under-

cover officers randomly pulled guns on protesters and acted as provocateurs in Oakland, California, a development ignored by corporate media.[146] Similarly, after Gray's death in Baltimore, violence erupted once police showed up in riot gear and blocked streets.[147]

With selective violence erupting in Baltimore, the corporate media jumped at the opportunity to bring images of the sensationalistic violence to viewers rather than the actions of thousands of peaceful protesters. In an interview on CNN, anchor Wolf Blitzer demanded that a protester denounce what Blitzer framed as protester violence. Instead, the protester noted that the press was hypocritical for condemning protester violence, and not the police violence that provoked public reaction.[148] While Blitzer saw protesters as violent actors, CNN anchor Erin Burnett referred to them as "thugs."[149] When MSNBC tried to get Baltimore activist Danielle Williams to admit that violence accomplished nothing, she reminded MSNBC that there was no national attention during the peaceful protests because the corporate media only showed up when the protests turned violent.[150] Fox News was targeted for its perceived bias as protesters shouted and attempted to stop Geraldo Rivera's live coverage, which sensationalized the demonstrations as mass looting.[151] A Baltimore congresswoman lambasted Fox while in an interview with them for only focusing on looters.[152]

Not only did the corporate media frame protests as violent, they even attacked those who protested peacefully. In late 2014, Fox News verbally attacked the St. Louis Rams players for silently protesting police violence as they entered the football field with their hands raised (a reference to "Hands up, don't shoot," relating to yet another incident of the death of an unarmed African-American at the hands of police in New York, Eric Garner).[153] Fox News host Bill O'Reilly claimed the players were not "smart enough to know what they're doing."[154]

The very same acts that corporate media decry as rioting by people of color are framed in a very different way when committed by whites. Violence against property as part of "celebrations" surrounding sporting or other public events is not held to the same standard as when executed by African-Americans. For example, in 2013, surfers descended upon Huntington Beach, California, for a day of surfing that turned into rioting and looting. Most of those involved were white.[155] In fact, in 2014, *New York* magazine published a collection of photos showing whites rioting and committing acts of violence in celebration of sporting events and other relatively trivial matters.[156] For example, a 2014 football game in Denver and a 2012 World Series in San Francisco resulted in large groups of individuals taking to the streets, lighting fires, and destroying property with little police action. Similarly, in New Hampshire, college students fought for their right to party at the Keene Pumpkin Festival, smashing windows, slashing tires, overturning dumpsters, and hurling liquor bottles; CNN called them "unruly," but no one was called a "thug" like in Baltimore or Ferguson. According to the corporate media, these events were unfortunate, but they never received the negative attention reserved for events in Ferguson or Baltimore.

The corporate press did not widely deride these events or denounce white "family culture" as the culprit, like O'Reilly had with African-Americans. In fact, these examples undermine Fox's argument that "the police would not be there if you were not committing crimes." Further, no one was asked to denounce the acts as part of "white culture." The message of the corporate media is clear: if you are an African-American protesting civil liberty violations, you are a thug; if you are white and engaged in wanton public property destruction or legal violations, you may only be letting off steam or celebrating a recent sporting event or festival.

CONCLUSION

The press has the power to stimulate people to clean up the environment, prevent nuclear proliferation, force crooked politicians out of office, reduce poverty, provide quality health care for all people, and even to save the lives of millions of people as it did in Ethiopia in 1984. But instead we are using it to promote sex, violence, and sensationalism and to line the pockets of already wealthy media moguls.

—Dr. Carl Jensen[157]

Carl Jensen invited students, scholars, and community members to not only examine the news critically, but to also examine themselves and their media habits. Despite the criticism Jensen leveled at the corporate media, he did it constructively and as a former newsman, with an eye on improving the quality of professional journalism. Where individuals get their information and the manner in which it is framed impacts the decisions people make politically, socially, and economically. Jensen's contributions and the subsequent work of Project Censored have proven that the corporate press works to obfuscate reality and reduce viewers' knowledge through trivial stories and disinformation campaigns. To carry on Jensen's legacy of media literacy education is to continue giving citizens knowledge and agency for positive change that affects us all.

NOLAN HIGDON is an assistant professor of history in the San Francisco Bay Area. He sits on the board of Project Censored as well as Action Coalition for Media Education (ACME), where he acts as the Global Critical Media Literacy Project coordinator.

MICKEY HUFF is the director of Project Censored and professor of social science and history at Diablo Valley College.

ELLIE KIM is an intern with Project Censored and a junior at Reed College. She is the student club officer for the Global Critical Media Literacy Project, a subset of Project Censored and Action Coalition for Media Education (ACME).

Notes

1. Mary Elizabeth Williams, "Shirley Manson Perfectly Nails What's Wrong with Kanye," *Salon*, February 10, 2015, accessed February 15, 2015, http://www.salon.com/2015/02/10/shirley_manson_perfectly_nails_whats_wrong_with_kanye/?utm_source=facebook&utm_medium=socialflow.
2. "Family Values Shocker: Pro-Life, Gun-Loving Tea Partier Holly Fisher Admits Cheating on Husband," Democratic Underground, January 19, 2015, accessed March 10, 2015, http://www.democraticunderground.com/10026107992.
3. LeftofCenter, "'It's Not My Job' Chuck Todd Admits He Can't Ask Tough Questions," Crooks and Liars, December 28, 2014, accessed March 10, 2015, http://crooksandliars.com/2014/12/todd-admits-he-wont-ask-tough-questions-so.
4. Micheal Calderone, "Hillary Clinton Team Holds Off-The-Record Journalist Dinner Ahead of 2016 Announcement," *Huffington Post*, April 10, 2015, accessed April 20, 2015, http://www.huffingtonpost.com/2015/04/10/hillary-clinton-journalists-2016_n_7039814.html.
5. Micheal Calderone, "Obama Met Privately with Journalists Amid Iran Deal Media Push," *Huffington Post*, April 7, 2015, accessed April 20, 2015, http://www.huffingtonpost.com/2015/04/07/obama-journalists-iran_n_7016400.html.
6. Frank Rich, "All the President's Press," *New York Times*, April 29, 2009, http://www.nytimes.com/2007/04/29/opinion/29rich.html.
7. "President Barack Obama's Top 10 Jokes at 2015 White House Correspondents' Dinner," Fox 13, April 26, 2015, accessed April 30, 2015, http://q13fox.com/2015/04/26/president-barack-obamas-top-10-jokes-at-2015-white-house-correspondents-dinner/.

Bonnie Faller, "WHCD Best Dressed: Chrissy Teigen, Sophia Bush, Michelle Obama & More," Hollywoodlife.com, April 27, 2015, a http://hollywoodlife.com/2015/04/27/whcd-best-dressed-2015-white-house-correspondents-dinner-pics/.

8. Paige Lavender, "Obama Uses White House Correspondents' Dinner Speech To Take A Jab At Dick Cheney," *Huffington Post*, April 25, 2015, http://www.huffingtonpost.com/2015/04/25/obama-dick-cheney_n_7144652.html.

9. Renee Hobbs, "Digital and Media Literacy: A Plan of Action," *Aspen Institute*, 2010.

10. Amy Mitchell, Jeffrey Gottfried, Katerina Eva Mats, "Millennials and Political News: Social Media—the Local TV for the Next Generation," Pew Research Center, June 1, 2015, accessed June 4, 2015, http://www.journalism.org/2015/06/01/millennials-political-news.

11. Ibid.

12. Ibid.

13. "The Invisible Hand of the Media," Williambova.net, September 18, 1997, accessed March 7, 2015, http://uts.cc.utexas.edu/~wbova/fn/gov/media.htm.

14. Aaron Couch,"Jon Stewart Mocks Fox News Outrage Over 'American Sniper' Oscar Snub (Video)," *Hollywood Report*, February 25, 2015, accessed March 4, 2015, http://www.hollywood-reporter.com/live-feed/jon-stewart-mocks-fox-news-777961.

15. Courtney Duckworth, "How Accurate is American Sniper," *Slate*, January 23, 2015, accessed February 7, 2015, http://www.slate.com/blogs/browbeat/2015/01/23/.

16. Sarah Gray, "Sean Hannity and Others are Freaking Out About 'American Sniper's Oscar Loss," *Salon*, February 22, 2015, accessed March 7, 2015, http://www.salon.com/2015/02/23/.

17. Andrew Kirell, "Fox & Friends Brings Out Ex-Marine to Answer: Was American Sniper 'Snubbed'?," *Mediaite*, February 23, 2015, accessed March 7, 2015, http://www.mediaite.com/tv/fox-friends-brings-out-ex-marine-to-answer-was-american-sniper-snubbed.

18. Amy Goodman and Juan Gonzalez, "Headlines," *Democracy Now!*, February 23, 2015, accessed March 7, 2015, http://www.democracynow.org/2015/2/23/headlines.

19. Eliott McLaughlin, "What the Heck Is Deflategate Anyway?" CNN, January 23, 2015, accessed February 10, 2015, http://www.cnn.com/2015/01/22/us/nfl-patriots-deflategate-rules.

20. Ian Rapoport, "More Details on the Investigation of Patriots' Deflated Footballs," NFL.com, February 1, 2015, accessed March 7, 2015, http://www.nfl.com/news/story/0ap3000000466783/article/more-details-on-the-investigation-of-patriots-deflated-footballs.

21. Christopher Gasper, "Joe Montana Thinks Tom Brady Responsible for Deflategate," *Boston Globe*, January 30, 2015.

22. Igor Mello, "WATCH: Daily Show's Jon Stewart Weighs in on Deflategate," CBSSports.com, January 31, 2015, accessed February 10, 2015, http://www.cbssports.com/nfl/eye-on-football/25013578/watch-daily-shows-jon-stewart-weighs-in-on-deflategate.

23. Jaisal Noor and Walid Al-Saqaf, "US Resumes Drone Strikes in Yemen Despite the Political Leadership Vacuum," *Real News*, January 28, 2015, accessed March 10, 2015, http://therealnews.com/t2/index.php?option=com_content&task=view&id=31&Itemid=74&jumival=13063.

24. Ken Dilanian, "The Collapse of Yemen's Government Took the US Totally by Surprise," *Business Insider*, February 12, 2015, accessed February 20, 2015, http://www.businessinsider.com/ken-dilanian-us-surprised-by-collapse-of-yemeni-government-2015-2.

25. "Get the Data: Drone Wars," Bureau of Investigative Journalism, accessed March 10, 2015, http://www.thebureauinvestigates.com/category/projects/drones/drones-graphs.

26. "Obama, Hagel Pay Tribute to Robin Williams," Fox News, August 12, 2014, accessed March 4, 2015, http://www.foxnews.com/entertainment/2014/08/12/obama-robin-williams-was-one-kind.

27. Steve Almasy et al., "Sarah Michelle Gellar, Conan O'Brien Pay Tribute to Robin Williams," CNN, August 11, 2014, accessed March 7, 2015, http://edition.cnn.com/2014/08/11/showbiz/robin-williams-reactions/index.html#em3.

28. Catherine Taibi, "ABC News Apologizes for Streaming Video of Robin Williams' Home," *Huffington Post*, August 12, 2014, accessed March 9, 2015, http://www.huffingtonpost.com/2014/08/12/abc-news-robin-williams-home-camera_n_5671709.html?utm_hp_ref=tw.

29. Dylan Stableford, "HANGED," Yahoo! News, August 13, 2014, accessed March 9, 2015, http://news.yahoo.com/robin-williams-death-media-coverage-225459533.html.

30. Gareth Porter, "US Kept Mum for Weeks on Israel's Civilian Targeting in Gaza," Common Dreams, August 12, 2014, accessed March 6, 2015, http://www.commondreams.org/news/2014/08/12/us-kept-mum-weeks-israels-civilian-targeting-gaza.

31. Sandy Tolan, "Blown Chances in Gaza: Israel and the U.S. Miss Many Chances to Avoid War," Common Dreams, March 7, 2015, accessed March 15, 2015, http://www.commondreams.org/views/2014/08/12/blown-chances-gaza-israel-and-us-miss-many-chances-avoid-war.

32. Ibid.

33. Ibid.

34. Ibid.

35. Lizzie Dearden, "Israel-Gaza Conflict: 50-day War by the Numbers," Independent, August 27, 2014, http://www.independent.co.uk/news/world/middle-east/israelgaza-conflict-50day-war-by-numbers-9693310.html.

36. "Jeb Bush's New Hints 2016," CNN, December 14, 2014, accessed March 15, 2015, http://www.cnn.com/videos/politics/2014/12/14/ip-jeb-bushs-new-hints-about-2016.cnn.

37. Stephen Collinson and Alexandra Jaffe, "Mitt Romney Exit Widens Path for Jeb Bush," CNN Politics, January 30, 2015, accessed March 15, 2015, http://www.cnn.com/2015/01/30/politics/mitt-romney-exit-jeb-bush.

38. Joe Romm, "Can Koch Brothers Lock in Fatal Climate Delay for $889 Million in 2016 Election?," ThinkProgress, January 27, 2015, accessed February 10, 2015, http://thinkprogress.org/climate/2015/01/27/3615930/koch-brothers-climate-delay-889-million-2016-election/.

39. "Unreliable Sources: How the News Media Help the Koch Brothers and ExxonMobil Spread Climate Disinformation," Union of Concerned Scientists, May 13, 2013, accessed February 10, 2015, http://www.ucsusa.org/global_warming/solutions/fight-misinformation/news-media-helps-koch-brothers-exxon-mobil-spread-climate-disinformation.html.

40. Amy Chozick, "Economic Plan is a Quandary for Hillary Clinton's Campaign," New York Times, February 7, 2015, accessed February 14, 2015, http://www.nytimes.com/2015/02/08/us/politics/economic-plan-is-a-quandary-for-hillary-clintons-campaign.html?_r=0.

41. Andrew Stiles, "Hillary Clinton's Top Corporate Donors Are Among the Most Hated Companies in America," Fox Nation, February 8, 2015, accessed February 14, 2015, http://nation.foxnews.com/2015/02/07/hillary-clinton-s-top-corporate-donors-are-among-most-hated-companies-america.

42. Ed Mazza, "Jon Stewart Watches the Media Freak Out Over Hillary's Burrito Order," Huffington Post, April 15, 2015, accessed April 20, 2015, http://www.huffingtonpost.com/2015/04/15/jon-stewart-hillary-burrito_n_7068268.html?utm_hp_ref=tw.

43. Jessica Weiss, "Miami Fast-food Workers Strike Today to Demand $15 per Hour," Miami New Times, April 15, 2015, accessed April 20, 2015, http://www.miaminewtimes.com/news/miami-fast-food-workers-strike-today-to-demand-15-per-hour-7570918.

44. Sarah Lazare, "'I Know We Will Win': Largest Ever Low-Wage Worker Protest Sweeps United States," Common Dreams, April 16, 2015, accessed April 20, 2015, http://www.commondreams.org/news/2015/04/16/i-know-we-will-win-largest-ever-low-wage-worker-protest-sweeps-united-states.

45. Ibid.

46. Carl Jensen with Project Censored, Censored: The News that Didn't Make the News—and Why: The 1996 Project Censored Yearbook (New York: Seven Stories Press, 1996), 13.

47. Rick Kissell, "Fox News Dominates Cable News Ratings in 2014; MSNBC Tumbles," Huffington Post, December 30, 2014, accessed January 15, 2015, http://www.huffingtonpost.com/2014/12/30/fox-news-cable-news-ratings_n_6398220.html.

48. Anthony Zurcher, "Did Censorship Charge Help Fox News Best DISH?," BBC, January 16, 2015, accessed January 23, 2015, http://m.bbc.com/news/blogs-echochambers-30821317.

49. "Scahill: White House Attempt to Control Who Journalists Source Is Assault on Press Freedoms," Common Dreams, January 18, 2015, accessed February 1, 2015, http://commondreams.org/news/2015/01/18/scahill-white-house-attempt-control-who-journalists-source-assault-press-freedoms.

50. Gabriel Arana, "Blogger Resigns from the Daily Caller after Tucker Carlson Pulls Column Critical of Fox News," *Huffington Post*, March 18, 2015, accessed March 20, 2015. http://www.huffingtonpost.com/2015/03/18/daily-caller-tucker-carlson-fox-resign_n_6893596.html?utm_hp_ref=tw.

51. Travis J. Tritten, "NBC's Brian Williams Recants Iraq Story after Soldiers Protest," *Stars and Stripes*, February 4, 2015, accessed April 23, 2015, http://www.stripes.com/news/us/nbc-s-brian-williams-recants-iraq-story-after-soldiers-protest-1.327792.

52. Howard Kurtz, "Why NBC's Suspension is Brian Williams' Last Hope for Remaining Anchor," Fox News, February 11, 2015, accessed April, 23, 2015, http://www.foxnews.com/politics/2015/02/11/why-nbcs-suspension-is-brian-williams-last-hope-for-remaining-anchor.

53. Karen Brooks, "Brian Williams Cancels Letterman Appearance: NBC Source," Yahoo! News, February 2, 2015, accessed April 23, 2015, http://news.yahoo.com/brian-williams-cancels-letterman-appearance-nbc-source-225611784.html.

54. Lisa de Moraes, "'NBC Nightly News' Wins February Sweep in All Metrics, Despite Brian Williams Suspension," *Deadline*, March 3, 2015, accessed April 23, 2015, http://deadline.com/2015/03/nbc-nightly-news-february-sweep-win-brian-williams-1201385139.

55. See Jim Naureckas, "Some Other Tall Tales Brian Williams Might Want to Apologize For," FAIR, February 5, 2015, accessed April 23, 2015, http://fair.org/blog/2015/02/05/some-other-tall-tales-brian-williams-might-want-to-apologize-for; and Emily Smith, "Brian Williams Also Told Iffy Tales of Rescuing Puppies from Fires," *Page Six*, February 6, 2015, accessed April 23, 2015, http://pagesix.com/2015/02/06/brian-williams-also-told-iffy-tales-of-rescuing-puppies-from-fires.

56. Gabriel Sherman, "(Actually) True War Stories at NBC News," *New York*, March 8, 2015, accessed April 23, 2015, http://nymag.com/daily/intelligencer/2015/03/nbc-news-brian-williams-deborah-turness.html.

57. See David McGrath, "St. Pat's Day: Time to Pardon Brian Williams and Bill O'Reilly," *Chicago Sun Times*, March 12, 2015, accessed April 23, 2015, http://chicago.suntimes.com/news/7/71/429848/st-patricks-day-time-pardon-williams-mcdonald-oreilly; and Douglas Brinkley, "The Brian Williams Case—That's the Way it Wasn't," CNN, February 11, 2015, accessed April 23, 2015, http://www.cnn.com/2015/02/10/opinion/brinkley-brian-williams-cronkite.

58. Ravi Somaiya, "Brian Williams Inquiry Is Said to Expand," *New York Times*, April 24, 2015, http://www.nytimes.com/2015/04/25/business/media/nbc-inquiry-said-to-find-that-brian-williams-embellished.html.

59. Dylan Byers, "Bill O'Reilly Defends Brian Williams," Politico, February 10, 2015, accessed March 1, 2015, http://www.politico.com/blogs/media/2015/02/bill-oreilly-defends-brian-williams-202381.html.

60. David Corn and Daniel Schulman, "Bill O'Reilly Has His Own Brian Williams Problem," *Mother Jones*, February 19, 2015, accessed April 23, 2015, http://www.motherjones.com/politics/2015/02/bill-oreilly-brian-williams-falklands-war?dg.

61. Ibid.

62. David Corn and Daniel Schulman, "O'Reilly Cameraman Disputes Fox News Host's Falklands 'War Zone' Story," *Mother Jones*, March, 30, 2015, accessed April 23, 2015, http://m.motherjones.com/politics/2015/03/cameraman-disputes-bill-oreilly-falklands-war-story.

63. Jon Greenberg, "Bill O'Reilly: 'I Never Said I was on the Falkland Islands,'" *PunditFact*, March 3, 2015, accessed April 23, 2015, http://www.politifact.com/punditfact/statements/2015/mar/03/bill-oreilly/oreilly-i-never-said-i-was-falkland-islands.

64. See Olivia Marshall, "Another Fabrication: O'Reilly Never Witnessed the Murder of Nuns in El Salvador (Updated)," Media Matters, February 25, 2015, accessed April 23, 2015, http://mediamatters.org/blog/2015/02/25/another-fabrication-oreilly-never-witnessed-the/202667; and Jeremy Holden and Joe Strupp, "As O'Reilly Spins, News Sources Further Undermine His JFK Story," Media Matters, February 26, 2015, accessed April 23, 2015, http://mediamatters.org/blog/2015/02/26/as-oreilly-spins-new-sources-further-undermine/202691iams.html.

65. Matt Gertz, "Media Matters Presents Killing Truth, an eBook Of O'Reilly's Legends," Media Matters, April 7, 2015, accessed April 20, 2015, mediamatters.org/blog/2015/04/07/media-matters-presents-killing-truth-an-ebook-o/203182.

66. Jackson Connor, "Here's Every Claim Made Against Bill O'Reilly So Far," *Huffington Post*, February 27, 2015, accessed April 23, 2015, http://www.huffingtonpost.com/2015/02/27/bill-oreilly-every-claim-so-far_n_6760320.html?utm_hp_ref=tw.

67. Paul Farhi, "Bill O'Reilly Exaggerated War-Zone Experiences, Mother Jones says," *Washington Post*, February 19, 2015, accessed April 23, 2015, http://www.washingtonpost.com/lifestyle/style/mother-jones-accuses-bill-oreilly-of-hyping-his-war-zone-experiences/2015/02/19/ddbfaf70-b88f-11e4-aa05-1ce812b3fdd2_story.html?tid=ptv_rellink.

68. Glenn Greenwald, "NBC's Conduct in Engel Kidnapping Story is More Troubling than the Brian Williams Scandal," *Intercept*, April 16, 2015, accessed April 21, 2015, https://firstlook.org/theintercept/2015/04/16/nbcs-conduct-richard-engel-kidnapping-serious-brian-williams-scandal/.

69. See Denise Robbins, "NY Times Fails to Disclose Oil Funding Behind Pro-Oil Op-Ed," Media Matters, March 12, 2015, accessed April 21, 2015, http://mediamatters.org/blog/2015/03/12/ny-times-fails-to-disclose-oil-funding-behind-p/202883; and Action Alert, "The Washington Post Should Tell You When Its Columnists Are Paid to Disinform You," FAIR, April 23, 2015, accessed April 26, 2015, http://fair.org/home/the-washington-post-should-tell-you-when-its-columnists-are-paid-to-disinform-you/.

70. Scott Kaufman, "'Tea Party' Protestors Opposed to Florida Land Deal Were Mostly Actors Hired by Big Sugar," *Raw Story*, April 3, 2015, accessed April 15, 2015, http://www.rawstory.com/rs/2015/04/tea-party-protesters-opposed-to-florida-land-deal-were-mostly-actors-hired-by-big-sugar.

71. Judith Miller, "The Iraq War and Stubborn Myths," *Wall Street Journal*, April 3, 2015, accessed April 15, 2015, http://www.wsj.com/articles/the-iraq-war-and-stubborn-myths-1428087215.

72. *Real Time with Bill Maher*, season 13, episode 350, aired April 17, 2015 (Los Angeles, CA: HBO, 2015).

73. Jackson Connor, "NYT's Nick Confessore Grills Judith Miller On WMD Reporting: 'Your Stories Were Wrong,'" *Huffington Post*, April 20, 2015, http://www.huffingtonpost.com/2015/04/20/nick-confessore-judith-miller-stories-were-wrong_n_7101398.html?utm_hp_ref=tw.

74. Dennis Bernstein, "Silencing Donahue and Anti-War Voices," *Consortium News*, January 15, 2012, accessed May 3, 2015, http://consortiumnews.com/2012/01/15/silencing-donahue-and-anti-war-voices; James Poniewozik, "In the Obama Era, Will the Media Change, Too?" *Time*, January 15, 2009, accessed March 3, 2015, http://content.time.com/time/magazine/article/0,9171,1871916,00.html; Eric Roper, "Ventura Says MSNBC Nixed His Show for Not Supporting Iraq War," *Star Tribune*, November 30, 2009, accessed March 3, 2015, http://www.startribune.com/politics/blogs/78150302.html; Shindu Parameswaran, "War, Devastation, and Who's Cashing in On Them," *Arbitrage Magazine*, April 2013, accessed March 3, 2015, http://www.arbitragemagazine.com/features/profiting-vs-profiteering.

75. Project Censored, "#1. Over One Million Iraqi Deaths Caused by US Occupation," April 30, 2010, accessed March 15, 2015, http://www.projectcensored.org/1-over-one-million-iraqi-deaths-caused-by-us-occupation/; Michael B. Kelly, "The Iraq War Could Cost More Than $6 Trillion," *Business Insider*, March 14, 2013, accessed March 15, 2015, http://www.businessinsider.com/why-the-iraq-war-cost-2-trillion-2013-3.

76. "Cases of Ebola Diagnosed in the United States," Centers for Disease Control and Prevention, December 16, 2014, accessed March 3, 2015, http://www.cdc.gov/vhf/ebola/outbreaks/2014-west-africa/united-states-imported-case.html.

77. Ibid.

78. Dana Ford, "First Diagnosed Case of Ebola in US," CNN, September 30, 2014, accessed March 3, 2015, http://www.cnn.com/2014/09/30/health/ebola-us/index.html; Mannie Fernandez, "Texas Health Care Worker Tests Positive for Ebola," *New York Times*, October 12, 2014, accessed March 3, 2015, http://www.nytimes.com/2014/10/13/us/texas-health-worker-tests-positive-for-ebola.html; "Ebola Outbreak: Second Texas Health Worker 'Tests Positive,'"

BBC News, October 15, 2014, accessed March 3, 2015, http://www.bbc.com/news/world-us-canada-29628622; Maggie Fox, "New York Doctor Just Back From Africa Has Ebola," NBC News, October 23, 2014, accessed March 3, 2015, http://www.nbcnews.com/storyline/ebola-virus-outbreak/new-york-doctor-just-back-africa-has-ebola-n232561.

79. Ellie Sandmeyer, "Right-Wing Media Exploit Ebola Fears to Attack Immigration," Media Matters, October 2, 2014, accessed March 5, 2015, http://mediamatters.org/research/2014/10/02/right-wing-media-exploit-ebola-fears-to-attack/200995.

80. Adam Serwer, "Like Obama, George W. Bush Let Illegal Immigrants Stay and Work," *Mother Jones*, July 6, 2012, accessed March 13, 2015, http://www.motherjones.com/politics/2012/07/obama-bush-immigration-enforcement.

81. Sandmeyer, "Right-Wing Media."

82. Staff, "Fox Guest Stokes Ebola Fears Due To 'Uninspected' Immigrants," Media Matters, July 29, 2014, accessed March 13, 2015, http://mediamatters.org/video/2014/07/29/fox-guest-stokes-ebola-fears-due-to-uninspected/200245.

83. Ibid.

84. Tom Boggioni, "O'Reilly Calls On 'Propagandist' CDC Director to Step Down: 'Resign! Have a Little Dignity,'" *Raw Story*, October 13, 2014, accessed March 15, 2015, http://www.rawstory.com/rs/2014/10/oreilly-calls-on-propagandist-cdc-director-to-step-down-resign-have-a-little-dignity/.

85. James Jackson, "Ebola Story Puts Old Fears in New Virus," FAIR, December 1, 2014, accessed March 15, 2015, http://fair.org/extra-online-articles/ebola-story-puts-old-fears-in-new-virus/.

86. Ibid.

87. David Edwards, "Fox News Host Proposes Ebola Quarantine 'Centers' for Every City in the US," *Raw Story*, October 13, 2014, accessed March 15, 2015, http://www.rawstory.com/rs/2014/10/fox-news-host-proposes-ebola-quarantine-centers-for-every-city-in-the-us/.

88. Joaquim Moreira Salles, "Ebola is Bringing Out the Worst in Cable News," *ThinkProgress*, October 7, 2014, accessed March 15, 2015, http://thinkprogress.org/health/2014/10/07/3576799/ebola-cable-news-coverage/.

89. Jackson, "Ebola Story."

90. Ellie Sandmeyer, "CNN Turns to Outbreak Fiction Writer For Ebola Coverage," Media Matters, October 10, 2014, accessed March 15, 2015, http://mediamatters.org/blog/2014/10/10/cnn-turns-to-outbreak-fiction-writer-for-ebola/201113.

91. Robert Wallace, "The Neoliberal Outbreak of Ebola," *Real News*, November 2, 2014, accessed March 15, 2015, http://therealnews.com/t2/index.php?option=com_content&task=view&id=31&Itemid=74&jumival=12596.

92. Matt Gertz and Rob Savillo, "REPORT: Ebola Coverage on TV News Plummeted after Mid-terms," Media Matters, November 19, 2014, accessed March 15, 2015, http://mediamatters.org/research/2014/11/19/report-ebola-coverage-on-tv-news-plummeted-afte/201619.

93. Efraim Karsh, "The Palestinians, Alone," *New York Times*, August 1, 2010, accessed March 1, 2015, http://www.nytimes.com/2010/08/02/opinion/02karsh.html?_r=0; "Does the NY Times Factcheck Op-Eds?," FAIR, August 10, 2010, accessed March 1, 2015, http://fair.org/take-action/action-alerts/does-the-ny-times-factcheck-op-eds/; Isabel Kershner and Fares Akram, "Ferocious Israeli Assault on Gaza Kills a Leader of Hamas," *New York Times*, November 14, 2012, accessed March 1, 2015, http://www.nytimes.com/2012/11/15/world/middleeast/israeli-strike-in-gaza-kills-the-military-leader-of-hamas.html?pagewanted=2&ref=opinion; Peter Hart, "Media Hype and Gaza's 'Terror' Tunnels," FAIR, July 29, 2014, accessed March 1, 2015, http://fair.org/blog/2014/07/29/media-hype-and-gazas-terror-tunnels/.

94. Patricia Davis, "We Called It Genocide in Guatemala. Why Not in Gaza Too?," Common Dreams, October 7, 2014, accessed March 1, 2015, http://www.commondreams.org/views/2014/10/07/we-called-it-genocide-guatemala-why-not-gaza-too; Stephen Zunes, "Obama's Mideast Speech: Two Steps Back, One Step Forward," Common Dreams, May 20, 2011, accessed March 1, 2015, http://www.commondreams.org/views/2011/05/20/obamas-mideast-speech-two-steps-back-one-step-forward.

95. Colin Cavell, "America's Dependency on Middle East Oil," Global Research, April 11, 2012, accessed June 4, 2015, http://www.globalresearch.ca/america-s-dependency-on-middle-east-oil/30177#sthash.jgu1rTzM.dpuf.

96. "Global Connections: Middle East," PBS, accessed June 4, 2015, http://www.pbs.org/wgbh/globalconnections/mideast/questions/resource/#american_dependence; US Energy Information Administration, "Frequently Asked Questions," http://www.eia.gov/tools/faqs/faq.cfm?id=727&t=6.

97. "Global Connections: Middle East," PBS, 2015.

98. Ibid.

99. David Vine, "America Still Has Hundreds of Military Bases Worldwide. Have They Made Us Any Safer? How Our Global Military Presence Works to Facilitate, Not Prevent, War," Mother Jones, November 14, 2014, accessed June 4, 2015, http://www.motherjones.com/politics/2014/11/america-still-has-hundreds-military-bases-worldwide-have-they-made-us-any-safer.

100. Ibid.

101. "Global Connections: Middle East."

102. Jaweed Kaleem, "Obama's Anti-Extremist Strategy Criticized As Wrongly Singling Out Muslims," Huffington Post, February 13, 2015, accessed March 4, 2015, http://www.huffingtonpost.com/2015/02/13/muslims-white-house-summit-extremism_n_6680952.html.

103. Ibid.

104. "12 Years Post 9/11, Islamophobia Still Runs High," Real News, video, 11:50, September 12, 2013, accessed March 4, 2015, http://therealnews.com/t2/index.php?option=com_content&task=view&id=31&Itemid=74&jumival=10698.

105. "#MuslimLivesMatter Shock and Outrage as 3 Muslim Students Gunned Down in N. Carolina," Russia Today, February 11, 2015, accessed March 4, 2015, http://rt.com/usa/231451-muslim-lives-matter-triple-homicide.

106. Pooja Podugu, "From Charlie Hebdo to Chapel Hill," Harvard Political Review, February 27, 2015, accessed March 4, 2015, http://harvardpolitics.com/world/portrayals-violence-abroad-dehumanization-home.

107. Ibid.

108. Michael Hirst et al., "Paris Attacks: Millions Rally for Unity in France," BBC News Europe, January 11, 2015, accessed March 5, 2015, http://www.bbc.com/news/world-europe-30765824.

109. Ibid.

110. Rana F. Sweis, "Jordanians See US Reporting Bias in Coverage of Student Killings," New York Times, February 13, 2015, http://www.nytimes.com/2015/02/14/world/middleeast/online-commenters-see-reporting-bias-in-killing-of-3-muslims.html?_r=0.

111. Podugu, "From Charlie Hebdo to Chapel Hill."

112. Ibid.

113. Ibid.; "Reporting the Baga Massacre," Al Jazeera, January 24, 2015, accessed March 17, 2015, http://www.aljazeera.com/programmes/listeningpost/2015/01/reporting-baga-massacre-150124095659185.html.

114. George Washington [pseud.], "Non-Muslims Carried Out More than 90% of All Terrorist Attacks on U.S. Soil," ZeroHedge, May 1, 2013, accessed March 17, 2015, http://www.zerohedge.com/contributed/2013-05-01/non-muslims-carried-out-more-90-all-terrorist-attacks-us-soil.

115. Garikai Chengu, "How the US Helped Create Al Qaeda and ISIS," CounterPunch, September 19, 2014, accessed March 3, 2015, http://www.counterpunch.org/2014/09/19/how-the-us-helped-create-al-qaeda-and-isis/; "What Is 'Islamic State'?" BBC News, September 29, 2014, accessed March 14, 2015, http://www.bbc.com/news/world-middle-east-29052144.

116. Kurt Nimmo, "ISIS Domestic Terror Threat Created by CIA and U.S. Military," Global Research, June 20, 2014, accessed March 14, 2014, http://www.globalresearch.ca/isis-domestic-terror-threat-created-by-cia-and-u-s-military/5387874.

117. Paul Lewis, Spencer Ackerman, and Ian Cobain, "Steven Sotloff: ISIS Video Claims to Show Beheading of US Journalist," Guardian, September 3, 2014, accessed June 30, 2015, http://www.theguardian.com/world/2014/sep/02/isis-video-steven-sotloff-beheading.

118. Peter Hart, "No Debate and the New War," FAIR, November 14, 2014, accessed March 14, 2015, http://fair.org/press-release/no-debate-and-the-new-war/.

119. Ronn Torossian, "Giuliani, O'Reilly: Stand With the NYPD," Newsmax, January 7, 2015, accessed February 27, 2015, http://www.newsmax.com/RonnTorossian/NYPD-Blasio-Giuliani-O-Reilly/2015/01/07/id/616975.

120. Stephen A. Crockett Jr., "Young Black Men 21 Times More Likely Than Whites to Be Shot Dead by Police," Root, October 10, 2014, accessed March 2, 2015, http://www.theroot.com/articles/culture/2014/10/young_black_men_21_times_more_likely_to_be_shot_dead_by_police_than_whites.html.

121. Peter Phillips, Diana Grant, and Greg Sewell, "Law Enforcement Related Deaths in the US: 'Justifiable Homicides' and the Impacts on Families," Project Censored, September 10, 2014, accessed March 1, 2015, http://www.projectcensored.org/law-enforcement-related-deaths-us-justifiable-homicides-impacts-families.

122. "You're Nine Times More Likely to be Killed by a Police Officer than a Terrorist," Washington's Blog, August 15, 2014, accessed March 1, 2015, http://www.washingtonsblog.com/2014/08/youre-nine-times-likely-killed-police-officer-terrorist.html.

123. Nolan Higdon, "Justice For Sale," Project Censored, February 6, 2015, accessed May 25, 2015, http://www.projectcensored.org/justice-sale-part-1-declining-faith-rising-police-violence.

124. "Arrest to Death: What Happened to Freddie Gray," CBS News, May 1, 2015, accessed May 1, 2015, http://www.cbsnews.com/news/arrest-to-death-what-happened-to-freddie-gray.

125. Ibid.

126. See Janine Jackson, "FAIR TV: Fox News & Ferguson, Cop Euphemisms and Disney 'News,'" FAIR, December 5, 2014, accessed February 27, 2015, http://fair.org/blog/2014/12/05/fair-tv-fox-news-ferguson-cop-euphemisms-and-disney-news/; and Peter Hart, "Michael Brown, According to the New York Times," FAIR, August 25, 2014, accessed February 27, 2015, http://fair.org/blog/2014/08/25/michael-brown-according-to-the-new-york-times.

127. Jim Naureckas, "Give Killer Cops a Break, Says NYT," FAIR, August 25, 2014, accessed February 27, 2015, http://fair.org/blog/2014/08/25/give-killer-cops-a-break-says-nyt.

128. Jack Mirkinson, "Megyn Kelly Schools Bill O'Reilly about White Privilege. No, Really," Huffington Post, August 26, 2014, accessed March 1, 2015, http://m.huffpost.com/us/entry/5714619?ncid=fcbklnkushpmg00000018.

129. "O'Reilly: Juries Give Police 'Benefit Of The Doubt' Because Stats Show Blacks Commit More Crimes," Media Matters, December 8, 2014, accessed March 1, 2015, http://mediamatters.org/video/2014/12/08/oreilly-juries-give-police-benefit-of-the-doubt/201801.

130. Steve Chapman, "The Problem with Blaming Black Crime for Police Shootings," Reason, December 8, 2014, accessed May 21, 2015, http://reason.com/archives/2014/12/08/black-crime-and-police-killings.

131. Nick Wing, "When the Media Treats White Suspects and Killers Better Than Black Victims," Huffington Post, August 14, 2014, accessed March 25, 2015, http://www.huffingtonpost.com/2014/08/14/media-black-victims_n_5673291.html.

132. Jackson Connor, "Fox News' Keith Ablow Tries to Blame Michael Brown's Stepfather for his Death," Huffington Post, December 3, 2014, accessed March 1, 2015, http://www.huffingtonpost.com/2014/12/03/keith-ablow-michael-brown-step-father-blames-for-death_n_6262002.html.

133. Danielle Paquette, "Giuliani: 'White Police Officers Wouldn't Be There If You Weren't Killing Each Other,'" Washington Post, November 23, 2014, accessed March 1, 2015, http://www.washingtonpost.com/blogs/post-politics/wp/2014/11/23/giuliani-white-police-officers-wouldnt-be-there-if-you-werent-killing-each-other.

134. Alexandrea Boguhn and Coleman Lowndes, "Geraldo Rivera and the Victim-Blaming of Black Teenagers," Media Matters, August 20, 2014, accessed March 1, 2015, http://mediamatters.org/blog/2014/08/20/geraldo-rivera-and-the-victim-blaming-of-black/200489.

135. Paul Rosenberg, "Fox News is Tearing Us Apart: Race Baiting and Divisiveness Hits Disgusting New Low," Salon, August 23, 2014, accessed March 1, 2015, http://www.salon.com/2014/08/28/fox_news_is_tearing_us_apart_race_baiting_and_divisiveness_hits_disgusting_new_low.

136. Ezekiel Edwards, "Walter Scott's Killing Is a Direct Result of the Current State of Policing in America," Common Dreams, April 10, 2015, accessed June 4, 2015, http://www.commondreams. org/views/2015/04/10/walter-scotts-killing-direct-result-current-state-policing-america-today; Brendan James, "Stewart Unloads On Hannity For Blaming Ferguson On Obama, Sharpton," Popist, December 2, 2014, accessed February 27, 2015, http://popist.com/s/c727a30.

137. Wing, "When the Media Treats."

138. Dan Elliot and Michael R. Blood, "Colorado Suspect Was Brilliant Science Student," Yahoo! News, July 21, 2012, accessed March 1, 2015, http://news.yahoo.com/colorado-suspect-brilliant-science-student-230349806.html.

139. Ibid.

140. Adam Nagourney, Michael Cieply, Alan Feuer, and Ian Lovett, "Before Brief, Deadly Spree, Trouble Since Age 8," New York Times, June 1, 2014, accessed March 1, 2015, http://www.nytimes. com/2014/06/02/us/elliot-rodger-killings-in-california-followed-years-of-withdrawal.html; Alan Duke, "Five Revelations from the 'Twisted World' of a 'Kissless Virgin,'" CNN, May 27, 2014, accessed March 1, 2015, http://www.cnn.com/2014/05/25/justice/california-shooting-revelations/; Alexandra Berzon, "Isolated Son Worried Parents," Wall Street Journal, May 26, 2014, accessed March 1, 2015, http://www.wsj.com/articles/portrait-of-california-shooter-a-troubled-son-1401136376; "Elliot Rodger Killings Show Difficulty Of Policing YouTube," Huffington Post, May 27, 2014, accessed March 1, 2015, http://www.huffingtonpost.ca/2014/05/27/elliot-rodger-youtube_n_5395933.html.

141. Ibid.

142. Ibid.

143. "Former College Professor Pleads Guilty to Attempted Murder Charge," CNN, September 11, 2012, accessed March 1, 2015, http://www.cnn.com/2012/09/11/justice/alabama-college-shooting/; "Motive in Question as Professor Faces Murder Charge in Alabama Campus Shooting," Fox News, February 13, 2010, accessed March 1, 2015, http://www.foxnews.com/ story/2010/02/13/motive-in-question-as-professor-faces-murder-charge-in-alabama-campus-shooting/.

144. Paula Mejia, "Ferguson, Eric Garner Protests Spread Worldwide," Newsweek, December 14, 2014, accessed February 26, 2015, http://www.newsweek.com/ferguson-eric-garner-protests-sprawl-worldwide-289867.

145. Josmar Trujillo, "CNN Attempts Actual Journalism—But Reverts to Embedded Reporting," FAIR, August 19, 2014, accessed February 27, 2015, http://fair.org/blog/2014/08/19/cnn-attempts-actual-journalism-but-reverts-to-embedded-reporting.

146. Taylor Berman, "Undercover Cop Pulls Gun at Eric Garner-Michael Brown Protest in Oakland," Gawker, December 11, 2014, accessed February 26, 2015, http://gawker.com/under-cover-cop-pulls-gun-at-eric-garner-michael-brown-p-1669866054.

147. "Media Blackout: How Baltimore Cops Turned a Peaceful Student Protest into a Riot," Anti-Media, April 28, 2015, accessed April 29, 2015, http://theantimedia.org/media-blackout-how-baltimore-cops-turned-a-peaceful-student-protest-into-a-riot/; Sam Brodey and Jenna McLaughlin, "Eyewitnesses: The Baltimore Riots Didn't Start the Way You Think," Mother Jones, April 28, 2015, accessed June 4, 2015, http://www.motherjones.com/politics/2015/04/how-baltimore-riots-began-mondawmin-purge.

148. Julia Craven, "Wolf Blitzer Fails to Goad Protester into Condemning Violence," Huffington Post, April 29, 2015, http://www.huffingtonpost.com/2015/04/29/wolf-blitzer-baltimore-protests_n_7168964.html.

149. Simon McCormack, "Baltimore Councilman Eviscerates Erin Burnett for Calling Teens 'Thugs,'" Huffington Post, April 29, 2015, accessed March 1, 2015, http://huff.to/1JB402g.

150. Nick Wing, "Protester Schools MSNBC Anchor about Coverage of Baltimore Riots," Huffington Post, April 28, 2015, http://huff.to/1GCWu3l.

151. Catherine Taibi, "Geraldo Rivera Battles Protesters Who Want Fox News to Leave Baltimore," Huffington Post, April 29, 2015, http://huff.to/1JBpcoU.

152. Christopher Mathias, "Fox News Wanted to Focus on Looters, But This Baltimore City Council Member Wasn't Having It," Huffington Post, April 28, 2015, http://huff.to/1GCZMU5.

153. Joanna Rothkopf, "Bill O'Reilly: St. Louis Rams Who Protested Aren't 'Smart Enough to Know What They're Doing,'" *Salon*, December 2, 2014, accessed February 27, 2015, http://www.salon.com/2014/12/02/bill_oreilly_st_louis_rams_who_protested_arent_smart_enough_to_know_what_theyre_doing.

154. Ibid.

155. "Riots in Huntington Beach, CA," *Daily Kos*, July 30, 2013, accessed March 1, 2015, www.dailykos.com/story/2013/07/31/1227834/-Riots-in-Huntington-Beach-CA.

156. Jessica Roy, "White People Rioting for No Reason," *New York*, November 26, 2014, accessed March 1, 2015, http://nymag.com/daily/intelligencer/2014/11/white-people-rioting-for-no-reason.html.

157. Peter Phillips with Project Censored, *Censored 2000: The Year's Top 25 Censored Stories* (New York: Seven Stories Press, 2000), 185.

CHAPTER 4

Media Democracy in Action

Compiled by Andy Lee Roth and Mickey Huff, with contributions by
Steven Wishnia (Dissent NewsWire), Alexander Reid Ross (Earth
First! Newswire), and Sue Udry (Defending Dissent Foundation);
Beatrice Edwards (Government Accountability Project); Adam
Jonas Horowitz (*Nuclear Savage*); Ian Thomas Ash (*A2-B-C*);
Arlene Engelhardt and Mary Glenney (*From a Woman's Point of
View*); Crystal Bedford, Lisa Davis, Darian Edelman,
Lauren Freeman, and Ellie Kim (Project Censored
student interns); and Jyarland Daniels,
and Rebekah Spicuglia (Race Forward/*Colorlines*)

*We are what we do, and above all what we do to change
what we are: our identity lies in action and struggle.
That is why the revelation of what we are implies
denunciation of what prevents us being what we can
be. We define ourselves through defiance and through
opposing obstacles.*

—Eduardo Galeano (September 3, 1940–April 13, 2015)[1]

Censored 2004 was the first volume in which we featured a chapter
titled "Media Democracy in Action." Documenting a growing media
democracy movement that offered a sharp contrast to the top-down
corporate model, the chapter's authors framed it as "a report on the
everyday activism of grassroots media groups all across the nation."[2]
Subsequent *Censored* volumes have continued and expanded this
coverage to include organizations and individuals whose work fosters more informed publics, promotes direct participation in political
decision making, and contributes to a more robust civil society.

The contributors to this year's chapter continue that tradition.

Engaged in the action and struggle that Eduardo Galeano identified as crucial to positive social change, the issues and organizations represented here deserve your keen attention and support.

MOBILIZING INDEPENDENT MEDIA TO HALT FBI HARASSMENT IN CASCADIA

Steven Wishnia, Alexander Reid Ross, and Sue Udry

On December 19, 2014, Idaho environmental activist Helen Yost received a text message from a Federal Bureau of Investigation (FBI) agent named Travis Thiede. "Helen, I am trying to get a hold of you to speak with you," he wrote. "An issue has come up, and I need to speak with you. Please give me a call. I am an FBI agent."

The text followed several phone calls from an unfamiliar number that she'd ignored. Yost, whose response was "NO!," had her ideas about why she was being sought out. She was active in Wild Idaho Rising Tide (WIRT), which had been fighting "megaloads," giant trucks that haul equipment for processing tar-sands oil and can be longer than a football field, since 2011. On the day the first calls were placed, she had just returned to her home in Moscow from a weekend organizing trip.

Yost wasn't the only activist being bothered.

The development of Alberta's tar-sands oil—the massively polluting oil slated to be shipped through the planned Keystone XL pipeline—has drawn a strong response from environmentalists in the Pacific Northwest, also known as the Cascadia Bioregion. In 2013, a coalition of settler-descendants and Native Americans blocked megaloads traveling through the Nez Perce reservation in Idaho. In turn, the FBI and local police have begun reviving the surveillance and infiltration tactics used on a larger scale in the "Green Scare" operations of the late 1990s and early 2000s.

In October 2014, FBI agents had visited Herb Goodwin, a Rising Tide activist who often worked with Yost, at his home in Bellingham, Washington, questioning him about another environmentalist group. Idaho anti-fracking activist Alma Hasse was jailed for a week without being charged after her questions at a public meeting annoyed members of a county commission.

Alexander Reid Ross, who had broken stories about the megaloads as a writer for *Earth First! Journal,* approached Dissent NewsWire in November with an idea for a story on government harassment of activists in Cascadia. Devoted to dissent and civil liberties news, Dissent NewsWire was started in 2014, but its publisher, the Defending Dissent Foundation, has a long history; it was founded in 1960 by Frank Wilkinson, a Los Angeles activist who'd helped organize a working-class Chicano neighborhood that was about to be evicted in order to build the Dodgers stadium. At the time, Wilkinson was about to go to prison for contempt of Congress: when the House Un-American Activities Committee asked him its perennial question—"Are you now or have you ever been a member of the Communist Party?"— he'd responded by taking the *First* Amendment instead of the Fifth.

We launched Dissent NewsWire to provide authoritative, comprehensive coverage of the repression of dissent in the United States. It complements our advocacy work by ensuring that stories of repression are made public. When you put it all together in one place— police cracking down on protesters of every stripe, the FBI infiltrating activist groups or harassing activists without any reasonable suspicion, and the government collecting data on everyone's phone calls, along with government secrecy and the war on whistleblowers—the scope of the problem is evident.

Udry passed Ross's query on to Dissent NewsWire editor Steven Wishnia. They both agreed it was a good story, but not yet ready for publication.

At the time, all we had was a couple of FBI visits, Alma Hasse's arrest, and a lot of background information on Green Scare. There was smoke there, but not enough solid information yet for us to go with it. We wanted to document more specific instances of government harassing activists.

We were working on the story for about a month when it seemed as though it had gone cold. Ross recalled frustratedly putting down his pen for a day or two when suddenly his friend Helen received the postmodern equivalent of a knock on the door.

The FBI phone calls and texts to Helen Yost gave the story the hook it needed. Ross reworked the article, and Wishnia and Udry combed the burrs out of the verbiage. Dissent NewsWire published it on January 5,

2015, under the headline "Why Is the FBI Harassing Activists in Cascadia?" Ross, using relationships he'd developed as both a journalist and an activist, got it reposted immediately by the *Ecologist*, CounterPunch, the Global Justice Ecology Project, GreenIstheNewRed.com, *Earth Island Journal*, and more.

Meanwhile, Yost had e-mailed Spokane *Spokesman-Review* reporter Becky Kramer in late December, trying to get her interested in doing a story. Kramer was interested enough to begin reporting it, but got "sidetracked" by the breaking news of a northern Idaho woman being fatally shot by her two-year-old son, who'd pulled her gun out of her purse.

Yost kept reminding her, sending her a copy of Ross's Dissent NewsWire article, and putting her in touch with Bellingham lawyer Lawrence Hildes, who in turn put her in touch with Herb Goodwin. Eventually Kramer got back on the story.

The *Spokesman-Review* article ran on January 23, 2015. It got picked up by the Associated Press, through which it was disseminated to Oregon Public Broadcasting, the *Houston Chronicle*, the *Washington Times*, and other newspapers around the nation. In early February, it got picked up by the Canadian Press news agency, which recast it with a more Canadian orientation. From there, it made its way to the Toronto-based *Globe and Mail* and other international sites.

Since the article was published, activists have not reported any additional FBI visits. "I haven't heard of any contact in at least the last month—at least since the story broke," Hildes, who has represented Northwestern environmental activists for twenty-five years, told Ross in February. "The FBI's only comment is 'We don't contact people unless there's a criminal investigation,' which they kept telling me there wasn't. I think at this point . . . they slunk back off into the corner they came out of."

It's a small victory, but we'll take it.

For more on the Defending Dissent Foundation and its Dissent NewsWire, see defendingdissent.org.

Follow the Earth First! Newswire at earthfirstjournal.org/newswire.

STEVEN WISHNIA is a New York–based journalist who has written extensively on civil liberties, housing, labor, and drug policy issues. Currently editor of Dissent NewsWire (defendingdissent.org), national reporter for LaborPress (laborpress.org), and editor of the New York City housing monthly *Tenant/Inquilino* (metcouncilonhousing.org), he has won two New York City Independent Press Association awards for his coverage of housing issues. His work has appeared in the *Nation, In These Times*, Daily Beast, AlterNet, *Salon*, the *Indypendent, Gothamist*, and numerous others, and he has worked as an editor at *High Times, PC Magazine*, and *Junior Scholastic*. He is also the author of two novels, *When the Drumming Stops* and *Exit 25 Utopia*, as well as *The Cannabis Companion*, and he coedited the anthology *Imagine: Living in a Socialist U.S.A.* Bassist in the 1980s punk band False Prophets, he still plays music quasi-professionally.

ALEXANDER REID ROSS, MA, is a cofounding moderator of the Earth First! Newswire. His master's thesis, "Politics and the People," and his latest book, *Against the Fascist Creep*, are both due out in 2015. He edited the anthology *Grabbing Back: Essays Against the Global Land Grab*, featuring Noam Chomsky and Vandana Shiva, and his work has been featured in the Cambridge University Strategic Initiative in Global Food Security, Climate and Capitalism, CounterPunch, Defending Dissent, the *Ecologist*, Green Social Thought, Third World Resurgence, Toward Freedom, and Upping the Anti. Updates and links to his writing can be found at alexanderreidross.com.

SUE UDRY, executive director of the Defending Dissent Foundation, won her high school's "Best Citizen" award in 1978 and has been working to earn that title ever since. She played a leadership role in her campus peace group, and after graduate school, she began knocking on doors in neighborhoods around the country as a canvasser for SANE, the Committee for a Sane Nuclear Policy, now Peace Action. Prior to joining the Defending Dissent Foundation, she served as the executive director of the Chicago Committee to Defend the Bill of Rights and as an organizer for the Coalition for New Priorities and the Day Care Action Council of Illinois. She was the legislative coordinator for United for Peace and Justice, a coalition of over 1,600 groups opposing the wars in Iraq and Afghanistan. Sue currently serves on the board of the National Coalition to Protect Civil Freedoms and the National Coalition to Protect Student Privacy, as well as the advisory board of the Charity and Security Network. She is a cofounder of the Montgomery County Civil Rights Coalition and treasurer of the Washington DC chapter of the National Lawyers Guild.

THE GOVERNMENT ACCOUNTABILITY PROJECT

Beatrice Edwards

Nearly forty years ago, the Institute for Policy Studies (IPS) created the Government Accountability Project (GAP) in response to whistleblowers such as Daniel Ellsberg, who approached IPS for help releasing the Pentagon Papers. In the years since then, as the US has privatized what were once basic public services and then deregulated the private sector, whistleblowers have come to be the last voice of the public interest in an increasingly secretive and undemocratic government/corporate complex.

Since 1977, GAP has grown to over twenty lawyers and investigators who work to promote occupational free speech. While protecting whistleblowers from retaliation, GAP helps them release crucial information that serves the public interest and the common good—information that, in the absence of whistleblowers, the public would never know.

Working through Congress, the courts, and the press, GAP has developed a method of exposing government and corporate secrets responsibly. We support our whistleblowing clients in creating an advocacy agenda surrounding their concerns, and developing, then implementing, broad whistleblower protection policy reforms both domestically and internationally. Over the course of the past thirty-eight years, we have represented over 5,000 whistleblowers and achieved highly public results.

In the aftermath of the Enron meltdown in 2001, GAP worked to include whistleblower protection provisions in the reform legislation known as Sarbanes-Oxley. Similarly, GAP ensured that the Dodd-Frank Wall Street reforms, adopted after the financial crisis of 2008 and 2009, included strong whistleblower protection provisions so that whistleblowers in banking would not have to fear reprisal if they reported illegal risk and trading by their employers.

Because of GAP's work with Congress, comprehensive whistleblower protections now apply to federal workers, private sector employees, and nearly all federal government contractors. In addition, food production facilities regulated by the Food and Drug Administration (FDA), manufacturing or retailing companies that make products regulated by the federal government, health insurance companies, airline and surface transportation companies, and any firms receiving federal stimulus funds are all obliged to afford their workers protection from retaliation should they lawfully disclose corruption, fraud, illegality, abuse of authority, or danger to the public health and safety.

In recent years, GAP has become especially active in protecting whistleblowers who disclose crimes and misdemeanors in the environmental sphere, where corporate and government secrecy intersect. For example, since 2001, we have brought to the world's attention White House efforts to allow oil lobbyists to rewrite scientific reports on climate change to make the government's own empirical research appear tentative and dubious. With a former client, the late whistle-blower Rick Piltz, GAP launched Climate Science Watch in 2005, and since then, CSW has become a compelling voice in opposing those who claim climate change is a hoax or not man-made. Our program has expanded to include scientists and policy makers who monitor and expose the contradiction between effective climate policy and accelerated fossil fuel development. Put simply, GAP and its environmental program whistleblowers highlight the collision course between current climate change mitigation efforts and overt efforts to expand fracking, tar-sands extraction, and deepwater oil drilling.

Of course, the intelligence community and the national security state are at the heart of government secrecy and overreach, and GAP is working there to secure whistleblower protections for both federal workers and intelligence community contractors. As unconstitutional government programs have obliged American taxpayers to fund the surveillance operations that illegally seized their private communications, we represent a group of National Security Agency (NSA) whistleblowers, including Edward Snowden. We are working to obtain legislative protection for national security whistleblowers that would allow them to mount a public interest defense when they are charged as criminals for exposing the clandestine corruption of the military–surveillance complex.

Deregulation has also become an increasingly serious issue in food production, especially as corporate food producers have successfully transferred routine food safety inspections to the industry itself. We are working with whistleblowers in poultry and hog production facilities to expose the dangers of high-speed meat inspection and the reality behind bogus "humane handling" claims. With guidance from whistleblowers, GAP is submitting targeted Freedom of Information Act requests to secure information about inadequate food safety safeguards and to publicize the documents that the government is forced to release.

Internationally, GAP has worked to secure and then strengthen whistleblower protection policies at intergovernmental organizations, where senior management typically operate beyond the reach of national legal systems. At the United Nations, the World Bank and the Inter-American Development Bank, where management enjoys legal immunities similar to those of the diplomatic corps, an atmosphere developed where fraud flourished, until staff members could claim protection from reprisal when they report illegality and abuse. High-level abuse of authority became routine in this climate, but guided by whistleblowers, GAP demonstrated that even the most influential senior officials could be held accountable. In May 2007, Paul Wolfowitz, then president of the World Bank, was attempting to engage the Bank in Iraq, in violation of institutional operating principles that prohibited projects in countries at war. Before he could reach this goal, however, Wolfowitz was forced to resign when whistleblowers helped GAP expose his personal corruption.

In 2015, although much has been accomplished to protect whistleblowers and reveal their disclosures, much remains to be done. As managers find it more difficult to retaliate in the face of stronger free speech rights in the workplace, they are increasing their use of a forceful new method of retribution: referring whistleblowers for criminal investigation and prosecution when they make what should be protected disclosures. Although most of these retaliatory criminal investigations find no wrongdoing by the whistleblower, the chilling effect is real. While under investigation, whistleblowers' reputations can be irreparably harmed and they can accumulate ruinous legal costs. To combat this form of career-wrecking reprisal, GAP is now promoting measures that provide whistleblowers with an affirmative defense to challenge criminal charges. As employees of conscience work to ensure that the public interest is protected, even behind the veil of government and corporate secrecy, GAP is actively working to establish that it must never be a crime to report a crime.

BEATRICE EDWARDS is the executive director and international program director of GAP. As executive director, she heads the organization's efforts to defend whistleblowers in Congress, the media, and the courts. She has thirty years' experience working on labor issues, anticorruption measures, and public-service reforms within both domestic and international frameworks. Bea is a previous contributing writer for the *Texas Observer*, and holds a master's degree in Latin American studies from the University of Texas and a PhD in sociology from American University.

NUCLEAR SAVAGE: THE ISLANDS OF SECRET PROJECT 4.1

Adam Jonas Horowitz

In early May 2013, I opened a bottle of champagne to celebrate the long delayed national broadcast of my documentary film, *Nuclear Savage: The Islands of Secret Project 4.1.* The Public Broadcasting Service (PBS) in the US announced in advertisements across the country that the film that I had written, directed, and produced, would be aired on May 28 by PBS flagship station WGBH's broadcast division World Channel, on PBS affiliate stations from New York to California.

PBS held exclusive US broadcast rights to the film, and by then had already had the finished film in its hands for more than a year and a half. PBS had already scheduled and then abruptly canceled another broadcast of the film in 2012, and I feared the film might be permanently shelved. So I was elated to see that the film had actually been advertised widely on the websites of individual PBS affiliate stations. My sister in California had seen large Web advertisements for my show on KQED San Francisco, and indeed I found similar advertisements on other PBS affiliate stations in California, Oregon, Washington, New Mexico, Vermont, and elsewhere. The broadcast was official, and it was public.

But on the advertised day and time, I switched on KNME, my local affiliate station, and the film was not there. It had been replaced by another program. The same thing had happened on KQED San Francisco, and all across the country. The broadcast had been killed, apparently from the top, without notice or explanation.

The reason for the cancellation was unstated but obvious. *Nuclear Savage* is "controversial"—the euphemism for telling an unpalatable and inconvenient truth in the mainstream media. The film tells the story of American Cold War nuclear testing in the Marshall Islands of the South Pacific, and how US government scientists deliberately exposed populations of local islanders to massive fallout radiation, in top secret human guinea pig experiments that lasted for more than three decades. The nuclear testing permanently contaminated dozens of islands, and resulted in deadly cancers and horrendous birth defects that continue to this day. It's a shocking tale of US government–sanctioned human rights abuse, and it's all true, proven by reams of declassified official government documents, direct survivor testimony, and formerly top secret motion picture films.

Nuclear Savage also reveals the devastating human impact of ongoing US nuclear and strategic missile testing in the Marshall Islands on Kwajalein Atoll, which the Pentagon has renamed Ronald Reagan Ballistic Missile Defense Test Site, a division of the US Army Space and Missile Defense Command/Army Forces Strategic Command.

Nuclear Savage was partially funded by PBS and the Corporation for Public Broadcasting's "Minority Consortia" member, Pacific Islanders in Communications (PIC), in exchange for exclusive US public media broadcast rights. The film was delivered to PIC in October 2011, the same month it had its world premiere at the Amsterdam International Documentary Film Festival, where it was nominated for Best Environmental Film. PIC immediately asked me for permission to cut the film down to fifty-six minutes specifically to meet "PBS broadcast standards," and I agreed to let them do the 35 percent content cut, on the condition that PBS could remove material, but could not add anything without my approval. The recut was completed under PIC's sole supervision using their own editor. To any reasonable observer, PBS now had a final version of the show that met their own specific editorial standards, because they alone supervised and produced the new fifty-six-minute version.

American Public Television (APT), another division of PBS, selected the film for their national series called "Pacific Heartbeat," but then asked me for narration changes, which they never sent, and instead decided to cancel *Nuclear Savage* from their series altogether. APT's final series lineup for that season included shows about hula dancing, Tonga, and one about Royal Hawaiian Music, but they had no place for the subject of Pacific Island human radiation experiments.

Since then, *Nuclear Savage* has become a hit on the international film festival circuit, and has received impressive reviews from numerous sources. *Chicago Tribune*'s Robert Koehler said it was "one of the most disturbing documentaries I have ever seen," and that it "does a stunning job juxtaposing our smug ignorance of South Sea culture with the reality of what we did to it." *Variety* writer Richard Kuipers said that the film was "highly charged and well assembled" and "assumes the

qualities of a detective thriller with massive moral and political implications. . . . Few will be left unmoved." *Variety* also wrote that "the TV-
hour version is sure to trigger discussion when broadcast on PBS in
2013."

The film went on to win top jury prizes and audience awards in
places such as Paris, Chicago, Rio de Janeiro, Tahiti, Berlin, and Mexico
City, and has now been screened in more than twenty-six countries.

Nuclear Savage was also screened by special invitation at the Film
Society of Lincoln Center in New York City, and in spring 2015 was
given an official screening at the United Nations' Dag Hammerskold
Auditorium at the United Nations Headquarters complex, hosted by the
UN Permanent Forum on Indigenous Issues, in conjunction with the
nuclear Non-Proliferation Treaty conference in New York in April 2015.

PBS was not impressed. PBS executive Cheryl Hirasa wrote to me:
"We all recognize the success the film has had (and still has) in festivals and the reception it's gotten from festival goers. Having said
that, the public television audience is quite a different animal. With
public television, viewers expect a high level of authenticity and trust
in regards to fair and balanced storytelling. . . . While this isn't a news
piece the same level of journalistic integrity is of the utmost importance."

While implying, or rather, stating, that *Nuclear Savage* lacks "journalistic integrity" and "authenticity," PBS has still not identified a
single fact or journalistic claim in this film that is wrong or incor-
rect. They promised the producer lists of "fact-check" issues after both
the APT broadcast cancellation in 2012, and the last-minute WGBH
World Channel cancellation in 2013, but they have never found or
identified a single questionable fact, let alone a list, in the three and
a half years that PBS has been suppressing the broadcast of this film.

In May 2013, PBS sent me a certified legal letter informing me that
Nuclear Savage failed to meet PBS's "minimum broadcast standards,"
and that I must now produce and deliver a twenty-six-minute version of
the film meeting those unwritten standards, within two months, or be
officially in "breach of contract," with various potentially damaging and
expensive implications. This proposed twenty-six-minute show would
be a 65 percent cut down from the original eighty-six-minute program.

I spoke by telephone with an experienced PBS documentary producer in San Francisco, who offered to "help" me with the situation by intervening with PBS. He was also a well-known distributor of environmental films, and knowing little more than this I initially trusted him. My trust was misplaced.

He spoke with PBS execs and told me that he got them to offer $15,000 to pay for the new proposed reedit of *Nuclear Savage*, under the condition that he act as "executive producer" of the new twenty-six-minute show, and he also said that he would oversee all aspects, including scripting and all actual editing, which he said must be done at his private postproduction facility near San Francisco.

This self-proclaimed "executive producer" also told me that he would "hire outside writers," under his supervision, to rewrite the narration and edit the script of the new show, and that I, who was the producer, writer, and director of the original eighty-six-minute show, would have essentially no oversight, participation, or payment whatsoever in this new, severely truncated version.

He told me that my show, and indeed PBS's own fifty-six-minute version, needed to be "sanitized," to remove any traces of "liberal bias," and he said repeatedly, "It is in your best interest to cooperate fully" with whatever he and PBS wanted. He warned me: "It's not wise to bite the hand that feeds you." There were other vague, and veiled, threats (or "recommendations," depending on your interpretation). I wondered if I was not actually dealing with a Joe Pesci gangster character from a Martin Scorsese movie. He proposed that I be paid a total of $250 as an "honorarium," for my symbolic role in the new recut and sanitization, and that he would keep, or spend, the rest of the $15,000 budget as he saw fit. He also proposed that his own company would receive the worldwide distribution rights to the new twenty-six-minute show.

In a telephone conference call between this "executive producer," a PBS executive, and me, I asked them both point-blank if the proposed, truncated twenty-six-minute show would be allowed to keep its basic premise: that the US had deliberately exposed people to radiation in order to study them, and had lied and covered this up. The "executive producer" replied, "Well, that's the 600-pound gorilla in the room."

No, that's the point and original premise of the film, which PBS funded twice, for production, and postproduction, based on this original premise, until executives changed their minds, even suppressing their own completed fifty-six-minute internally produced recut. The current PBS demand to sanitize and truncate the film yet again, under officially sanctioned threat of "breach of contract," reeks of both thuggery and coercion.

PBS's handling of *Nuclear Savage* is now being watched by various private attorneys, including civil rights and First Amendment lawyer and nationally recognized expert John Boyd, who wrote, "Whether you look at these events from the perspective of Horowitz's contractual rights or his civil rights or, for that matter, from the perspective of the public's abhorrence of censorship, PBS's behavior is pretty outrageous."

My experience with *Nuclear Savage* and PBS is not unique, and similar stories of censorship at that network have been leveled several times in recent years. *The New Yorker*'s Jane Mayer did a story in 2010, titled "Public Television's Attempts to Placate David Koch," and in 2014 the TV satirist Stephen Colbert did a brilliant send-up of PBS censorship and how the network has become "more and more dependent on viewers nothing like you." *Harper's* did a piece in October 2014 alleging widespread PBS corporate sellout and government censorship in the story "PBS Self-Destructs," and my own film, *Nuclear Savage*, was the subject of a detailed censorship exposé by the media watchdog group Fairness and Accuracy in Reporting (FAIR) in 2014. That story, by Lane Wollerton, is titled "Nuclear Stalemate: When will PBS air exposé on deadly Pacific Bomb Tests?"

The answer, sadly, seems to be never. PBS is not only suppressing the broadcast of *Nuclear Savage*, but the network is also attempting to restrict and censor my own free speech and public discussion of it. After the FAIR story, the PIC/PBS executive Leanne Ferrer wrote to me asking that I "Stop sicking reporters" [sic] on them.

The San Francisco "executive producer" that PBS demanded I hire in their new written contract told me to observe a "gag order" (his words) in dealing with any members of the press and media regarding this program, and told me to direct any media or reporter inquiries to him for comment. PBS executive Cheryl Hirasa wrote to me that "communication to the press about this particular situation should be simply expressed by letting them know that we are moving forward with continuing to find a home on public television—no more, no less." PBS's handling of both *Nuclear Savage* and me appears like episodes out of novels by Franz Kafka and George Orwell, or the real-life exploits of the infamous World War II propaganda minister Joseph Goebbels. I did not remotely expect this kind of behavior from officials of the US "public" media establishment.

In March 2015, I was watching an episode of *Nova*, the premier PBS science program, and the show began with narrated, actual sponsor commercials: "*Nova*. Brought to you by the David Koch Foundation, Boeing, Lockheed Martin, Sandia Nuclear Laboratories, Northrop Grumman, the US Department of Energy, and viewers like you!" These are the kingpins of the US military–industrial complex. You can't make this stuff up.

Remember that Boeing and Lockheed make the missiles and interceptor rockets tested at the Ronald Reagan Ballistic Missile Defense Test Site on Kwajalein Atoll, which the US government controls by military lease until at least the year 2086.

And remember, too, that the US Department of Energy is the same agency that built the sixty-seven nuclear bombs detonated in the Marshall Islands, and is the same agency that conceived and carried out the deadly and secret human-radiation experiments depicted in *Nuclear Savage*.

Is there really any question about why this film is having trouble getting a broadcast on PBS? In July 2015, PBS informed me that they had officially declined the film, meaning that they would neither try to make a twenty-six-minute version, nor ever show any version of the film at any length.

ADAM JONAS HOROWITZ is a conceptual artist, documentary filmmaker, and sculptor, who has focused much of his life work and career on ideas surrounding human rights, free speech, and the environment. His first feature documentary film, released in 1990, told the story of a Pacific Island chieftain who occupied lands at the top secret US Ronald Reagan Ballistic Missile Defense Test Site in the Marshall Islands for six months after the US lease expired. He is also the creator of Fridgehenge, a gigantic, satirical public art project and sculptural monument constructed (and reconstructed) in Santa Fe, New Mexico, between 1997 and 2007. At first approved and then later repeatedly damaged and finally destroyed by city government officials, Fridgehenge became a controversial and infamous conceptual anti-monument to a range of ideas about consumer society, hubris, and ultimately censorship. He received dual degrees in journalism and humanities at the University of California, Berkeley, and currently resides in Santa Fe, New Mexico.

FREEDOM OF MEDIA, POST-FUKUSHIMA

Ian Thomas Ash

Has the increasingly polarized debate over nuclear energy led private distributors of documentary media in Japan to embrace self-censorship? This is the question I am left asking myself following the recent cancellations of all domestic screenings of my film *A2-B-C* (2013, Japan), which documents the health of children living in contaminated areas of Fukushima following the nuclear meltdown on March 11, 2011.

A2-B-C is the second film in my series about children living in Fukushima, following *In the Grey Zone* (2012, Japan), which documented children living within twenty to thirty kilometers (twelve to eighteen miles) of the damaged power plant, just one month after the nuclear meltdown. While *In the Grey Zone* depicts parents' fears about potential health consequences for their children, *A2-B-C*, filmed just eighteen months later, documents an increase in nosebleeds as well as thyroid cysts and nodules in the children living in these areas.

Domestic Distribution and Protecting Families Who Speak Out

Sensing it would be difficult to find a distributor in Japan that would take on a film documenting mothers speaking out against the government's claims that children living in contaminated areas are not in danger, I decided to try "reverse importing," gaining attention for something abroad with the aim of eventually bringing it back to the country of origin. My goal was to make *A2-B-C* so recognized abroad that the problems it documented could no longer be ignored in Japan.

After receiving the top prize in the Nippon Vision category at the film's world premiere in the Nippon Connection Film Festival in Frankfurt, Germany, in 2013, *A2-B-C* went on to screen in more than twenty-five festivals around the world, receiving multiple awards along the way. My idea to "reverse import" worked, and in autumn 2013, the rights to distribute the film in Japan were acquired by a Japanese company on behalf of a newly formed group called the *A2-B-C* Screening Committee.

Working to secure a theatrical release in Japan, the committee met with several cinema programmers in Tokyo but were told that, although as private citizens the programmers felt the film needed to be screened, as business owners they could not handle a film that was perceived as being so controversial. The committee then turned to smaller art house cinemas, and beginning in May 2014, a countrywide theatrical release of the film began in Tokyo, eventually moving on to nine cities in Japan.

At the request of the families who appeared in *A2-B-C*, I had agreed the film would not be uploaded to the Internet and a DVD would not be released in Japan. This was to protect them as much as possible from becoming the targets of harsh criticism for having spoken out in a country where, as the expression goes, "the nail that sticks up gets hammered down." Already the recipients of cruel bashing and Internet bullying by often-anonymous attackers, the families would be exposed to even more criticism, potentially leading to a concern for their safety, if the film were to be released online.

Japan's Secrecy Law

As is customary in Japan following the theatrical release of a film, a series of "private screenings," a process by which citizen groups can rent the film and organize their own screenings, was held. In the six months following the theatrical release, there were over eighty private screenings of the film held across Japan, and importantly, these screenings provided a significant revenue source for the screening committee, which served as an incentive to help keep the film off the Internet, thereby protecting the families to a greater degree.

After nearly a year of screening the film, in March 2015, during the week to mark the March 11 disaster's fourth anniversary, the company advising the *A2-B-C* Screening Committee suddenly pulled its support for the distribution of the film and abruptly canceled all domestic screenings of the film, including dozens of confirmed contracts for private screenings and those in consideration. This was followed a week later by the dissolution of the *A2-B-C* Screening Committee. In a blog post that went on to be widely shared on social media, I suggested that this was an act of self-censorship possibly influenced by the Designated Secrets Bill.

Also known as the Secrecy Law, the Designated Secrets Bill grants the Japanese government the power to arrest, imprison, and/or fine anyone accused of revealing "state secrets." While ostensibly to protect issues deemed to be of national security, the Japanese government's intentions were called into question when it used cases of whistleblowing abroad as examples of why such a law was needed.

During the debate before the bill was passed into law, opposition lawmaker Mizuho Fukushima, concerned with the vague definition of what would be considered secret, asked the lawmakers in the ruling party for clarification. "What is considered secret," she was told, "is secret."

With my recent filming being almost exclusively about Fukushima, I began to wonder if work like mine—interviewing doctors in Fukushima, collecting data, and recording testimonies—would be considered a "state secret."

Screenings of A2-B-C Canceled Due to Accusation of Violent Far-Left Extremism

Following the cancellations of all the screenings of A2-B-C in Japan, rumors circulated, including the suggestion that the topic of the health of children in Fukushima was "taboo." While a reason such as this would be understandable although still objectionable, the real reason is simply unbelievable: the company advising the A2-B-C Screening Committee canceled all screenings of the film after hearing a rumor that one of the mothers appearing in the film speaking out about her fears for the health of children in Fukushima is a violent extremist tied to a communist political group. The medical clinic where the thyroid examinations of children are carried out in the film was also said to be tied to this group, whose tactics in the past have included confrontations with the authorities.

It should be noted that in Japan the two main accusations that are hurled at someone to discredit them are that they are either ethnically Korean or communist. Accusing someone speaking out of being a communist is a rhetoric often employed in Japan when no other logical explanation can be found.

The mere rumors of a connection to communism proved to be

more powerful than money and resulted in the cancellation of the distribution of the film when the *A2-B-C* Screening Committee willfully chose to turn down guaranteed-profit private screenings rather than make any attempt to clarify or confirm the accusations.

Whether a member of a communist political group appears in *A2-B-C* should be discussed, as well as why this group may have established in Fukushima a medical clinic offering independent testing of children for radiation-related health issues. This is something that should be debated, not hidden. But it seems that the fate of my film is in the hands of people who can look at a scene of a child receiving a thyroid examination following a nuclear meltdown and still attempt to turn the focus onto the rumored political views of that child's mother.

Self-Censorship and Fukushima

During my work on the follow-up to *A2-B-C*, I have been finding it extremely difficult to meet people who are willing to be filmed speaking out. One woman I met told me that she would formerly share and "like" her friends' Facebook posts about radiation issues, but that since the Secrecy Law has come into effect she has been afraid of being identified as antinuclear, and thus no longer shares or "likes" posts about Fukushima.

At a press conference before the Secrecy Law was passed, independent lawmaker Taro Yamamoto expressed his disbelief at the lack of media coverage that the proposed bill was receiving. "By not providing coverage of this bill," Yamamoto said, "the media is putting a noose around its own neck." Sadly, his prediction appears to be coming true.

It is not clear to me how much of the decision to cancel the screenings of *A2-B-C* was the result of actual censorship and how much was simply self-censorship. My feeling is that it is self-censorship based on the fear of a potential censorship problem at some point in the future. If this is the case, then it is an example of the terrifying and wide-reaching effect of the Secrecy Law. This law does not even need to be enforced for its effect to be felt: its mere existence causes people to engage in self-censorship, imposing on themselves the very crackdown that the drafters of the legislation surely envisioned.

It seems it is no longer possible to have honest, open discussions and debates about what is happening in Fukushima, and the cancellation of all domestic screenings of *A2-B-C* is merely the symptom of a disease that has infected free speech in Japan.

An Unresolved Ending

The mothers in *A2-B-C* are not violent extremists, and the clinic is not a terrorist staging ground. But if they are allowed to be convicted in a court of public opinion based solely on rumor and innuendo, and my film is discredited by association, then the single most important issue that we should be focusing on will have been overlooked: the health and the future of children living in areas contaminated by radiation.

If our actions contribute to a climate of fear and the suppression of free speech, it will not be the extremists, whether they are left or right, that we defeat, but rather it will be ourselves.

References

Ian Thomas Ash, "Can You Keep a Secret?," *Documenting Ian Blog*, November 15, 2013, http://ianthomasash.blogspot.jp/2013/11/can-you-keep-secret.html.

Ian Thomas Ash, "Interpreting Secrets," *Documenting Ian Blog*, March 12, 2014, http://ianthomasash.blogspot.jp/2014/03/interpreting-secrets.html.

Ian Thomas Ash, "Censorship? Self-Censorship?," *Documenting Ian Blog*, March 14, 2015, http://ianthomasash.blogspot.jp/2015/03/censorship-self-censorship.html.

Ian Thomas Ash, "'A2-B-C' Screening Committee Dissolved," *Documenting Ian Blog*, March 23, 2015, http://ianthomasash.blogspot.jp/2015/03/a2-b-c-screening-committee-dissolved.html.

Born in New York, filmmaker IAN THOMAS ASH is the director of the Japanese feature documentaries *In the Grey Zone* (2012), *A2-B-C* (2013), and *-1287* (2014). He is currently in postproduction for *MSM*, about male sex workers in Tokyo, and in production for his third feature documentary about children living in Fukushima. Both films are scheduled for release in 2016. More information about his documentaries can be found on his website, DocumentingIan.com.

FROM A WOMAN'S POINT OF VIEW—WMNF

Mary Glenney and Arlene Engelhardt

We host a weekly radio show, *From a Woman's Point of View*, on WMNF, in Tampa, Florida. We have hosted the show for nearly twenty years. WMNF is a community radio station that allows programmers tremendous freedom as long as they adhere to the station's mission—giving voice to the voiceless and supporting social justice and equality. We could say that the show is of and about women, but that is pretty trite and meaningless. Hillary Clinton stated the obvious twenty years ago in Beijing when she said, "Human rights are women's rights—and women's rights are human rights." If one has to state the obvious, it gives an idea of the focus of our show.

We feel that in the media women's voices are not heard and their expertise not valued. Why? If you listened to our show you would be aware of the competency and brilliance of our guests—all women. We cover the gamut of issues of concern to us all: the environment, climate change, toxins, militarism, the economy, equality, and violence against women—and we never have problems getting qualified guests. Unfortunately, we rarely see or hear them on major media.

One example is Sandra Steingraber. She has been a major fighter for environmental issues for years. We hope you are familiar with her and her work. She has been a guest on our show many times. We remember our first interview with Sandra—we were talking about long-standing toxins and heavy metals in children. Sandra mentioned lead, and she told us that she was a lover of old books and would thumb through them in used bookstores. She happened to see a copy of the tenth edition of *Holt's Diseases of Infancy and Childhood*, published in 1936. She picked it up and opened it to the page describing the symptoms of lead poisoning in children. There, she said, she clearly saw the list of the symptoms—the doctors were well aware of them then. Sandra told us that the levels of lead in children's bodies did not change markedly until the federal government passed laws in 1973 regulating the exposure of children to lead in paints, etc. Sandra concluded by saying, "I cannot be a HEPA filter for my children." And I think that is one of the reasons that women are not heard as commonly as men. Women such as Sandra are not only the scientists, but they are also not afraid to talk about that science in the context of the real world of their children.

Helen Caldicott also comes to mind. She was a young emergency room pediatrician when president Ronald Reagan asked all the emergency rooms in the country to prepare contingency plans for the US in the event of a nuclear attack. While the other doctors got busy on the plans, Helen said it was impossible—we cannot have contingency plans for a nuclear attack, we have to prevent it. Helen is still fighting nuclear power and weapons. Helen told us that when her grandbabies ask why the world didn't do something about this, Helen said she could look them in the eyes and say, "I tried, I tried." In the 1970s, she gave new life to Physicians for Social Responsibility.

Women have been at the foreground in these battles and we have been fortunate to have interviewed them as guests on our show. Jodi Williams has fought land mines; Medea Benjamin, drones; and on and on. Women speak truth to power because, among many reasons, they know the future depends on it. They do not avoid the searching eyes of their children.

Let's explore militarism a little more. Most of us are aware of the excessive use of militarism and power. We know that you can't bring peace with the barrel of a gun and yet how many of us speak out? How many of us give peace a chance? Many, many women historically have had the courage to stand up against war, endangering their lives to build bridges to peace. There are almost too many to count, yet how many do you know? They spoke out not only because they were tender hearted. They saw the carnage for what it was and had the courage to define it.

We are all aware of the Nobel Peace Prize, which, incidentally, very few women have received. But do you know anything about its history? Alfred Nobel was a chemist, engineer, inventor, and armaments manufacturer. He developed dynamite, which was used in war. To use part of his fortune to fund prizes in chemistry, physics, and medicine was obvious, but why the Peace Prize? Guilt that his inventions were immediately used for war? What most of us do not know is that he had a close friendship with Bertha von Suttner, a peace activist who argued that his inventions would make peace impossible. Nobel believed that nations that felt secure would not need to make war, but Bertha felt the opposite. Nobel and von Suttner corresponded for years and there is little doubt that she had great influence on his creation of the Peace Prize. Do you think that if there had been more emphasis on her views, we might have a world that is less in need of awards, one with a more deeply ingrained sense of justice? Baroness von Suttner was the first woman to receive the Nobel Peace Prize.

Let's look at another area, the economy. We have all played Monopoly. Did you learn anything about monopolies and trusts and trying to keep out of jail while playing this game? And did you know that Monopoly was actually invented by Elizabeth Magie and not Charles Darrow, who sold it to the Parker Brothers? Magie was born in 1866 and was a stenographer with a passion for politics and inventing. She lived in the Gilded Age in which the excesses of the privileged were as obvious as they are today. Elizabeth hoped that from the game people could learn something about slumlords, monopolies, trusts, and the whole sense of capital, with spaces on the board for rental properties, electricity, water, etc. Players earned wages, paid taxes, and the players who did well were the ones who could foil the attempts of the wealthy to send them to the poorhouse or to jail. Wouldn't it have been interesting to have known more about Elizabeth Magie's ideas?

So with the show *From a Woman's Point of View* we make the effort—not to bring Elizabeth Magie, but to broadcast women of today. We feel they are brilliant, passionate, funny, and truly necessary visionaries. We do not feel that women are any more brilliant or visionary than men—we do not see women as morally superior or more altruistic. We do not believe in genetic or biological superiority or inferiority. But none of us lives in a vacuum. We are all shaped in the social, psychological, and cultural milieu of our times, and those conditions have made women, in large measures, outsiders. This has disadvantaged women in positions of power, but we believe it has also given them unique perspectives as outsiders. Not a detached outsider, but the passionate, caring, intelligent observer of the familiar. Particularly at this time in our history, we need the genius and brilliance of many of those "outsiders."

MARY GLENNEY is cohost and principal interviewer on *From a Woman's Point of View* on WMNF, a well-known community radio station in Tampa, Florida. She began doing a segment called "Life Choices" on the show more than twenty years ago and within two years became the cohost. She spent much of her life doing research and writing about genetics. Mary has an MD degree from the University of Illinois. She has been an activist most of her life, focusing on the environment, politics, social justice, and equality for women and minorities.

ARLENE ENGELHARDT is also cohost of *From a Woman's Point of View* on WMNF. She was president of the board of directors at WMNF during the station's capital campaign and construction of their new facility. Previously, Arlene was the executive director of the Pacifica Radio network, directly supervising the national office, five stations, the archives, and the affiliates. Prior to that she was vice president of a multimedia publishing company. She has a Bachelor of Arts degree from the University of Illinois. She, too, has been an activist most of her life, focusing on the environment, politics, social justice, and equality for women and minorities.

THE MALE GAZE AND ITS IMPACT ON GENDER PORTRAYALS IN MEDIA

Crystal Bedford, Lisa Davis, Darian Edelman, Lauren Freeman,
and Ellie Kim

Celebrations filled the halls of Congress and cities across America in 1868 as the Fourteenth Amendment to the US Constitution was ratified. The centuries-long struggle of African-Americans and the decades-long struggle of abolitionists had led to this moment. The amendment provided citizenship status to black men in the US. Many of the abolitionists who made this day possible had been women. Many of those same women assumed that they would enjoy the sweet taste of equality with their African-American brothers and sisters. However, female activists were shocked that the Fourteenth Amendment only guaranteed citizenship rights for males. In fact, it was the first time the word *male* appeared in the Constitution. Women had been integral to the success of the abolitionist movement. The lack of rights granted to women created a bitter divide between abolitionists and advocates for women's rights that worsened when the Fifteenth Amendment only guaranteed voting rights for males. In response, longtime abolitionists and women's rights activists such as Susan B. Anthony and Elizabeth Cady Stanton turned to anti-abolitionists to fund their movement for gender equality.[3]

In 2015, debate over gender equality in the US continues. At the 2015 Oscars, Patricia Arquette echoed history by explaining that it was time for "all the gay people and people of color that we've all fought for to fight for us [women] now." This immediately created friction, as supporters of LGBT and racial equality argued that Arquette was incorrectly assuming that they owe white women anything.[4] The lack of context for Arquette's comments, such as women's central role in most social movements in US history, contributes to the coverage women receive. However, by disingenuously representing women and their rights, the corporate press also plays an influential role.

In our study, which this article previews, we argue that the corporate press is operated by and for the interests of men. Despite males making up only half the population, 97 percent of media outlets are male owned and 64 percent of journalists are men.[5] Scholars have argued that this inevitably produces a patriarchal dominant view of media, known as the male gaze theory.

The Male Gaze Theory in Media

The central concept in our study is male gaze theory, which posits that, because men control the creation of media, media messages are dominated by a male point of view. The CEOs of the six companies that own 90 percent of media are all white males.[6] Those same corporations are also heavily invested in the entertainment industry. Thus, male gaze theory argues that, with men controlling the media and entertainment industries, women are the passive objects of the gaze.[7] Although originally applied to narrative cinema, this article postulates that the male gaze is present in all forms of contemporary media, including the music and news industries, in which women are objectified and sexualized.

Even when women are given positions of power within male-dominated media organizations, they face pressure to maintain narratives constructed on the basis of the male gaze. Men outpace women in every news media position, making up two-thirds of newsrooms, and consistently hiring and sourcing men more often than women.[8] The saturation of the male gaze in corporate media ensures that women who attain power are met with multifaceted resistance. For example, in an attempt to break the male-dominated landscape, NBC News chair Patricia Fili-Krushel hired Deborah Turness as president of NBC News.[9] Yet as the first woman to hold the position, Turness wielded less power than previous presidents and experienced conflicts with anchors Matt Lauer and Brian Williams, including Lauer dictating network decisions to Turness.[10] The incident suggested that men dominate media even when women are seemingly given power to direct it.

Studying the Impacts

This study examines the impact of the male gaze on media representations of women and women's issues. The study argues that the male-dominated media environment contributes to misleading depictions of feminism and women in coverage of sexual violence, race, and politics, as well as in the entertainment industries, including music and film. These distorted representations leave the public uninformed, or misinformed, about crucial topics such as sexual assault as well as the roles of female artists, professionals, and politicians. Thus, the public is unaware of, insensitive to, and unresponsive to the many issues that impact women's lives.

These findings are important because the corporate media not only inform the public about current events, but also help shape the values and realities shared by the public. Since the corporate for-profit model and white male influence dominate news and entertainment, it is these interests and messages that are packaged for public consumption. In turn the skewed frames constructed by corporate media limit what women can and cannot do in American society, due in part to the perception of women that results from such framing. However, history shows that women of all types have been integral in the major social advancements of human beings, around the world and in the US. Thus, a strong movement comprised of diverse women needs to undermine and eliminate the dominant influence of the white male gaze. What is in the best interest of people in general, and women specifically, is for the public to be informed about the issues that concern women, without a male filter on that information. Women number slightly more than half of US society. If their concerns are not heard, how can the US call itself a free and equal nation?

The full version of this report is available online at http://www. projectcensored.org/male-gaze-and-its-impact-on-gender-portrayals-in-media.

The authors would like to acknowledge the editorial assistance of professors Laura Wing, Nolan Higdon, and Mickey Huff.

CRYSTAL BEDFORD is completing a Transfer Associate of Science degree in mathematics at Diablo Valley College while in the process of transferring to UC Davis as an economics major. She is the current president of DVC's Project Censored Club.

LISA DAVIS is completing her Bachelor of Arts in political, legal, and economic analysis at Mills College. Her research interests include the intersectionality of race and gender issues in the American education system.

DARIAN EDELMAN is transferring from Diablo Valley College and will be working toward a Bachelor of Arts in political science at the University of California, Berkeley, in Fall 2015. She plans to eventually attend law school in order to fight for environmental rights.

LAUREN FREEMAN is a student at Las Positas College in Livermore, California.

ELLIE KIM is an intern with Project Censored and a junior at Reed College. She is the student club officer for the Global Critical Media Literacy Project, a subset of Project Censored and Action Coalition for Media Education (ACME).

RACE FORWARD: THE CENTER FOR RACIAL JUSTICE INNOVATION

Jyarland Daniels and Rebekah Spicuglia

We Are: The Center for Racial Justice Innovation

Race has played and still plays a significant role in our country's political conversation. Although our country has made progress, there is still so much work to be done. Now more than ever, we need to be explicit about race, have productive conversations, and come up with systemic solutions to create positive and lasting change. Too often our national conversations about race focus on individual actions and identifying who is a racist, or who is not. Race Forward is unique in that we offer a systemic perspective to move the conversation on race forward, in a multiracial, multi-issue, intergenerational way.

Since 1981, Race Forward has brought a systemic analysis and an innovative approach to complex race issues to help people take effective action toward racial equity. We envision a vibrant world in which people of all races create, share, and enjoy resources and relationships equitably, unleashing individual potential, embracing collective responsibility, and generating global prosperity. We define racial justice as the systemic fair treatment of people of all races, resulting in equitable opportunities and outcomes for all.

We work to advance racial justice in several ways—media, research, and practice. *Colorlines* is an award-winning daily news site, published by Race Forward (see colorlines.com). Our research is cutting-edge, original, and broadly accessible on pressing racial justice issues. We present Facing Race, the country's largest multiracial conference on racial justice, and offer training on racial justice within our Racial Justice Leadership Institute.

We Are: Committed to the Racial Justice Movement

There are many ideas about what makes a movement. We believe that a movement doesn't necessarily begin with us, but it is about using the resources we have to bring people together to advance a common cause.

One example of our movement work was the Drop the I-Word Campaign, launched in September 2010, which sought to eliminate the widespread usage of the inhumane and derogatory word *illegal* in reference to immigrants, because of the link between racially charged language and racially unjust policies.[11] By Spring 2013, the Associated Press, *USA Today*, the *Los Angeles Times*, *San Francisco Chronicle*, and many other news outlets dropped the I-Word, affecting millions of readers daily nationwide. Drop the I-Word continues to advocate for change at the *New York Times*, the *Washington Post*, and media outlets everywhere. This movement has been successful because it engaged and enlisted others, to whom we provided tools and resources for them to use within their communities. Due to the collective efforts of so many individuals, Race Forward was able to influence how the media, one of our most powerful institutions, talk about individuals who are undocumented, and how to do so in a way that centers on their humanity and leadership.

Another example of our movement work is Life Cycles of Inequity: A *Colorlines* Series on Black Men.[12] Using the power of storytelling, investigative reporting, and the voices of those impacted by structures and systems, Race Forward and *Colorlines* helped change the narrative on black men. Throughout seven installments of articles, videos, and photo essays, the series explored the ways in which inequity impacts the lives of black men. Each installment focused on different life stages or events, from school discipline to fatherhood and employment. Our strength in investigative reporting and storytelling provided us with the tools to support the movement for racial justice in changing the narrative about black men during a time when honest and humane discussion around people of color is more necessary than ever. The series was especially timely due to events such as those in Ferguson and Baltimore, which, sadly, continue to happen every day.

We also contribute to the movement by bringing those who are committed to this work together to learn, grow, share their experiences, and strengthen their skills. Our largest ongoing contribution to the racial justice movement is Facing Race. Facing Race is the largest multiracial and intergenerational national conference on race, where nearly 2,000 people from multiple countries and continents, convene. This biennial conference is a unique collaborative space for racial justice movement making, featuring talks, panels, workshops, films, and performances by established and rising leaders in the racial justice arena. It brings together advocates, students, academics, journalists, community organizers, and artists.

At Race Forward, we support advocacy and action on complex racial justice issues in several ways. Our work includes mobilization, skill-building, leadership development, organization- and alliance-building, issue framing, messaging, and advancing solutions. Through the Race Forward Racial Justice Leadership Action Network, we provide targeted online and in-person training and consulting services in these areas. We also provide a team of seasoned speakers who can address public audiences on a range of racial justice issues.

We Are: Leaders with a Systemic Approach

A key component to a systemic approach is reframing the conversation on race. In 2014, Race Forward conducted a comprehensive analysis of media coverage in over 1,200 articles and transcripts in a variety of topic areas seeking to identify the extent to which media coverage was "systemically aware," meaning the coverage highlighted policies and practices that lead to racial disparities. The findings were released in "Moving the Race Conversation Forward," a multipart report that describes some of the major impediments to racial discourse in the United States, and profiles initiatives that can make racial discourse more productive.[13]

Continuing to serve as a resource to media, we released "The Race Forward Media Reference Guide" to serve as an accessible and concise tool for journalists and thought leaders in the United States who talk and write about race, racism, and racial justice. Our Media Reference Guide aims to provide critical support for the use of responsible language and story framing that reflects our most basic values and affirms the dignity and human rights of people of all races.

Racial justice work is necessary to continue the efforts to make our democracy live up to its promise. However, this work cannot only be done by people of color, it cannot only be done by racial justice organizations, it cannot only be done by those in positions of power or authority. The work of racial justice is important for all of us; therefore all of us must engage in it.

To learn more about Race Forward's mission to advance racial justice through research, media, and practice, see raceforward.org.

JYARLAND DANIELS is director of marketing and communications at Race Forward, where she is responsible for all branding and communication initiatives. Prior to her work at Race Forward she held senior positions in marketing and public relations at several major corporations. She holds a Master of Business Administration degree from the University of Michigan and a law degree from Wayne State University in Detroit.

REBEKAH SPICUGLIA is Race Forward's senior communications manager. She has worked previously as media and programs director at the Women's Media Center, and as a Media Field Strategy Fellow at GLAAD. Spicuglia has a background in film, a Bachelor of Arts degree in mass communications from University of California, Berkeley, and has dedicated herself to solutions-focused media advocacy that lifts up underrepresented voices and challenges systemic inequities.

Notes

1. Eduardo Galeano, "In Defence of the Word," *Index on Censorship* 6, no. 4 (July 1977): 15–20, quote at 19.
2. Peter Phillips, DaveyD, Marc Sapir, and Project Censored, "Media Democracy in Action," in *Censored 2004*, ed. Peter Phillips and Project Censored (New York: Seven Stories Press, 2003), 181–217, quotes at 181.
3. "Debating Conflicting Rights, United States, 1867–69," Women in World History Curriculum, 2013, http://www.womeninworldhistory.com/TWR-16.html; Christine Stansell, *The Feminist Promise: 1792 to the Present* (New York: Random House, 2010).
4. Kay Steiger, "Patricia Arquette Calls For Wage Equality During The Oscars," *ThinkProgress*, February 22, 2015, http://thinkprogress.org/culture/2015/02/22/3625691/patricia-arquette-calls-wage-equality-oscars.
5. "The Status of Women in the U.S. Media 2014," Women's Media Center, 2014, http://www.womensmediacenter.com/pages/2014-statistics.
6. Ashley Lutz, "These 6 Corporations Control 90% of the Media in America," *Business Insider*, June 14, 2012, http://www.businessinsider.com/these-6-corporations-control-90-of-the-media-in-america-2012-6. The CEOs include Comcast's Brian L. Roberts, NBC's Jeff Zucker, News Corporation's Rupert Murdoch, Disney's Bob Iger, CBS's Leslie Moonves, Time Warner's Robert D. Marcus, and Viacom's Philippe Dauman.
7. Laura Mulvey, "Visual Pleasure and Narrative Cinema," *Screen* 16, no. 3 (Autumn 1975).
8. Women's Media Center, "The Status of Women in the U. S. Media 2014."
9. Gabriel Sherman, "(Actually) True War Stories at NBC News," *Daily Intelligencer*, March 8, 2015, http://nymag.com/daily/intelligencer/2015/03/nbc-news-brian-williams-deborah-turness.html.
10. Ibid.
11. "Drop the I-Word," *Colorlines*, http://www.colorlines.com/droptheiword.
12. Kai Wright, "Life Cycles of Inequity: A Colorlines Series on Black Men," *Colorlines*, May 11, 2014, http://www.colorlines.com/articles/life-cycles-inequity-colorlines-series-black-men-0.
13. "Moving the Race Conversation Forward," *Colorlines*, January 22, 2104, https://www.raceforward.org/research/reports/moving-race-conversation-forward.

CHAPTER 5

A Vision for Transformative Civic Engagement
The Global Critical Media Literacy Project

Julie Frechette, Nolan Higdon, and Rob Williams

In September 2015, two long-standing media organizations, Project Censored and Action Coalition for Media Education (ACME), will be launching the Global Critical Media Literacy Project (GCMLP). The project is the first of its kind in its use of a service-learning-based media literacy education model to teach digital media literacy and critical thinking skills, as well as to raise awareness about corporate and state-engineered news media censorship around the world. The goal of the GCMLP is to create more equitable democratic and economic participation in our twenty-first–century public spheres.

THE NEED FOR THE GCMLP

We are now a networked global society, one in which key social activities and structures are organized around digital information networks. This shift has altered the skills required for economic and democratic participation in the twenty-first century. Currently, 70 percent of jobs in the United States require specialized knowledge and skills, up from only 5 percent at the start of the last century. Twenty-first–century jobs often require skills that are vital and that many see as attainable mostly through colleges and universities, such as the ability to design, evaluate, and manage one's own work; frame, investigate, and solve problems using a wide range of tools and resources; collaborate strategically with others; communicate effectively in many forms (i.e., multiple platforms); find, analyze, and use information for multiple and often overlapping purposes; and develop new products and ideas. Further, the type of work and skill sets needed in the twenty-first century will likely change rapidly. In fact, although the top three-quarters of job fields with the fastest growth require postsecondary education, the US has dropped from first in the world to sixteenth in college participation.[1]

With the arrival of Web 2.0, the potential emergence of Web 3.0 (the "Internet of Things"), the rise of new digital and social media platforms, and the ubiquity of mobile forms of communication technology, changes in how democracy operates in the US and around the world are happening at a rapid pace. However, students are not being trained to navigate and participate in this new digital democracy in part due to a deficit in media literacy education. In 2012, a *Journal of Personality and Social Psychology* study found that when compared to previous generations, the millennials (the generation born between 1982 and 2004) are less civically engaged than their predecessors. The article defines civic engagement as having an "interest in social problems, political participation, trust in government, taking action to help the environment and save energy."[2]

Indeed, most students are unaware of how to participate in the democratic process. Fewer than 20 percent of states in the United States mandate civics testing in order to graduate high school.[3] As a result, most young citizens get their understanding of the democratic process from the "news." This "news" comprises a series of programming, 90 percent of which is controlled by six US-based transnational corporations.[4] Concentrated ownership creates a host of problems: lack of diversity, as well as a lack of equity in perspectives. Not only are millennials receiving from corporate-owned media an increasingly homogenous, limited, and ethnocentric version of news and the world, they are not being trained to recognize this slant or to understand its impact, particularly when these are normalized through a process that labels hegemonic media values as the "mainstream."[5] Developing and spreading critical media literacy skills among this population is one antidote to these challenges.

OUR NETWORKED "TRUTH EMERGENCY"

Recent data suggest a "truth emergency"—we live and work in a world in which really vital news stories that shape our future are routinely downplayed, misreported, or ignored altogether.[6] As a result, millennial-era voters are widely uninformed, misinformed, and disinformed about political happenings. The press is supposed to be the institution that prevents the public from being uninformed or misinformed by providing them with transparently sourced, fact-based information. However, the US corporate press consistently engages in disinformation campaigns. Disinformation is a form of propaganda disseminated by world leaders and media outlets, with an aim to plant false ideas in the public discourse to fulfill an ulterior motive.

Since the latter part of the twentieth century, authors including Neil Postman, Edward S. Herman and Noam Chomsky, Morris Berman, and Chris Hedges have documented Americans' dismal political and social knowledge.[7] A 2012 Pew Research study found that Americans were largely *uninformed* about basic civil issues concerning the nation. For example, just half of those polled knew that the Republican Party's platform supports "reducing the size and scope of the federal government." This has been a basic foundation of the Republican platform for decades.[8] Similarly, polls in 2010 showed a slew of American voters were *misinformed*. High numbers of those polled believed the following falsehoods: the stimulus legislation lost jobs (91 percent), health reform will increase the deficit (72 percent), income taxes increased under President Barack Obama (49 percent), stimulus legislation did not include any tax cuts (63 percent), and President Obama was not born in the United States (63 percent).[9] That the facts contradict these views demonstrates that US citizens misunderstand some of the most important issues facing the US.

In addition to the problem of uninformed and misinformed citizens, a large contingent of US citizens are *disinformed*. The corporate press largely acts as a vehicle to disinform the public in service of its funders, the funders' political allies, and all of their interests. For example, the 2003 US invasion of Iraq was in large part supported by the public based on the corporate media's disinformation campaign. The corporate media falsified information concerning Iraq in order to produce public approval for war.[10] The war produced massive profits for defense industries and increased political capital for the politicians who supported intervention.[11]

How did the media convince the public to support the war? A Fairness and Accuracy in Reporting (FAIR) study found that, in the weeks leading up to the war, "Nearly two thirds of all [news] sources, 64 percent, were pro-war, while 71 percent of U.S. guests favored the war. Anti-war voices were 10 percent of all sources. . . . Thus viewers were more than six times as likely to see a pro-war source as one who was anti-war."[12] The FAIR study's findings matched the resulting public opinion. Sixty-eight percent of US citizens supported the war under the false pretense that Iraq had weapons of mass destruction (WMDs).[13] By a ratio of twenty-five to one, the vast majority of US news media commentators and guests proclaimed the presence of WMDs in Iraq.[14] By 2005, the Central Intelligence Agency (CIA) had admitted there were no WMDs in Iraq, but by then the war had already begun, taking thousands of US lives and over one million Iraqi lives.[15]

The lies perpetrated by the media took on a life of their own. For example, three years after the invasion of Iraq and a full year after the CIA admitted there were no WMDs in Iraq, over 50 percent of Americans still believed they existed.[16] In fact, in 2015, four out of ten Americans and over 50 percent of self-identifying Republicans still believe there were WMDs in Iraq.[17] Equally alarming is that, to convince the public to support the 2003 war in Iraq, the media repeated the false message from pro-war US politicians that Iraqi President Saddam Hussein was involved in the attacks of September 11, 2001.[18] This led to nearly 70 percent of Americans in 2003 believing that Hussein was personally involved in the 9/11 attacks.[19] By 2011, nearly 40 percent of US citizens polled still believed the falsehood that Hussein was involved in the 9/11 attacks.[20]

Disinformation is a powerful tool to cajole or deceive citizens into voting against their interests. The days of violently forcing individuals to succumb to the will of elites may be decreasing, only to be replaced by disinformation campaigns that produce similar results. In fact, in 2004, journalist Thomas Frank was astounded when he pored over the voting data from the state of Kansas. What immediately jumped out at him was that the citizens consistently voted against their own economic interests.[21] At a time when income inequality is at its highest levels since the Great Depression, citizens need to be informed in order to position themselves and their loved ones for survival.[22]

The development of the Internet and digital technologies will not alleviate the problems with television and print news. In 2013, media scholar Robert W. McChesney found that the Internet's promise of widespread information is declining as a few monopolies dominate the majority of its economy: Google owns 97 percent of the mobile search market, for example, while Microsoft controls 90 percent of operating systems.[23] Like television, a few major corporations dominate the popular Internet news sites, which re-post and aggregate articles from the same six corporations that own 90 percent of traditional media.[24] Thus, the Internet is drawing citizens to be informed by the same culprits who corrupted television news. In fact, Eli Pariser, the board president of the progressive public policy advocacy group MoveOn.org, found that search engines reinforce rather than challenge people's beliefs as companies such Google, AOL, Facebook, and ABC News personalize searches based around past search history.[25] Thus, those surfing the Web are being led to find stories that support rather than challenge their (false) beliefs.[26]

The GCMLP aims to address the growing networked truth emergency and seeks to move beyond teaching students how to use new technologies, to a critical media education that teaches students the impact and opportunity costs of the digital world. This is key in the time of a truth emergency, because citizens need to be armed with the skills to recognize duplicitous claims and use new technologies to make alternative narratives, to create and navigate media with a critical lens. The ultimate goal is to develop a core set of critical competencies to directly tackle the truth emergency that has ensued due to misinformation and disinformation within the corporate news media.

WHAT IS CRITICAL MEDIA LITERACY?

An important branch of media education is *critical* media literacy. Critical media literacy (CML) not only aims to provide students with the skills necessary to participate in democratic self-government, but it also seeks to provide them with the skills required to participate in the production of a more equitable twenty-first–century digital economy. This approach has been shown to increase students' understanding of democratic processes and to spur their own civic engagement.[27] In fact, a study of 400 American high school students found that "students in a selective-admission media literacy program have substantially higher levels of media knowledge and news and advertising analysis skills than other students," which independently "contributed to adolescents' intent toward civic engagement."[28]

CML courses seek to teach students a critical awareness of power in media, the production of alternative media, and the relationship between media and audiences. Specifically, through institutional analysis, students are asked to analyze who gets to tell the stories or news in media, how noncommercial media diversify media narratives and perspectives, and how audiences have unique demographic qualities that enable them to interpret media messages differently. In the twenty-first century, propaganda, often disguised as legitimate and normalized political discourse, is far more sophisticated than it was in the past (in part due to media communications technology). Students are often bombarded with carefully constructed hegemonic messages related to personal and political subjects on and off campus without a critical awareness of the influences of the power behind them (for example, ads targeting students to participate in spring break or leisure travel that encourages rampant drinking, drugs, and sex).

Educators and librarians continue to find that students trust the information they obtain from websites, and that they struggle to differentiate between trustworthy sources and their unreliable or even dishonest counterparts, especially when students undertake academic research.[29] This problem is exacerbated by the visually seductive layouts of well-funded websites that persuade by appearances rather than by substance. Likewise, data mining and targeted advertising on the Internet and via mobile technologies continue to marginalize educational news and public affairs information in favor of commercial content. When students allow these messages—across social media, gaming, television, film, music, and streaming cloud-based content—to go unchallenged, powerful elites benefit in terms of increased control of public perceptions, further limitations on what is not—or cannot be—discussed, and enhanced capacities to set public agendas. These processes undermine democracy by thwarting students' desires to be informed about and engaged in the issues that affect them and their communities.

As a means of countering these challenges, academic institutions must strive to make students media literate within our twenty-first-century political economy. CML is a vital part of local-to-global education, in that it provides "the tools through which to examine the political, cultural, historical, economic and social ramifications of all media" in a holistic way.[30] The process begins by encouraging students to analyze the unprecedented amount of media content and digital technology that targets them; to recognize the ways that corporate media seek to colonize their time, money, and intellectual focus; and to track the differences in how commercial messages solicit them as consumers rather than citizens—and thus getting to the root of the ideological, capitalistic motivations that drive the production of corporate media content.

Across social media, gaming, television, film, music, and streaming cloud-based content, the goal is for students to discover how advertising, public relations, and marketing imperatives define and delimit perspectives in news and entertainment. The critical learning process continues as students discover the political and economic goals of content creators and media industries, which target both niche and mass audiences in national and international contexts. On an institutional level, students learn to identify how media production is part of a transnational global market in which six media corporations dominate news and entertainment worldwide. The result is a contested media landscape in which some individuals and groups have the power to access, shape, and define the public issues and narratives of their cultures, while others remain relatively powerless and marginalized. Ultimately, the goal for CML is to analyze how media industries reproduce sociocultural structures of power by determining who gets to tell the stories of a society, what points of view and organizational interests will shape the construction of these stories, and who the desired target audience is.

CML focuses on a set of *multi-literacies* that includes digital literacy skills and competencies for engaging as citizens of the digital world.[31] This pedagogical model begins by arguing that humanistic objectives should determine the technological choices we make, not the other way around. In lieu of a market-driven paradigm of cultural participation, CML focuses on using technology for transformational self-expression and meaningful relationships that enhance the self as well as one's own social and civic participation. To ensure that the marketplace of apps and tools does not usurp the ways we want to use them for cultural and civic participation, curricula that use technology for its own sake are questioned.

As an antidote to digital information overload, students must learn to maintain a critical approach toward the knowledge presented to them. By questioning how sources, underwriters, sponsors, and advertisers influence digital content, students become empowered to judge whether the references cited and the claims made deserve to be trusted. Although the Internet has dramatically increased the diversity of perspectives available by undermining the old distinction between active media producers and relatively passive consumers, the timeliness, scope, and depth of digital media messages must still be verified (using both online and offline sources) to ensure their validity and reliability.

Does networked social interaction promote meaningful human agency? Or, by encouraging adherence to narcissistic, commercial values, do social media function as a means of social control? These are important questions for today's learners to confront and consider. Such questions encourage them to assess whether or not online platforms truly diversify content or simply reproduce new forms of homogeneity through more diverse platforms.

CML also encourages evaluation of how algorithmic trends in mobile and online technology affect social behaviors and perceptions. Issues concerning targeted marketing, privacy, and the consequences of our digital footprints are also critically analyzed through a proactive social media curriculum—one that reflectively considers questions of access, analysis, evaluation, and production, and that encourages students to develop an awareness of their online behaviors and practices.

While social media tools have promoted cultural production among a wide range of amateurs, critical inquiry is needed to assess the extent to which users are encouraged and taught to "become the media." For example, in what ways are audiences encouraged to use technology as knowledge creators who publish their own blogs and Web pages, upload videos or audio that they have created, and post articles and stories that they authored? Are users encouraged to distribute their content through the Creative Commons, which allows others to copy, share, perform, and remix digital works? Or does copyright displace collective knowledge in favor of private profit and proprietary domains? These are some of the pressing questions that CML encourages students to address. Naturally, issues concerning the digital divide are examined within this context to determine whether technology providers and educational institutions offer equitable training and resources across all communities.

Finally, with increasing amounts of time spent with digital and online media, CML assesses the benefits and costs associated with engaging in the digital media world. Specifically, the concepts of "fun" and "play" associated with virtual playgrounds are critically examined, as they often overshadow the costs of cybernetic amusements, which include how time and creative talent are colonized by large, for-profit transnational corporations (i.e., Google, Facebook, Twitter, YouTube).[32] There are also ethical issues associated with digital media and the gaming community, as some individuals are encouraged to engage in cultural production and play, while others are threatened and intimidated on the basis of their sex, gender, race, class, sexuality, and more (see #Gamergate). Other costs include mineral mining, labor exploitation, and the safety of those who work in the factories that produce the tools used for digital entertainment. Finally, growing awareness of privacy issues must include the analysis and application of best practices to ensure that advertisers and government sources don't exploit the very democratic rights and benefits that decentralized media promise.

Given these important issues, educational institutions must strive to make students media literate in the twenty-first–century political economy. Canada, England, and Australia have about a thirty-five–year jump on the US in implementing media literacy courses as a crucial component of public education.[33] The result? While millennials have been exposed to more media content and are using more digital media tools than previous generations, the US falls behind the rest of the world in providing a viable critical media literacy component to its educational curricula. The United States' twenty-first-century education standards—including No Child Left Behind and Common Core—lack specific mandates for any media literacy education, much less the kind of *critical* media literacy education we advocate. The GCMLP seeks to close this significant learning gap by providing equitable access to a critical media literacy education.

SERVICE LEARNING

The GCMLP recognizes that the US is behind other nations in critical media literacy education. Realizing that it is up to educators, working with students, to lead the way in producing and implementing an accessible critical media literacy education, Project Censored and ACME are committed to a course of action centered on service-learning programs. Service learning is a form of pedagogy that emphasizes student participation in course-relevant community service to enhance their learning experience.[34] The concept of service learning derives from the early twentieth-century educational theorist and philosopher John Dewey, who reasoned that students learn more and become more engaged through a pedagogy of embedded experience.[35] Service-learning courses allow students to attain skills while helping them create meaningful and positive change in their community. These courses are typically credit bearing and an important factor in college completion.[36]

Service learning is a promising pedagogy believed to increase student success more than traditional pedagogical methods.[37] There are various models for service-learning programs, all of which usually include face-to-face interactions between students and community members with the goal of bringing benefits to the community through the restoration or accumulation of needed supplies.[38] These models provide students with the opportunity to become engaged, validated, and integrated into the campus.

Service learning through the GCMLP will not only teach students to navigate through the vast world of media but also to create locations of truth within which to disseminate their own work to the communities they serve and to broader publics. In a society largely dominated by individualism, justified in the neoliberal economic model, educators need to teach students the value of collaboration as a method for creating meaningful change. Thus, service learning with a focus on critical media literacy has the potential to not only inform students, but to position them as their own agents of meaningful change.

PROJECT CENSORED

The GCMLP will be based upon the service-learning model of Project Censored, which has demonstrated its success for nearly forty years at over twenty colleges and universities around the US and in six countries. In addition to writing and researching their annual book on media democracy, conducting a weekly national radio show, and working with students and faculty around the US, Project Censored has long been dedicated to community outreach programs, orchestrating community events, creating digital and print media (including blogging and short documentary filmmaking), partnering with local media (such as community radio and campus newspapers), and providing opportunities for students to publish research about current media stories and other academic works in books and on the Internet.

Project Censored affords students the experience and opportunity to hone their public speaking and researching skills while moving from basic to advanced writing skills and addressing social justice issues in their community and beyond. In each of the past three annual books by Project Censored (published by Seven Stories Press in New York), more than 250 students and fifty faculty members from over twenty campuses nationwide have been included. The Project itself is a huge collaborative and interdisciplinary effort aimed at attracting students in the interest of growing their awareness and passion for civic engagement, citizen journalism, and public service.

ACME: ACTION COALITION FOR MEDIA EDUCATION

Project Censored brings its successful track record as an independent news watchdog and a proponent of press freedoms to the table, while the Action Coalition for Media Education offers a complementary set of skills focused on critical digital media literacy education. As we move into the twenty-first century, just a few multinational corporations (Big Media) own much of the media that shape our twenty-first–century culture. Independently funded media literacy education plays a crucial role in challenging Big Media's monopoly over our culture, helping to move our world toward a more just, democratic, and sustainable future. Free of any funding from Big Media, ACME is part of an emerging SmartMediaEducation network, a global coalition run by and for media educators that champions a three-part mission:

1. Teaching media education knowledge and skills—through keynotes, trainings, and conferences—in classrooms and communities to foster more critical media consumption and more active participation in our democracy.
2. Supporting media reform. No matter what one's cause, media reform is crucial for the success of that cause, and since only those who are media educated support media reform, media education must be a top priority for all citizens and activists.
3. Democratizing our media system through education and activism.

ACME Action-In-Media-Education (AIME) trainings—built around several core critical thinking areas—focus on three arenas of professional development for teachers, journalists, public health professionals, and other interested citizen groups.

Arena #1, KNOWLEDGE of how our twenty-first–century media culture works—locally, nationally, and globally. Rather than prepackaged content or curricula, ACME provides a number of accessible resources focused on core questions, concepts, and themes to provide a foundation of critical knowledge.

Arena #2, SKILLS provide the tools needed to more effectively access, analyze, evaluate, and produce media.

Arena #3, ACME's emphasis on ACTIVISM encourages the development of real-world hands-on projects and initiatives designed to engage students in moving critical media literacy education from the realm of theory into the world of practice. ACME's skills-driven interdisciplinary approach considers a wide variety of "windows" into the teaching and learning of critical media literacy education: the power of symbols and stories (language arts and history), the centrality of the human brain and neurocognitive development to the storytelling process (psychology); the big shifts and trends that have defined our twenty-first–century media landscapes (sociology, technology, and political economy); the role of critical questioning (philosophy and the Socratic method); the importance of persuasive forms of language (rhetoric), and the need for various production methods (social media, journalism, and digital storytelling) in sharing the power of stories within public and media spaces. This evolving organic approach is flexible and can be easily tailored to meet the needs of any organization.

GLOBAL CRITICAL MEDIA LITERACY PROJECT

Students who participate in the GCMLP will be well poised for educational success through the synthesis of community-based employment and academic opportunities. Moving forward, the GCMLP will work with numerous campuses around the country, providing students with the opportunity to collaborate with instructors and to network with community-based organizations. Studies have shown that students who have participated in service-learning programs are more likely to remain in college, including students who are traditionally underrepresented in college;[39] thus, the GCMLP will provide equitable pathways to student success. The GCMLP will also provide networking opportunities via cross-campus project collaboration, enabling students to continue their academic careers via internships where they can gain job skills and meet potential employers, leading to future employment opportunities. Lastly, the digital-projects component of the GCMLP allows students to hone their coding and software design skills to increase their economic viability in the twenty-first century.

The resources created from these collaborative student/teacher programs—including research studies, curricula, open software, and music—will be available digitally and in print, for public and classroom use. Planned approaches include:

1. Student Opportunities
   ‣ Publish local investigative journalism

- Create memes of resistance
- Publish in annual book and on website
- Nominate Validated Independent News Stories
- Research and write published articles with faculty
- Certificate/degree in emerging field of critical media literacy

2. Educator Opportunities
- Publish academic works in a forthcoming PC/ACME journal, website, and annual book
- Receive lecture notes, slideshows, and curriculum for an array of disciplines
- Present at conferences
- Create relevant programs and design related courses
- Lead and take part in staff development
- Become a GCMLP officer presiding over multiple campuses

CONCLUSION

Educators of all kinds have an obligation to prepare their students for success in the world in which they live. In the increasingly digitally mediated twenty-first century, that means providing them with the skills and knowledge necessary to participate in what are now thoroughly networked democratic and economic spheres. Given the current truth emergency, fulfilling this obligation has never been more vital. Critical media literacy education is needed not only to make people aware that commercial online news is overdetermined by algorithmic trends, advertising, and structural forces, similar to traditional media, but also to provide people with the tools to navigate and create space for transparently sourced, fact-based information to be shared and considered.[40] The union of two long-standing organizations, Project Censored and ACME, to form the GCMLP, is the first step in fulfilling educators' important obligation to the students they educate, and in helping to extend that body of students to include the public at large.

The authors would like to thank Peter Phillips, Mickey Huff, and Andy Lee Roth for their consultation and feedback on this chapter as it developed.

JULIE FRECHETTE, PHD, is professor of communication at Worcester State University, in Massachusetts, where she teaches courses on media studies, critical cultural studies, media education, and gender representations. She is the author of the book *Developing Media Literacy in Cyberspace* and is the coauthor and coeditor of the book *Media In Society*. She serves as copresident of the Action Coalition for Media Education.

NOLAN HIGDON is a professor of history in the San Francisco Bay Area. His work focuses on nationalism, propaganda, and critical media literacy education. He sits on the boards of the Media Freedom Foundation and ACME as the GCMLP coordinator.

ROB WILLIAMS, PHD, is a professor of media, global studies, and communications in the Burlington, Vermont, area. He has authored numerous articles on critical media literacy education and has lectured around the world, and is currently the board copresident of the Action Coalition for Media Education (ACME).

Notes

1. Linda Darling-Hammond, *The Flat World and Education: How America's Commitment to Equity Will Determine Our Future* (New York: Teachers College Press, 2010).
2. Jean Twenge, Keith Campbell, and Elise Freeman, "Generational Differences in Young Adults' Life Goals, Concern for Others, and Civic Orientation, 1966–2009," *Journal of Personality and Social Psychology* 102, no. 5 (2012): 1045.
3. "Civics Education Testing Only Required in 9 States for High School Graduation: CIRCLE Study," *Huffington Post*, October 12, 2012, http://www.huffingtonpost.com/2012/10/12/circle-study-finds-most-s_n_1959522.html.
4. Ashley Lutz, "These Six Corporations Control 90% Of Media In America," *Business Insider*, June 2012, http://www.businessinsider.com/these-6-corporations-control-90-of-the-media-in-america-2012-6; Patrick Morrison, "Media Monopoly Revisited: The 20 Corporations That Dominate Our Information and Ideas," Fairness and Accuracy in Reporting, October 1, 2011, http://fair.org/extra-online-articles/media-monopoly-revisited/; Ben H. Bagdikian, *The New Media Monopoly* (Boston: Beacon Press, 2004).
5. Robert W. McChesney, *Digital Disconnect: How Capitalism Is Turning the Internet against Democracy* (New York: New Press, 2013).
6. See Peter Phillips, Mickey S. Huff, Carmela Rocha et al., "Truth Emergency Meets Media Reform," in *Censored 2009*, eds. Peter Phillips, Andrew Roth, and Project Censored (New York: Seven Stories Press, 2008), 281–295.
7. Neil Postman, *Amusing Ourselves to Death: Public Discourse in the Age of Show Business* (New York: Penguin, 2006 [1985]); Edward S. Herman and Noam Chomsky, *Manufacturing Consent: The Political Economy of the Mass Media* (New York: Random House, 2010 [1988]); Morris Berman, *The Twilight of American Culture* (New York: W. W. Norton & Company, 2001); Morris Berman, *Dark Ages America: The Final Phase of Empire* (New York: W. W. Norton & Company, 2007); and Chris Hedges, *Empire of Illusion: The End of Literacy and the Triumph of Spectacle* (New York: Nation Books, 2009).
8. Mark Blumenthal, "What Americans Know: Pew Research Finds Most Can Identify Where the Parties Stand," *Huffington Post*, April 11, 2012, http://www.huffingtonpost.com/2012/04/11/what-americans-know-pew-research-party-positions-leaders_n_1418489.html; "What the Public Knows about the Political Parties," Pew Research Center, April 11, 2012, http://www.people-press.org/2012/04/11/What-The-Public-Knows-About-The-Political-Parties.
9. "Voters Say Election Full of Misleading and False Information," World Public Opinion, December 9, 2010, http://www.worldpublicopinion.org/pipa/articles/brunitedstatescanadara/671.php. *Note:* Income taxes did increase under president Barack Obama, but those increases took place after this poll was conducted.

10. James Bamford, "The Man Who Sold the War," *Rolling Stone*, November 17, 2005, http://www.commondreams.org/headlines05/1118-10.htm.

11. Samuel Weigley, "Ten Companies Profiting Most from War," 24/7 Wall Street, March 6, 2013, http://247wallst.com/special-report/2013/03/06/ten-companies-profiting-most-from-war-2; Thom Hartmann, "George W. Bush's Noble Cause—'Political Capital,'" Common Dreams, August 29, 2005, http://www.commondreams.org/Views/2005/08/29/George-W-Bushs-Noble-Cause-Political-Capital.

12. Steve Rendall and Tara Broughel, "Amplifying Officials, Squelching Dissent," Fairness and Accuracy in Reporting, May 1, 2003, http://fair.org/Extra-Online-Articles/Amplifying-Officials-Squelching-Dissent.

13. Steven Kull, Clay Ramsay, and Evan Lewis, "Misperceptions, the Media, and the Iraq War," *Political Science Quarterly* 118, no. 4 (Winter 2003–04): 569–598; Sheldon Rampton and John Stauber, *Weapons of Mass Deception: The Uses of Propaganda in Bush's War on Iraq* (New York: Penguin, 2003).

14. Rendall and Broughel, "Amplifying Officials, Squelching Dissent."

15. Julian Borger, "There Were No Weapons of Mass Destruction in Iraq," *Guardian*, October 7, 2004, http://www.theguardian.com/world/2004/oct/07/usa.iraq1; "Over One Million Iraqi Deaths Caused by US Occupation," *Censored 2009*, 20–25; for an update, see Dahr Jamail, "Report Shows US Invasion, Occupation of Iraq Left 1 Million Dead," *Truthout*, April 13, 2015, http://www.truth-out.org/news/item/30164-report-shows-us-invasion-occupation-of-iraq-left-1-million-dead.

16. "Percentage of Americans Believing Iraq Had WMD Rises," World Public Opinion, August 9, 2006, http://www.worldpublicopinion.org/pipa/articles/brunitedstatescanadara/238.php.

17. "4 in 10 Americans Erroneously Believe US Found Active WMDs in Iraq–Survey," Russia Today, January 7, 2015, http://rt.com/usa/220667-wmds-iraq-americans-poll/; "Ignorance, Partisanship Drive False Beliefs about Obama, Iraq," Fairleigh Dickinson University's PublicMind Poll, January 7, 2015, http://publicmind.fdu.edu/2015/false. Kendall Breitman, "Poll: Half of Republicans Still Believe WMDs Found in Iraq," Politico, January 7, 2015, http://www.politico.com/story/2015/01/poll-republicans-wmds-iraq-114016.html.

18. Kull, Ramsay, and Lewis, "Misperceptions, the Media, and the Iraq War."

19. "Poll: 70% Believe Saddam, 9-11 Link," *USA Today*, September 6, 2003, http://usatoday30.usatoday.com/News/Washington/2003-09-06-Poll-Iraq_X.Htm.

20. Nick Rivera, "Ten Years Later, Belief in Iraq Connection with 9/11 Attack Persists," *Moderate Voice*, September 9, 2011, http://themoderatevoice.com/121921/Ten-Years-Later-Belief-In-Iraq-Connection-With-911-Attack-Persists; Shibley Telhami and Steven Kull, "The American Public on the 9/11 Decade: A Study of American Public Opinion," Program on International Policy Attitudes, University of Maryland, September 8, 2011, http://www.sadat.umd.edu/911Anniversary_Sep11_rpt.pdf.

21. Thomas Frank, *What's The Matter With Kansas? How Conservatives Won The Heart Of America* (New York: Henry Holt and Company, 2004).

22. Mark Gongloff, "Key Inequality Measure the Highest Since the Great Depression," *Huffington Post*, October 14, 2014, http://www.huffingtonpost.com/2014/10/14/inequality-recession-credit-suisse-wealth-report_n_5982748.html.

23. McChesney, *Digital Disconnect*, 123–40.

24. Lutz, "These Six Corporations"; Morrison, "Media Monopoly Revisited"; Bagdikian, *New Media Monopoly*; Robert W. McChesney and John Nichols, *The Death and Life of American Journalism: The Media Revolution Will Begin the World Again* (New York: Nation Books, 2010).

25. Eli Pariser, *The Filter Bubble: What the Internet Is Hiding from You* (New York: Penguin Press, 2011).

26. See Mickey Huff, Frances A. Capell, and Adam Bessie, "Manufacturing Distraction: Junk Food News and News Abuse on a Feed to Know Basis," *Censored 2011*, eds. Mickey Huff and Peter Phillips (New York: Seven Stories Press, 2010), 159–91.

27. Richard P. Adler and Judy Goggin, "What Do We Mean by 'Civic Engagement'?," *Journal of Transformative Education* 3, no. 3 (July 2005): 236–53; Scott W. Lester et al., "Does Service-

Learning Add Value? Examining the Perspectives of Multiple Stakeholders," *Academy of Management Learning & Education* 4, no. 3 (September 2005): 278–94; Catherine Mobley, "Breaking Ground Engaging Undergraduates in Social Change through Service Learning," *Teaching Sociology* 35, no. 2 (April 2007): 125–37.

28. Hans Martens and Renee Hobbs, "How Media Literacy Supports Civic Engagement in a Digital Age," *Atlantic Journal of Communication* 23, no. 2 (May 2015): 120–37.

29. Bettina Fabos, *Wrong Turn on the Information Superhighway: Education and the Commercialization of the Internet* (New York: Teachers College Press, 2004).

30. Julie Frechette, *Developing Media Literacy in Cyberspace: Pedagogy and Critical Learning for the Twenty-First-Century Classroom* (Westport CT: Praeger, 2002), xvii.

31. Julie Frechette, "Top Ten Guiding Questions for Critical Digital Literacy," *Journal of Media Literacy* 61, nos. 1–2 (2014), http://www.academia.edu/10640340/Top_Ten_Guiding_Questions_for_Critical_Digital_Literacy.

32. Christian Fuchs, *Social Media: A Critical Introduction* (London: Sage, 2014).

33. Renee Hobbs and Richard Frost, "Measuring the Acquisition of Media-Literacy Skills," *Reading Research Quarterly* 38, no. 3 (2003): 330–55. Hobbs and Frost found that the US was about twenty-five years behind other countries in media literacy education in 2003. Thus, we estimate that the gap today is approximately thirty-five years.

34. Amanda Taggart and Gloria Crisp, "Service Learning at Community Colleges: Synthesis, Critique, and Recommendations for Future Research," *Journal of College Reading and Learning* 42, no. 1 (2011): 24–44. See also Michael I. Niman, "Service Learning: The SUNY-Buffalo State and Project Censored Partnership," in *Censored 2015: Inspiring We the People*, eds. Andy Lee Roth, Mickey Huff, and Project Censored (New York: Seven Stories Press, 2014): 193–98. Niman emphasizes how service learning is distinct from both academic internships and traditional volunteerism.

35. Dwight E. Giles Jr. and Janet Eyler, "The Theoretical Roots of Service-Learning in John Dewey: Toward a Theory of Service-Learning," *Michigan Journal of Community Service Learning* 1, no. 1 (1994): 77–85.

36. Taggart and Crisp, "Service Learning at Community Colleges."

37. Ibid; George D. Kuh et al., "Unmasking the Effects of Student Engagement on First-Year College Grades and Persistence," *Journal of Higher Education* 79, no. 5 (September–October 2008): 540–63.

38. Cathryn Berger Kaye, *The Complete Guide to Service Learning: Proven, Practical Ways to Engage Students in Civic Responsibility, Academic Curriculum, & Social Action* (Minneapolis MN: Free Spirit Publishing, 2004); Mark G. Chupp and Mark L. Joseph, "Getting the Most Out of Service Learning: Maximizing Student, University and Community Impact," *Journal of Community Practice* 18, nos. 2–3 (2010): 190–212.

39. Michal Kurlaender, "Choosing Community College: Factors Affecting Latino College Choice," *New Directions for Community Colleges* 2006, no. 133 (spring 2006): 7–16; Mitchell J. Chang et al., "The Contradictory Roles of Institutional Status in Retaining Underrepresented Minorities in Biomedical and Behavioral Science Majors," *Review of Higher Education* 31, no. 4 (summer 2008), 433–64; Theresa Ling Yeh, "Service Learning and Persistence of Low-Income, First-Generation College Students: An Exploratory Study," *Michigan Journal of Community Service Learning* 16, no. 2 (spring 2010): 50–65.

40. Douglas Rushkoff, *Present Shock: When Everything Happens Now* (New York: Penguin, 2013).

CHAPTER 6

Modern Herlands
The Significance of Gilman's *Herland* for the Next 100 Years

Sheila Katz

Mother's Day 2015: I'm writing this chapter in a café about 2,400 miles from my mother, and am pondering a short hundred-year-old book. In 2015, Charlotte Perkins Gilman's *Herland*[1] celebrates its one hundredth birthday, and this presents an opportunity to examine its legacy and relevance for current audiences.

All over my Facebook feed this morning are tributes to mothers. Most women my age have children of their own and most are also lucky enough to have their mothers still alive. For some, today is painful—many have suffered losses around reproduction, deaths of children, or mothers. For others, it's disappointing. For me—it's a day of mixed emotions. I intentionally don't have children. I'm proud of that. I do work I love: I teach at a university and do research with low-income single mothers, and I value their motherhood and choices. I research their experiences to inform social policies that could help their lives.[2] I made a different choice about motherhood and it works for me. I also have a good relationship with my mother, but given my job, I am almost never in the same city as her on Mother's Day, which is disappointing for both of us. So, as I contemplate *Herland*'s contemporary relevance, this is my positionality (as feminists say . . .).

Herland is a book I adore. It is a short treatise on a society of women who abolish patriarchy, create a mostly socialist society, and value women and their contributions to society in a holistic way. A central feature in this intentionally created world is that the women hold motherhood to be the highest achievement of their society. However, Gilman's conception of motherhood in *Herland* is a society that values the roles of all of the women in the society and ensures that everyone has an education, food, shelter, meaningful work, and a place within their community. I've been playing with these concepts and working on this chapter for a couple of months, pondering the significance of this book for our contemporary society, reread the book a couple of times, assigned it to my students this semester in a sociology of gender undergraduate course to get their feedback, and read what others have written about it.[3] I've started this chapter several times. Yet, I still was not quite sure what I wanted to make the central focus of my piece, and here it found me on Mother's Day.

MOTHER'S DAY(S)

Mother's Day in the United States. Instead of taking one day each year and turning it into an over-commercialized holiday that exalts the hard work mothers do, why not consider how our society could value women's work, women's contributions, women as people, motherhood and parenting, and "women's place" *every day*? And challenge the power structures that exist within patriarchy and under capitalism that devalue women and mothers all the *other* days of the year.

In 2014, Mother's Day celebrated its hundredth birthday in the United States.[4] Anna Jarvis founded it as a way for children to celebrate their own mothers by spending time with them, writing them handwritten notes, and thanking their mothers for all they did for their daughters and sons. In 1914, president Woodrow Wilson officially made the second Sunday in May Mother's Day. Florists, candy makers, and greeting card companies quickly converted the holiday into a commercialized celebration of motherhood. Jarvis worked until her death fighting against the holiday's commercialization in hopes of returning it to her original intent. The over-commercialization of the celebration continues to the present, and Mother's Day is the most popular day to eat out in the United States according to the National Restaurant Association. However, if we consider Jarvis's intent for Mother's Day and Gilman's utopian society in *Herland*, we discover similarities.

Herland gives us glimpses of a society that attempts to deconstruct gendered assumptions, and it doesn't matter if the book is a week old or a hundred years old, we can learn many lessons about masculinity, femininity, parenthood, capitalism, community, education, and valuing humanity from her novel—lessons that contemporary societies could learn and implement, but have chosen not to, particularly in the US. These concepts are not new—Gilman wrote about them a hundred years ago—but they are as relevant today as they were in 1915. And that to me is deeply frustrating. As a woman, as a daughter, as a feminist, as a teacher, as a gender and poverty researcher, and as a human.

I first read *Herland* in graduate school, when I was exploring a genre of fiction called "feminist dystopias," which borders science fiction and fantasy in many ways, but from a feminist perspective.[5] In *Herland*, three young male American explorers, Van, Jeff, and Terry, discover a "civilized" society of all women who procreate through asexual reproduction. The men are captured, then educated about the society's language, culture, history, traditions, and values. After a failed attempt at escaping, the men are gradually allowed more freedoms during their education. They build relationships with the women, starting with their "tutors" and then with others in the society. Through their tale, the story uncovers the gendered assumptions and stereotypes held by the young men, and Gilman uses those moments to deconstruct the "masculine" and "feminine" in her story of their adventures among the society of women.

Herland is the middle book in a trilogy that starts with *Moving the Mountain* (1911) and ends with *With Her in Ourland* (1916).[6] Gilman's trilogy was largely overlooked in the middle of the twentieth century, but has been republished since. Today, *Herland* is recognized within the feminist community for its role in the first wave of the women's movement.[7]

ABOLISHING GENDER BINARIES

Herland gives us the opportunity to step outside the patriarchy and explore a society comprised entirely of women. Gilman presents this society in ways that directly challenge normative assumptions about masculinity and femininity, and that playfully poke fun of those assumptions. She also gives a biting critique of capitalism—of economic systems that create poverty and vast inequality.

As I teach sociology of gender each semester, students continue to wonder, what would society be like without patriarchy? In *Herland*, Gilman "maps women's refusal to accept patriarchal inscriptions."[8] Many assume that without patriarchy, matriarchy is the sole alternative. But that leaves us in the same binary that creates unequal power structures. Let me be clear. In no way am I suggesting that we abolish patriarchy to establish a matriarchy. As long as feminism has existed, feminists have been accused of this. But that is just an ignorant and inaccurate understanding of feminism. Abolish patriarchy: yes, that is a goal of feminism—but in its place create a system not based on any gendered oppression. Instead, feminism uncovers and explores how power is distributed based on gender, and challenges those assumptions. Feminism fights for equality for men and women and for abolishing gendered oppressions. Although *Herland* is about a society of only women, Gilman is not suggesting a matriarchy either. *Herland* instead calls for an abolishment of gender binaries. Gilman "utilizes the utopian tradition to exemplify her critique of the institutionalized separate spheres" and works to "deconstruct the sexual division of labor" and "redefine and remodel womanhood and motherhood."[9]

As much as we talk in feminism, sociology, and gender studies about women's status, rights, and roles, the core of gender studies and feminism is a critique of gendered inequalities: how we socially construct masculinity and femininity; how we "do" gender;[10] and how power is embedded and imbued in gender identity, gender roles, and gendered institutions.[11] Further, many feminists, such as myself, also are concerned with other power-based oppressions, and work through an intersectional approach to challenge systems of sexism, classism, racism, homophobia, and ageism, among others.[12] Therefore, we also examine, question, and challenge men's roles, rights, and privileges. We question multiple systems of oppression. In order to change gender inequality, we have to rethink both men's and women's gender roles and understand egalitarianism more directly. We need to understand how those gender roles vary by race, class, age, and sexuality. This is both a timeless and very current quandary.

WHY *HERLAND* IS A CENSORED STORY

How does *Herland* fit in *Censored 2016* among the top censored news stories of 2014 and 2015? As we consider *Herland*'s relevance for our present lives, three themes stand out to me in relation to Project Censored's mission.

First, *Herland* was a lost volume, ignored for many years by scholars, feminists, and the general public after it was first published as a serial in Gilman's periodical *The Forerunner*, until it appeared as a book in 1979. Its contributions to current feminism and sociology and its relevance for social theory are only recently being fully understood and appreciated.

Second, it presents a critique of patriarchal and capitalist social orders that devalue, silence, and minimize women's contributions—those of a hundred years ago, but in terms that are relevant to the public issues of our times. By creating a utopian society, Gilman centers those values and women's voices, perspectives, and views in a society that is free from many of the social problems that the rest of *Censored 2016* covers.

Third, as we think about women's contributions—which is my main theme in this chapter—including especially *Herland*'s celebration of "motherhood," we must ask ourselves, what other life choices are censored in that celebration? "Motherhood" in *Herland* celebrates women's contributions to society and to the education of the next generation of citizens in ways that contemporary motherhood does not. *Herland* acknowledges the many roles that women who have biological children—and those who do not—play in contributing, each in their own way, to a society that works together to raise the next generation, in an imagined society premised on shared resources and devoid of income inequality or poverty.

Yet, our present society does not conceptualize motherhood this way. So, unless a woman is a mother in a limited, contemporary sense (defined by having given birth, adopted, or some similar conception of raising children in her household), her work contributing to the raising of the next generation is not recognized. Her contribution to the future common good of a society is overlooked. Often women without children are shamed and called selfish for being childless.

I have read a lot about being childless lately. Some women write about how they have always known they did not want to bear children. Others came to that conclusion later in life. Some struggled with infertility for many years before turning to other options such as adoption or surrogacy, or deciding to stop trying. However, many women's stories about motherhood are even more complicated. Our contemporary public conversation about motherhood does not fully cover their experiences and perspectives. It ignores their choices or experiences. It censors their voices on the topic.

So, while motherhood is a central theme in *Herland*, Gilman discusses it in a way that more fully captures what I have been pondering lately about the silencing and shaming of women who are childless. We need to understand how our society effectively censors many perspectives on childlessness. Gilman's novel provides one basis for developing an expanded understanding of motherhood that recognizes and values how all members of a society work to raise and contribute to the education of the next generation and the future of a society. Since our society devalues women in many areas (unequal pay, unequal responsibility for home and children, higher rates of poverty, less political representation, declining access to reproductive health services, sexual objectification, etc.), women's contributions are not fully recognized and continue to be marginalized. Some women make the decision between a career and motherhood, others try to do both. We expect them to "lean in"[13] instead of exposing this systemic sexism (and racism and classism) that requires women and minorities to be exceptional in order to achieve at levels similar to those of white men. And, too often, we criticize them when they fail.

Instead of continuing debates premised on faulty assumptions about gender, motherhood, economy, and social structure, we have the opportunity to reconsider the utopia that Gilman creates in *Herland*, and to learn from Gilman's fundamental sociological insights involving gender roles, the economy, social change, and the value of social roles not organized in terms of gendered assumptions. These lessons illuminate two main areas: motherhood and the economy. Her critique is both of gender roles and of socioeconomic structures and access to resources—*Herland* is conceptualized through the intersecting lenses of gender and class.

Gilman works to illustrate how all women in a society can contribute in a variety of ways. As Li-Wen Chang explains, Gilman shows "each Herlander as a productive agent in the open and collective society."[14] So, in addition to a critique of gender roles in the home, Gilman is critiquing a capitalist social order that devalues or undervalues women's work outside the home and contributions to society. "*Herland* presents industrious cooperation that forges a non-hierarchical community offering an alternative different from the present invalid society reigned by men."[15] Those human qualities, when incorporated in a system that does not distribute resources according to capitalist principles, can create societies that truly value individual contributions, and provide people with opportunities to live fuller lives.

TEACHING *HERLAND*

This spring, I assigned *Herland* to my undergraduate sociology of gender course. All semester we read scholarly research about gender, gendered inequalities, and social problems caused by gendered inequalities. We ended the semester with two books, Jessica Taft's *Rebel Girls*, an ethnography about girls' activism in the US, Canada, and Latin America.[16] We finished the semester with *Herland*.

As I introduced *Herland*, I asked my students if they had read any other feminist dystopias. Only one or two students raised their hands. They knew *The Handmaid's Tale* by Margaret Atwood.[17] I pushed the students to name other examples. Recently, several youth fiction trilogies have enjoyed popularity, such as Veronica Roth's *Divergent* trilogy and Suzanne Collins's *Hunger Games* series. Among the labels that we could give them, both could be called feminist dystopias. When I suggested this to my students, they were shocked. They barely use the term *feminist*, much less read this obscure genre called feminist dystopias!

Our exchange went along these lines: "No," they tell me, "those books are about class and socioeconomic status."

"Really?" I ask. "Those books are only about class conflict?"

"Yes," they enthusiastically reply.

But some students look skeptical, wondering where I am going with this.

"Really? Does it matter that the lead character is a young woman?" I wait a beat. "Who is challenging gender roles as she fights the oppressive class structure?"

"Oh! Wait! Well maybe . . ." I smile as this realization dawns on them. However, as a feminist, teacher, researcher, and someone who devotes her life to work on social justice issues, it pains me that they have read these books, seen the movie adaptations, and yet the gendered component of the stories has mostly escaped their attention.

The *Divergent* and *Hunger Games* trilogies are much more dystopian than *Herland*, which my millennial students remarked had an "approachable style for a book this old." Students reported reading it in a couple sittings or a long afternoon. While not as "action packed" as the more recent dystopian fictions, they felt that it was still an engaging story that flowed with depth and nuance. They wondered why Gilman didn't discuss sexuality more, but also found many aspects of the book quite relevant. Specifically, they found her archetypes of the men as illustrated in the characters of Van, Jeff, and Terry fairly represented today's spectrum of men. Although in no way all-encompassing, they found the trio of hapless men who Gilman introduces to her female utopia to be representative of typical attitudes of today's men.

So, go explore *Herland* for yourself. Choose it for your next book club meeting, assign it to your students, and start a conversation about gender inequality. Its relevance to our contemporary struggles is poignant. We can all use *Herland* to better understand gender inequality, socioeconomic inequality, and the potential for significant social change. As a sociological theorist, this was Gilman's goal. As a contemporary sociologist, this is my goal too.

This piece is dedicated to my mother, Gail Baker Katz. Happy Mother's Day, Momma, I wrote you a chapter instead of buying a card; thanks for teaching me to be a feminist, and let's keep this fight going!

SHEILA MARIE KATZ, PHD, is an assistant professor of sociology at the University of Houston, who specializes in gender, poverty, and social policy. She earned her MA and PhD in sociology from Vanderbilt University and her BA in sociology and women's studies from the University of Georgia. She is currently writing a book based on her research: *Reformed American Dreams: Welfare Mothers in Higher Education During the Great Recession*. Based on her work in this area, Dr. Katz was named an Emerging Scholar in 2011 by the US Department of Health and Human Services' Administration for Children and Families' Office of Planning, Research, and Evaluation. From 2003 to 2013, Dr. Katz collaborated with the community-based organization Low Income Families' Empowerment through Education (LIFETIME), conducting community-based participatory research. She also works nationally with the ACLU's Reproductive Freedom project and is a board member of the Commission on the Accreditation of Programs in Applied and Clinical Sociology (CAPACS). She lives in Houston, Texas, in a hundred-year-old house with her three cats, Tiberius, Cleo, and Athena.

Notes

1. *Herland* is available free online through Project Gutenberg (www.gutenberg.org).
2. For example, Sheila Katz, "'Give Us a Chance to Get an Education': CalWORKs Mothers' Survival Narratives and Strategies," *Journal of Poverty* 17, no. 3 (2013): 273–304; Sheila Katz, "TANF's 15th Anniversary: Are Low-Income Mothers Celebrating Upward Economic Mobility?," *Sociology Compass* 6, no. 8 (2012): 657–70.
3. Haley Salinas, "A Sociological Analysis of Charlotte Perkins Gilman's *Herland* and *With Her in Ourland*," *Discourse of Sociological Practice* 6, no. 2 (fall 2004): 127–36.
4. On the history of Mother's Day, see Brian Handwerk, "Mother's Day Turns 100: Its Surprisingly Dark History," *National Geographic*, May 9, 2014, http://news.nationalgeographic.com/news/2014/05/140508-mothers-day-nation-gifts-facts-culture-moms/; and Emily Cohn, "The Founder of Mother's Day Hated What the Holiday Became," *Huffington Post*, May 8, 2014, http://www.huffingtonpost.com/2014/05/08/anna-jarvis-mothers-day_n_5282952.html.
5. My first feminist dystopia was Starhawk's *Fifth Sacred Thing* (New York: Bantam, 1994), which I read as a senior in a feminist philosophy class at the University of Georgia. It blew my mind, and I wanted to read more in this area. This started a journey that led me to *Herland*—which, though similar, is more utopian. When I first read *Herland*, I did not actually know about Charlotte Perkins Gilman's contributions to sociological theory. I had only read her short story, "The Yellow Wallpaper." But as I was devouring other feminist dystopias, her novel came across my path. If you want my recommendations for other feminist dystopian fictions check out Octavia Butler's work, especially *Parable of the Sower* (New York: Four Walls Eight Windows, 1993). If you have feminist dystopian titles to recommend, e-mail me at smkatz@uh.edu.
6. Charlotte Perkins Gilman's *Herland* first appeared in serial form in *The Forerunner*, a journal Gilman edited from 1909 to 1916. It was not published in book form until 1979. Charlotte Perkins Gilman, *Moving the Mountain* (New York: Charlton, 1911); *Herland: A Lost Feminist Utopian Novel* (New York: Pantheon, 1979 [1915]); *With Her in Ourland* (Westport CT: Praeger/Greenwood Press, 1997 [1916]). The version I read for this chapter was the 1979 version.
7. Li-Wen Chang, "Economics, Evolution, and Feminism in Charlotte Perkins Gilman's Utopian Fiction," *Women's Studies* 39, no. 4 (2010): 319–48.
8. Ibid., 324.
9. Ibid., 319–20.
10. Candace West and Don H. Zimmerman, "Doing Gender," *Gender and Society* 1, no. 2 (June 1987): 125–51.
11. Joan Acker, "From Sex Roles to Gendered Institutions," *Contemporary Sociology* 21, no. 5 (September 1992): 565–69.
12. On "intersectionality," see for example Patricia Hill Collins, "Knowledge, Consciousness, and the Politics of Empowerment," in *Black Feminist Thought: Knowledge, Consciousness, and the Politics of Empowerment* (New York: Routledge, Chapman and Hall, 1991), 221–38.
13. Sheryl Sandburg, *Lean In: Women, Work, and the Will to Lead* (New York: Knopf, 2013).
14. Chang 326.
15. Chang 328.

16. Jessica K. Taft, *Rebel Girls: Youth Activism Across the Americas* (New York: New York University Press, 2010).

17. Margaret Atwood, *The Handmaid's Tale* (New York: Houghton Mifflin, 1985).

CHAPTER 7

"Dark Alliance"

The Controversy and the Legacy, Twenty Years On

Brian Covert

[T]he presentation of truth is awesome; to speak it requires courage, to write the truth is very often dangerous, to live it guarantees an early death.

—Reverend Wyatt T. Walker[1]

It was one of the most explosive news stories of 1993: Officials of the United States government's Central Intelligence Agency (CIA) had been caught red-handed in helping years earlier to import more than a ton of pure cocaine worth an estimated billions of dollars from Venezuela into the US, destined for American streets.

The CIA, denying any criminal complicity, acknowledged the whole affair as "a most regrettable incident" involving "instances of poor judgment and management on the part of several CIA officers" that resulted in lots of cocaine slipping into the country.[2] The US Department of Justice launched a major investigation into the case.[3]

The media outlet that broke this big story? The CBS News program *60 Minutes*, in a hard-hitting, thirteen-minute segment titled "The CIA's Cocaine," which named names and was televised nationwide.[4] The episode went on to earn *60 Minutes* a prestigious American journalism award for "perform[ing] a vital public service" in the airing of such stories.[5]

A mere three years later in November 1996, around the time of a US federal indictment against a top Venezuelan military official in that case,[6] a journalist covering a much different angle of the CIA and international drug trafficking was receiving his own recognition. Gary Webb, a staff reporter for the *San Jose Mercury News*, the daily newspaper of record in northern California's Silicon Valley, strode up to the podium to receive a "Journalist of the Year" award from a local chapter of the Society of Professional Journalists, one of the oldest and most respected press-support organizations in the US. He was given a round of applause by his peers in the audience, a number of them rising to their feet in a standing ovation.[7]

The groundbreaking three-part series Webb investigated and reported for the *Mercury News* had by then been dominating the nation's headlines and airwaves in the US for several months. "Dark Alliance: The Story behind the Crack Explosion," as the series was billed, incited passionate debate and public outrage nationwide not only about the American government's role in drug trafficking, but also about the ongoing outbreak of crack cocaine use across the US and the government's highly touted "war on drugs" at home and abroad.

Standing alongside Webb and basking in the glow that evening was his boss, *Mercury News* executive editor Jerry Ceppos. "There's still a lot more life in this story," Ceppos reassured the audience of media people, promising even more disclosures to come in the "Dark Alliance" reportage.[8]

But within a few months, the celebratory mood would dramatically change: the "Dark Alliance" series would be killed off by Ceppos's own hand and, in stark contrast to the widespread media approval of the CBS report on the CIA and cocaine trafficking just three years before, Webb and his investigative series would be maligned by some of America's most influential news media companies. The US corporate press, by the mid-1990s, had become its own worst enemy.

August 2016 marks two decades since Webb's "Dark Alliance" investigation took the world by storm as one of the most compelling US news stories in the latter half of the twentieth century. This report takes a critical look back at the controversy that was "Dark Alliance," zooming in for a close-up view of specific episodes and events that were overlooked or omitted in US corporate media reporting. The critical lens is also zoomed-out to reveal the much wider media landscape surrounding "Dark Alliance"—vital context and background that have been all but invisible in the US establishment press over the past twenty years.

And lastly, this report looks at the long-term legacy of Gary Webb's "Dark Alliance" investigation and its place among the acts of journalistic truth-seeking in modern times.

SIGNIFICANCE OF THE SERIES

"Dark Alliance" was originally published in three parts from August 18 to 20, 1996, in the *San Jose Mercury News* and carried on its high-tech Mercury Center website.[9] This was significant because it marked the first time for a US newspaper to make use of the new technology known as the Internet as part of a major news investigation.

Webb had wanted to use the newspaper's website particularly to show the hard evidence and detailed documentation he had amassed as a way to counterbalance what he called the "high unbelievability factor" of his investigation—a true story that the public would literally find too hard to believe unless it was documented in great detail.

And that is where the next significant aspect of "Dark Alliance" comes in: it was the first news media investigation to expose the links between the CIA, the contras, and the rise of crack cocaine use in the United States.

Other journalists, most notably Associated Press (AP) reporters Brian Barger and Robert Parry in the mid-1980s, had reported on the ties between the CIA and large-scale cocaine trafficking by the anti-communist paramilitary forces in Nicaragua known as the "contras."[10] In his "Dark Alliance" investigation a decade later in the summer of 1996, Webb provided the crucial missing piece of the puzzle: what happened to the powdered cocaine once it had been smuggled into the United States by Nicaraguan contra supporters and turned into dried "crack" cocaine, and how the money made from such crack sales on American streets made its way back to the contras in their CIA-sponsored campaign to overturn the new socialist government of Nicaragua.

While "Dark Alliance" did not implicate the CIA in specific incidents of drug smuggling into and within the United States—a point Webb was always clear in publicly emphasizing—his series did present strong circumstantial evidence that the CIA at least knew of the cocaine smuggling into the US by the Nicaraguans and did not act to stop it. As Webb also demonstrated in "Dark Alliance," some US government agencies went as far as offering bureaucratic cover and legal protection to some of the most infamous cocaine traffickers in the Western hemisphere.

Webb had specifically documented in his series how the crossing of paths of three main characters—Nicaraguan wholesale drug traffickers Norwin Meneses and Danilo Blandón, along with a young African-American street-level drug dealer named "Freeway" Rick Ross—had eventually led to an outbreak of crack cocaine use and abuse in Los Angeles that then spread to other US cities, hitting African-American communities the hardest.

Webb's "Dark Alliance" series was also significant in the way it was treated by the influential Big Three newspapers. Instead of building on Webb's groundbreaking investigation and moving the story forward, the *Washington Post*, the *Los Angeles Times*, and the *New York Times* attacked the "Dark Alliance" series for often self-serving reasons and sought to tarnish both Webb's credibility as a journalist and his investigation. This was unprecedented, certainly in contemporary US press history.

THE GREAT AMERICAN LAPDOG ATTACK

In October 1996, a month and a half after "Dark Alliance" had been published in the *San Jose Mercury News*, igniting a firestorm of public protest over its findings, the Big Three newspapers started striking back. They gave an abundance of column inches in their pages to news and opinion articles that dismissed the core facts of the "Dark Alliance" series, often relying on the weakest of sources, and essentially defended the US government in its denial of complicity in the entire affair.

A review of the attacks by the three newspapers reveals the astounding amounts of time, space, and human resources they had invested in debunking the "Dark Alliance" story. Far from serving the role of a watchdog for the public over centers of political and corporate power, the Big Three newspapers were now ready to prove themselves as media lapdogs guarding the gates of such power from public intruders and from smaller, rival news organizations.

The *Washington Post*: "No CIA Plot"

Howard Kurtz, media affairs reporter for the *Washington Post*, took aim at "Dark Alliance" in early October with a critical opinion column that paved the way for the big media attacks to follow.[11]

"Allegations" of CIA involvement in narcotics trafficking were old news that had been laid to rest a long time ago, Kurtz maintained. What Kurtz conveniently left out was the fact that big newspaper companies such as the *Washington Post* had downplayed or ignored that very same controversy a full decade earlier—both the AP news reports at the time by reporters Parry and Barger, as well as a congressional investigation into the matter in 1988 by then-Massachusetts senator John Kerry.[12] Kurtz also cast the first stone of doubt at Gary Webb's journalistic credibility.

Two days later on October 4, the *Washington Post* brought out its big guns in a major five-story takedown of the *Mercury News'* "Dark Alliance" series. It was led by a front-page story cowritten by the *Post*'s veteran national security affairs reporter, Walter Pincus, under the headline, "The CIA and Crack: Evidence is Lacking of Alleged Plot."[13] The 4,000-word story cleverly rejected claims of a CIA "plot" that Webb's investigation had never made.

The CIA links to Nicaraguan coke trafficker Danilo Blandón, as well as Blandón's influence on Los Angeles-based drug dealer "Freeway" Rick Ross, and Ross's influence in turn on the crack cocaine market at the time, were all rejected out of hand by the *Post*. The story also contained the curious assertion that no more than five tons of cocaine were ever smuggled into South Central Los Angeles over the course of a decade (challenging the much higher figures that "Dark Alliance" reported). And who were the sources cited by the *Post* for all these claims? Anonymous government officials.

Included in that set of five stories by the *Post* attacking "Dark Alliance" was another shorter article by *Post* staff reporter Douglas Farah from Managua, Nicaragua, which focused mainly on jailed Nicaraguan drug kingpin Norwin Meneses and his connections with the CIA-sponsored contra forces.[14] Farah's story, by and large, corroborated what Webb had reported in "Dark Alliance" about Meneses as a major trafficker and his dubious relationship with the US government's Drug Enforcement Administration (DEA) back in the 1980s—which may well be the reason why the *Post* substantially cut Farah's article and buried it deep inside the newspaper that day.[15]

Farah remembers having to fight like hell with *Post* editors back in Washington DC, and with Pincus in particular, to get his story into the paper. Farah attributed the closeness of the *Post* to the national power structure in Washington DC as a factor in how the newspaper had handled such news reports by him in the past: "There was so much Washington influence [at the *Post*] that it ends up dominating the story no matter what the reality on the ground was."

Looking back today, Farah, who has since left the *Washington Post*, acknowledges Gary Webb's reporting in "Dark Alliance" as accurate and on target. "The contra-drug stuff, I think, was there," Farah said. "Largely, I think it [Webb's story] was right."[16]

The Los Angeles Times: "Get Gary Webb"

A couple weeks after the *Post*'s takedown of "Dark Alliance," the *Los Angeles Times* was next to check in with a hefty three-day series of articles titled "The Cocaine Trail" that ran from October 20 to 22, 1996. The newspaper enlisted fifteen reporters and two editors—a "get Gary Webb team," as one *Times* staffer called it—to go after the *Mercury News*' "Dark Alliance" investigation as well as its author.[17] The idea behind this group effort had reportedly come from the very top: *Los Angeles Times* editor in chief Shelby Coffey III.[18]

The three-day series opened with a lengthy article by Jesse Katz, the *Times*' self-described gang reporter, that focused on "Freeway" Rick Ross.[19] Katz's story downplayed the role of Ross, the young African-American dealer of crack cocaine, in the nationwide crack cocaine outbreak as outlined in "Dark Alliance." But what the *Times* ended up revealing even more with this article was how low a newspaper would stoop to disprove a journalistic competitor that stepped onto its own turf, even if it meant rewriting history.

Katz had reported two years earlier in 1994 on Ross's dominance of the Los Angeles crack market in an article with this lead paragraph: "If there was an eye to the storm, if there was a criminal mastermind behind crack's decade-long reign, if there was one outlaw capitalist most responsible for flooding Los Angeles' streets with mass-marketed cocaine, his name was Freeway Rick [Ross]."[20] Two years later in 1996, kicking off the *Times'* serial knockdown of Webb's "Dark Alliance" investigation, Katz totally reversed himself with this front-page lead paragraph: "The crack epidemic in Los Angeles followed no blueprint or master plan. It was not orchestrated by the Contras or the CIA or any single drug ring. No one trafficker, even the kingpins who sold thousands of kilos and pocketed millions of dollars, ever came close to monopolizing the trade."[21]

Doyle McManus, the *Times* bureau chief in Washington DC, opened the second day of coverage with a long article that challenged Webb's assertion in "Dark Alliance" that "millions [of dollars] in drug profits" had been funneled from the sale of crack on American streets to the CIA-sponsored Nicaraguan contras.[22] Quoting three anonymous Nicaraguan associates of drug dealers Norwin Meneses and Danilo Blandón, McManus put Webb's figure of "millions" of dollars down much lower to a questionable figure of $50,000, thus reducing in one fell swoop the huge impact of the cocaine smuggled by the Nicaraguans into the US on the overall American crack market.

Two decades after "Dark Alliance," the only journalist among the US major news companies to express anything remotely resembling regret for the way in which Webb and his investigation were treated back then was, appropriately enough, the reporter who had arguably gone the farthest in rewriting the facts of the CIA-contra-crack cocaine story: Jesse Katz, then of the *Los Angeles Times*.

"Overkill" is how Katz today describes his ex-newspaper's three-day attack on Webb's series back in October 1996. "[W]e did it in a way that I think most of us who were involved in it would look back on that and say it was overkill. We had this huge team of people at the *L.A. Times* and we kind of piled on to one lone muckraker [Webb] up in northern California. . . . But we really didn't do anything to advance his work or add or illuminate much to the ['Dark Alliance'] story," Katz said. "It was a really kind of tawdry exercise."[23]

The New York Times: "Only Bit Players"

The last of the Big Three newspapers to jump into the fray was the *New York Times* on October 21, with a well-timed takedown of "Dark Alliance" that was published on the middle day of the *Los Angeles Times'* three-day series. *The New York Times* gave one of its top reporters, Tim Golden, a full news page inside the paper to do the hatchet job with two lengthy articles.

In one of the stories, Golden followed the course laid by the earlier *Washington Post* knockdown of "Dark Alliance" in citing one current or former US government or narcotics official after another—but not disclosing their names.[24] Readers of the story were left to take the word of those CIA, DEA, and other US government sources that the major Nicaraguan cocaine traffickers Webb had exposed in "Dark Alliance" were seemingly "only bit players" in the whole controversy and not a major influence in the overall spread of crack cocaine in the US during the 1980s.

The longer of the two *New York Times* articles by Golden was datelined Compton, California—the area at the center of the crack cocaine outbreak in Los Angeles—and fed into what was perhaps the most disreputable aspect of the whole US establishment media furor over "Dark Alliance": the racial profiling of the African-American community.

"BLACK PARANOIA"

A key component of the US corporate media response to "Dark Alliance" was a steady flow of news and opinion stories that reduced the justified public outrage to little more than the paranoid imaginings of a secret US government plan to destroy African-American lives. Black America, or at least part of it, was in effect being disparaged right alongside journalist Gary Webb for being gullible enough to believe the contents of Webb's "Dark Alliance" reporting.

The Washington Post was the first of the big US news companies to set the "black paranoia" tone in national coverage.[25] This was done in an article carried in the *Post* in mid-September 1996, nearly a month after "Dark Alliance" was published.

In the story, reporter Michael A. Fletcher quoted an authoritative source, a black university professor of political science, who had an explanation for all the fuss being made over "Dark Alliance": "When these horrible things happen in the black community, people feel there must be someone behind it. Being unable to explain it, it becomes a conspiracy theory, the work of an unseen hand."[26] Cited as proof of this were the "suspicions" still lingering in the 1990s over the actual Tuskegee Institute syphilis experiment of the 1930s to 1970s, in which hundreds of African-American men went untreated for syphilis by US government researchers studying the disease.

Another shot came from *Time* magazine a couple weeks later, in an article by reporter Jack E. White.[27] In addressing the black public reaction to "Dark Alliance," White belittled "conspiracy theorists, who blame every plague that afflicts the black community on racist government plots." He took particular aim at both black talk-radio programs and the so-called "black telegraph"—the informal word-of-mouth network of communication long used in the African-American community—for recently being "a font of bizarre fantasies."

A few days later on October 4, Michael A. Fletcher of the *Washington Post* returned with another story on black paranoia—this time on the front page, as part of the *Post*'s major five-story takedown of the *Mercury News* "Dark Alliance" investigation.[28] Fletcher once again trotted out the Tuskegee syphilis experiment as a factor in black paranoia, and also pointed to unfounded suspicions in black America of a conspiracy in tainted food such as fast-food fried chicken and soft drinks, not to mention the longstanding suspicions of a US government hand in the creation of the AIDS virus and the 1968 assassination of Reverend Martin Luther King Jr. "Dark Alliance," Fletcher wrote, had "highlight[ed] an inclination, born of bitter history and captured in polls, to accept as fact unsubstantiated reports or rumors about conspiracies targeting blacks."

A second article on black paranoia, carried the same day in an inside section of the *Washington Post* by staff reporter Donna Britt, assumed a less subtle tone.[29] The whole CIA-contra-crack cocaine scenario "just may not have happened," Britt surmised, but that would not stop paranoia, among both blacks and whites, from rearing its ugly head. "They know the truth, or one truth, anyway: It doesn't matter whether the ['Dark Alliance'] series' claims are 'proved' true. To some folks—graduates of Watergate, Iran-contra and FBI harassment of Malcolm X and Martin Luther King Jr.—they feel so true that even if they're refuted, they'll still be fact to them."

The Associated Press wire service chimed in on black paranoia the very next day, citing, like the other stories, the Tuskegee experiment and adding a few more items to the list of "black fears."[30] "For years, rumors have swirled about body bags of black GIs being sent home [from overseas] laden with opium to resupply drug sellers of the ghetto," the AP explained.

Then came the massive three-day knockdown of "Dark Alliance" by the *Los Angeles Times*, from October 20 to 22, which included a lengthy article with graphics on black paranoia. In a front-page story that led the *Times'* third and final day of its series, reporters John L. Mitchell and Sam Fulwood III wheeled out once more the example of Tuskegee, among others, often interweaving African-American suspicions over factual incidents like US government spying on Martin Luther King Jr. and the radical Black Panthers group with suspicions over other unrelated issues like tainted food.[31]

Not to be outdone, the main story by the *New York Times*—in its full-page, two-story hatchet job on "Dark Alliance" by reporter Tim Golden on October 21, 1996—opened with the issue of black paranoia.[32] Just how much of the truth the *New York Times* was willing to stretch was evident in reporter Golden's assertion that back in 1990, "long before any major news organizations had connected crack and the CIA," a joint telephone poll with the *Times* and a local television station of about a thousand African-American New Yorkers had found that some respondents suspected a US government role in the flow of drugs into poor black neighborhoods, and that more blacks than whites believed in a US government role behind the AIDS epidemic.

But what the *Times* failed to remind readers of this story on black paranoia is that by 1990, other news outlets such as the Associated Press and CBS News (not to mention a host of credible published books on the subject) had already reported on CIA ties to international drug trafficking.[33] This was not something new.

In the meantime, the *Washington Post* kept the momentum of black paranoia going with an October 24 opinion article by columnist Richard Cohen, whose rants were widely syndicated to other news media.[34] Cohen made this sweeping racial observation: "It should come as no surprise, then, that a piece of black America remains hospitable to the most bizarre rumors and myths—the one about the CIA and crack being just one." Cohen took the media's argument on black paranoia one step further by tying it into religious discrimination, blasting the African-American Muslim leader Louis Farrakhan, head of the Nation of Islam, and other influential black leaders who "embrace his every paranoid theory, including his anti-Semitism."

From inside the distorted bubble of white American racism, what routinely looks like black paranoia is actually a high degree of black consensus on given issues, according to writer/activist Bruce A. Dixon, and it was that strong consensus that the major media companies sought to diminish in regard to the "Dark Alliance" story. "A gargantuan, racist lie was deployed to swallow and conceal the truths that Gary Webb had labored so diligently to bring to light. 'Black paranoia' was a very useful diagnosis, tailor-made to convince the white public that further examinations of the CIA connection to crack cocaine were pointless," Dixon noted.[35]

Yet one fact complicated the whole black paranoia clamor in the press as being just another case of racism: some of the worst offenders in the corporate media's rush to play up black paranoia in attacking "Dark Alliance" were themselves of African-American heritage—reporters Fletcher and Britt of the *Washington Post*, reporters Mitchell and Fulwood of the *Los Angeles Times*, and reporter White of *Time* magazine. In explaining why he and other African-American journalists had played the black paranoia card at the time, White later pleaded pressure from white colleagues in the media who were dismissing the veracity of the original "Dark Alliance" series on one side, and angry conspiratorial blacks on the other.[36] He did recognize, though, that "to many blacks, pushing the paranoia angle looked like a plot to write off their suspicions as delusions."

Beyond the race of the reporters who wrote the stories, however, the issue over black paranoia in the sustained media bashing of "Dark Alliance" raises a fundamental question: is the racial profiling of an entire group of people any more acceptable in society when it is done in the press than by police on the street? The answer, of course, is no, with the final responsibility resting with the elite, white-owned media conglomerates that promoted such racially offensive stories on black paranoia in the first place.

ADVANCING THE STORY

With the Big Three newspapers' attacks on Gary Webb's investigation now concluded by November 1996, and the follow-up stories by these and other major US news companies continuing to tag the "Dark Alliance" investigation with the D-word—"discredited"—the American public could be forgiven for thinking that "Dark Alliance" was now gone for good.

It was not. Within the United States, among the few journalists who were consistently following the "Dark Alliance" series and/or advancing forward its original investigation were, on the East Coast, former Associated Press reporter Robert Parry (who had first broken the story on Nicaraguan contras and cocaine trafficking back in 1985), and weekly newspaper reporter Nick Schou, who had cooperated with Webb on part of the "Dark Alliance" investigation, on the West Coast.[37]

In late November 1996, two reporters from the *Dallas Morning News* in Texas, David LaGesse and George Rodrigue, broke a related story that revived the contra-drug issue from a decade earlier in the 1980s.[38] The story focused on former DEA agent Celerino Castillo III and how he had confirmed links between the CIA-supported Nicaraguan contras and cocaine trafficking while investigating an airport in the Central American nation of El Salvador—and how he had come under internal DEA pressure to back off his investigation.

More importantly, outside the United States, the "Dark Alliance" investigation had been read worldwide on the Internet and was being followed with particular interest by news organizations in Europe. The December 12, 1996 edition of the *Independent*, one of the major British newspapers, gave a heads-up to its readers about a television documentary to be aired that same evening on the Independent Television (ITV) network of England that would advance the CIA-contra-crack cocaine story beyond what had already been reported by Gary Webb in the *San Jose Mercury News*.[39]

When the half-hour documentary, titled "The Crack Conspiracy," aired that night on ITV's *The Big Story* program, potentially watched by millions of viewers in Europe, it lived up to the British print media publicity, and then some. The ITV report (an archived copy of which was obtained by this author) included on-camera interviews with the

CENSORED 2016

key players in the still-unfolding "Dark Alliance" drama—*Mercury News* reporter Gary Webb, "Freeway" Rick Ross in prison in California, cocaine trafficker Norwin Meneses in prison in Nicaragua, Castillo of the DEA, and others related to the story.[40] The program respectfully addressed African-American beliefs about the CIA and the rise of crack cocaine as natural concerns rather than as illogical symptoms of black paranoia.

While Webb's "Dark Alliance" series had shown that the CIA, at the very least, knew about contra drug trafficking into the US and let it continue, the ITV report went further with what it called "major new revelations": the CIA, it asserted, was an active participant in that drug smuggling. ITV's prime witness was one that Gary Webb had not yet tracked down in his "Dark Alliance" investigation (but soon would)—Carlos Cabezas, a Nicaraguan attorney and former pilot who had trafficked cocaine into the United States in the 1980s and served time for that in a US prison. Cabezas told ITV in an off-camera interview in Nicaragua that he had had dealings directly with a Costa Rican-based CIA agent, a Venezuelan named Ivan Gómez, who was making sure that drug profits from the sales of cocaine within the US ended up going back to the CIA-sponsored Nicaraguan contras in Central America instead of into the pockets of Nicaraguan drug traffickers. Said Cabezas: "They told me who he [Gómez] was and the reason that he was there. It was to make sure that the money was given to the right people and nobody was taking advantage of the situation and nobody was taking profit that they were not supposed to. And that was it. He was making sure that the money goes to the contra revolution."[41]

ITV also did an on-camera interview with the ex-CIA official who oversaw the agency's Nicaraguan contra-support program back in the 1980s, Duane Clarridge. He denied knowing anything about such cocaine smuggling under his watch at the time. When the ITV reporter, Dermot Murnaghan, suggested to Clarridge that he was being less than truthful, Clarridge thrust his fist in front of the reporter, threatening with an expletive to physically assault him in the face. Clarridge ended up walking out of the interview, more expletives flying.

The British television report had backed up Webb's "Dark Alliance" series and taken it even further. But American media on the whole were not interested. The ITV report barely registered on the radar of US independent/alternative media at the time, and no US corporate press company appears to have acknowledged the ITV program and its major advance of Webb's story. One US government agency, on the other hand, had no such trouble gaining the attention of the American media when it came to "Dark Alliance."

THE PRESS AND "PRODUCTIVE RELATIONS"

Just how closely the CIA was monitoring the public firestorm over the *Mercury News* investigative series back in 1996 as it played out in real time was revealed by an in-house CIA journal report on the "Dark Alliance" investigation that was declassified and released in 2014. The report, originally written in 1997, also gives a glimpse into how the CIA milked the relationships it had built over time with journalists to effectively help shift the media glare away from the message—the CIA-contra-crack cocaine connections outlined in "Dark Alliance"—and onto Gary Webb and the *Mercury News* as the messenger.[42]

The six-page CIA report showed how, from the start, the agency went about deceiving and manipulating the news media during the press inquiries that began filtering in just after "Dark Alliance" was published.[43] ". . . CIA media spokesmen would remind reporters seeking comment that this series represented no real news, in that similar charges were made in the 1980s and were investigated by the Congress and were found to be without substance," stated the report.[44] In fact, "Dark Alliance" broke new investigative ground on several counts, and both the AP news reports and congressional Kerry investigation of the 1980s had uncovered much substantial evidence linking the CIA-backed Nicaraguan contras to cocaine trafficking.

A number of news organizations across the United States, to their credit, found "Dark Alliance" newsworthy enough when it first came out to reprint excerpts of the series in their own publications. But on at least one occasion, the CIA report noted, "one major news affiliate, after speaking with a CIA media spokesman, decided not to run the ['Dark Alliance'] story."

Then in late September 1996, after about a month of CIA assurances to journalists nationwide that there was no substance at all to the "Dark Alliance" series, the media tide started turning in the agency's favor. "Respected columnists, including prominent blacks, began to question the motives of those who uncritically accepted the idea that CIA was responsible for destroying black communities," the report said. "Others took a hard look at the evidence provided by the *Mercury News*—something [CIA] Public Affairs encouraged from the beginning—and found it unconvincing."[45]

The back-to-back attacks on "Dark Alliance" by the Big Three newspapers in October 1996, "especially the *Los Angeles Times*," the CIA report said, were the decisive turning point. After that, other news stories in the US corporate press grew more skeptical of the claims of a CIA-drug conspiracy than they were of the CIA itself by a three-to-one margin.[46]

And the CIA was not beyond breaking its own institutional rule of neither confirming nor denying a suspected person's links to the agency, the report divulged, when it came to helping the media to "undermine" Webb's series: "[I]n order to help a journalist working on a story that would undermine the *Mercury News* allegations, [CIA] Public Affairs was able to deny any affiliation of a particular individual—which is a rare exception to the general policy that CIA does not comment on any individual's alleged CIA ties."

While media companies were inclined to take the CIA's word, that kind of trusting attitude apparently cost some reporters their credibility among an angry public that was not fully buying the official denials. "Journalists who wrote articles skeptical of the charges against CIA were pilloried in print—one was accused of serving as a CIA lackey—and even threatened with physical harm over their articles," according to the report.[47]

Understanding the decades-long relationship between the press and the US government's premier spy agency goes a long way toward explaining such American public skepticism of the media during the "Dark Alliance" firestorm. In at least one case, there was a direct link between a former CIA asset in the media and the corporate press attacks on the "Dark Alliance" series. That link was in the person of Walter Pincus, the veteran national security affairs reporter for the *Washington Post*, the newspaper that did the most to let the CIA off the hook during the "Dark Alliance" controversy. It was Pincus who cowrote the first extensive takedown of "Dark Alliance" in October 1996 that would be followed in short order by other media companies.

Assets in the Media

As Gary Webb continued investigating "Dark Alliance" in the wake of those media attacks, he was tipped off to a news article in the archives of his own newspaper, the *San Jose Mercury News*, written by none other than *Washington Post* reporter Walter Pincus. In the lengthy article, which had been syndicated by the *Post* and carried in several American newspapers in February 1967, Pincus essentially outed himself as an ex-CIA media asset in the late 1950s and early 1960s.[48]

In that 1967 article he wrote how, as a young freelance writer, he had been recruited by a US-based student organization funded by the CIA to infiltrate an international youth conference in Vienna, Austria, and did so, later volunteering to testify if necessary about what he had observed to the anticommunist House Un-American Activities Committee (HUAC) in the United States.[49] Pincus also traveled to the African nations of Ghana and Guinea, and reported back to his CIA handler on the international youth conferences he joined there. "No one openly questioned my presence," Pincus wrote of his Ghana experiences. "But I had been briefed in Washington on each of them. None was remotely aware of CIA's interest." Back home in the USA, Pincus added, he was offered steady work with the CIA but turned the job down.[50]

No matter. By the time that "Dark Alliance" came out in 1996, three decades later, *Washington Post* reporter Pincus had built up something of a reputation within the CIA, according to the right-wing *Washington Times* newspaper, as "the CIA's house reporter."[51]

The CIA and its network of cooperative media assets—both institutional and individual, and within the United States and internationally—has been the subject of several well-documented exposés in US news media circles in past decades, most notably in the respected *Columbia Journalism Review* by the late Stuart H. Loory, a former *Los Angeles Times* White House correspondent; in *Rolling Stone* magazine by former *Washington Post* Watergate reporter Carl Bernstein; and even in a front-page series over a few days in the *New York Times*.[52]

But despite those and other revelations in past years, ties between the press and the CIA have persisted at varying levels, with neither party being too eager to have the facts behind those longstanding links made public.

To be very clear: the only evidence that has surfaced so far of a direct link to a CIA media asset, past or present, in the "Dark Alliance" saga is that of Walter Pincus of the *Washington Post*. In any case, as the CIA's recently released in-house journal report on "Dark Alliance" also makes clear, the agency's "ground base of already productive relations with journalists" had paid off and the CIA managed to "prevent this story from becoming an unmitigated disaster."[53] The US government could claim a limited victory in the battle over the truth. "In the world of public relations, as in war," the report stated, "avoiding a rout in the face of hostile multitudes can be considered a success."

DISAPPEARING ACT

December 31, 1996, marked the end of a tumultuous year for the *San Jose Mercury News* and reporter Gary Webb. It was also the day that the last article under his name would make it into print in the newspaper as part of his "Dark Alliance" investigation.[54] Webb later submitted four additional follow-up stories to his editors as part of the investigation, but the stories never ran.

By May 1997, nine months after "Dark Alliance" had first appeared, the combined weight of the continuing public outrage over suspected US government involvement in the crack cocaine outbreak, the government's vehement denials, and the corporate media's discrediting of "Dark Alliance" was taking its toll. On May 11, *Mercury News* executive editor Jerry Ceppos announced in a 1,200-word open letter to the paper's readers that he had reexamined the series and found several "shortcomings" in the presentation and wording of "Dark Alliance."[55]

Ceppos's personal column, carried on the front page of the paper's Sunday opinion section, stands out as surely one of the oddest editorial retreats from a legitimate news story from among a long line of such retreats throughout US press history. Ceppos did not openly apologize to readers for anything in the article. He did not offer a

full retraction or recantation of the series or, for that matter, even a detailed correction of what Webb had originally investigated in "Dark Alliance."

What he did do was list four relatively minor points on which the "Dark Alliance" series came up short in his view: omitting a single instance of conflicting court testimony that should have been included in the story (but which had been removed by Webb's editors during the editing process); failing to explain that the figure of "millions" of dollars raised by the Nicaraguan traffickers in street drug sales in the US was just an estimate, not a hard fact; overestimating the influence of the Nicaraguan drug traffickers on the origins of the crack cocaine outbreak in Los Angeles and nationwide; and implying CIA knowledge of the whole thing. "I feel that we did not have proof that top CIA officials knew of the relationship," Ceppos wrote, although the "Dark Alliance" series never alleged that they had known.

But in a key point, he emphasized that the "shortcomings" of the series did not detract from an otherwise well-done job: "Does the presence of conflicting information invalidate our entire effort? I strongly believe the answer is no, and that this story was right on many important points."

In the end, that was not enough to save the story, and with Ceppos's final words on the matter—"But ultimately, the responsibility was, and is, mine"—the newspaper abandoned the "Dark Alliance" investigation. The entire "Dark Alliance" website was pulled down not long afterward. One of the most significant news stories in decades had disappeared without a trace in the vast digital expanse known as the information superhighway.

If that was not a white flag of journalistic surrender, it was certainly how other corporate media giants viewed it. *The New York Times* played up Ceppos's retreat in a lengthy, front-page news article, the first time that the *Times* apparently found the snit over "Dark Alliance" worthy of printing on page one. "It is gratifying to see that a large segment of the media . . . has taken a serious and objective look at how this story was constructed and reported," a thankful CIA spokesman was quoted as saying.[56]

"The Mercury News Comes Clean" gloated the headline of an editorial carried in the *Times* the next day.[57] America's newspaper of record had nothing but praise for the way in which the *Mercury News* editor had handled the problem, saying, "His candor and self-criticism set a high standard for cases in which journalists make egregious errors."

A few days later, the *New York Times* rolled out the royal carpet on its op-ed pages for Massachusetts Institute of Technology (MIT) chemistry professor John M. Deutch, the beleaguered director of the CIA at the time of the uproar over "Dark Alliance."[58] Deutch sniffed in an opinion article that he was "not impressed"—neither with the original "Dark Alliance" series and its suggestion of CIA links to drug trafficking, nor with the *Mercury News*' retreat from the series now. The establishment press, he said, was missing the real story: the way that "Dark Alliance" had somehow managed to gain credibility among African-Americans. Raising once more the black paranoia specter, Deutch proffered the Tuskegee syphilis experiment and recalled an enraged black audience of hundreds that he had encountered a few months earlier during an unprecedented public appearance by him in South Central Los Angeles, ground zero of the crack cocaine outbreak.[59] The ex-CIA chief also used his free podium in the *Times* to once again deny, unchallenged, that the agency ever "directed or knowingly condoned drug smuggling into the United States."

One voice that was noticeably absent from the opinion pages of the *New York Times* and other corporate press at the time of the *Mercury News* retreat from "Dark Alliance" was that of Gary Webb. Denied a chance to respond in his own newspaper and virtually blacklisted by the big US media companies, Webb used the Internet to issue a formal rebuttal on behalf of himself and his colleague in the "Dark Alliance" investigation, Nicaragua-based Swiss journalist Georg Hodel—a rebuttal that seems to have gone unreported in both corporate and independent news media in the years since then. "The only 'shortcoming' in our Dark Alliance series is that it didn't go far enough," Webb wrote in a message posted to Usenet discussion groups.[60] "What Mr. Ceppos' column fails to mention is that, as a result of our continuing investigation, we DO have evidence of direct CIA involvement with this Contra drug operation. . . . Perhaps one day Mr. Ceppos will allow us to share this information with the public."

"Despite the efforts of the biggest newspapers in the country to discredit our work," Webb continued, "our central findings [in 'Dark Alliance'] remain unchallenged: After being instructed by a CIA agent to raise money in California for the Contras, two Contra drug dealers began selling vast amounts of cocaine in inner-city Los Angeles, primarily to the Crips and Bloods [street gangs]. Some of the profits went to pay for the CIA's covert war against the Sandinistas. We wrote last year that the amounts were in the millions and we stand by that statement. . . . Only a fool could argue that this wasn't a critical factor in the spread of crack from South Central to the rest of the country."

A LEGACY OF RESISTANCE

Gary Webb was later removed from the "Dark Alliance" investigation altogether by his editors, and ended up resigning from the *San Jose Mercury News* in disgust in December 1997. He got a job as an investigative writer for the California state government and continued to follow up the "Dark Alliance" leads on his own, eventually getting the whole CIA-contra-crack cocaine story told in a book published in 1998 by New York–based Seven Stories Press (publisher of this *Censored* volume).

But the gilded gates to the US daily newspaper business that had raised Webb as one of the best investigative journalists of his generation were now closed, and he would never be accepted back there again. A slow, deep slide by Webb into financial instability and emotional depression followed. On December 10, 2004—seven years to the day after leaving the *San Jose Mercury News*—Webb was found dead at age forty-nine in his home in Sacramento, California, of two gunshot wounds to the head. The coroner's office ruled the death a suicide.

Three months after he died, the *Los Angeles Times*, not to be denied the last word on "Dark Alliance," published a lengthy, often-unflattering feature article about Webb in the entertainment section of the newspaper that continued to besmirch the reputation of a fellow journalist who could no longer respond.[61]

Webb's rise and fall from corporate media grace was later told in the well-documented book *Kill the Messenger* by journalist Nick Schou and was dramatized in 2014 in a Hollywood movie of the same name. A nonfiction film by director Marc Levin that revisited "Dark Alliance" and the US crack cocaine explosion, *Freeway: Crack in the System*, was broadcast on the Al Jazeera America cable television network in March 2015.[62]

Looking back twenty years on the media brushfire of a controversy that was "Dark Alliance," what did Gary Webb's investigative series achieve and what did it fail to do?

The groundswell of public opinion over "Dark Alliance," especially from the African-American community, forced three separate US government investigations that eventually resulted in four internal reports being released: two by the CIA in 1998, one by the US Department of Justice that same year, and another by the US congressional House Intelligence Committee in 2000.[63] All the reports, not surprisingly, absolved the US government of wrongdoing and denied any illicit CIA connections to the main characters in "Dark Alliance." But in their attempt at whitewashing history, the official reports contained valuable facts and background information that could be gleaned in validating the central findings in "Dark Alliance," showing that in many ways Webb's series had only scratched the surface of ties between the CIA, the contras, and crack cocaine. Webb, through his investigation, did a commendable public service in recovering a piece of America's recent lost history.

If "Dark Alliance" is remembered for any one thing, it is perhaps for the astonishing sight of the head of the CIA taking time out from other pressing top-secret priorities like military coups and proxy wars overseas to go and face reality on the American inner-city streets of Los Angeles. CIA director John M. Deutch had been invited on November 15, 1996, to address a town hall meeting called by African-American congresswoman Juanita Millender-McDonald (D-Carson), whose congressional district included the area where the crack cocaine explosion was shown by "Dark Alliance" to have first erupted.[64] Deutch was compelled to address the issues raised by "Dark Alliance" before a disbelieving, jeering crowd of hundreds of mostly African-American citizens—a rare display of US government accountability directly to the public.

What Gary Webb's "Dark Alliance" series failed to do, despite much public assumption to the contrary, was offer a "smoking gun" of proof that conclusively tied together the US government and international drug trafficking. The evidence presented in "Dark Alliance" was strong and persuasive, but it was mostly circumstantial. "Dark Alliance" was not perfect in its presentation and there were several points on which the story could have been expanded or tightened up before publishing, oversights for which the San Jose Mercury News editors arguably deserved more blame than reporter Webb. Those editors, to this day, have not been called to account for their role in the whole debacle; all of them have instead gone on to illustrious careers in the media field and academia.[65]

Nearly two decades after "Dark Alliance" had been put in its proverbial grave by the influential US media establishment, an opinion poll found that public trust in the Fourth Estate had sunk to yet another all-time low.[66] Webb's hard-hitting "Dark Alliance" investigation, meanwhile, has stood the test of time as a classic, high-quality work of investigative journalism.

But it would be a mistake to view the "Dark Alliance" controversy as an isolated incident. Rather, the real legacy of Gary Webb's ground-breaking investigation is to be found as part of a continuum of resistance to the censorship of news and the suppression of truth that dates far back in the North American experience—from well before African-American journalist Ida B. Wells and her perilous reporting on lynchings in US southern states in the late 1800s,[67] to well after *New York Times* reporter Seymour M. Hersh being "reviled" by peers in the big news media companies for his 1974 front-page exposé of illegal CIA spying on US citizens.[68] Hersh, in 2015, would once again find himself before the US corporate media firing squad for a lengthy exposé, published in Britain, that reported the US government's account of its courageous killing of renowned Saudi Arabian evildoer Osama bin Laden to be untrue.[69]

As Columbia University professor and former journalist Anya Schiffrin has chronicled in her 2014 book *Global Muckraking*, wherever in the world there have been attempts to keep the truth from being reported, there have also been journalists, writers, editors, and other muckrakers who take great risks to report the truth, often in defiance of powerful corporate media interests.[70]

The "Dark Alliance" investigation of the 1990s is but one part of a long tradition of seeking out the truth and resisting news censorship and suppression, a tradition that continues up to the present day. Gary Webb, the author of that controversial series of twenty years ago, may have fallen, but in the Internet age of investigative journalism, which his "Dark Alliance" story helped to inaugurate in such a meaningful way, future generations of journalists are inspired to keep that rich tradition of international muckraking alive by continuing to investigate, report, and expose the truths that those in authority would rather keep hidden away. That, in the end, is the ultimate karmic justice.

BRIAN COVERT is an independent journalist and author based in western Japan. He has worked for United Press International (UPI) news service in Japan, as a staff reporter and editor for English-language daily newspapers in Japan, and as a contributor to Japanese and overseas newspapers and magazines. He is currently a lecturer in the Department of Media, Journalism, and Communications at Doshisha University in Kyoto.

Notes

1. US civil rights movement leader Wyatt T. Walker, "Reflections on Crime, Vietnam and God," *Negro Digest*, December 1967, 9.

2. Tim Weiner, "Anti-Drug Unit of CIA Sent Ton of Cocaine to US in 1990," *New York Times*, November 20, 1993, http://www.nytimes.com/1993/11/20/world/anti-drug-unit-of-cia-sent-ton-of-cocaine-to-us-in-1990.html.

3. Michael Isikoff, "US Probes Narcotics Unit Funded by CIA," *Washington Post*, November 20, 1993, A1, http://www.washingtonpost.com/archive/politics/1993/11/20/us-probes-narcotics-unit-funded-by-cia/08e49ab4-b23a-4143-ace9-baebab212284/.

4. *60 Minutes*, "The CIA's Cocaine," CBS News, November 21, 1993, http://www.cbsnews.com/videos/the-cias-cocaine.

5. "60 Minutes: The CIA's Cocaine (CBS)," Peabody Awards, 1993, http://www.peabodyawards.com/award-profile/60-minutes-the-cias-cocaine.

6. "Report: Venezuelan Official Indicted," United Press International (UPI), November 23, 1996, http://www.upi.com/Archives/1996/11/23/Report-Venezuelan-official-indicted/1801848725200/.

7. M.L. Stein, "Embattled Reporter Wins Award amidst Controversy," *Editor & Publisher*, November 30, 1996, 7. See also "MN Reporters Honored for Journalism Excellence," *San Jose Mercury News*, November 13, 1996, 4B.

8. Stein, "Embattled Reporter Wins Award amidst Controversy."

9. Gary Webb, "Dark Alliance: The Story behind the Crack Cocaine Explosion," *San Jose Mercury News*, August 18–20, 1996, http://web.archive.org/web/19970409180523/http://www2.sjmercury.com/drugs/.

10. Brian Barger and Robert Parry, "Reports Link Nicaraguan Rebels to Cocaine Trafficking," Associated Press, December 20, 1985, http://www.apnewsarchive.com/1985/Reports-Link-Nicaraguan-Rebels-to-Cocaine-Trafficking/id-c69eaf370de9884f907a39efd90337d3. For an archived draft of the original AP story, see https://archive.org/details/AP-CIA-Contras-Cocaine-1985.

11. Howard Kurtz, "Running with the CIA Story; Reporter Says Series Didn't Go as Far as Readers Took It," *Washington Post*, October 2, 1996, B1, http://www.washingtonpost.com/pb/archive/lifestyle/1996/10/02/running-with-the-cia-story/0364290d-d2d1-42a6-85df-768c375b2a0f/?resType=accessibility.

12. For the congressional Kerry report, see https://www2.gwu.edu/~nsarchiv/NSAEBB/NSAEBB113/north06.pdf.

13. Roberto Suro and Walter Pincus, "The CIA and Crack: Evidence is Lacking of Alleged Plot," *Washington Post*, October 4, 1996, A1, http://people.duke.edu/~ldbaker/clippings/cia.html.

14. Douglas Farah, "Drug Dealer Depicted as Contra Fund-Raiser," *Washington Post*, October 4, 1996, A18, http://www.washingtonpost.com/archive/politics/1996/10/04/drug-dealer-depicted-as-contra-fund-raiser/f38da99e-04fe-4f8e945b-4899b3e9df54.

15. Ryan Grim, *This is Your Country on Drugs* (Hoboken, New Jersey: John Wiley & Sons, 2009), 185-187. For online excerpts, see http://www.huffingtonpost.com/2014/10/10/kill-the-messenger_n_5962708.html.

16. Grim, *This is Your Country on Drugs*, 187.

17. Quoted in Peter Kornbluh, "The Storm over 'Dark Alliance,'" *Columbia Journalism Review*, January/February 1997, 37–38, https://www2.gwu.edu/~nsarchiv/NSAEBB/NSAEBB113/storm.htm.

18. Rick Barrs, "A Barracuda Tries to Eat the Messenger," *New Times Los Angeles*, October 31, 1996, https://web.archive.org/web/19970111145357/http://www1.sjmercury.com/drugs/postscript/controversy/controversy1031.htm.

19. Jesse Katz, "Tracking the Genesis of the Crack Trade," *Los Angeles Times*, October 20, 1996, A1, http://articles.latimes.com/1996-10-20/news/mn-59169_1_crack-cocaine.

20. Jesse Katz, "Deposed King of Crack," *Los Angeles Times*, December 20, 1994, A20, http://articles.latimes.com/1994-12-20/news/mn-11084_1_master-marketer.

21. Katz, "Tracking the Genesis of the Crack Trade." For an explanation by Katz on his contradictions in those two *Times* articles, as well as a long profile of Ross, see Jesse Katz, "The Rise and

Fall and Rise and Fall of Ricky Ross," *Texas Monthly*, July 1998, http://www.texasmonthly.com/content/rise-and-fall-and-rise-and-fall-ricky-ross.

22. Doyle McManus, "Examining Charges of CIA Role in Crack Sales," *Los Angeles Times*, October 21, 1996, A1, http://articles.latimes.com/1996-10-21/news/mn-59232_1_cia-officials.

23. Jesse Katz, quoted in "Will the Real & Reformed Rick Ross Please Stand Up?," KPCC *Air-Talk* radio program, May 23, 2013, http://www.scpr.org/programs/airtalk/2013/05/22/31915/will-the-real-reformed-rick-ross-please-stand-up. See also Nick Schou, "Ex-LA Times Writer Apologizes for 'Tawdry' Attacks," *LA Weekly*, May 30, 2013, http://www.laweekly.com/news/ex-la-times-writer-apologizes-for-tawdry-attacks-2614004.

24. Tim Golden, "Pivotal Figures of Newspaper Series May be Only Bit Players," *New York Times*, October 21, 1996, A14, http://www.nytimes.com/1996/10/21/us/pivotal-figures-of-newspaper-series-may-be-only-bit-players.html.

25. According to the author's review of "Dark Alliance"–related articles listed in the *Washington Post* online archives (www.washingtonpost.com) and other news media sources.

26. Michael A. Fletcher, "Black Caucus Urges Probe of CIA-Contra Drug Charge; Newspaper Articles Fan Conspiracy Suspicions," *Washington Post*, September 13, 1996, A20, http://www.washingtonpost.com/pb/archive/politics/1996/09/13/black-caucus-urges-probe-of-cia-contra-drug-charge/fefe4c2e-b0b5-4da7-9630-0bdb99e00fcd/?resType=accessibility

27. Jack E. White, "Crack, Contras and Cyberspace: When It Comes to the CIA and Drugs, Are the Paranoids on the Right Track?," *Time*, September 30, 1996, 59, http://content.time.com/time/magazine/article/0,9171,136590,00.html.

28. Michael A. Fletcher, "Conspiracy Theories Can Often Ring True; History Feeds Blacks' Mistrust," *Washington Post*, October 4, 1996, A1, http://people.duke.edu/%7Eldbaker/clippings/cons.html.

29. Donna Britt, "Finding the Truest Truth," *Washington Post*, October 4. 1996, B1, http://www.washingtonpost.com/archive/local/1996/10/04/finding-the-truest-truth/d62ccf2a-51a8-4a47-89fc-94b44dd7ad2f/.

30. Paul Shepard, "CIA-Drug Allegations Revive Black Fears of Anti-Black Conspiracy," Associated Press, October 5, 1996, http://www.apnewsarchive.com/1996/CIA-Drug-Allegations-Revive-Black-Fears-of-Anti-Black-Conspiracy/id-ae0e79ce0ce81e3114742b6ef68d35e8.

31. John L. Mitchell and Sam Fulwood III, "History Fuels Outrage over Crack Allegations," *Los Angeles Times*, October 22, 1996, A1, http://articles.latimes.com/1996-10-22/news/mn-56455_1_crack-cocaine.

32. Tim Golden, "Though Evidence is Thin, Tale of CIA and Drugs Has a Life of Its Own," *New York Times*, October 21, 1996, A14, http://www.nytimes.com/1996/10/21/us/though-evidence-is-thin-tale-of-cia-and-drugs-has-a-life-of-its-own.html.

33. Jim Naureckas, "That Delusional Mindset," *Extra!*, Fairness and Accuracy in Reporting (FAIR), January/February 1997, 16. For FAIR's overview of the media attacks on "Dark Alliance," see http://fair.org/extra-online-articles/snow-job.

34. Richard Cohen, "Crack and the CIA: Why the Story Lives," *Washington Post*, October 24, 1996, A21. For an online version of the column, see http://articles.philly.com/1996-10-26/news/25662920_1_black-soldiers-black-leaders-tuskegee-study.

35. Bruce A. Dixon, "Gary Webb, African-American Paranoia and the Black Consensus," *Black Commentator*, January 6, 2005, http://www.blackcommentator.com/120/120_dixon_webb.html.

36. Jack E. White, "Caught in the Middle: The CIA-Crack Story Put Black Reporters in a Bind," *Time*, May 26, 1997, 82, http://content.time.com/time/magazine/article/0,9171,986403,00.html.

37. See archives of Parry's *Consortium News* website (https://consortiumnews.com/), as well as Nick Schou, "New Dope on the Contra-Crack Connection," *LA Weekly*, December 20, 1996, 16, https://archive.is/MdDA3.

38. David LaGesse and George Rodrigue, "Claims Linking Contras, Drugs, El Salvador Revived," *Dallas Morning News*, November 30, 1996, http://web.archive.org/web/19970409203856/http://www2.sjmercury.com/drugs/postscript/update1130.htm.

39. Christopher Bellamy, "CIA 'was Embroiled' in Contra Drug Fund," *Independent*, December 12, 1996, http://www.independent.co.uk/news/world/cia-was-embroiled-in-contra-drug-fund-1314147.html.

40. Dermot Murnaghan (reporter), "The Crack Conspiracy," Independent Television (ITV), December 12, 1996. The author obtained an archived copy of the video from ITV headquarters in London in May 2015.

41. Ibid.

42. Ryan Devereaux, "Managing a Nightmare: How the CIA Watched over the Destruction of Gary Webb," *Intercept*, September 26, 2014, https://firstlook.org/theintercept/2014/09/25/managing-nightmare-cia-media-destruction-gary-webb/.

43. Nicholas Dujmovic, "CIA Public Affairs and the Drug Conspiracy Story," Central Intelligence Agency, *Studies in Intelligence* 41, no. 3 (1997): 9–14, http://www.foia.cia.gov/sites/default/files/DOC_0001372115.pdf.

44. Ibid., 10.

45. Ibid., 11.

46. Ibid., 11–12.

47. Ibid., 13.

48. Gary Webb, *Dark Alliance* (New York: Seven Stories Press, 1999), 464-466. For the original article, see Walter Pincus, "How I Traveled Abroad on CIA Subsidy," *San Jose Mercury News*, February 18, 1967.

49. Walter Pincus, "'I was Subsidized by the CIA,'" *Boston Globe*, February 17, 1967, 11.

50. Ibid. For more on the Pincus-CIA connection, see also Hugh Wilford, *The Mighty Wurlitzer: How the CIA Played America* (Cambridge, Massachusetts: Harvard University Press, 2008) and especially Karen M. Paget, *Patriotic Betrayal* (New Haven, Connecticut: Yale University Press, 2015).

51. John McCaslin, "Inside the Beltway: Drink to Your Health," *Washington Times*, July 31, 1996, A10.

52. See Stuart H. Loory, "The CIA's Use of the Press: A Mighty Wurlitzer," *Columbia Journalism Review*, September/October 1974, 9–18. See also Carl Bernstein, "The CIA and the Media," *Rolling Stone*, October 20, 1977, 55–67, http://www.carlbernstein.com/magazine_cia_and_media.php. For the three-day *New York Times* series by reporter John M. Crewdson, titled "CIA: Secret Shaper of Public Opinion," see "The CIA's 3-Decade Effort to Mold the World's Views," *New York Times*, December 25, 1977, A1, A12; "Worldwide Propaganda Network Built by the CIA," *New York Times*, December 26, 1977, A1, A37; and "CIA Established Many Links to Journalists in US and Abroad," *New York Times*, December 27, 1977, A1, A40.

53. Dujmovic, "CIA Public Affairs and the Drug Conspiracy Story," 9.

54. According to the author's review of "Dark Alliance"-related articles listed in the *San Jose Mercury News* online archives (www.mercurynews.com). For the story, see Gary Webb, "US Gave Visa to Nicaraguan Drug Trafficker," *San Jose Mercury News*, December 31, 1996, 11A, http://web.archive.org/web/19970409203834/http://www2.sjmercury.com/drugs/postscript/update1231.htm.

55. Jerry Ceppos, "To Readers of Our 'Dark Alliance' Series," *San Jose Mercury News*, May 11, 1997, https://web.archive.org/web/19971119070955/http://www.sjmercury.com/drugs/column051197.htm. See also "Newspaper Admits Shortcomings in Drug Series," Associated Press, May 11, 1997, http://www.apnewsarchive.com/1997/Newspaper-admits-shortcomings-in-drug-series/id-0d1607f2a63b4b584ab668f5ca4a0250.

56. Todd S. Purdum, "Exposé on Crack was Flawed, Paper Says," *New York Times*, May 13, 1997, A1, http://www.nytimes.com/1997/05/13/us/expose-on-crack-was-flawed-paper-says.html.

57. "The Mercury News Comes Clean," *New York Times*, May 14, 1997, A20, http://www.nytimes.com/1997/05/14/opinion/the-mercury-news-comes-clean.html.

58. John M. Deutch, "A Time to Open Up the CIA," *New York Times*, May 18, 1997. For a transcript of the article online, see http://www.rave.ca/en/news_info/197703/all.

59. "CIA Drug Trafficking Town Hall Meeting," C-SPAN, November 15, 1996, http://www.c-span.org/video/?76861-1/cia-drug-trafficking-town-hall-meeting.

60. Gary Webb, "Mercury News Retraction," Usenet group, May 16, 1997, http://to.or.at/scl/scl1/msg03567.html. (For a correctly dated version, see http://www.rense.com/political/ciacrack.htm.) A reposting of Webb's message on Usenet can also be found at https://archive.is/EG6ym. The author, Brian Covert, was subscribed to Usenet groups at the time, and can vouch for the authenticity of Webb's posting.

61. Tina Daunt, "Written in Pain," Los Angeles Times, March 16, 2005, E1, http://articles.latimes.com/2005/mar/16/entertainment/et-webb16.

62. "Freeway: Crack in the System," Al Jazeera America, http://america.aljazeera.com/watch/shows/ajam-presents-freeway.html. For the film's official website, see http://crackinthesystem.com.

63. For the two CIA inspector general reports, see "Report of Investigation—Volume I: The California Story," January 28, 1998, https://www.cia.gov/library/reports/general-reports-1/cocaine/report, and "Volume II: The Contra Story," October 8, 1998, https://www.cia.gov/library/reports/general-reports-1/cocaine/contra-story/contents.html. For the Department of Justice inspector general report, see "The CIA-Contra-Crack Cocaine Controversy: A Review of the Justice Department's Investigations and Prosecutions," July 23, 1998, https://oig.justice.gov/special/9712. For the House Intelligence Committee report, see "Report on the Central Intelligence Agency's Alleged Involvement in Crack Cocaine Trafficking in the Los Angeles Area," February 2000, https://archive.org/details/House-Intelligence-Report-Crack-Cocaine-CIA.

64. Millender-McDonald died in 2007, with the CIA director's public appearance that day in 1996 now etched into her political legacy. See http://www.washingtonpost.com/wp-dyn/content/article/2007/04/22/AR2007042201358.html.

65. San Jose Mercury News executive editor Jerry Ceppos, for example, was among the recipients of the first "ethics in journalism" award by the Society of Professional Journalists in October 1997, a few months after having killed the "Dark Alliance" series. See Tracy Seipel, "Journalists Honor MN Editor; Ethics Award Cites Ceppos' Column on 'Dark Alliance' Series," San Jose Mercury News, October 7, 1997, 4A. Ceppos today serves as dean of the journalism department at Louisiana State University; see http://www.manship.lsu.edu/staff/jerry-ceppos/.

66. Justin McCarthy, "Trust in Mass Media Returns to All-Time Low," Gallup.com, September 17, 2014, http://www.gallup.com/poll/176042/trust-mass-media-returns-time-low.aspx.

67. A recommended source is Miriam DeCosta-Willis, ed., The Memphis Diary of Ida B. Wells (Boston: Beacon Press, 1995). See also http://www2.webster.edu/~woolflm/idabwells.html.

68. Seymour M. Hersh, "Huge CIA Operation Reported in US against Antiwar Forces, Other Dissidents in Nixon Years," New York Times, December 22, 1974, A1, http://goodtimesweb.org/covert-operations/2013/nyt-cia-operation-antiwar-forces-dec-22-1974.html. For related follow-up stories by Hersh, see also "Proxmire to Seek Inquiry on CIA over Role in US," New York Times, December 23, 1974, A1; and "Underground for the CIA in New York: An Ex-Agent Tells of Spying on Students," New York Times, December 29, 1974, A1. Hersh is quoted in Kathryn S. Olmsted, Challenging the Secret Government: The Post-Watergate Investigations of the CIA and FBI (Chapel Hill: University of North Carolina Press, 1996), 34.

69. Seymour M. Hersh, "The Killing of Osama bin Laden," London Review of Books, May 21, 2015, 3-12, http://www.lrb.co.uk/v37/n10/seymour-m-hersh/the-killing-of-osama-bin-laden. See also Trevor Timm, "The Media's Reaction to Seymour Hersh's Bin Laden Scoop Has been Disgraceful," Columbia Journalism Review, May 15, 2015, http://www.cjr.org/analysis/seymour_hersh_osama_bin_laden.php.

70. Anya Schiffrin, Global Muckraking: 100 Years of Investigative Journalism from around the World (New York: New Press, 2014), https://thenewpress.com/books/global-muckraking. For equally inspiring stories, see also Carl Jensen, Stories that Changed America: Muckrakers of the 20th Century (New York: Seven Stories Press, 2002), http://catalog.sevenstories.com/products/stories-that-changed.

CHAPTER 8

Twenty-First-Century Fascism
Private Military Companies in Service to the Transnational Capitalist Class

Peter Phillips, Ray McClintock, Melissa Carneiro,
and Jacob Crabtree

Globalization of trade and central banking has propelled private corporations to positions of power and control never before seen in human history. Under advanced capitalism, the structural demands for a return on investment require an unending expansion of central-ized capital in the hands of fewer and fewer people. The financial center of global capitalism is so highly concentrated that less than a few thousand people dominate and control $100 trillion of wealth.[1] At the same time half of the world's population lives on less than three dollars a day and some 40,000 people die daily from malnutrition and easily curable diseases. This gross inequality is what William Rob-inson calls the crisis of humanity.[2] This crisis of capitalism threatens humanity in an unprecedented manner not only by increasing mass poverty, but also in terms of environmental and spiritual poverty. The world faces a new dark age of neo-feudal totalitarianism unlike any previously known.[3]

The few thousand people controlling global capital amount to less than 0.0001 percent of the world's population. They are the transna-tional capitalist class (TCC), who, as the capitalist elite of the world, dominate nation-states through international treaty agreements and transnational state organizations such as the World Bank, the Bank for International Settlements, and the International Monetary Fund.[4] The TCC communicates their policy requirements through global networks such as the G-7 and G-20, and various nongovernmental policy organizations such as the World Economic Forum, the Trilateral Commission, and the Bilderberger Group. The TCC represents the interests of hundreds of thousands of millionaires and billionaires who comprise the richest people in the top 1 percent of the world's wealth hierarchy. Ironically, the extreme accumulation of concentrated capital at the top creates a continuing problem for the TCC, who must continually scour the world for new investment opportunities that will yield adequate returns.

War is one use for over-accumulated capital. A permanent war on terror offers a unique opportunity for the TCC to loan capital at a profit to governments for military actions, and to participate in rebuilding efforts made necessary by war. The collection of taxes on working people's incomes to pay for permanent war results in increasing pressure toward neoliberal governmental austerity measures, which further impoverish the 99 percent and transfer yet more wealth to the global 1 percent.

The TCC are keenly aware of both their elite status and their increasing vulnerabilities to democracy movements and to unrest from the teeming masses. The military empire dominated by the US and the North Atlantic Treaty Organization (NATO) serves to protect TCC investments around the world.[5] Wars, regime changes, and occupations performed in service of empire support investors' access to natural resources and their speculative advantages in the market place.

When the empire is slow to perform or faced with political resistance, private security firms and private military companies increasingly fulfill the TCC's demands for the protections of their assets. These protection services include personal security for TCC executives and their families, protection of safe residential and work zones, tactical military advisory and training of national police and armed forces, intelligence gathering on democracy movements and opposition groups, weapons acquisitions and weapon systems management, and strike forces for military actions and assassinations.[6]

Private military companies (PMC)—known less formally as mercenaries—have been part of armies as far back as the Roman Empire. To protect their interests throughout the Mediterranean, the wealthy city-states of Florence, Genoa, and Venice, which lacked large populations for raising armies, hired mercenaries under a contract (*condotta*) system. The Dutch East India Company and the British East India Company hired private soldiers to protect their investments around the world.[7] However, a newer form of PMC has been emerging in the past few decades, one that involves the penetration of private capital into the security business of protecting the TCC's interests and global capitalism. The expanding crisis of desperate masses, alienated work forces, and environmental exhaustion means an unlimited opportunity for PMCs to engage in the enforcement of TCC dictates.[8]

The Iraq War opened the opportunity for a rapid increase of PMCs. The US spent billions annually on security, with some 150 PMCs in the Iraq and Afghanistan war zones.[9] By 2008, there were more PMC mercenaries than actual US government troops in Iraq.[10] In 2010–11, the Department of Defense (DOD) had 90,339 contractor personnel in Afghanistan and 64,250 in Iraq. From 2005 to 2010, the DOD spent $146 billion on PMCs in the Afghan/Iraq war theater. The majority of the private contracting was for base support and logistics; however, 18 percent of the private contractors in Iraq—roughly

www.CORPWATCH.ORG

10,000 people—were listed as working in security. A third of these security contracts involved US citizens, 15 percent were locals, and the balance consisted of third-country nationals.[11] Many of the PMCs in Middle East wars were opportunistic organizations that withdrew as the war scaled down, but the largest PMCs not only maintain presences there today but also have expanded their services to other countries and private corporations worldwide.

Actual expenditures by the US government for PMCs remain high as the US scales down its troop presence in the region.[12] Some of the largest and most famous firms have merged and/or reconfigured in order to hide negative reputations. They are increasingly integrated in ways that expand their abilities to offer security and safety to the TCC while generating profits. "The newest wave of private military agents are commercial enterprises first and foremost. They are hierarchically organized and registered businesses that trade and compete openly (for the most part) and are vertically integrated into the wider global marketplace."[13]

In this chapter we evaluate six of the current largest PMCs in terms of their history, growth, and stability. We examine (1) Aegis; (2) Academi (better known by its previous name, Blackwater) and Triple Canopy, which merged to form Constellis Holdings; (3) Military Professional Resources Inc. (L-3 MPRI); (4) Erinys; (5) G4S; and (6) DynCorp. We identify trends and commonalities that demonstrate the increasing militarization of capitalism and the transnational capitalist class.

AEGIS DEFENSE SYSTEMS

Tim Spicer, a British citizen, founded Sandline International in 1995. Calling Sandline a "private military company," Spicer arranged a three-month, $35-million contract with Papua New Guinea to provide mercenaries, intelligence, weapons (including attack helicopters), and troop training in support of the government's civil war against separatist rebels. One month into the war, the regular army, supported by the Australian government, staged a coup, and arrested Spicer and his forty-seven mercenaries and expelled them from the country.[14] Spicer went on to found Aegis Defense Systems in 2002, now a multimillion-dollar PMC. Based in London, Aegis boasts "project experience in over 60 countries."[15]

Aegis offers private security services to governments, international agencies, and corporations. On its website, Aegis reports that it "now provides a wide breadth of complimentary service streams including Kidnap for Ransom Support, technology integration, advisory and intelligence, training, consultancy, strategic communications and protective services."[16] Aegis is registered as a United Nations contractor and is a main security provider to the US government. Over the past decade, its contracts with the United States Department of Defense exceed $1.3 billion in services. For instance, it is under contract with the DOD to provide security support services for the US Project and Contracting Office that manages the US reconstruction program in Iraq.[17] Additionally, "[i]n separate contracts, AEGIS provides security protection to a number of significant blue chip companies operating in Iraq."[18] A November 2014 DOD document reports that Aegis has a $12.7 million contract to provide private security services at Kandahar Airfield in Afghanistan through September 2015.[19]

Aegis's twelve board members are all men and include nine high-ranking former military officers, three international finance and banking people, two former members of British Parliament, and president Ronald Reagan's national security advisor, Robert McFarlane.[20]

BLACKWATER

Blackwater is probably the best-known private security company in the world. Started in 1997 by Erik Prince, an ex-Navy SEAL (Sea, Air, Land teams), the company was established to provide top-level training for the United States military and law enforcement. Their training center was 7,000 acres of swampland on the border of North Carolina and Virginia. Blackwater was awarded its first government contract after the bombing of the USS *Cole* in October 2000. It opened another training center in 2001 with indoor and outdoor shooting ranges, urban city reproductions, a man-made lake, and several driving tracks.

In early 2002, Blackwater USA established a branch specifically devoted to fulfilling security contracts. One of its first big contracts was to provide twenty men with top-secret security clearances to protect the Central Intelligence Agency (CIA) headquarters in Kabul, Afghanistan, which was tasked with hunting down Osama bin Laden.[21]

Soon thereafter, Blackwater was firmly footed in America's business overseas, especially in Iraq and Afghanistan. In addition to governmental affairs, Blackwater has also been the recipient of numerous private contracts, most of which have been kept secret. In the aftermath of Hurricane Katrina, 200 Blackwater employees deployed to the devastated areas. There are conflicting reports as to their actual business in the areas affected by Katrina. Blackwater insisted they were there to provide humanitarian aid, free of charge, while others note that many Blackwater employees were under contract to protect government buildings. Either way, Blackwater was an undeniable presence in Katrina's aftermath.[22]

In May 2006, the US government awarded Blackwater, DynCorp, and Triple Canopy contracts to provide diplomatic security in Iraq, establishing an unprecedented number of hired guns working overseas for this purpose.[23]

Perhaps the most notorious event involving Blackwater took place at Nisour Square in Baghdad on September 16, 2007, when Blackwater employees killed seventeen Iraqi civilians. According to Iraqi government sources, a convoy of US State Department diplomats was approaching Nisour Square when their Blackwater guards spotted an unidentified car traveling on the wrong side of the road. The US convoy opened fire on the vehicle and also threw stun grenades to clear the scene. Nearby Iraqi police mistook the stun grenades for fragmentation grenades and returned fire on the convoy. The Iraqi government holds firmly that the Iraqi civilians were fired upon without provocation.[24]

Blackwater claimed that its guards gave multiple warnings to the car by means of verbal commands, hand gestures, and throwing water bottles at the car. The vehicle had slowed but failed to stop when an Iraqi police officer approached the car and appeared to push it toward the convoy. With insurgents commonly disguising themselves as police, the Blackwater guards feared the convoy was under attack and they fired on the car, killing the driver, a passenger, and the police officer. As more police officers returned fire on the convoy, the situation grew increasingly chaotic, and the convoy ultimately needed support to exit the scene.[25]

When the smoke settled, altogether seventeen Iraqi civilians were dead and twenty more had been wounded. The following day the Iraqi government suspended Blackwater operations in the country. The incident fueled Iraqi rage over American involvement, severely weakened political ties, and created a backlash in the US over private security firms.[26] In October 2014, a US federal district court found that the deaths were not a battlefield tragedy, but the result of criminal acts. The court convicted four of the Blackwater guards on charges of murder, manslaughter, and using a machine gun. All of the convicted face several decades, potentially up to life, in prison.[27]

Following the Nisour Square incident, Blackwater began a process of restructuring its public image. In October 2007, Blackwater USA changed its name to Blackwater Worldwide, altered its company logo, and started shifting resources away from security contracting. In 2009, Blackwater Worldwide changed its name yet again to Xe Services LLC, and also began another round of restructuring. Founder and CEO Erik Prince resigned as CEO and Joseph Yorio took over daily operations, while Prince continued as chairman of the board. In 2010 a private group of investors purchased Xe and renamed the company Academi. The new company instituted a new management system, created a compliance and governance program, and assembled a leadership team characterized by "deep experience with crisis management" and prior experience in senior government positions.[28] The members of Academi's board of directors all serve on the corporate board of Constellis, which has controlled Blackwater and Triple Canopy since 2014.

TRIPLE CANOPY

Triple Canopy is a private security-and-risk-management company founded in 2003 by former US Special Forces soldiers Tom Katis and Matt Mann. The name Triple Canopy references the layered canopies of jungles where the company's founders received training. Triple Canopy secured its first government contracts in 2004, following the US invasion of Iraq. Like many PMCs, most of its early contracts were to protect high-ranking government officials, as well as troops in transportation. Soon, contracts included the protection of high-risk US embassies around the world, and in Iraq a growing presence beyond Baghdad.[29] After the 2007 Nisour Square massacre, Triple Canopy's profile in Iraq increased. The investigation of its PMC rival, Blackwater, gave Triple Canopy the chance to take over lucrative contracts previously fulfilled by Blackwater.[30]

To differentiate itself from Blackwater, Triple Canopy championed a code of conduct for private security forces. According to CEO Ignacio Balderas, "While governments and clients play an important role in regulating the sector, the industry itself must be willing to take a stand and set standards."[31] Triple Canopy's website promotes Balderas and the company as being at the forefront of developing an international code of conduct for private security contractors.[32]

Although Triple Canopy has tried to present itself as an ethical company, they have issues of their own. For example, on July 8, 2006, four Triple Canopy guards on duty in Baghdad were involved in multiple shootings of civilians. The incident centered around one guard in particular, Jacob C. Washbourne, who was accused of firing on Iraqi civilians in three separate incidents that day. Although the incident's details are unclear, in part due to a nearly impenetrable protective curtain that shields private contractors from blame, the *Washington Post* put together most of the pieces of the story. The day before Washbourne was due to return home, he and three other guards went on typical runs up and down Baghdad's Airport Road. Those three reported that Washbourne told them, "I want to kill somebody today." Later, Washbourne opened fire on two civilian trucks, stating that he felt threatened by them, and at close range on a taxi.[33]

The fates of those Washbourne opened fire on that day are unknown because Triple Canopy conducted the only known inquiry into the situation. The three other guards with Washbourne that day described him as a man on a rampage who, as their team leader, instructed them to not disclose what happened that day. Washbourne denied all responsibility for firing on the trucks and denies that the shooting on the taxi ever occurred. He and two of the other guards were terminated for not properly reporting the incidents.[34] Realizing the possible severity of the incident, Triple Canopy reported it to the director of security for the Green Zone in Iraq, who declined to investigate and referred the case to Joint Contracting Command for Iraq, who in turn also declined to investigate what happened. The case went cold when a spokesperson for the US Central Command said, "This is not a Centcom issue. It's whoever was running that contract. We're fighting a war here."[35]

Although Triple Canopy may present itself as a paragon of ethical practices in the private security and contracting world, it is still complicit in the broader issue of the unchecked power that private security companies have over civilians. Triple Canopy, along with dozens of other private security, logistics, and reconstruction contractors, were the beneficiaries of $138 billion allocated by the US for the Iraq War.[36] As Triple Canopy continued to gain prominence following the Iraq War, it joined with rival firm Academi (Blackwater) under a new management team, Constellis Holdings, which has consolidated some of the private security world's biggest players into a single firm.

CONSTELLIS HOLDINGS

Constellis Holdings is a leading provider of security, support, and advisory services to the US government, foreign governments, multinational corporations, and international organizations. Constellis Holdings came into existence in June 2014 with the merger of Academi (Blackwater) and Triple Canopy. At the time, the conglomerate acquired numerous other prominent companies that were under the former Constellis Group, including Strategic Social, Tidewater Global Services, and National Strategic Protective Services.[37]

While all of the Constellis Group companies, including Academi and Triple Canopy, remain officially separate, they are under the control of the larger umbrella of Constellis Holdings. With the merger, all of these companies are able to utilize each other's resources, most notably Academi's world-class training facility. The majority of the new board of directors are from Academi,[38] which makes it hard to overlook that this may be yet another attempt by its leadership to distance the company from its tarnished Blackwater past. In any event, the resources and manpower now consolidated as Constellis likely make it the most powerful PMC firm.

Red McCombs leads the all-male board of directors. With an estimated net worth of $1.78 billion, he ranks no. 1,054 on the *Forbes* list of the world's billionaires.[39] He is a former owner of the Minnesota Vikings, Denver Nuggets, and San Antonio Spurs, as well as a cofounder of Clear Channel Communications.[40] Joining McCombs on the board is John Ashcroft, the former attorney general under George W. Bush, and one of the driving advocates of the war on terror after September 11, 2001. The board also includes retired admiral Bobby Inman and two leading finance managers, Dean Bosacki and Jason DeYonker. The final two men on the board are Jack Quinn, a leading Democratic advisor for many years, who served as chief of staff to vice president Al Gore from 1993 to 1995 and as counsel to President Clinton from 1995 to 1997, and Tom Katis, the cofounder of Triple Canopy and a decorated Special Forces veteran who earned a Bronze Star as a Green Beret.[41]

ERINYS

Jonathan Garrett, a former British Army officer, founded Erinys in 2002. Garrett graduated from the Royal Military Academy–Sandhurst in 1983 and began working in the private sector in 1992 with Defence Systems Limited (now ArmorGroup International), mostly in Africa. He is the CEO of Erinys, which is incorporated in the British Virgin Islands and headquartered in Dubai, with offices and subsidiaries in Africa, Iraq, and England. The name Erinys comes from the avenging goddesses of Greek mythology, Erinyes, who punish crimes against the natural order.

Erinys was awarded a lucrative contract by the US Army Corps of Engineers to protect Iraqi oil fields in 2003.[42] The contract was awarded to Erinys's subsidiary Erinys Iraq Ltd., which was a surprise to many observers at the time. However, a member of the Iraqi National Congress was one of Erinys Iraq Ltd.'s founding partners, and its director, Faisal Daghistani, was the son of one of Iraqi politician Ahmed Chalabi's most trusted friends. Chalabi had close ties with neoconservatives in the Bush administration and reportedly acted as the middleman in dealings with Erinys Iraq, which resulted in them getting the contract.[43] Erinys employed up to 1,000 people in Iraq.

The company faced a lawsuit over the death of an American soldier who was killed by an Erinys convoy in 2005. The suit was the first case of its kind.[44] It was involved in a shooting incident in 2008 with an Iraqi taxi, which left three unarmed civilians wounded.[45]

Outside Iraq, Erinys has significant, if troubling, connections across Africa, including the founders' ties dating back to apartheid-era South Africa and white supremacist Rhodesia (now Zimbabwe), as well as operations in Nigeria and Ghana.[46]

An undated page on the company's Web site indicates: "Following recent changes in control the board is currently being reconstituted."[47] Previously, an all-male board of directors has led Erinys.[48] Its past members include John Holmes, a former Special Air Services (SAS) commando in the British Army; Alastair Morrison, the cofounder of Defence Systems Ltd., and another former SAS officer, who is famous for his involvement in the rescue of hostages held on a Lufthansa jet in Mogadishu, Somalia, in 1977; and Michael Hutchings, a career soldier in the British Army. Sean Cleary, a former South African military intelligence operative, served on the board of Erinys South Africa.

MILITARY PROFESSIONAL RESOURCES INC. (MPRI)

Retired US major general Vernon B. Lewis Jr. founded MPRI in 1987. By 2002 it had grown to forty administrators, 800 field agents, and 12,500 personnel on call, with over $100 million in contracts. In 1997, MPRI's all-male board consisted of thirteen US generals and an admiral.[49]

MPRI provided military consulting on security services and tactical operations in several countries in the 1990s, including Bosnia, Croatia, Macedonia, Colombia, Angola, and Nigeria. In 1994, MPRI served as consultants to the Croatian army. Though the firm denies helping to conduct offensive operations against Bosnian Serbs—which would have been in violation of a 1991 UN Security Council arms embargo that made direct military assistance illegal—analysts believe that MPRI directly supported the Croatian army's Operation Storm in August 1995, which "utilized typical American operational tactics, including integrated air, artillery and infantry movements, and the use of maneuver war fighting techniques to destroy Serbian command and control networks."[50]

The Croat surprise attack was described as "a lighting five pronged offensive, integrating air power, artillery, and rapid infantry movements . . . classic US Army textbook tactics."[51] The Croatian success led to some 200,000 to 300,000 Serbs fleeing the region, creating the worst refugee crisis of the Yugoslav war.[52]

In 2000, L-3 Communications acquired MPRI for $40 million. Under L-3, MPRI won numerous contracts. In 2001, it serviced both sides of the Balkan war: MPRI provided consultants to the Macedonian government, while MPRI trainers worked with a branch of the Kosovo Liberation Army (KLA), rebels opposed to the Macedonian forces. Under the auspices of NATO, US forces "saved" 500 rebels from Macedonian forces, including seventeen MPRI instructors, relocated them to another area, and allowed them to keep their US-made weapons.[53] In 2005, MPRI received a six-year contract with the Department of Justice to support the International Criminal Investigative Training Assistance Program in providing personnel and facilities for law enforcement programs in foreign countries. That contract was reported to be worth up to $400 million. In 2008, MPRI was one of a handful of PMCs contracted by the US military for "information operations" in Iraq and possibly Afghanistan.[54]

MPRI was quietly disappeared by L-3 Communications in 2014 after agreeing to pay $3.2 million for false labor charges in supporting the US Army in Afghanistan. The US Department of Justice proved that MPRI billed for employees who had not worked because they were on leave outside the country. The false billing occurred between March 2005 and October 2010.[55] By the end of 2014, MPRI was no longer listed on the L-3 Communications website. Its offices in Virginia were closed and its website was no longer active. L-3 now lists CyTerra as its primary securities division.[56] CyTerra has also had difficulties with proper billing.[57]

G4S

With roughly 625,000 employees spanning five continents in more than 120 countries, G4S is one of the largest private-sector employers in the world. Some of its more important contractors are the governments of the UK, the US, Israel, and Australia; in the private sector it has worked with corporations such as Chrysler, Apple, and the Bank of America.[58]

According to its own website, the company known today as G4S traces its roots back to a Danish security firm established in 1901. That company, through a series of mergers, became Securicor in 1951. It then became Group 4 Securicor in 2004 when Securicor merged with Group 4 Falck. In 2002, Group 4 Falck had entered the US security market by acquiring the Wackenhut Corporation, which was the second largest US security services company at the time.[59] Since its beginnings, Wackenhut had strong ties to the US government and especially its military.[60] Group 4 Securicor became known as G4S in 2006.

The second-largest private employer in the world, G4S offers security guards, alarms, management and transportation of cash and valuables, prison management, and electronic monitoring of offenders in 120 countries worldwide.[61] G4S's annual revenue in 2014 was nearly $10.5 billion.[62] Increasingly, G4S operates in "complex environments" and accepts jobs that national armies are not trained to do.[63]

In Nigeria, Chevron contracts with G4S for counterinsurgency operations including fast-response mercenaries. G4S undertakes similar operations in South Sudan, and has provided surveillance equipment for checkpoints and prisons in Israel and security for Jewish settlements in Palestine.[64]

The G4S board of directors consists of nine men and two women, and, unlike board members of the previously described PMCs, none of G4S's board members list prior military service, instead encompassing a broad range of backgrounds, including finance, media, accounting, and logistics.[65]

G4S has been plagued with problems in the last decade, including most noticeably its botched contract at the 2012 London Olympic Games. G4S failed to provide the 10,000-plus trained employees it had promised under contract. Instead G4S provided roughly 2,000 properly trained personnel, with many more receiving only a few weeks' preparation. The result led to the British military being called on to provide some 13,000 troops to maintain security alongside G4S during the Games.[66]

In June 2014, G4S was accused of violently removing protesters from outside its own London offices, a claim the company denied. A few months later G4S had to pay $100,000 for unlawfully restraining youths in a secure training facility. In 2011, a double amputee was improperly secured in one of G4S's ambulance services and died while he was being transported to the hospital. An inquest found that G4S staff had not been sufficiently trained to move patients safely from their homes to hospitals. And as far back as 2004, a fifteen-year-old died when three G4S employees at Rainsbrook Secure Training Center restrained him. None of the officers were charged in that incident.[67]

As of July 2012, the financial core of the transnational capitalist class was heavily invested in G4S.[68] Nine of the thirteen largest, most-connected money management firms and banks in the world have direct investment holdings in G4S.[69] The financial core of the TCC is directly linked to and invested in the world's largest PMC.

DYNCORP

DynCorp originated with two companies formed in 1946, an aviation maintenance business named Land-Air Inc., and a cargo business started by World War II pilots, California Eastern Airways.[70] After mergers and resulting name changes, the company became known as DynCorp in 1987. By 1994, it reported over one billion dollars in annual revenues; after merging with or acquiring some forty additional companies, DynCorp earned revenues of $2.4 billion in 2003.[71] In 2003, the Computer Sciences Corporation purchased DynCorp for $914 million, then two years later sold part of the company to Veritas Capital Fund LP for $850 million. After being a privately held company since 1988, the company went public in 2006.[72] In 2010, Cerberus Capital Management acquired DynCorp International for $1.5 billion.[73]

DynCorp currently employs 22,300 people, offering services in "global stabilization" that include international policing and police training, judicial support, immigration services, base operations, and security for diplomats and senior governmental officials.[74] In 2005, CorpWatch described DynCorp as "the world's premier rent-a-cop business," which "runs the security show in Afghanistan, Iraq, and the US–Mexico border. They also run the coca crop-dusting business in Colombia, and occasional sex trafficking sorties in Bosnia."[75]

DynCorp remains under the control of Cerberus Capital Management LP. Cerberus describes itself as a leading private investment firm with an investment team consisting of nine primary advisors. The all-male team consists mostly of Ivy League graduates, including high-level finance capital advisors and two lawyers. The most politically connected advisors are John Snow, former US secretary of the treasury (2003–06) and chairman of the Business Roundtable; and former US vice president Dan Quayle (1989–93).[76]

ANALYSIS

In *Global Capitalism and the Crisis of Humanity*, William Robinson devotes a chapter to the policing of global capitalism in the twenty-first century. He describes transnational capitalist class elites' responses to democracy movements, including their reliance on militarism, masculinization, racism, and scapegoats as ideological justifications for police state repression.[77]

Robinson hypothesizes that continuing the concentration of capital and massive poverty will lead to nation-states facing legitimation crises that would require them to employ a vast host of coercive control mechanisms, including mass incarceration, various levels of martial law, and an increasing separation of classes into restrictive geographical zones.[78]

Private military contractors would play an essential role in the enforcement of this future neofascist capitalist world that Robinson foresees. Capital would be free to travel instantly and internationally to anywhere that profits are possible, while nation-states would become little more than population containment zones with increasingly repressive labor controls. For these reasons, many scholars have come to understand PMCs as a component of neoliberal imperialism that now supplements nation-states' police powers and could eventually substitute for them.[79] Estimates are that over $200 billion is spent on private security globally, with higher annual expenditures anticipated. The industry currently employs some fifteen million people worldwide. Many of the security companies are smaller versions of G4S, offering a range of services from guarding banks and private buildings to armed security and outright warfare.[80]

The firms we reviewed offer the full range of PMC services. The larger firms are increasingly integrated within the world of transnational capital. PMC boards of directors and advisors—almost exclusively male—represent some of the most powerfully connected people in the world with multiple sociopolitical interlocks to governments, military, finance, and policy groups.[81]

The trend toward privatization of war is a serious threat to human rights, due process, and democratic transparency and accountability.[82] The US/NATO military empire sets the moral standards for denial of human rights by using pilotless drones to kill civilians without regard for international law in various regions of resistance to empire. Labeling dead civilians as insurgents and terrorists, the complete lack of due process and human rights belies any standard of governmental moral legitimacy. This lack of moral legitimacy in turn sets standards for private military companies to operate with much the same malice in the shadow of the empire.

The globalization of PMC operations alongside transnational capital investment, international trade agreements, and an increasing concentration of wealth in the TCC means that the repressive practices of private security and war will inevitably come home to roost in the US, the European Union, and other first-world nations.

The 99 percent of us without wealth and private police power face the looming threat of overt repression and complete loss of human rights and legal protections.[83] We see signs of this daily with police killings (now close to a hundred per month in the US),[84] warrantless electronic spying, mass incarceration, random traffic checkpoints, airport security/no-fly lists, and Homeland Security compilations of databases on suspected radicals.

We must recognize that among the 99 percent are reactionary elements characterized by extreme racism, homophobia, and xenophobia that will be encouraged and unleashed by the empire to disrupt emerging democracy and human rights movements. The resulting chaos and fear will be used to justify even more repression and martial law. The rapid deployment of repressive shock forces remains imminently possible in coming years, requiring only natural disaster, actual security threats, or false flag operations in order to be implemented. The massive police lockdown of segments of the city of Boston after the marathon bombings on April 15, 2013, is one example of the rapid deployment of thousands of police and the implementation of de facto martial law. Boston residents seemingly accepted government orders for them to stay indoors and shelter in place.[85]

Each time we look past the crimes of the empire we lose a portion of our integrity of self. Ignoring repression becomes part of continuing compromise in our daily lives leading to a moral malaise and increased feelings of helplessness. It becomes easier to accept as normal the presence of the police state and PMC agents in our daily lives—after all, they are keeping us "safe" from the evil ones. As humanitarian activists we must continue to personally address these issues openly and honestly by asking the individuals in control of global capital for moral legitimacy, structural mediation, and systemic reform.

There seems little possibility that the electoral process in the US or most nation-states will allow for elected officials—even progressive and fair-minded ones—to forestall capitalism's need for continued growth. Even progressive tax reform and adjustments in income inequality would likely be inadequate to offset the rapid deterioration of the global environment and the massive poverty facing half of humanity.

It is time to address the capitalist elite, the one-thousandth of 1 percent, by directly appealing to their humanity. Given the emerging research on the transnational capitalist class—the few thousand individuals who control $100 trillion worth of capital—it would seem that an organized group of nongovernmental organizations and civil society leaders could seek to negotiate directly with the financial core of the TCC to explore ways of addressing war, fascism, global poverty, and environmental collapse.[86] After all, these managers of global capital have names, physical addresses, and online presences. They also have families (including, in many cases, children and grandchildren) and friends who are increasingly threatened by global chaos. The financial core of the TCC is in a position of power to make corrections to the formation and use of capital, which could serve humanity's needs rather than simply drive profits. This isn't an all-or-nothing agenda, but rather an attempt to mediate the massive negative consequences of the path of continuing capitalist concentration of wealth in the desire to prevent global socioeconomic and/or environmental collapse. In actuality, humankind is faced with extinction, at least to life as we know it, and any attempt to forestall this global certainty seems worth the effort.

PETER PHILLIPS is a professor of sociology at Sonoma State University, and president of Media Freedom Foundation, the nonprofit of which Project Censored is a program.

RAY MCCLINTOCK, MELISSA CARNEIRO, and JACOB CRABTREE are seniors at Sonoma State University.

Notes

1. Peter Phillips and Brady Osborne, "Exposing the Financial Core of the Transnational Corporate Class," *Censored 2014: Fearless Speech in Fateful Times*, eds. Mickey Huff and Andy Lee Roth (New York: Seven Stories Press, 2013), 313–30.
2. William I. Robinson, *Global Capitalism and the Crisis of Humanity* (New York: Cambridge University Press, 2014).
3. For a short review of William Robinson's work in his own words, listen to his interview on the *Project Censored Show* from April 26, 2015, http://www.projectcensored.org/sociologist-william-robinson-and-kathy-kelly.
4. Peter Phillips and Kimberly Soeiro, "The Global 1 Percent Ruling Class Exposed," *Censored 2013: Dispatches from the Media Revolution*, eds. Mickey Huff and Andy Lee Roth (New York: Seven Stories Press, 2012), 235–58.
5. See, for example, *Censored* story #13, "Pentagon and NATO Encircle Russia and China," in this volume.
6. Christian Davenport, "Companies Can Spend Millions on Security Measures to Keep Executives Safe," *Washington Post*, June 6, 2014, http://www.washingtonpost.com/business/economy/companies-can-spend-millions-on-security-measures-to-keep-executives-safe/2014/06/06/5f500350-e802-11e3-afc6-a1dd9407abcf_story.html; John Whitehead, "Private Police: Mercenaries of the American Police State," OpEd News, March 4, 2015, http://www.opednews.com/articles/Private-Police-Mercenarie-by-John-Whitehead-Police-Abuse-Of-Power_Police-Brutality_Police-Coverup_Police-State-150304-539.html.
7. Richard Godfrey et al., "Mapping the Terrain," *Organization* 21, no. 1 (2014): 106–25.
8. Luke McKenna and Robert Johnson, "A Look at the World's Most Powerful Mercenary Armies," *Business Insider*, February 26, 2012, http://www.businessinsider.com/bi-mercenary-armies-2012-2.
9. Shawn Engbrecht, *America's Covert Warriors: Inside the World of Private Military Contractors* (Washington DC: Potomac Books, 2011), 18.
10. Steve Fainaru, *Big Boy Rules: America's Mercenaries Fighting in Iraq* (Boston: Da Capo Press, 2008), 24.
11. Moshe Schwartz and Joyprada Swain, "Department of Defense Contractors in Afghanistan and Iraq: Background Analysis," Congressional Research Service, May 13, 2011, https://www.fas.org/sgp/crs/natsec/R40764.pdf.

12. David Francis, "U.S. Troops Replaced by an Outsourced Army in Afghanistan," *Fiscal Times*, May 10, 2013, http://www.thefiscaltimes.com/Articles/2013/05/10/US-Troops-Replaced-by-an-Outsourced-Army-in-Afghanistan.

13. P. W. Singer, *Corporate Warriors: The Rise of the Privatized Military Industry* (Ithaca NY: Cornell University Press, 2008), 45.

14. Rolf Uesseler, *Servants of War, Private Military Corporations and the Profit of Conflict* (Berkeley CA: Soft Skull Press, 2008), 126.

15. "Who We Are," Aegis, http://www.aegisworld.com.

16. Ibid.

17. "Aegis Defense Services," Source Watch (Center for Media and Democracy), May 30, 2014, http://www.sourcewatch.org/index.php/Aegis_Defence_Services#Corporate_Profile.

18. Ibid.

19. "Contracts," US Department of Defense (No: CR-224-14), November 21, 2014, http://www.defense.gov/contracts/contract.aspx?contractid=5423.

20. "Aegis Defense Services," Source Watch.

21. Jeremy Scahill, *Blackwater: The Rise of the World's Most Powerful Mercenary Army* (New York: Nation Books, 2007), 45.

22. James Ridgeway, "The Secret History of Hurricane Katrina," *Mother Jones*, August 28, 2009, http://www.motherjones.com/environment/2009/08/secret-history-hurricane-katrina.

23. "Iraq has become the largest single gathering of private armed men in recent history." Quoted from Robert Young Pelton, *Licensed to Kill: Hired Guns in the War on Terror* (New York: Crown Publishers, 2006), 343.

24. James Glanz and Sabrina Tavernise, "Blackwater Shooting Scene Was Chaotic," *New York Times*, September 28, 2007, http://www.nytimes.com/2007/09/28/world/middleeast/28blackwater.html.

25. Mike Nizza, "The Blackwater Gunner's Account," *Lede* (*New York Times* news blog), November 14, 2007, http://thelede.blogs.nytimes.com/2007/11/14/the-blackwater-gunners-account.

26. Over time, further evidence came to light and the facts of the incident became even fuzzier. While virtually all of the early reports blamed Blackwater for an overly aggressive response that resulted in the killing of unarmed civilians, subsequent reports affirmed aspects of the Blackwater version of the story. For instance, radio logs confirmed that Blackwater guards did indeed take fire from insurgents and Iraqi police. "No Forensic Match for Ammo in Blackwater Shooting," *USA Today*, April 1, 2009, http://usatoday30.usatoday.com/news/washington/2009-04-01-blackwater-report_N.htm.

27. Spencer S. Hsu, Victoria St. Martin, and Keith L. Alexander, "Four Blackwater Guards Found Guilty in 2007 Iraq Shootings of 31 Unarmed Civilians," *Washington Post*, October 22, 2014, http://www.washingtonpost.com/world/national-security/verdict-expected-in-blackwater-shooting-case/2014/10/22/5a488258-59fc-11e4-bd61-346aee66ba29_story.html; Matt Apuzzo, "Blackwater Guards Found Guilty in 2007 Iraq Killings," *New York Times*, October 22, 2014, http://www.nytimes.com/2014/10/23/us/blackwater-verdict.html.

28. Spencer Ackerman, "Blackwater 3.0: Rebranded 'Academi' Wants Back in Iraq," *Wired*, December 12, 2011, http://www.wired.com/2011/12/blackwater-rebrand-academi; "Blackwater Name Change: Private Security Firm Switches Name Again to Academi from Xe," *Huffington Post*, December 12, 2011, http://www.huffingtonpost.com/2011/12/12/blackwater-name-change-private-security-firm-academi_n_1143789.html.

29. "About Us," Triple Canopy, http://www.triplecanopy.com/about-us/company.

30. "Blackwater (Now Xe) Still Working in Iraq," CBS News, April 21, 2009, http://www.cbsnews.com/news/blackwater-now-xe-still-working-in-iraq.

31. "Triple Canopy Signs International Code of Conduct for Private Security Service Providers," Triple Canopy, November 9, 2010, http://www.triplecanopy.com/about-us/news/press-releases/article/news/triple-canopy-signs-international-code-of-conduct-for-private-security-service-providers.

32. Ibid.

33. Steve Fainaru, "Four Hired Guns in an Armored Truck, Bullets Flying, and a Pickup and a Taxi Brought to a Halt. Who Did the Shooting and Why?," *Washington Post*, April 16, 2007, http://www.washingtonpost.com/wp-dyn/content/article/2007/04/14/AR2007041401490.html. At the time he filed the story, Fairnaru noted, "Private contractors were granted immunity from the Iraqi legal process in 2004 by L. Paul Bremer, head of the Coalition Provisional Authority, the U.S. occupation government. More recently, the military and Congress have moved to establish guidelines for prosecuting contractors under U.S. law or the Uniform Code of Military Justice, but so far the issue remains unresolved."

34. C. J. Chivers, "Contractor's Boss in Iraq Shot at Civilians, Workers' Suit Says," *New York Times*, November 16, 2006, http://www.nytimes.com/2006/11/17/world/middleeast/17contractors.html.

35. Fainaru, "Four Hired Guns."

36. Anna Fifield, "Contractors Reap $138B from Iraq War," CNN, March 19, 2013, http://www.cnn.com/2013/03/19/business/iraq-war-contractors/index.html.

37. "Company Overview of Constellis Group Inc.," Bloomberg, June 2, 2015, http://www.bloomberg.com/research/stocks/private/snapshot.asp?privcapId=237562172.

38. Constellis Holdings, Inc., "Constellis Holdings, Inc. Acquires Constellis Group Inc.," PR News Wire, June 6, 2014, http://www.prnewswire.com/news-releases/constellis-holdings-inc-acquires-constellis-group-inc-262388561.html.

39. "The World's Billionaires: #1054 Billy Joe (Red) McCombs," *Forbes*, June 2, 2015, http://www.forbes.com/profile/billy-joe-red-mccombs.

40. "Red McCombs (Chairman)," Academi, https://www.academi.com/pages/about-us/board-of-directors/red-mccombs-chairman.

41. "Board of Directors," Constellis Group, http://www.constellisgroup.com/about/leadership/board-of-directors. As this volume goes to press, Constellis Group has just announced its merger with Olive Group, "a leading provider of innovative risk management solutions." Chris and David St. George, cofounders of Olive Group, were projected to join the Constellis board of directors. Constellis Group, "Constellis Group to Merge with Olive Group," PR News Wire, May 7, 2015, http://www.prnewswire.com/news-releases/constellis-group-to-merge-with-olive-group-300079518.html.

42. Suzanne Goldenberg, "UK Security Firm Sued Over US Soldier's Death," *Guardian*, October 29, 2007, http://www.theguardian.com/world/2007/oct/29/iraq.uk.

43. Pratap Chatterjee, *Iraq Inc.: A Profitable Occupation* (New York: Seven Stories Press, 2004), 121–22.

44. Goldenberg, "UK Security Firm Sued."

45. Mark Townsend, "Iraq Victims Sue UK Security Firm," *Observer* (UK), January 10, 2009, http://www.theguardian.com/world/2009/jan/11/iraq-uk-security-firms.

46. "Erinys International," Powerbase (Public Interest Investigations), http://powerbase.info/index.php/Erinys_International; also see Chatterjee, *Iraq Inc.*, 116–20.

47. "Board of Directors," Erinys, accessed June 2, 2015, http://www.erinys.net/#/board-of-directors/4577428102.

48. "Erinys International," Powerbase.

49. David Isenberg, *Soldiers of Fortune Inc.* (Washington DC: Center for Defense Information, November 1997), http://www.aloha.net/~stroble/mercs.html.

50. Ibid.

51. Singer, *Corporate Warriors*, 5.

52. Ethnic Serbs filed a class action lawsuit against MPRI in 2010, contending that it trained and armed Croatian troops that committed genocide in the Krajina region. The lawsuit sought billions of dollars from L-3 Communications and its subsidiary, MPRI. In 2014, the lawsuit was dismissed for lack of jurisdiction. "Victims of Genocide in Krajina Lawsuit Against MPRI Dismissed," InSerbia, September 29, 2014, http://inserbia.info/today/2014/09/victims-of-genocide-in-krajina-lawsuit-against-mpri-dismissed.

53. Srdja Trifkovic, "The Really Bad Dogs of War," Global Research, October 11, 2007, http://www.globalresearch.ca/the-really-bad-dogs-of-war/7052.

54. Source Watch, "Military Professional Resources Inc.," Center for Media and Democracy, http://www.sourcewatch.org/index.php/Military_Professional_Resources_Inc.

55. "MPRI Inc. Agrees to Pay $3.2 Million for False Labor Charges on Contract to Support Army in Afghanistan," United States Department of Justice, February 12, 2014, http://www.justice.gov/opa/pr/mpri-inc-agrees-pay-32-million-false-labor-charges-contract-support-army-afghanistan.

56. According to its website, CyTerra offers "today's soldiers and security professionals with increased situational awareness to protect lives and critical infrastructure." See http://www.cyterracorp.com/index.htm.

57. According to the Department of Justice, in July 2013, CyTerra "agreed to pay the federal government $1.9 million to resolve civil liability arising from its failure to provide the U.S. Department of the Army with accurate, complete and current cost or pricing data for its sales of mine detectors." See "CyTerra Corporation Agrees to Pay $1.9 Million to Resolve False Claims Act Allegations," US Department of Justice, July 2, 2013, http://www.justice.gov/opa/pr/cyterra-corporation-agrees-pay-19-million-resolve-false-claims-act-allegations.

58. "The Largest Company You've Never Heard of: G4S and the London Olympics," *International Business Times*, August 6, 2012, http://www.ibtimes.com/largest-company-youve-never-heard-g4s-london-olympics-739232.

59. "Our History," G4S, http://www.g4s.com/en/Who%20we%20are/History.

60. According to Source Watch, Wackenhut's "early board members included Capt. Eddie Rickenbacker, Gen. Mark Clark and Ralph E. Davis, a leader of the John Birch Society. Other members include former FBI director Clarence Kelley, former Defense secretary and CIA deputy director Frank Carlucci, former Defense Intelligence Agency director Gen. Joseph Carroll, former Secret Service director James J. Rowley, former Marine commandant P.X. Kelley, former CIA deputy director Adm. Bobby Ray Inman, and previous to becoming CIA director, William J. Casey as outside legal counsel." See "Wackenhut," Source Watch, http://www.sourcewatch.org/index.php/Wackenhut.

61. McKenna and Johnson, "A Look at the World's Most Powerful Mercenary Armies."

62. "G4S PLC (GFS: London Stock Exchange)," Bloomberg, http://www.bloomberg.com/research/stocks/financials/financials.asp?ticker=GFS:LN&dataset=incomeStatement&period=A&currency=US%20Dollar.

63. William Langewiesche, "The Chaos Company," *Vanity Fair*, April 2014, http://www.vanityfair.com/news/business/2014/04/g4s-global-security-company.

64. Ibid.

65. "Our Group Board," G4S, http://www.g4s.com/en/Who%20we%20are/Our%20people/Group%20board%20profiles.

66. Kim Sengupta and Nigel Morris, "Olympic Security: Now the Army is Giving Orders," *Independent*, July 17, 2012, http://www.independent.co.uk/news/uk/home-news/now-the-army-is-giving-the-orders-7946831.html.

67. Simon Hattenstone and Eric Allison, "G4S, The Company With No Convictions—But Does it Have Blood on its Hands?," *Guardian*, December 22, 2014, http://www.theguardian.com/commentisfree/2014/dec/22/g4s-convictions-deaths-employees-racial-overtones.

68. Corporate Watch's list of major corporate investors in G4S includes, but is not limited to, Blackrock, Prudential, UBS, Vanguard, Barclays, State Street, Allianz, J. P. Morgan Chase, Credit Suisse, and FMR. See "G4S: Finances & Investors," Corporate Watch, http://www.corporatewatch.org/company-profiles/g4s-finances-investors. Although Bank of America is not listed as an investor, it is a G4S client.

69. Phillips and Osborne, "Exposing the Financial Core."

70. "A Brief History of DynCorp International," http://www.dyn-intl.com/about-di/history.

71. T. Rees Shapiro, "Daniel R. Bannister Former President of DynCorp, Dies at 80," *Washington Post*, March 15, 2011, http://www.washingtonpost.com/local/obituaries/daniel-r-bannister-former-president-of-DynCorp-dies-at-80/2011/03/15/ABYVl9a_story.html.

72. "DynCorp International Prices Initial Public Offering," DynCorp International, May 3, 2006, http://ir.dyn-intl.com/releasedetail.cfm?releaseid=257939.

73. Will Daley, "DynCorp to Be Acquired by Cerberus for $1.5 Billion," Bloomberg Business, April 12, 2010, http://www.bloomberg.com/news/articles/2010-04-12/cerberus-will-buy-dyncorp-for-1-5-billion.

74. "Company Overview of DynCorp International LLC," Bloomberg Business, http://www.bloomberg.com/research/stocks/private/snapshot.asp?privcapId=13154196.

75. "CSC/DynCorp," CorpWatch, http://www.corpwatch.org/section.php?id=18.

76. "Senior Leadership," Cerberus Capital Management LP, http://www.cerberuscapital.com/the-team/senior-executive-leadership.

77. Robinson, Global Capitalism and the Crisis of Humanity, "Policing Global Capitalism," 158–213.

78. Ibid., 163–65.

79. See, for example, Godfrey et al., "The Private Military Industry and the Neoliberal Imperialism."

80. See, e.g., Langewiesche, "The Chaos Company."

81. In 1956, C. Wright Mills coined the term "interlocking directorate" to refer to "the community of interest, the unification of outlook and policy, that prevails among the propertied class." See C. Wright Mills, The Power Elite (Oxford and New York: Oxford University Press, 1956), 123; for a contemporary application of Mills's concept, see Phillips and Soeiro, "The Global 1 Percent Ruling Class Exposed."

82. Laura Dickinson, Outsourcing War and Peace: Preserving Public Values in a World of Privatized Foreign Affairs (New Haven CT: Yale University Press, 2011).

83. Whitehead, "Private Police: Mercenaries of the American Police State."

84. See the database "The Counted: People Killed by Police in the US," Guardian, http://www.theguardian.com/us-news/ng-interactive/2015/jun/01/the-counted-police-killings-us-database.

85. "Battlefield USA: De Facto State of Martial Law Has Been Declared in Boston," Before It's News, April 19, 2013, http://beforeitsnews.com/survival/2013/04/battlefield-usa-de-facto-state-of-martial-law-has-been-declared-in-boston-pics-from-the-war-zone-2470350.html.

86. For more on the 161 individuals who have been identified as the core of the TCC—i.e. the key players and board members in the PMCs discussed in this chapter—see Phillips and Osborne, "Exposing the Financial Core," http://www.projectcensored.org/financial-core-of-the-transnational-corporate-class.

CHAPTER 9

Existence is Resistance
Women in Occupied Palestine and Kashmir

Tara Dorabji and Susan Rahman

Exile is more than a geographical concept. You can be an
exile in your homeland, in your own house, in a room.

—Mahmoud Darwish

The occupations of Palestine and Kashmir are perhaps two of the most censored stories of our time. The voices of women living under occupation are even more silenced. For many Palestinian and Kashmiri women, their existence is resistance. How have women been instrumental in sustaining these independence movements? This chapter identifies some of the realities of life for women living under military occupation by examining the Israeli occupation of Palestine and the Indian occupation of Kashmir.

For Palestinians as a people living in a region that has been occupied since the 1500s—first by the Ottoman Empire, then by the British, and presently by the Israelis—occupation has been central to the ways in which their lives are circumscribed and conducted. Although the West Bank is still part of what was once historic Palestine and has not yet been colonized and renamed Israel, the Israeli government still occupies it. The Israeli military, under direction from the Israeli government, controls the movement of people and goods, makes policy that affects the residents, and usurps the land when Israel wishes to expand its territory. Since 1967, over 800,000 Palestinians—men, women, and children—have been arrested or detained in Israeli prisons, and their prison experience has been documented by numerous independent media sources—including Project Censored—as harsh and cruel.[1]

Despite the Israeli government's denial that there is currently a military occupation, facts on the ground prove otherwise: however one wishes to label the situation, restricted mobility through Israeli-only roads and long waits at checkpoints, forced demolition of homes and olive orchards, a separation wall, unsolicited military surveillance, and restrictions on import and export activities that do not apply to Israelis all indicate that military occupation is in fact occurring.[2]

The Kashmiri independence movement started in 1846 when the region came under Dogra rule.[3] It fortified under British colonization and has since evolved into the present-day movement for *azadi*, or freedom. In 1947, when the British carved up India under partitioning, an estimated ten million people were forced to move, creating the largest land migration in human history. An estimated one million civilian deaths resulted from violence sparked by displacement.[4] At the moment of independence, amid the bloodshed, it was unclear if Kashmir would go to India or Pakistan. But in 1947, the first Indo–Pakistani war took place, with India taking Kashmir. In 1948, India brought the case of Kashmir to the United Nations, and Kashmir was officially recognized as a disputed territory. Over time, the dispute eroded into a full-blown occupation from which arose a popular independence movement.

Thus in Kashmir, as in Palestine, the occupation is widely disputed and often framed as an internal dispute—albeit an "internal dispute" that has led to the deployment of over half a million armed military personnel in the region. Today Kashmir is the most densely militarized land in the world, with approximately 700,000 Indian military and paramilitary personnel policing a population of ten million.[5] That means that for every fourteen civilians there is about one military personnel. The bulk of the weaponry comes from Israel: between 2002 and 2008, India acquired $5 billion in arms from Israel to combat Islamic insurgents.[6]

The heavy military presence impacts Kashmiri civilian lives in staggering ways. According to Khurram Parvez, coordinator for the Jammu and Kashmir Coalition of Civil Society, torture is rampant, with over 60,000 documented cases in the valley of Kashmir. Methods of torture include such heinous acts as waterboarding, injecting petrol into anuses, rape, psychological abuse, and mutilation.[7] As of November 2012, an estimated 70,000 Kashmiris had died as a result of the Indian occupation.[8]

The Indian government has created a set of special laws that allows the killing and torture of Kashmiri civilians to continue. For example, the Public Safety Act (PSA) of 1978 permits the incarceration of civilians for up to two years on grounds of unconfirmed suspicion. Amnesty International reported that between 8,000 and 20,000 people have been held under the PSA over the past twenty years.[9] In 2012, more than 20,000 Kashmiri youth faced trials for protesting against the Indian government.[10] And the Armed Forces Special Powers Act allows security forces to preemptively shoot civilians to prevent future terrorist attempts.[11] In addition, it allows soldiers to detain residents without cause, search homes without warrants, and destroy houses.[12]

WOMEN OF RESISTANCE

In both Palestine and Kashmir, women have played pivotal roles in historic and present-day resistance. From holding vigils to remember the disappeared to organizing protests to stop the wall from being built in Palestine, women are on the front lines. In addition, women are often the keepers of the family stories, maintaining the language and culture and passing it along to the next generation.

For women in Palestine, resistance is not a choice. When asked, "Why do you resist occupation?" many women respond that it is inherent to their identies—Palestinians are resisters, especially of Israeli occupation. As one woman put it, "To resist is to exist." (All of the following interview quotations with Palestinian women are excerpted from the second author's doctoral dissertation, "To Exist Is To Resist: The Voices of the Women of Palestine."[13])

Nora, a mother, grandmother, lifelong activist, and refugee, has been in the movement since before the 1967 war, and her *sumud*—steadfastness or dedication to the resistance—serves as a reminder that there is always work to be done.

> I can tell you in all honesty if the resistance movement has gone on so far it is because of the women. Pre-1948, after

1948, with the coming of the PLO, with women's movements/organizations—we have not stopped, and of course after Oslo things have changed because we have a pseudo-government. And so you thought with the government they would really be doing the job that the organizations were doing, but there definitely is a role for women. As women in general we care about the world, we care about our children, we care about the environment, we care about creation . . . and very few of us care about our pockets or our prestige. . . . So in fact I think women's role is [a] very great part of what I've been doing in my work.[14]

Mothers feel it is their job to raise their children to always remember the history of Palestine. Their concern is that if the next generation does understand occupation and life before 1948, then occupied life will become normalized. Many participants place a great value on classical education and emphasize the importance of it both in their own lives and in the lives of the next generation. Popular Front for the Liberation of Palestine (PFLP) activist, former prisoner, and longtime women's advocate Myssar conceives of education as a weapon of resistance, for herself and others:

> I worked with Popular Front for Liberation of Palestine in university. My belief until now is that for women our weapon is not the gun, it is our certificate [education] and now I encourage all the kids to continue their studying.[15]

Teacher-activist Fulla hopes that, by keeping the culture alive, she will help to invigorate a new generation of resisters:

> I would like to mention that in my work as a private teacher I teach my students more than is in the textbooks. I try to answer the questions about occupation; I try to answer the questions about the corruption that is taking place and what we can do to not be ignorant or passive. I think this is a good thing to do so that the generation that is coming next will be very active when it comes to resistance, and [will] aim toward [a] free Palestine.[16]

Many women go out to the Friday protests and get hit with tear gas on a regular basis. Despite the repeated assaults that they face, these women continue to expose themselves to danger in order to pursue their goals. One activist in particular has been openly critical of the Palestinian Authority's failure to bring about an end to the occupation. She reports that both she and her family have been threatened by local Palestinian officials as a result of what she posts on social media.

Myssar has been incarcerated multiple times, and now advocates for the rights of prisoners who are held in Israeli prisons. While in prison herself, incarcerated without due process, she was subjected to cruel and unusual punishment including being blindfolded for days on end, kept in freezing quarters, and interrogated inhumanely. She now spends her days meeting with prisoners to learn about their treatment so she can raise awareness about what is going on inside Israeli jails. She works with the families of prisoners to help with their basic survival needs while their family member is incarcerated. She also participates in symbolic acts of solidarity with prisoners. When tents were set up in cities around the West Bank during the time of the prison hunger strike (April–June 2014), she spent much of her time there to show solidarity with the prisoners. Myssar explained the centrality of her work to her self-identity.

> Now I am working in the GUPW [the General Union of Palestinian Women]. I am a member of the high committee of the prisoners. All the time I am at the tent. I am active in prisoner's issues including all of the writing about them, both men and women. I visit the families of the prisoners. It is my aim that I will continue until my death.[17]

Lidia's husband is serving a twenty-five-year jail sentence after participating in the second intifada. He is currently in his twelfth year and, while they have one daughter, she knew that by the time he was released she would be too old to have more children. Her act of resistance was to ask him to provide her with his sperm so that she could get it inseminated in the hopes of becoming pregnant. She visited him in jail one day and smuggled out his sperm, which she immediately took to the doctor to have artificially inseminated in her. Her creative act of resistance resulted in the birth of her now two-year-old son. She plans to do it again. She explained:

> I am the second successful example of sperm smuggling from my husband's prison. It was a very nice, amazing experience for me. At the beginning of the idea I refused to do it, but when I heard about the first successful woman (O Muhammad), I was encouraged to do it. . . . My husband will be fifty years old when he will leaves the prison, and I will be fifty too, so I told him about this idea and he agree[d] with me. Then he sent the sperm sample. . . . It was very successful from the first time and I'm very proud of it. . . . I did this to challenge the occupation, but also I love be[ing] a mom. . . . The way we [got the] sperm sample was very hard, and then the test was very long, but I was very happy when [it was a] successful one.[18]

Kashmiri women also continue to play vital roles in resistance. Many women are part of the Association of Parents of Disappeared Persons (APDP), making up more than half of its membership and board,[19] and they lead monthly vigils to remember those who have disappeared. Between 1989 and 2012, an estimated 8,000 Kashmiris disappeared as a result of the Indian occupation.[20] The APDP was founded by Parveena Ahangar, also known as the Iron Lady of Kashmir, to organize families of the disappeared. The mother of a seventeen-year-old boy who disappeared under the custody of the Indian forces, Ahangar has been beaten, intimidated, and harassed for her work,[21] but her group continues to hold vigils despite these dangers.

Meera Shah, whose husband disappeared, explained why she continues to visibly organize:

> I joined the Association of Parents of Disappeared Persons and we are protesting every month in the square. I am not afraid. I must protest not just for my husband or for my sons, but for all the families and the men who are disap-

peared. There are 10,000 disappeared people in Kashmir . . .
I want freedom for the people and for all those who are disappeared, those killed and those in jail. With freedom, the
mass graves, crackdowns, and disappearances will all stop.
We will continue to protest until we get freedom for all those
dead, alive, and disappeared.[22]

Women's participation in resistance goes beyond the present day.
They have long been a critical part of indigenous Kashmiri opposition. Women were also on the front lines of mass protests for clean
elections in 1990. During this time the militants revolted and many
papers reported on women's spirited and extensive participation.[23]
Women's resistance took on a cultural flavor and many women would
sing, mixing traditional Kashmiri songs of celebration with new
phrases praising the militant fighters.[24] In *Between Democracy and
Nation: Gender and Militarisation in Kashmir*, Seema Kazi interviewed
a government teacher, whose son was detained without charges,
about why she took part in protests:

We [women] participated in demonstrations for freedom
and self-determination out of a sense of the great injustice
and subordination of Kashmir's Muslims. The historical
memory of injustice is strong and enhanced by the present
conflict . . . I walked with hundreds of women and men in
1990 during protests against the Indian government.[25]

Women's roles in resistance have not been limited to protests.
They have cared for the wounded and provided food and water to
militants. They have monitored escape routes, allowing militants to
take flight. In 1991, during a six-month curfew, women organized
the food supply lines.[26] In 2000, Kashmiri Women in Peace and
Disarmament was founded and they began to publish a monthly
newsletter, *Voices Unheard*, that provided women's perspectives on
the conflict.[27] In 2007, Kashmiri women's protests around unemployment, water scarcity, and human rights abuses prompted the
chief minister of Kashmir to announce that a women's police battalion would be formed to "help the state to tackle women pro-

testors."[28] During the massive nonviolent summer uprisings of 2008–11, when millions of Kashmiris took to the streets and the army enforced weeks of curfew, women were prominent participants.[29] These summer actions were the first time that women led massive protests and participated in stone throwing.[30] In summer 2010, 110 civilians, including several women, were killed, and over 2,000 were injured. Most of the people were fired on by the police, though several were hit by tear gas shells or rubber bullets. Women whose sons were killed by the police joined the protests, bringing their children with them.[31] In the International Peace Research Association Foundation's report, "Kashmir: Militarization, Protest, and Gender," Ather Zia explained how the police violence has drawn women into active, visible protest:

> "Fear can get us nowhere, it has not helped Kashmir thus far," says a mother activist who has been searching for her son missing since 18 years, "We have to come out on streets otherwise no one will see what is being done to us inside our homes and alleys, we have to make noise, only then will we get justice, it will be handed to us."[32]

Not only do women show innovation and resilience at the forefront of the independence movement but they also continue to display it in their daily existence, keeping their families together and their households running.[33]

KASHMIRI WOMEN UNDER OCCUPATION

The impacts of occupation on Kashmiri women are staggering. One of the gravest ways that militarization affects women are enforced disappearances—a key strategy used by the Indian state to suppress the Kashmiri resistance.[34] There are about 32,000 widows and 97,000 orphans in the valley.[35] None of the thousands of cases of disappeared people have been solved.[36] Khansa Bashir's father disappeared, and she took his case all the way to India's Supreme Court. She explains how she sees the occupation.

This occupation is affecting women. Over the years, I have seen many women raped by the armed forces. No one is taking serious action. In this way, women are suffering. I don't think there has ever been a conviction. It's all a government game to destroy Kashmir. Another difficult thing for women is that when her husband is working, she is always worried, wondering if he is dead or alive. I saw several cases of women tortured by the Indian army. I am also threatened with calls telling me not to bring forward my dad's case, or I will pay for it. But me, I am not afraid. I am strong. I will file this case and never stop. I have been threatened, but they do not misbehave with me. I know how to handle these things. There are many other ways that women are affected by the army, but these things are difficult to prove. . . . When we have independence we'll be free of this. With the independence of Kashmir, maybe the women will feel free. If she is out late, she'll be free—nobody will touch her. This would be a big freedom for women. Right now women are threatened, if I walk out on the road and the armed forces are there, they could touch me, or a disappearance could happen.[37]

Bashir's mother is considered a half widow, a woman whose husband disappeared but has not yet been declared dead. By conservative estimates, at least 1,500 half widows live in Kashmir. Half widows are ineligible for pensions, rarely remarry, and face severe economic hardships.[38] They generally become the breadwinners for their family and often are unable to qualify for social services.[39]

Because half widows who lack death certificates can't prove that their husbands are dead, they are ineligible to receive ration cards or have their husband's land or bank accounts transferred to them,[40] which is problematic because a key indicator of a woman's power and vitality within her community is whether she owns land.[41] Even if a woman can prove her husband is dead, Muslim personal law says that if the father-in-law survives the husband, the wife and children can make no claims to the family property.[42] Thus, the disappearance or death of a woman's husband can further marginalize her status.

Women not only join but often lead the search for their missing husbands.[43] In some cases, the women face community backlash. Some are blamed for their husband's disappearance and are told that they have brought bad luck on the family.[44] In addition, some half widows face sexual harassment when visiting army camps and prisons to search for their husbands.[45] Making matters more difficult, when women frequent military camps and interrogation centers, they are often perceived as militants. In 2003, APDP member Dilshada was killed by militants. Silence shrouded her murder as neighbors believed that she was a government informant.[46] Haleema Begum and her son were shot dead by unidentified gunmen. Many locals believe that her murder was linked to her persistent attempts to find her disappeared son.[47] Yet, despite the continued hardships and grave dangers, many of these women, mostly Muslim mothers and half widows, have become tireless fighters for human rights.[48]

Sexual violence is perhaps the greatest underreported phenomenon in Kashmir. Although there are no reliable statistics on rape,[49] a Doctors Without Borders survey found that Kashmiris reported experiencing much higher levels of sexual violence than residents of other militarized zones.[50] In addition, surveys found that one in seven Kashmiris has witnessed a rape.[51] However, in South Asia there is a taboo around sexual violence, so few women report the crimes.[52] Rape is used by the occupying force as a collective punishment and a "cultural weapon" to inflict dishonor on men.[53] The Indian security forces often rape civilians in retaliation for militant ambushes.[54]

The Indian army raided the Kashmiri village of Kunan Poshpora in 1991, and members of the Fourth Rajputana Rifles Unit allegedly raped more than forty women between the ages of thirteen and eighty.[55] When the then director general of police was asked about the number of rapes in the Kupwara district, he said it was "a badly infested terrorist area."[56] The local magistrate confirmed that the women suffered from sexual violence inflicted by the army on March 5, 1991.[57] As a result of the gang rape, at least eighteen out of the forty survivors had to have their uteruses removed. Mothers were raped in front of their daughters and little girls in front of their mothers. A pregnant woman gave birth a few days after being raped and the child was born with fractured arms.[58]

There have been no convictions to date—after twenty-four years, survivors continue to plead their case in court. The women who were violated not only have failed to see justice in the courts, but have also experienced backlash within their own community. As Seema Kazi explains in *Between Democracy and Nation:*

> Three years after the incident, no marriage had taken place in the village. All young women, raped or not, were single; all married women who were raped had been deserted. Two husbands did take their wives back, one on the condition that they have no conjugal relations, the other that he live in the city far away from his wife.[59]

In February 2015, the surviving women marked the twenty-fourth anniversary of the tragic rapes, demanding justice. *Daily Kashmir* quoted a survivor who spoke at the anniversary gathering.

> It has been twenty-four years since the incident took place and justice has not been delivered yet. It is really embarrassing that in the court we are questioned about the incident again and again. I have cried a lot in the courtroom when the same questions are posed. They only play with our emotions and no decision has been given yet.[60]

EFFECTS OF ISRAELI OCCUPATION ON PALESTINIANS

The effects of the Israeli occupation of Palestine take many forms, from restricted movement to segregated roads to the deaths of loved ones. All of the interviewed women experienced trauma as a result of living under military occupation. Risk of death at the hands of Israeli soldiers and illegal settlers is something Palestinians have come to expect. Wadid, who has been fighting forced expulsion from her home of over forty years, told the story of losing her son:

> The other children are married but my one son passed away. He was about to turn sixteen. He was going on the bus; during the vacation the students work a little bit. The settlers

chased him after he got off the bus in Mamaela and stabbed him. I was sitting here, and it was his time to come at four o'clock, and he didn't come. I was worried at that time, all the time making bombs on the buses, so I called all the hospitals, Bethlehem and Beit Jama and here French Hospital in Jerusalem. . . . I called the police. . . . At nine, some men came asking for my family name. My husband went outside and they told him, "The police want you." I had a feeling something happened to my son. [My son] was with two other Arab boys but they couldn't do anything because there were more Jewish boys, so they ran away and they left him alone. So one of the journalists passed by and took the picture, and this picture is what the artist used to paint the picture of my son. The boys who stabbed my son were not charged with anything. They targeted him because he was wearing a Palestinian flag on his clothing so they started teasing him. He knew he did not have a chance, so he got off the bus and ran.[61]

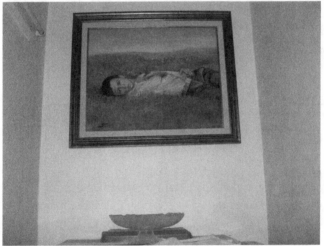

Painting of a photograph of Wadid's sixteen-year-old son, a victim of a hate crime: stabbed to death by Israeli settlers because he was Palestinian. Summer 2014.
PERSONAL PHOTO

Another mother, Sintia, lost two children to the occupation. She lives in Bil'in, where both locals and internationals gather for Friday protests.

I lost my son who was a very good man and everybody loved him. When he would see a woman doing farming he would help. All the trees that you see on the road—he planted and he used to water. He spent four years going to the demos against the apartheid wall in Bil'in. He used to get injured and he used to get teargassed and keep going. On a Friday I was farming, and the first thing he did was he said, "Where is Mother?" So he went to find me and said to me, "What are you doing in this hot weather? Come home and have lunch with me." So we went home, but he was in a hurry, so he did not have lunch with me. He told me to "put a dish for me" and he ate in a hurry, and this was the first time he did that. On that day they had hot water, and he took his brother out of the shower and said, "Okay, I need to take a shower first." And he did and I said, "Why are you in such a hurry?" And he said, "I need to go to the Friday prayer and then go to the demo." After the prayer he was smoking *shisha* and he asked a friend, "Would you take a photo of me because we may get shot today?" Like he had a feeling. And he did get shot. He went to the demo. And I don't go to the demos anymore because I am old. But I was watching TV, and as I was watching, my daughter came and said that my son was injured. I said okay, it is not the first time, but then my daughter said that this time it looks critical. The neighbors came and I thought they knew something I did not know. So I went to Ramallah. I felt something in my heart, and all the way to the hospital I kept praying. When I got to the hospital, I saw a lot of press and people, including my two sons. It was like I am here, and I don't know. They told me my son is martyr. So I went to the emergency room, and there was a tear gas canister in his chest. And it left a hole, so the doctors had to put some cotton in there. I was shocked, and I do not remember what happened after that. When I got home,

I asked the people not to cry, because we don't cry for martyrs—and he has always wanted to be a martyr and he got his wish. My son Basem was a good guy, and I didn't get to kiss him. Well, I only got to kiss one cheek and they took him away. He was a very good, kindhearted man, and he used to get money from rich people and give it to the students.[62]

Tear gas is touted as a non-life-threatening way to subdue a crowd. But, in the case of Sintia and many others, the practice of firing tear gas canisters at Palestinians often results in greater harm than is the purported objective. Sintia's pain at losing her son was coupled with yet another tragedy.

I also lost my daughter to the occupation. There was so much tear gas one day it felt like it was raining tear gas. My daughter said, "I cannot anymore, I am going home." So I said, "Okay, go home." A minute later, people were calling for me to come and check [on] my daughter. I came home and didn't see my daughter. She was at the neighbor's house. She wasn't breathing. I could see bubbles coming out of her mouth. I called my son and said we needed to take her to the hospital, and when we got there, the doctors kept asking me what it was she inhaled. . . . I told them it was only tear gas. My daughter started throwing up after that. The doctors inserted a tube into her stomach to pump out all of the poison, and they had to move her to an intensive care unit. One of my sons stayed with her and told me to go home. So the next day, early in the morning, my son called from the hospital and said to my other son . . . "Your sister is in critical condition." So my son went and did not take me. The doctors were surprised to see my daughter having such a strong reaction to tear gas, which she had been exposed to many times.

What we discovered was that the Israelis were experimenting with other chemicals and testing them on Palestinians who go to Friday demonstrations. Something went wrong with my daughter's heart and so the doctors assumed there was something extra in the gas because tear gas doesn't usually do that. By the time I got to the hospital, my daughter was dead. Since then I have been in shock and been under treatment. I feel like I have lost my mind and I cannot do anything on my own. It was such a huge loss. My daughter used to help around the house and Basem used to bring in money for the family. So everything has been really hard since then.[63]

An Israeli chemical plant that was originally in Netanya, inside Israel, had been proven to be an environmental hazard, both as an air pollutant and through soil and water contamination, and public outcry forced its closure. The plant was then relocated to Tulkarem, part of the occupied West Bank. A scientist at Khadoori University in Tulkarem explained that when the wind is blowing toward Israel, the factory is forced to stop production to prevent toxic air from reaching Israel. When it blows toward the West Bank, the plant continues to operate normally.[64]

Fulla, who lost her father to cancer as a result of environmental damage from this plant, has been through a lot of trauma due to byproducts of occupation. Losing her father has meant that she has become the main breadwinner for her family of four. Aside from the added burden of this, she misses her father dearly. She recalls what things were like in Tulkarem during the second intifada.

I remember when [during] times of curfew there was no bread in the house, there was nothing to eat, and I would ask my dad, "Hey Dad, why can't we open the curtain?" There was an Israeli sniper outside and if you would move the curtain he would shoot, so we would . . . try not to move so that they would not shoot at us. The most difficult time[s] were when the war planes would be shelling. . . . [What] I would do is I would take my brother and sister and run to hide downstairs, and I remember hearing the babies' cries . . . that scared me more than the bombing itself because I just know that these babies don't know what is going on and they just want their mother to calm them down. . . . When we would hide in this room we would keep the windows open in the winter, and I remember I asked my mom to close it because I was freezing. And she was like, "Well, Foo Foo, if you don't die from the bombings you may die from the broken glass. Do you want to die from broken glass?" . . . So I remember the winter was so difficult because we had to keep the windows and doors open all of the time. The curfew was so bad and we could not go anywhere. . . . We've been through a lot, and the fact [is] that now we [still] can't do much. Just because now our president thinks a third intifada is inconvenient, it seems like all the past pain was done in vain. Because you know the martyrs were lost. The wounded, we lived in horror. And it should not be done in vain—like, we knew that we were hanging in there because we wanted a free Palestine and we wanted the occupiers to leave but that didn't happen. Yet I hope it does. There are some days . . . I lose hope, like we are never going to get anywhere. I am just going . . . crazy—just go live my life, and I am going to forget about resistance and not do the work. But after some time I am like, okay, I need to do the work so I don't feel guilty that I don't do my part. And if everybody thinks that way, that I need to do my part, then no matter how small that was then . . . I miss my dad so much. He must be so proud of me.[65]

The chemical plant also affected Ameera, mother of seven, who lives in a refugee camp in Tulkarem. Her family has suffered immensely due to this factory: her son has chronic health problems related to exposure, and her husband has been unable to hold a job due to his ill health.

I have seven children. Occupation has affected me negatively in many ways. First, I lost my father. The factories posed issues and problems for the whole area, not just [for] my son. First of all they took the land that [the locals] owned to build the factory. We lost three *dunams* of land [approximately three quarters of an acre]. . . . We are farmers and cannot afford to lose the land. The canal that my son fell in is full of substances, and they are harmful for people and nature. . . . His lungs have shrunk and his stomach swelled up and his immune system is pretty weak. If anything bites him—like an insect—he has to go to the hospital. Since falling in, he has had to use special breathing treatments and cannot play or run like he used to. He is not the only one. In every home in this area, at least one or two people are suffering from the chemical exposure and are suffering with cancer. Since this, then, we call these factories the factories of death.[66]

Threats and harassment by Israeli military, intended to intimidate Palestinians, are another prevalent source of trauma. In Deir Dibwan, a small town about five miles outside of Ramallah, Faika recounts when the military came into their village during a peaceful time to run military exercises. Israeli Defense Force soldiers approached the household of a family downstairs from Faika.

Downstairs the family was sleeping and [the soldiers] . . . knocked on the door. [The family members] have to answer or [the soldiers] start shooting. They checked the house. They asked who was upstairs, and the son told them it was an old lady: "Please let me go tell her, you will scare her." They told him no and they came upstairs. I was sleeping and they came in my bedroom, six of them and six more in the hallway. One soldier put his dirty boot on my bed and aimed the gun at my chest and told me to get up. I said, "Why? What do you want? I'm sleeping, it's winter." All twelve were pointing their guns at me. They told me to go downstairs with the family. I went. They checked my house and then told all of us to go outside and sit in the cold rain. I told them I'm not going outside, I'm sick, and I can't. So they [said] okay, stay inside, but they made the husband [from downstairs] wait outside and told them all to wait there while they checked all over town. . . . I was scared. I told them, "Don't you have sisters? Don't you have daughters? You scared me like that. Didn't you think about your family?" And then they went away.[67]

During spring and summer 2014 in the West Bank, Palestinian prisoners throughout the region staged a hunger strike to protest administrative detention and overall unjust treatment. The prisoners ended their hunger strike after sixty-four days with no change to the administrative detention policy. For Palestinians, having a friend or relative imprisoned in the West Bank is the norm.[68]

VEILED IN THE MEDIA

Despite the power, organizing, and resilience that both Kashmiri and Palestinian women display, the media continue to portray them as oppressed victims. When women took to the streets in 2010, leading massive nonviolent demonstrations, the media dubbed them "the angry housewives of Kashmir."[69] When men protest are they called angry husbands? Although conflict in Kashmir has disproportionately affected women, Indian media portrayals of them as "detached" victims who are trapped in their homes undermine women's dignity and misrepresent their leadership roles.[70]

In 2009, human rights activist Mughli passed away after nearly two decades of searching for her disappeared son, a school teacher. The newspaper headlines were filled with words such as "lonely," "mother," "aging," and "grief." While these words do describe aspects of her, in an article titled "Remembering Mughli, Human Rights Activist," Ather Zia argued that these depictions of Mughli

> seemed overwhelmed by a pitying objectivity. This is a move which journalism often makes in all good faith to cover every angle of human interest, which is dangerously misread as victimology. In Mughli's case, this tone overshadowed the agency and activism she had practiced all her life.[71]

For decades Mughli filed court petitions and visited morgues, prisons, and interrogation centers. She was at the forefront of monthly protests and sought justice for those, like her son, who had disappeared. As Zia summarized, the Indian media keep women like Mughli, who protest government abuses and search for their disappeared sons and husbands, "conveniently out of the sight of [the] mainstream Indian audience."[72]

The Indian media also conventionally portray the Indian state as the only potential provider of the emancipation and empowerment that Kashmiri women seek.[73] The media fail to connect how the militarization of Kashmir has led to increased insecurity, which is then cited as a primary cause for the suspension of women's education and the increasing gap in literacy between men and women.[74] Women routinely marry earlier and drop out of college for fear that they will be sexually harassed or that their sexual integrity could be jeopardized by the security forces.[75]

Indian media representations of Kashmiri women as victims are a form of colonial feminism, which appropriates women's rights in the service of empire. Essentially much of the portrayal of Kashmiri women rests on what Deepa Kumar describes as "the construction of a barbaric, misogynistic 'Muslim world' that must be civilized by a liberal, enlightened West; a rhetoric also known as gendered Orientalism."[76]

Yet Kashmiri women continue to subvert the victim image in their own ways. Despite the popular Western image of women being oppressed and "forced" to cover their heads, Kashmiri women started wearing the hijab as a form of pride and identity. Although the hijab is historically not a traditional dress, Kashmiri women have appropriated it as a symbol of self-expression and a "politically aware Kashmiri Muslim female identity."[77]

In Palestine, too, occupation limits women's opportunities. Limited access to education is a routinely underreported phenomenon. Many women discuss how occupation restricts education or makes obtaining it more difficult. Hube was ready to start college when the first intifada began. At that point the Israelis closed all the West Bank schools so she never attended college.

I graduated in 1987. I got high marks and I wanted to go to university, so I went to Al-Quds in Jerusalem. [Then] started the first intifada. They closed the university and fired us from it, and so I stopped getting my education. Then when I came home, there [was] no school for the boys and the girls, there [was] nothing, they [were] staying at home. At that time I finished high school so we [made] a home group to teach the boys and the girls. . . . One of my son's teachers told him that "your mom taught me when I was a young boy." I remember we used to teach the girls and boys every day in their houses. We [taught] them Arabic, English, math, for more than one year. They wanted us to not learn. It's what they want. So we taught all the children and young teenagers, that's what we did. In all the villages all over Palestine, that's what we did. We were determined to teach our children because the occupier does not want us to learn. He wants us to be uneducated, but Palestinian people are very smart. They can study at home and get high grades. So we did what we thought was the right thing. When the school opened and they [got] back to school, they already learned all the stuff they needed to learn so we didn't lose any time.[78]

Denial of Palestinians' access to education has persisted throughout the sixty-seven years of Israeli occupation.[79] Ironically, Israel routinely touts its efforts to support women's education.[80] Yet the corporate media routinely marginalize Palestinian women and their roles in both current and past social movements. By contrast, Simona Sharoni's work highlights the Palestinian women's movement tracing its origins back to 1917 or even earlier.[81] She argues that lack of documentation has led many people to assume that women were not politically engaged until the first intifada in 1987. In part, this assumption is premised on the Orientalist myth that Arab women are submissive, controlled by their male counterparts, and unintelligent. Nevertheless, Sharoni documents a long history of women's resistance.[82] Women's engagement in the movement to end the Israeli occupation has been crucial.

Clearly the corporate media have failed to tell the whole story of what occupation looks like in occupied Palestine and occupied Kashmir. Contrary to Western assumptions and stereotypes, Palestinian and Kashmiri women continue to live with dignity and act in resistance. As storytellers, mothers, and organizers, women make up the backbone of these movements for sovereignty and independence.

TARA DORABJI is a writer, arts educator, mother, and radio journalist at KPFA. Her work is published or forthcoming in the *Tayo Literary Magazine, Huizache, Good*

Girls Marry Doctors, and *Midwifery Today*. Tara is working on her first novel, *Before We Remember*, which is set in Kashmir. Her projects can be viewed at dorabji.com.

SUSAN RAHMAN is a mother, activist, and professor of sociology, psychology, and behavioral sciences. Her doctoral research took her to the West Bank last summer where she connected with family and conducted interviews of women who resist the Israeli occupation. Her work is inspired by the people of Palestine, who show great strength, resiliency, and *sumud* (steadfastness).

Notes

1. "Political Prisoners in Israel/Palestine," If Americans Knew, no date, http://ifamericansknew. org/stat/prisoners.html; see also Alison Weir, "U.S. Media Coverage of Israel and Palestine: Choosing Sides," in *Censored 2005*, ed. Peter Phillips and Project Censored (New York: Seven Stories, 2004), 285–300; and Nora Barrows-Friedman, "Invisible Victims: US Corporate Media Censorship of Israeli International Law Violations in Palestine," in *Censored 2011*, ed. Mickey Huff, Peter Phillips, and Project Censored (New York: Seven Stories, 2010), 293–314.

2. Phyllis Bennis, *Understanding the Palestinian–Israeli Conflict: A Primer* (Northampton MA: Olive Branch Press, 2012).

3. The Dogras are an Indian Aryan ethnic group that is predominantly Hindu. Arguably, the Kashmiri independence movement started in 1846 when the British sold Jammu and Kashmir to the Dogras.

4. Crispin Bates, "The Hidden Story of Partition and Its Legacies," BBC, March 3, 2011, http:// www.bbc.co.uk/history/british/modern/partition1947_01.shtml.

5. Parvaiz Bukhari, "Summers of Unrest Challenging India," in *Until My Freedom Has Come: The New Intifada in Kashmir*, ed. Sanjay Kak (Chicago: Haymarket Books, 2013) 4–5.

6. Angana P. Chatterji, "The Militarized Zone," in *Kashmir: The Case for Freedom* (London: Verso, 2011), 112.

7. Khurram Parvez, interview by Tara Dorabji, *Morning Mix*, KPFA, December 26, 2011, http:// www.kpfa.org/archive/id/76361.

8. Parvez Imroz et al., *Alleged Perpetrators: Stories of Impunity in Jammu and Kashmir* (Srinagar: International People's Tribunal on Human Rights and Justice in Indian-administered Kashmir, 2012), 7.

9. Amnesty International, A "Lawless Law": Detentions under the Jammu and Kashmir Public Safety Act (London: Amnesty International Limited, 2011), 4.

10. Riyaz Masroor, "Kashmiri Youth Troubled by Frequent Court Trips," BBC News, March 30, 2012, http://www.bbc.com/news/world-asia-india-17558589.

11. Gowhar Fazili, "Kashmir Marginalities: Construction, Nature, and Response," in Kak, *Until My Freedom Has Come*, 218.

12. Bukhari, "Summers of Unrest," 4.

13. See http://www.amazon.com/dp/B010RF8JM8.

14. Nora Carimi, interview by Susan Rahman, Jerusalem, June 2014; here and in subsequent interviews with additional women, names have been changed in order to protect them.

15. Myssar, interview by Susan Rahman, Nablus, June 2014.

16. Fulla Jallad, interview by Susan Rahman, Tulkarem, June 2014.

17. Myssar, interview by Susan Rahman, Nablus, June 2014.

18. Lidia, interview by Susan Rahman, Beit Rama, June 2014.

19. Association of the Parents of Disappeared Persons (APDP), *Half Widow, Half Wife?: Responding to Gendered Violence in Kashmir* (Jammu and Kashmir Coalition of Civil Society, 2011), 5, available online, http://www.jkccs.net/wp-content/uploads/2015/02/Half-Widow-Half-Wife-APDP-report.pdf.

20. Imroz et al., *Alleged Perpetrators*, 7.

21. Ather Zia, "Kashmiri Women: Concerns, Milestones & Solutions," *Kashmir Affairs*, July 30, 2007, http://arabisto.pointsoftouch.com/2015/01/31/kashmiri-women-concerns-milestones-solutions.
22. Meera Shah, interview by Tara Dorabji, Srinagar, October 2011.
23. APDP, *Half Widow, Half Wife?*, 4.
24. Seema Kazi, *Between Democracy and Nation: Gender and Militarisation in Kashmir* (New Delhi: Women Unlimited, 2009), 139.
25. Ibid., 140.
26. Ibid., 141.
27. APDP, *Half Widow, Half Wife?*, 8.
28. Ather Zia, "Solution for Kashmir and Women's Empowerment," *Arabisto*, September 11, 2007, http://arabisto.com/2007/09/11/solution-kashmir-womens-empowerment.
29. APDP, *Half Widow, Half Wife?*, 4.
30. Ather Zia, "Kashmir: Militarization, Protest, and Gender," International Peace Research Association Foundation, UC Irvine, Abridged Summer Field Report, 2010, 5.
31. Ibid., 5.
32. Ibid., 6.
33. Ibid.
34. Ather Zia, "Women in Search for the Disappeared in Kashmir," UC Irvine Human Rights Fellowship, Summer 2009, 2.
35. Ibid., 2.
36. Ather Zia, "Disappeared Men and Searching Women: Human Rights and Mourning in Kashmir," *SAMAR Magazine*, Issue 36, August 30, 2011, http://samarmagazine.org/archive/articles/364.http://samarmagazine.org/archive/articles/364.
37. Khansa Bashir, interview by Tara Dorabji, Srinagar, October 2011.
38. APDP, *Half Widow, Half Wife?*, 1.
39. Zia, "Women in Search for the Disappeared in Kashmir," 2.
40. APDP, *Half Widow, Half Wife?*, 10.
41. Deborah Sick, "Property, Power, and the Political Economy of Farming Households in Costa Rica," *Human Ecology*, 26, no. 2 (June 1998): 189–212.
42. Kazi, *Between Democracy and Nation*, 153.
43. Zia, "Women in Search for the Disappeared in Kashmir," 2.
44. APDP, *Half Widow, Half Wife?*, 12.
45. Ather Zia, "The Spectacle of a Good-Half Widow: Performing Agency in the Human Rights Movement in Kashmir," *eScholarship*, UCLA Center for the Study of Women, *Thinking Gender Papers*, February 1, 2013, 2, http://escholarship.org/uc/item/3xx4n1zf.http://escholarship.org/uc/item/3xx4n1zf.
46. APDP, *Half Widow, Half Wife?*, 18.
47. Zia, "Disappeared Men and Searching Women."
48. Zia, "Militarization, Protest, and Gender," 2.
49. Asia Watch (Human Rights Watch) and Physicians for Human Rights, *Rape in Kashmir: A Crime of War* 5, no. 9, 3, http://www.hrw.org/sites/default/files/reports/INDIA935.PDF.
50. Médecins Sans Frontières, "Kashmir: Violence and Health," November 2006, 24.
51. Ibid., 3.
52. APDP, *Half Widow, Half Wife?*, 3.
53. Kazi, *Between Democracy and Nation*, 155.
54. Asia Watch, *Rape in Kashmir*, 1.
55. APDP, *Half Widow, Half Wife?*, 3.
56. Kazi, *Between Democracy and Nation*, 154.
57. Ibid., 155.
58. Huma Dar, interview on KPFA, July 16, 2013, http://dorabji.com/2013/07/kupwara-rape-investigation-in-kashmir.
59. Kazi, *Between Democracy and Nation*, 159.

60. Raihana Maqbool, "Kashmiri Women's Resistance Day Observed," *Daily Kashmir*, February 23, 2015, http://www.dailykashmirimages.com/news-%E2%80%98kashmiri-womens-resistance-day-observed-73233.aspx.

61. Wadid, interview by Susan Rahman, Jerusalem, June 2014.

62. Sintia, interview by Susan Rahman, Bil'in, June 2014.

63. Ibid.

64. Mazen Salman, interview by Susan Rahman, Tulkarem, June 2014.

65. Fulla Jallad, interview by Susan Rahman, Tulkarem, June 2014.

66. Ameera, interview by Susan Rahman, Tulkarem, June 2014.

67. Faika Eseed, interview by Susan Rahman, Deir Dibwan, June 2014.

68. The mass incarceration of Palestinians in the West Bank is strikingly similar to the mass incarceration of people of color in the United States, as documented in Michelle Alexander's *The New Jim Crow: Mass Incarceration in the Age of Colorblindness* (New York: The New Press, 2010). See Curtis Bell, "Jim Crow in Palestine: Parallels between US and Israeli Racism," *Electronic Intifada*, February 21, 2013, http://electronicintifada.net/content/jim-crow-palestine-parallels-between-us-and-israeli-racism/12216. In response to the August 2014 shooting of unarmed Michael Brown by a police officer in Ferguson, Missouri, Palestinians expressed their solidarity through Internet statements and communications about effective ways to demonstrate. See, for example, Rana Baker, "Palestinians Express 'Solidarity with the People of Ferguson' in Mike Brown Statement," *Electronic Intifada*, August 15, 2014, http://electronicintifada.net/blogs/rana-baker/palestinians-express-solidarity-people-ferguson-mike-brown-statement.

69. Zia, "Militarization, Protest, and Gender," 5.

70. Ather Zia, "Indian Media and Coverage of Kashmiri Women," *Arabisto*, November 23, 2007, http://arabisto.pointsoftouch.com/2007/11/23/indian-media-coverage-kashmiri-women.

71. Ather Zia, "Remembering Mughli, Human Rights Activist," *Kashmir Lit*, Winter 2011, http://www.kashmirlit.org/remembering-mughli-human-rights-activist.

72. Zia, "Indian Media and Coverage of Kashmiri Women."

73. Ibid.

74. APDP, *Half Widow, Half Wife?*, 7.

75. Kazi, *Between Democracy and Nation*, 167.

76. Deepa Kumar, "Imperialist Feminism and Liberalism," Open Democracy, November 6, 2014, https://www.opendemocracy.net/deepa-kumar/imperialist-feminism-and-liberalism.

77. APDP, *Half Widow, Half Wife?*, 7.

78. Hube Awad, interview by Susan Rahman, Deir Dibwan, June 2014.

79. Ilan Pappe, *The Ethnic Cleansing of Palestine* (Oxford UK: Oneworld Publishing, 2007).

80. Ibid.

81. Simona Sharoni, *Gender and the Israeli-Palestinian Conflict* (Syracuse NY: Syracuse University Press, 1995).

82. Ibid.

CHAPTER 10

The Contours of Long-Term Systemic Crisis and the Need for Systemic Solutions

Gar Alperovitz, James Gustave Speth, and Joe Guinan

You wouldn't know it from the corporate media, but evidence is mounting that the United States faces a systemic crisis, not simply political and economic difficulties. The economy is stagnating. The political system is stalemated. Communities are in decay. The lives of millions are compromised by economic and social pain. Violence is endemic among individuals, communities, and nations. Civil liberties are eroding. Near-record numbers of citizens remain incarcerated. Underemployment, inequality, and ecological despoliation deepen day by day. The planet itself is threatened by climate change. A generation of young people expects to be worse off than their parents. The very idea of building a cooperative community of caring responsibility has faded from public discourse and common understanding.

Traditional strategies to achieve equitable and sustainable social, economic, and ecological outcomes simply no longer work. Income and wealth disparities have become severe. The government no longer has much capacity to use progressive taxation to achieve equity goals or to regulate corporations effectively. Corporate power dominates decision making through lobbying, uncontrolled political contributions, and political advertising. Publicly listed, large-scale corporations are subject to Wall Street's first commandment—grow or die!—and increasing carbon emissions come with the territory of ever-expanding growth, both as an economic matter and as a political matter, where opposition to anything that adds costs is part and parcel of the basic corporate dynamic.

Across a range of socioeconomic indicators, the data make for grim reading. Real wages for 80 percent of American workers have been virtually flat for at least three decades.[1] Meanwhile, income for the top 1 percent has jumped from 10 percent of all income to more than 20 percent. Wealth is even more concentrated, with the top 10 percent now commanding over three quarters of the total.[2] The richest *four hundred individuals*—they could all be seated on a single airplane—together have more wealth than the *bottom 180 million Americans* combined.[3] For decades now, virtually all the gains to the economy have been captured by the very rich, while the vast majority have received a declining share of increasing productivity. Union density, historically an important measure of countervailing power, has fallen from a postwar high of 34.7 percent in 1954 to just 11.1 percent in 2014—and a mere 6.6 percent in the private sector.[4] For more than forty years there has been virtually no change in the percentage of Americans living in poverty (if anything, there is evidence of a worsening trend).[5] Over the same period, the proportion of the population in federal and state prisons has more than quintupled, from ninety-three to almost five hundred per hundred thousand.[6] The United States now criminalizes more conduct than most other countries in the world. These are the contours of long-term systemic crisis.

Unsurprisingly, a growing number of Americans have begun to ask ever more penetrating questions about the direction in which the country is headed. Washington is broken. Serious decisions capable of dealing with real problems cannot be made. Gestures and posturing fill the airwaves. Politics no longer even attempts to confront the issues that matter most. When long, long trends get steadily worse, year in and year out, it is clear that something profound is at work. When big problems emerge across the entire spectrum of national life, it is not for small reasons. A political economy is a system, and today's system is programmed not to meet basic needs but to prioritize the generation of corporate profits, the growth of GDP, and the projection of national power. It follows that if we are serious about addressing the challenges we face, we need to think through and then build a new system of political economy, however difficult the task, and however long it may take. Systemic problems require systemic solutions.

To this end, in March 2015 we launched the Next System Project, a concerted effort to break through the national media silence and to radically shift the national dialogue about the future away from narrow debates about policies that do not alter any significant decaying trends, and toward awareness that what must be changed is the nature of the political-economic system itself. The time has come to think boldly about what is required to deal with the systemic difficulties we are facing. It is time to begin a real conversation—locally, nationally, and at all levels—about genuine alternatives. It is time to develop thoughtful, system-building answers to system-threatening challenges. It is time to debate what it will really take to move in a new direction capable of producing sustainable, lasting, and more democratic social, economic, and ecological outcomes.

Rarely do important ideas matter in politics. What usually matters is the momentum of entrenched power. But not always. Sometimes— when the old ideas no longer explain the world, when it is obvious that something is wrong—new ideas can matter, and matter a great deal. Today, there is a need for, and hunger for, new understanding, new clarity, and a new way forward. We believe that the time is ripe for a major strategic intervention in public life aimed at putting "the system question" on the map and catalyzing a wide-ranging public debate about genuine systemic alternatives. Unless a plausible alternative system can be developed, fleshed out via research and debate, and ultimately embraced and implemented by theorists, practitioners, policymakers, activists, and citizens at all levels, the current downward trajectory of pain and decay will only continue.

AN UNDERREPORTED EXPLOSION OF
INSTITUTIONAL INNOVATION

The good news is that the inability of traditional politics and policies to address fundamental challenges has fueled an extraordinary amount of experimentation in communities across the United States and around the world. It has also generated increasing numbers of sophisticated and thoughtful proposals that build from the bottom and begin to suggest new systemic possibilities beyond both corporate capitalism and state socialism. It is becoming possible to bring together, project, and extend elements of innovative thinking and real-world practice in key areas to define the underlying structural building blocks of a range of new political-economic system models capable of rebuilding the basis for democracy, liberty, equality, sustainability, and community in the United States in the twenty-first century.

Unbeknownst to many, literally thousands of on-the-ground efforts have been developing. These include cooperatives, worker-owned companies, neighborhood corporations, and many little-known municipal, state, and regional efforts. Even experts working on such matters rarely appreciate the sheer range of activity. Practical and policy foundations have been established that offer a solid basis for future expansion. A body of hard-won expertise is now available in each area, along with support organizations, and technical and other experts who have accumulated a great deal of direct problem-solving knowledge.

The corporate press, of course, covers very little of this. A recent Democracy Collaborative study made a sample assessment of coverage of the emerging "new economy" by counting articles that appeared in the *Wall Street Journal*, the most widely circulated newspaper in the United States, between January and November 2012.[7] The study found ten times more references to caviar than to employee-owned firms, a growing sector of the economy that involves more than $800 billion in assets and over ten million employee-owners. Worker ownership was mentioned in a mere five articles. By contrast, 132 articles referred to golf clubs and sixty to horse racing and related equestrian activities. Although 2012 was designated by the United Nations as the International Year of Cooperatives—co-ops now boast more than a billion members worldwide—the *Journal*'s coverage was similarly thin. More than 120 million Americans are members of cooperatives of one form or another, thirty million more than are owners of mutual funds. But while the *Journal* devoted some seven hundred articles to mutual funds, only 183 pieces mentioned co-ops, of which the majority were concerned with high-end New York real estate. A mere fourteen articles gave co-op businesses more than passing mention, only one more than mentioned Dom Pérignon champagne. Moreover, while the study singled out the *Wall Street Journal*, a preliminary review suggested that much the same held true of other major national media outlets.[8]

This national media silence regarding the growth of economic alternatives is hardly surprising. The idea that we need a "new economy"—that the entire economic system must be radically restructured if critical social and environmental goals are to be met—runs directly counter to the American creed that capitalism as we know it is the best, and only possible, option. Most of the new projects, ideas, and research efforts have thus gained traction slowly and with little national attention. But in the wake of the financial crisis, they have proliferated and earned a surprising amount of support—and not only among advocates on the left. New terms have begun to gain currency in diverse areas with activist groups and constituencies, an indication that the domination of traditional thinking may be starting to weaken. Thus we encounter the sharing economy, the caring economy, the provisioning economy, the restorative economy, the regenerative economy, the sustaining economy, the collaborative economy, the solidarity economy, the gift economy, the resilient economy, the steady state economy, the new economy, and many, many more. There are calls for a Great Transition, or for a reclamation of the commons. Several of these approaches already have significant constituencies and work under way. Creative thinking by researchers and engaged scholars is also contributing to the ferment, and policies at the state and local level can help move projects into much more powerful-scale and community-wide impact. Larger-scale strategic options that build on what is being learned locally are beginning to be sketched as the basis for longer-term national strategies.

Such approaches cannot claim to provide all the answers. But a number of exploratory models have already been put forward that emphasize fundamental changes in underlying political-economic institutions. Important work has also been done in related arenas: on political and constitutional political structure and the future of parliamentary and non-parliamentary systems; on the impact of regional models of different scale on democratic institutions and practice; on new voting arrangements that better safeguard the rights and interests of minority communities; and many others. Developing detailed and sophisticated alternatives that can be refined over time is a prerequisite if we are to stimulate a serious and wide-ranging debate around a broader menu of institutional possibilities for future development than the narrow range of choices commonly discussed.

THERE ARE REAL ALTERNATIVES

The need for a major intervention in the national debate is increasingly obvious. Even in a time of economic crisis there has been little willingness among traditional progressive organizations to discuss system-changing strategies. Many organizations spend most of their time trying to put out fires in Washington and have little capacity to stand back and consider deeper strategic issues—particularly if they involve movement building and challenges to the current orthodoxy. Efforts to cobble together "solutions" to today's challenges commonly draw upon the very same institutional arrangements and practices that gave rise to the problems in the first place. What is required is a self-conscious effort to face the fact that the system itself has to be changed and a different kind of political economy created.

Although precisely what "changing the system" means is obviously a matter of debate, certain key points are clear. The new movements seek a cooperative, caring, and community-nurturing economy that is ecologically sustainable, equitable, and socially responsible—one that is based on rethinking and democratizing the nature of ownership at every level, and challenging the growth paradigm that is the underlying assumption of all conventional policies. In short, these movements seek an economy that gives true priority to people, place, and planet. Such an economy, so different from our own, requires a radical redefinition of terms beyond a narrow choice between "capitalism" and "socialism."

It's easy to overestimate the possibilities. Emerging ideas and institutional explorations are limited compared with the power of Wall Street banks and the other corporate giants of the American economy. On the other hand, precisely because the existing structures of power have created enormous economic problems and fueled public anger, the opportunity for a more profound shift exists. Unexpectedly rapid change is not out of the question. We have already seen how, in moments of crisis, the nationalization of auto giants such as General Motors and Chrysler can suddenly become a reality. Such crises are likely to be repeated in the future, possibly with more far-reaching outcomes over time. When the next financial breakdown occurs, huge injections of public money may well lead to the breakup or de facto takeover of major financial institutions. At the same time, various forms of larger institutional experimentation—and pressure for further experimentation—are also clearly in the cards. Twenty states have seen legislation introduced to establish a public bank like the one that has been operating successfully in North Dakota for almost a century.

In a nation in which a tiny group of elites controls the lion's share of productive wealth, new approaches are already showing considerable appeal to the young—the people who will shape the next political era. Polls show that they are clearly open to something new, whatever it may be called. "Socialism," once a banned term, has in recent years been slightly more favorably received among young people than the word "capitalism."[9] Non-statist, community-building, institution-changing, democratizing strategies could very well capture the imaginations of younger generations and channel their desire to heal the world. Such strategies could open the way to a great era of renewal, even of step-by-step evolutionary systemic change—a time of ferment and explosion that could expand upon the periods of major unrest that have repeatedly occurred in the United States from the time of the Revolution onward.

The attempt to place "the system question" firmly back on the table can build upon a number of past precedents for an ambitious opening of public debate. The civil rights movement, the environmental movement, the feminist movement, and the LGBTQ rights movement all radically shifted both activist and academic directions—developing new strategies and action as the change agendas began to impact academic, organizational, and other decision making. Our goal is not to answer all the questions, a project that is indeed impossible. Rather, we seek to define sufficiently clear options for "the next system" so that we can radically expand the boundaries of political debate in the United States and help give greater clarity of long-term direction to activists, researchers, and practitioners—and to millions of others, young and old, who are increasingly angered by the immorality and insecurity of the existing system and want to somehow realize America's long-unfulfilled promises of freedom and democracy.

We seek a far-ranging debate, out of which even more developed ideas and proposals may come. Ultimately, alternative system models will only have an impact if they are given a major public airing. Partial precedents for stirring such far-ranging public discussion include the Club of Rome's 1972 report, *Limits to Growth*, as well as the 1987 Brundtland Commission Report defining sustainable development. Through a guerrilla communications effort, including publications, conferences, webinars, independent news media, study groups, film, and social media, we aim to bring the system debate to a wide audience and challenge directly the deadly notion that nothing can be done. Through engagement with community activists, and in collaboration with labor unions and other groups, the hope is to help equip a new generation of activists and public intellectuals with the means to open up a much broader debate on America's future—and begin putting change into action.

There is inspiration to be found in unexpected quarters. Most people forget how marginal conservative thinkers and activists were in the 1940s and 1950s—and even after the Goldwater debacle of 1964. The ideas and beliefs that currently dominate American politics were once regarded as antique and ridiculous by the mainstream press, political leadership, and most of serious academic thought. Committed conservatives worked in very difficult circumstances to self-consciously develop and propagate their ideas, practices, and politics for the long haul, demonstrating what can be done against once seemingly long odds by those prepared to roll up their sleeves, get organized, and get serious.

ALTERNATIVE SYSTEM MODELS AND APPROACHES

The conversation on systemic change will be able to build upon an impressive body of existing work and work that is currently under way. In recent years, individual researchers have begun to set down, sometimes in considerable detail, the outlines of comprehensive models or partial models of systemic alternatives. A non-exhaustive list would include David Schweickart, Juliet Schor, Richard Wolff, David Korten, Michael Albert, J. K. Gibson-Graham, Marta Harnecker, Roberto Mangabeira Unger, Robin Hahnel, Jessica Gordon Nembhard, Erik Olin Wright, and Herman Daly—along with many, many others. Additional approaches are being developed at the Tellus Institute in Boston, at the Institute for Policy Studies, at the Schumacher Center, at York University in Canada, at the New Economics Foundation in the United Kingdom, and elsewhere. Although each has its own special features, many of these alternative systemic models may be understood as falling within a number of broad categories or "ideal types."

Several thinkers have posited models in which the worker-owned and/or self-managed enterprise becomes the dominant economic unit, replacing the privately owned firm and the publicly traded corporation in capitalism and state-owned industry in socialism. In place of hierarchical modes of production these visions build on existing experience with worker-owned cooperatives to institutionalize democracy at work as the economy's central principle and society's new foundation. In *After Capitalism*, David Schweickart sets out his latest iteration of a detailed system model he calls "Economic Democracy."[10] This model would preserve a role for markets in goods and services while extending democracy into the workplace and the linked spheres of finance and investment. In place of private ownership of the means of production with markets in capital, labor, and goods and services under capitalism, or state ownership and planning under socialism, Economic Democracy has a basic economic structure of socially owned, worker-controlled firms in a competitive market. The model has neither capital markets nor labor markets in the usual sense. Although workers control their own jobs and workplaces, productive resources would become the collective property of society and there would be social control over investment.

Given pressing ecological limits and the need to restore "human scale" to the economy, a number of writers and organizations have argued for an economic model based around a small-scale, decentralized, ecologically oriented sector of entrepreneurial individuals, small businesses, and households. These approaches also emphasize trading off consumption against increased free time and sociability, and are rooted in healthy, resilient local communities that are capable of sustaining high degrees of trust, reciprocity, and mutualism. Juliet Schor posits a shift to a locally oriented economic model based on new sources of wealth, green technologies, and different ways of living, including downshifting out of the "work-and-spend" cycle and diversifying sources of household income.[11] The four pillars of "plenitude" include time, with citizens using their newfound time affluence to invest in other sources of wealth; high-tech self-provisioning, meeting basic needs (income, food, housing, consumer goods, energy) through creative, smart, high-productivity technologies; consuming differently, giving people more time, more creativity, and more social connection, while also lowering ecological footprints and avoiding consumer debt; and connection, a rebirth of community through local economic interdependence through the trading of services and sharing of assets.

David Korten proposes a model predicated on organizing to meet human needs as members of Earth's community of life.[12] The current dominant system fails, he argues, because it takes money rather than life as its defining value and is designed to maximize financial returns. For Korten, the proper system design goal is an economy that maintains ecological balance between aggregate human consumption and the regenerative capacity of the biosphere while maintaining an equitable distribution of real wealth and supporting deep democracy. Guided by living system principles, the global human economy should thus be restructured around largely self-reliant bioregional economies in which decision making is predominantly local and each bioregional economy seeks to live within the means of the bioregional ecosystem. Higher system levels will be structured around the principle of subsidiarity and be supportive of predominantly local decision making.

A number of proposals being put forward by liberals and left liberals, if pursued, would effectively amount to a reinvigorated social democracy. Such a model would retain many of the features of current capitalism, especially concerning ownership of productive wealth, but it envisions a far more active role for the state in the economy, including—inter alia—strengthened regulation, the institution of a guaranteed jobs program of some kind to ensure a full employment economy, and elements of industrial policy and national economic planning. (Related to—though not always included in—such models are post-Keynesian approaches such as modern monetary theory, or MMT, which open the door to an array of different policy options regarding public-benefitting credit, debt, and money creation.) To address ecological problems, some have linked job guarantees to a "Green New Deal" and a restorative economics approach that would seek to rebuild natural capital and ecosystems while also increasing employment.

In *Back to Full Employment*, Robert Pollin argues that full employment as a policy was abandoned in the United States in the 1970s for the wrong reasons, and argues that it can be achieved again despite the serious political and economic challenges it now faces.[13] Pollin believes the biggest obstacle to creating a full-employment economy is politics. Putting an end to the prevailing neoliberal opposition to full employment, he argues, will require an epoch-defining reallocation of political power away from the interests of big business and Wall Street and toward the middle class, working people, and the poor, and strong defense of the environment. In the end, achieving full employment will be a matter of political will around the creation and institutionalization of a fundamental right to a decent job.

Several thinkers—most notably Michael Albert and Robin Hahnel, but also British academic Pat Devine and Latin American theorist Marta Harnecker—have argued that an alternative to market forces is necessary as a means of coordinating decentralized economic decisions while avoiding the pitfalls of authoritarian command economies.[14] Under such participatory planning models, consumption and investment decisions would be made consensually by citizens through iterative democratic processes—"participatory planning" for Albert and Hahnel, or what Devine calls "negotiated coordination." Proponents are able to point to preliminary but expanding experience with participatory budgeting in Brazil, India, Europe, and the United States as partial precedents for such a model.

Another set of proposals generated by environmentally minded thinkers focuses on the ecological limits to unending growth and even—given the looming climate disaster—the imperative for a shift, in the developed world at least, toward no-growth ("steady-state") or de-growth economies. Depending on the end goal, whether it is decoupling measures of well-being from natural resource consumption or managing throughput, the mechanisms of these ecological models differ widely, ranging from strict regulation of inputs and outputs to a shift away from a dependence on economic growth for the achievement of full employment, poverty elimination, and environmental protection. Proposals range from the prioritization of resource efficiency, renewable energy, and steady reductions in material throughput to consumption taxes, to deeper-level engagements with the basic structure of market economies. Writers associated with models focused on ecology and growth include Herman Daly, Tim Jackson, and Richard Heinberg—among many others.[15]

There is also a renewed focus on public ownership, in decentralized and democratized forms, as the central organizing principle of a "socialism fit for the twenty-first century." Responding to the often disastrous experience with neoliberal privatization as well as the massive and unprecedented nationalization of the financial sector around the world during the recent crisis, these authors draw upon research showing that the actual performance record of public ownership in the twentieth century was substantially better than has been made out—at least when viewed in narrow efficiency terms. At the heart of efforts to rehabilitate public ownership is a critique of the centralized forms of the past in which nationalized industries were undemocratic and unresponsive, as in the Soviet bloc, or largely utilized to stabilize capitalism, as in Western Europe and Asia. Proponents of such a reclaimed public ownership can now point to a wave of innovations, especially in Latin America, whereby state industry is being blended with worker self-management and a multi-stakeholder approach involving cooperatives, trade unions, and civil society groups in a growing number of "public–public partnerships."

In *Reclaiming Public Ownership*, Andrew Cumbers surveys the experience of nationalization in countries as diverse as Britain, France, Norway, and the Asian Tigers, and concludes with an argument for a more pluralist, decentralized, and democratic public ownership wedded to "economic democracy."[16] In this vision, community ownership, cooperatives, municipal enterprise, and a host of kindred institutional forms all represent ways in which capital can be held in common by small and large publics. Cumbers offers a preliminary sketch of what an economy organized around various forms of public ownership might look like, including accompanying institutional and regulatory arrangements and their application to different sectors of the economy. He suggests finance and land—both sectors of pronounced rent seeking and the site of recent crises that have caused so much social havoc—as the obvious places to begin an extension of democratic public ownership throughout the economy.

As has become painfully clear, we face a systemic crisis not only in connection with the economy, but also in connection with order policing ("stop and frisk," "zero tolerance," and "broken windows"), police brutality, structural and institutional racism, and America's racialized regime of mass incarceration. A range of studies and on-the-ground activist work aimed at the complex of issues surrounding discrimination, policing, racialized violence, and mass incarceration—what some have termed "the American Gulag"— point to important elements of political economic design focused on resolving long-standing underlying systemic injustices. Jessica Gordon Nembhard's widely discussed book *Collective Courage* documents an alternative tradition of political economy based on cooperation, mutualism, and self-help, with a lineage traceable from the African mutual aid societies and communes of the early American republic, through W. E. B. Du Bois's "cooperative commonwealth," to efforts today by the Malcolm X Grassroots Movement at rebuilding the crumbling economy of Jackson, Mississippi, through a variety of cooperative enterprises and initiatives.[17] Such African-American traditions, born of the necessity of finding strategies aimed at delivering independence, solidarity, and community self-preservation, offer models and partial models for alternative developmental paths that are rooted in long histories of political struggle and the everyday experience of ordinary people of color grappling with systemic problems.

Another set of approaches—encompassing two of this chapter's authors, Gar Alperovitz and Gus Speth—synthesizes many elements of the approaches above to suggest a pluralist model in which ownership is based in a variety of institutions with a special focus on the local community and a robust vision of community democracy as the necessary foundation for a renewal of democracy in general.[18] Such visions project the development over time of a variety of new ownership institutions, ranging from locally anchored worker-owned and other community-benefitting firms, on the one hand, to state, regional, and national wealth-holding institutions, on the other. These ultimately would take the place of current elite and corporate ownership of large-scale private capital.

TOWARD THE NEXT SYSTEM

The above is only a rough and partial typology, a sampling intended to give a sense of the range and level of sophistication of this growing body of new models and approaches. There are many, many others. Solidarity economy networks around the world, for instance, are developing a wide range of initiatives and strategies. Points of convergence among different models are already emerging and offer opportunities for useful dialogue and debate and for sharpening areas of divergence and honest disagreement. An increasingly sophisticated but little-publicized debate about longer-term democratic systemic options is developing just below the surface of public attention.

At the same time, there are clear limitations to existing discussions of systemic alternatives. Absent from many of the models is deep substantive engagement with questions of political and cultural theory, on the one hand, and of rights concerns related to race, ethnicity, gender, and sexual orientation, on the other. There is a great deal that must also be learned from discussions of deliberative democracy and of political institutions and legal frameworks, and from important cultural initiatives related to race, sexism, violence, and beyond. Violence in particular—from Hiroshima to wars of intervention to brutal attacks on ethnic minorities, women, and gay Americans—also reflects (and amplifies) underlying systemic tensions and failures, above all the failure to create decent, secure, and equitable livelihoods and a nurturing and supportive community of common responsibility, caring, and respect.

The Next System Project, then, is an ambitious multiyear initiative aimed at thinking boldly about what is required to deal with the systemic challenges the United States faces now and in coming decades. Our goal is to put the central idea of system change, and the idea that there can be a "next system," on the map. Working with a broad group of researchers, theorists, and activists, we seek to launch a national debate on the nature of "the next system" using the best research, understanding, and strategic thinking, on the one hand, and on-the-ground organizing and development experience, on the other, to refine and publicize comprehensive alternative political-economic system models that are different in fundamental ways from the failed systems of the past and capable of delivering superior social, economic, and ecological outcomes. By defining issues systemically, we believe we can begin to move the political conversation beyond current limits with the aim of catalyzing a substantive debate about the need for a radically different system and how we might go about its construction. Despite the scale of the difficulties, a cautious and paradoxical optimism is warranted. There are real alternatives. Arising from the unforgiving logic of dead ends, the steadily building array of promising new proposals and alternative institutions and experiments, together with an explosion of ideas and new activism, offers a powerful basis for hope.

To learn more, please visit thenextsystem.org.

GAR ALPEROVITZ is cochair of the Next System Project, former Lionel R. Bauman Professor of Political Economy at the University of Maryland, and cofounder of the Democracy Collaborative. His most recent book, *What Then Must We Do?: Straight Talk About the Next American Revolution*, was published in 2013 by Chelsea Green.

JAMES GUSTAVE "GUS" SPETH is cochair of the Next System Project and a Senior Fellow at the Democracy Collaborative, Distinguished Senior Fellow at Demos, and Associate Fellow at the Tellus Institute. His recent memoir, *Angels by the River*, was published in 2014 by Chelsea Green.

JOE GUINAN is a Senior Fellow at the Democracy Collaborative and executive director of the Next System Project.

The authors would like to thank Thomas M. Hanna for help with data issues.

Notes

1. Real average wages for production workers in manufacturing and nonsupervisory workers in other sectors (accounting for 80 percent of employment) were $18.74 an hour in 1973 ($690.63 per week) in 2011 dollars. In 2011 they were $19.47 an hour ($654.87 per week). See Lawrence Mishel et al., "Table 4.3: Hourly Wage and Compensation Growth for Production/ Non-supervisory Workers, 1947–2011," in *The State of Working America*, 12th ed. (Washington DC: Economic Policy Institute, 2012), 184.
2. The income share (including capital gains) for the top 1 percent was 9.16 percent in 1973. In 1980 it was 10.02 percent. In 2013 it was up to 20.08 percent. See Facundo Alvaredo et al., "The World Top Incomes Database," *Paris School of Economics*, no date, accessed May 4, 2015, http://g-mond.parisschoolofeconomics.eu/topincomes. Using net worth as a measure, in 2010 the top 1 percent had a 35.4 percent share, the top 5 percent had a 63.1 percent share, and the top 10 percent had a 76.7 percent share. Using non-home wealth, in 2010, the top 1 percent had a 42.1 percent share, the top 5 percent had a 71.7 percent share, and the top 10 percent had

a 84.9 percent share. See Edward N. Wolff, "The Asset Price Meltdown and the Wealth of the Middle Class," New York University, August 26, 2012, 58.

3. See Gar Alperovitz, "Inequality's Dead End—And the Possibility of a New, Long-Term Direction," *Nonprofit Quarterly*, March 10, 2015, note 5, https://nonprofitquarterly.org/policysocial-context/25753-inequality-s-dead-end-and-the-possibility-of-a-new-long-term-direction.html.

4. Bureau of Labor Statistics, US Department of Labor, "Union Members—2014," news release, January 23, 2015, www.bls.gov/news.release/pdf/union2.pdf.

5. In 1973, the official poverty rate hit an all-time low of 11.1 percent. In 2013, the rate was 14.5 percent. For historical rates, see US Census Bureau, "Table 2: Poverty Status, by Family Relationship, Race, and Hispanic Origin," in *Historical Poverty Tables—People* (Washington DC: US Census Bureau, no date), www.census.gov/hhes/www/poverty/data/historical/people.html. For 2013, see Carmen DeNavas-Walt and Bernadette D. Proctor, *Income and Poverty in the United States: 2013* (Washington DC: US Census Bureau, September 2014), accessed November 18, 2014, https://www.census.gov/content/dam/Census/library/publications/2014/demo/p60-249.pdf.

6. For the 93 figure, see Kathleen Maguire, ed., *Source Book of Criminal Justice Statistics: 2002* (Washington DC: Government Printing Office, 2004), 495, http://www.albany.edu/sourcebook/pdf/section6.pdf. For 2013, see E. Ann Carson, *Prisoners in 2013* (Washington DC: US Department of Justice, September 30, 2014), 6, http://www.bjs.gov/content/pub/pdf/p13.pdf.

7. Gar Alperovitz and Keane Bhatt, "Revealed: Wall Street Journal More Interested in Caviar and Foie Gras Than Employee-owned Firms," AlterNet, December 3, 2012, http://www.alternet.org/economy/revealed-wall-street-journal-more-interested-caviar-and-foie-gras-employee-owned-firms.

8. Project Censored highlighted the growth of cooperatives as one of the most underreported news stories of 2011–12. See "2012: The International Year of Cooperatives" in *Censored 2013: Dispatches from the Media Revolution*, eds. Mickey Huff and Andy Lee Roth (New York: Seven Stories Press, 2012), 37, 79–80.

9. In a December 2011 Pew poll, 49 percent of Americans under thirty had a favorable reaction to "socialism," as compared to 46 percent who had a favorable reaction to "capitalism." See "Little Change in Public's Response to 'Capitalism,' 'Socialism,'" Pew Research Center for the People and the Press, December 28, 2011, http://www.people-press.org/files/legacy-pdf/12-28-11%20Words%20release.pdf.

10. David Schweickart, *After Capitalism*, 2nd ed. (Lanham, MD: Rowman & Littlefield, 2011).

11. Juliet B. Schor, *True Wealth: How and Why Millions of Americans Are Creating a Time-Rich, Ecologically Light, Small-Scale, High-Satisfaction Economy* (New York: Penguin, 2011).

12. David C. Korten, *Change the Story, Change the Future: A Living Economy for a Living Earth* (Oakland: Berrett-Koehler, 2015).

13. Robert Pollin, *Back to Full Employment* (Cambridge, MA: MIT Press, 2012).

14. Michael Albert, *Parecon: Life After Capitalism* (New York: Verso, 2003); Robin Hahnel, *Of the People, By the People: The Case for a Participatory Economy* (Oakland: AK Press, 2012); Pat Devine, *Democracy and Economic Planning* (Oxford, UK: Polity, 2010 [1988]); Marta Harnecker, *A World to Build: New Paths Toward Twenty-First Century Socialism* (New York: Monthly Review Press, 2015).

15. Herman E. Daly, *Steady-State Economics: The Economics of Biophysical Equilibrium and Moral Growth* (W. H. Freeman & Co., 1978); Tim Jackson, *Prosperity without Growth: Economics for a Finite Planet* (New York: Earthscan, 2009); Richard Heinberg, *The End of Growth: Adapting to Our New Economic Reality* (Gabriola Island, BC: New Society, 2011).

16. Andrew Cumbers, *Reclaiming Public Ownership: Making Space for Economic Democracy* (London: Zed Books, 2012).

17. Jessica Gordon Nembhard, *Collective Courage: A History of African-American Cooperative Economic Thought and Practice* (University Park, PA: Pennsylvania State University Press, 2014).

18. Gar Alperovitz, *What Then Must We Do?: Straight Talk About the Next American Revolution* (White River Junction VT: Chelsea Green, 2013); James Gustave Speth, *America the Possible: Manifesto for a New Economy* (New Haven: Yale University Press, 2013).

ACKNOWLEDGMENTS

Mickey Huff and Andy Lee Roth

Many remarkable people contributed, directly or indirectly, to make *Censored 2016* possible. We are grateful to all involved.

To the courageous independent journalists and vital independent news organizations—without your reporting, the Project would be pointless. Faculty evaluators and student researchers at the Project's college and university affiliate campuses make it possible for us to cover the increasingly extensive, dynamic networked fourth estate. The authors who contributed to chapters and sections to *Censored 2016* inspire us with challenging questions and new perspectives. The members of our international panel of judges once again assure that our Top 25 list includes only the best, most significant independent news stories.

At Seven Stories Press, our extraordinary publishers in New York—Dan Simon, Veronica Liu, Jon Gilbert, Liz DeLong, Stewart Cauley, Georgia Phillips-Amos, Lauren Hooker, Ruth Weiner, Ian Dreiblatt, Noah Kumin, Silvia Stramenga, and interns Nick Campanella, Rachel Nam, Nehal Aggarwal, Elena Watson—have our deepest respect and gratitude for their steadfast commitment to publish the Project's research once again.

Thanks to Hilary Allison whose original artwork graces the cover of *Censored 2016*. We also are indebted to the inimitable Khalil Bendib, whose cartoons once again add punch to our annual volume.

We offer our most heartfelt thanks and deepest respect to the founder of Project Censored, Carl Jensen, who passed away April 23, 2015. His pioneering vision and consummate optimism continue to inspire us. We dedicate *Censored 2016* to Carl, and we heed his admonishment to never stop "raking muck and raising hell!"

To Peter Phillips, whose wisdom, passion, and unrelenting support of the Project and its ideals make him a major force for social justice and equality in the world. Peter is an inspiration to all of us.

The members of the Media Freedom Foundation's board of directors (listed below) continue to provide organizational structure and invaluable counsel. You keep us on course in pursuing Project Censored's mission. We also thank our board bookkeeper, Cathy McKenna.

Adam Armstrong is our extraordinary webmaster. He maintains our online presence at projectcensored.com, as well as our sister sites, including dailycensored.com and proyectocensurado.org. We could not reach our increasingly global Internet audience without his great skills and dedication to our shared cause.

We thank Christopher Oscar and Doug Hecker of Hole in the Media Productions for their vision and support as filmmakers and allies. Their award-winning documentary, *Project Censored The Movie—Ending the Reign of Junk Food News*, brings Project Censored's message to new audiences. In the coming year, we look forward to working with them in encouraging student and classroom production of video shorts on Project Censored news stories and analysis.

We are grateful to our friends and supporters at Pacifica Radio, especially KPFA in Berkeley, California. *The Project Censored Show*, coming up on its fifth year on air, continues to broadcast live every Friday owing to the skills and dedication of our amazing producer Anthony Fest and engineers present and past, including Erica Bridgeman, Kirsten Thomas, Pedro Reyes, Rod Akil, and the late Wesley Burton. We also wish to thank all the volunteers there who support the overlapping missions of Project Censored and Pacifica, and all of the twenty-five stations that carry our weekly public affairs program across the US.

We are grateful to the people who have hosted Project Censored events or helped to spread the word about the Project's mission over the past year, including: Jacob Van Vleet and everyone at Moe's Books in Berkeley; Raymond Lawrason and all at Copperfield's Books in Petaluma; everyone at Book Passage in Corte Madera; John Bertucci of Petaluma Community Access Television; Kyle Williams for his videography; Chris McManus, Jim Geraghty, and the Community Media Center of Marin; John Crowley, Diane Gentile, Linda Lau, Paul Coffman, and everyone at Aqus Café and Community in Petaluma; Larry Figueroa, Carolyn Slater, and the crew at Lagunitas Brewing Company; Katie MacBride and Kristin Clark at the Mill Valley Public Library; Michael Nagler, Stephanie Van Hook, and the Metta Center for Nonviolence; David Rovics and Adam Carpinelli; Margli Auclair, Sergio Lub, and everyone at the Mount Diablo Peace and Justice Center; Steven Jay of What's Possible; Ken Walden of What the World Could Be; and Abby Martin of Media Roots—each of whom help the Project to reach a broader audience.

We are excited about partnering with Rob Williams and Julie Frechette at Action Coalition for Media Education (ACME; smartmediaeducation.net), as well as Bill Yousman and Lori Bindig at Sacred Heart University's graduate program in media literacy and digital culture. With the help of ACME and Project Censored board member Nolan Higdon, we are creating a Global Critical Media Literacy Project to further our organizations' joint missions.

We thank Michael McCray, Marcel Reid, Arlene Engelhardt, Mary Glenney and all those involved with the National Whistleblower Summit held in Washington DC. Project Censored is honored to be a cohost and supporter of this important annual event. We are also proud members of the National Coalition Against Censorship and a cosponsor of Banned Books Week. We are inspired by our allies who stand against censorship in its many guises.

Colleagues and staff at Diablo Valley College provide Mickey with tremendous support and informed dialogue. Thanks to Hedy Wong, history department cochairs Matthew Powell and Melissa Jacobson, Greg Tilles, Manual Gonzales, Katie Graham, Nolan Higdon, John Corbally, Jacob Van Vleet, Adam Bessie, David Vela, Lyn Krause, Steve Johnson, Jeremy Cloward, Amer Araim, Mark Akiyama, and Social Sciences Dean, Obed Vazquez, along with current and former teaching assistants and Project interns Ellie Kim, Sierra Shidner, Darian Edelman, Crystal Bedford, Lisa Davis, Miya McHugh, Caitlin McCoy, Bri Silva, Jaideep Singh, Clifton Damiens, Kira McDonough, Shelby Wade, Lauren Freeman, Emilee Mann, Tereese Abuhamdeh, Devin Rasmussen, Austin Heidt, Jasen Wallace, Melanie Voorsanger, Celina Hicks, Bryan Brennan, Jack Smith, Emma Durkin, Edwin Sevilla, Janet Hernandez, and Mark Yolango. Mickey would also like to thank all of his classes for the inspiration they provide, as they are a constant reminder of the possibilities of the future and how privileged we are as educators to have such an amazing role in contributing to the public sphere.

Andy thanks the students in his Fall 2014 Sociology of Mass Media seminar and his fall and spring semester sections of Introduction to Sociology at Pomona College for their intellectual curiosity and abiding enthusiasm.

The generous financial support of donors and subscribers, too numerous to mention here, literally sustain the Project. This year we are especially grateful to Julie Andrzejewski, Doug Durst, Jeremy Forcier, Chris Giuntoli, Chris Gulick, Michael Hansen, David Harris, Said Huber, Neil Joseph, Sergio and Gaye Lube, Robert Manning, Gregory McCarron, Sandi Maurer, Edwin Phillips, Donald Plummer, Barry Preisler, John and Lyn Roth, Basja Samuelson, Marc Sapir, David Schultz, T. M. Scruggs, Josh Sisco, Linda Sylvester, Mark and Debra Swedlund, Elaine Wellin, and Richard and Barbara Wells.

On a personal note, we are indebted to and thankful for the love and support of our families and close friends, as they oft make sacrifices in the shadows so we can continue to do the work we do. Mickey especially thanks his wife, Meg, as he could not do all that he does without her amazing work, counsel, and patience. Andy would like to thank Larry Gassan, Nick Wolfinger, and Liz Boyd for encouragement, inspiration, and loyalty.

Finally, we are grateful to you, our readers, who cherish and demand a truly free press. Together, we make a difference.

MEDIA FREEDOM FOUNDATION/PROJECT CENSORED BOARD OF DIRECTORS

Peter Phillips (president), Mickey Huff, Andy Lee Roth, Bill Simon, Derrick West, Elaine Wellin, Kenn Burrows, Abby Martin, T. M. Scruggs, Nolan Higdon, and Arlene Engelhardt

PROJECT CENSORED 2014–15 NATIONAL AND INTERNATIONAL JUDGES

JULIE ANDRZEJEWSKI. Professor Emeritus of Human Relations and cofounder of the Social Responsibility Program, St. Cloud State University. Publications include *Social Justice, Peace, and Environmental Education* (2009).

ROBIN ANDERSEN. Professor of Communication and Media Studies at Fordham University. She has written dozens of scholarly articles and is author and coauthor of four books, including *A Century of Media, A Century of War* (2006), winner of the Alpha Sigma Nu book award. She writes media criticism and commentary for the media watch group Fairness and Accuracy in Reporting (FAIR), the Vision Machine, and *Antenna Blog*.

OLIVER BOYD-BARRETT. Professor Emeritus, Bowling Green State University, Ohio, and California State Polytechnic University, Pomona. Publications include *The International News Agencies* (1980), *Contra-Flow in Global News* (1994), *The Globalization of News* (1998), *Media in Global Context* (2009), *News Agencies in the Turbulent Era of the Internet* (2010), *Hollywood and the CIA* (2011), and *Media Imperialism* (2015).

KENN BURROWS. Faculty member for the Institute for Holistic Health Studies, Department of Health Education, San Francisco State University. Director of the Holistic Health Learning Center and producer of the biennial conference, Future of Health Care.

ERNESTO CARMONA. Journalist and writer. Chief correspondent, Telesur-Chile. Director, Santiago Circle of Journalists. President of the Investigation Commission on Attacks Against Journalists, Latin American Federation of Journalists (CIAP-FELAP).

ELLIOT D. COHEN. Professor and chair, Department of Humanities, Indian River State College. Editor and founder, *International Journal of Applied Philosophy*. Recent books include *Technology of Oppression: Preserving Freedom and Dignity in an Age of Mass, Warrantless Surveillance* (2014); *Theory and Practice of Logic-Based Therapy* (2013); and *Philosophy, Counseling, and Psychotherapy* (2013).

JOSÉ MANUEL DE-PABLOS. Professor, University of La Laguna (Tenerife, Canary Islands, Spain). Founder of *Revista Latina de Comunicación Social* (RLCS), a scientific journal based out of the Laboratory of Information Technologies and New Analysis of Communication

GEOFF DAVIDIAN. Investigative reporter and editor, *The Putnam Pit* (Cookeville TN) and MilwaukeePress.net. Publications include the *Milwaukee Journal, Houston Chronicle, Arizona Republic*, Reuters, *Chicago Sun-Times, New York Daily News, Albuquerque Journal, Seattle Post-Intelligencer*, and the *Vancouver Sun*.

LENORE FOERSTEL. Women for Mutual Security, facilitator of the Progressive International Media Exchange (PRIME).

ROBERT HACKETT. Professor, School of Communication, Simon Fraser University (in Vancouver). Codirector of News Watch Canada since 1993; cofounder of Media Democracy Day (2001) and openmedia. ca (2007). Publications include *Expanding Peace Journalism* (coedited with I. S. Shaw and J. Lynch, 2011), and *Remaking Media: The Struggle to Democratize Public Communication* (with William K. Carroll, 2006).

KEVIN HOWLEY. Professor of Media Studies, DePauw University. Author of *Community Media: People, Places, and Communication Technologies* (2005), and editor of *Understanding Community Media* (2010) and *Media Interventions* (2013).

NICHOLAS JOHNSON.* Author, *How to Talk Back to Your Television Set*. Commissioner, Federal Communications Commission (1966–73). Former media and cyber law professor, University of Iowa College of Law. More online at nicholasjohnson.org.

CHARLES L. KLOTZER. Founder, editor, and publisher emeritus of *St. Louis Journalism Review* and *FOCUS/Midwest*. The *St. Louis Journalism Review* has been transferred to Southern Illinois University, Carbondale, and is now the *Gateway Journalism Review*. Klotzer remains active at the *Review*.

NANCY KRANICH. Lecturer, School of Communication and Information, and special projects librarian, Rutgers University. Past president of the American Library Association (ALA), convener of the ALA Center for Civic Life. Author of *Libraries and Democracy* (2001) and *Libraries and Civic Engagement* (2012).

DEEPA KUMAR. Associate professor, Media Studies at Rutgers University. Author of *Outside the Box: Corporate Media, Globalization and the UPS Strike* (2007) and *Islamophobia and the Politics of Empire* (2012). She is currently working on a book on the cultural politics of the war on terror.

MARTIN LEE. Investigative journalist and author. Cofounder of Fairness and Accuracy in Reporting, and former editor of FAIR's magazine, *Extra!* Director of Project CBD, a medical science information service. Author of *Smoke Signals: A Social History of Marijuana, The Beast Reawakens,* and *Acid Dreams: The Complete Social History of LSD: The CIA, the Sixties and Beyond.*

DENNIS LOO. Associate professor of Sociology at California State University Polytechnic University, Pomona. Coeditor (with Peter Phillips) of *Impeach the President: The Case Against Bush and Cheney* (2006).

PETER LUDES. Professor of Mass Communication, Jacobs University Bremen. Founder in 1997 of German initiative on news enlightenment, publishing the most neglected German news (Project Censored, Germany); and editor, *Algorithms of Power: Key Invisibles* (2011).

WILLIAM LUTZ. Emeritus Professor of English, Rutgers University. Former editor of *The Quarterly Review of Doublespeak.* Author of *Doublespeak Defined* (1999); *The New Doublespeak: Why No One Knows What Anyone's Saying Anymore* (1996); *Doublespeak: From Revenue Enhancement to Terminal Living* (1989); and *The Cambridge Thesaurus of American English* (1994).

SILVIA LAGO MARTINEZ. Professor of sociology, Universidad de Buenos Aires; Codirector, Gino Germani Research Institute Program for Research on Information Society.

CONCHA MATEOS. Faculty in the Universidad Rey Juan Carlos (Madrid). Journalist for radio, television, and political organizations in Spain and Latin America. Coordinator for Project Censored Research in Europe and Latin America.

MARK CRISPIN MILLER. Professor of Media, Culture, and Communication, New York University, Steinhardt School of Culture, Education, and Human Development. Author, editor, activist.

JACK L. NELSON.* Distinguished Professor Emeritus, Graduate School of Education, Rutgers University. Former member, AAUP Academic Freedom Committee. Author of seventeen books, including *Critical Issues in Education,* 8th ed. (2013) and about 200 articles.

PETER PHILLIPS. Professor of sociology, Sonoma State University. Director, Project Censored, 1996–2009. President, Media Freedom Foundation. Editor or coeditor of fourteen editions of *Censored*. Coeditor (with Dennis Loo) of *Impeach the President: The Case Against Bush and Cheney* (2006).

T. M. SCRUGGS. Professor Emeritus (and token ethnomusicologist), University of Iowa. Executive producer, the Real News Network.

NANCY SNOW. Professor Emeritus of Communications at California State University, Fullerton, and now part-time resident of Tokyo, Japan. Snow is Public Affairs and Media Relations Advisor to Langley Esquire, a leading public affairs firm. Author or editor of ten books, including *Information War* and the *Routledge Handbook of Critical Public Relations*.

SHEILA RABB WEIDENFELD.* President of DC Productions Ltd. Emmy award winning television producer. Former press secretary to Betty Ford.

ROB WILLIAMS. Copresident (with Julie Frechette) of the Action Coalition for Media Education (ACME). Teaches media, communications, global studies, and journalism at the University of Vermont, Champlain College, and Saint Michael's College. He has authored numerous articles on media and media literacy education, as well as coedited an anthology entitled *Most Likely to Secede* (2013) about the Vermont independence movement.

*Indicates having been a Project Censored judge since our founding in 1976.

ANNUAL REPORT FROM THE PRESIDENT FOR MEDIA FREEDOM FOUNDATION/PROJECT CENSORED

Founded in 2000, the Media Freedom Foundation (MFF) is a non-profit 501(c)(3) corporation that sponsors Project Censored and all our various programs. MFF has an eleven-person board of directors that is responsible for monitoring the budget and setting policy for our operations. Mickey Huff is the director of Project Censored and has overall responsibility for the daily management of the corporation and coproduction of the *Censored* yearbook. Associate director Andy Lee Roth serves in a similar administrative capacity and coordinates the Project's Validated Independent News program.

Carl Jensen founded Project Censored at Sonoma State University in 1976. The Project has remained a distinguishing aspect of the university's curriculum for thirty-nine years. Carl's pioneering program of hands-on student training in independent journalism has now been adopted at dozens of college and university campuses across the country and around the world. Today, Project Censored is the longest-running research project on news media censorship in the United States. We were saddened to learn that Carl's free spirit passed away on April 23, 2015; but we are proud to carry on his tradition of advocating for democracy, human rights, and a better world. Carl believed in the First Amendment of the US Constitution and the importance of an informed public as the best protectors of democracy and freedom. In his 2002 book, *Stories That Changed America: Muckrakers of the 20th Century*, Carl wrote, "We need skeptical journalists giving us the facts, courageous publishers providing the necessary soapbox, [and] an outraged public demanding change."

Our good friend Danny Schechter—television producer, filmmaker, and media critic—passed away on March 19, 2015. Danny was a supportive, longtime advisor to Project Censored. In the introduction to *Censored 1998*, he wrote, "Each day at thousands of newspapers and TV newsrooms, editors and producers gather to make their picks from a menu of story possibilities . . . despite the plethora of news sources and the size of the 'news army' there is a sameness to the choices. American Journalism owes Project Censored a debt . . . Project Censored warns that journalism as we have known it is sinking ever deeper in a sludge of sleaze, slime, and sensationalism—news that does not belong in the news." Project Censored remembers Danny for his crucial work on behalf of media freedom.

Since Project Censored's founding we have worked with students and the public through radio, television and film; and in print, via books and the Internet—to promote public understanding of the crucial roles that free speech and a free press play in making democratic government possible. We strive to achieve our mission in numerous ways. Since 1993, we have researched and written an annual book of the top censored news stories and media analysis. Our book *Censored* is published annually by Seven Stories, an independent press in New York City.

We produce and broadcast a weekly one-hour public affairs program, *The Project Censored Show*, for Pacifica Radio, every Friday at 1:00 PST on KPFA 94.1 FM and online at KPFA.org. Our twenty-five affiliate stations include in part: WBAI—New York; WPFA—Washington DC; WPRR—Grand Rapids MI; KSKQ—Ashland OR; KFCF—Fresno CA, WRFN—Radio Free Nashville TN; Progressive Radio Network; No Lies Radio; and various other Pacifica radio stations around the country. Please ask your local public/nonprofit radio station to air our weekly shows. See projectcensored.org/category/radio for a full listing of our shows and guests.

Over the past three *Censored* volumes, our campus affiliates program has involved an average of 220 students and 45 faculty members annually, from approximately 18 college and university campuses, who have reviewed approximately 224 independent news stories each year. This network of professors, students, and community members is a cornerstone of the Project's mission to educate students and the public in media literacy and the crucial role that a free press plays in democracy. Our affiliates program, now in its sixth year, is not only a model of how we can all *be* the media, it is also a unique contribution of the Project: As far as we know, no other media watchdog organization in the US has a larger, more systematic student training program than Project Censored. Faculty from additional college and university campuses have expressed interest in joining our affiliates program, and with enhanced funding we could expand the program and bring in many other campuses.

Our various campuses produce year round Validated Independent News Stories (VINs), which are news stories ignored by corporate media and covered by the independent press, which have been vetted by students and professors affiliated with Project Censored. These news stories are posted on line and become the nominees for the Project's annual listing of the twenty-five most important censored news stories. Any college campus can participate in this process. Teaching college classes and working with students to learn about alternative news outlets is a major part of our efforts to create a more media literate society.

In September 2015, Project Censored and the Action Coalition for Media Education (ACME) will be launching the Global Critical Media Literacy Project (GCMLP). The project is the first of its kind, teaching digital media literacy education and critical thinking skills, as well as raising awareness about corporate and state-engineered news media censorship around the world. The goal of the GCMLP is to use a service-learning-based media literacy education to create more equitable democratic and economic participation in our twenty-first–century public and civic spheres. Rather than wait for states or the nation to mandate media education, the GCMLP will provide educators with training, course materials, and a national network of colleagues to provide college level media education.

Adam Armstrong continues as the webmaster for all the MFF/ Project Censored websites, including our Spanish language site at proyectocensurado.org. He has responsibility for maintaining and protecting our websites and building traffic to each one. Unique views on our sites run some 400,000 each month with millions of monthly hits. Adam also manages the *Daily Censored* blog—dailycensored.com—that now features over fifty regular contributors, posting original news stories and opinion pieces. Adam is a vital part of the Project Censored team.

Our award-winning documentary film, *Project Censored The Movie: Ending the Reign of Junk Food News,* continues to be shown worldwide. Six years in the making, the film was cowritten, codirected, and coproduced by Doug Hecker, a Project Censored alum, and Chris Oscar, with editing by Mike Fischer. The film has won awards, including Best Director of a Documentary and Best Editing of a Documentary at the 2013 Madrid International Film Festival, as well as being honored as the Most Viewed Film at the 2013 Sonoma International Film Festival. The film is a vehicle to engage people who do not already know about the Project and to reach those who our annual books may not. It also is an excellent resource for high school and college teachers to use in their classrooms and is now available for downloading to own or rent online at projectcensoredthemovie.com.

The Project Censored team is regularly invited as speakers to community events, college campuses, academic conferences, and independent bookstores worldwide. We address the issues of media censorship, propaganda, and the importance of accurate independent media in society. To arrange for a member of our speaking team to come to your community or campus see projectcensored.org/speakers.

These efforts and others too numerous to list are part of our annual activities at Media Freedom Foundation/ Project Censored. We currently do all of this on less than $85,000 a year. In addition to annual revenues from book sales and royalties, our primary financial support comes from individual donors around the world. A developing support option has been for donors to pledge five dollars or more a month. Currently over 255 folks act as vital monthly contributors, giving five to fifty dollars a month online. Please consider making a monthly pledge at projectcensored.org. If you are affiliated with a nonprofit foundation or can make a larger gift in support of one or more of our activities, we would sincerely appreciate hearing from you.

At present, ninety percent of our operating budget comes from the support of individual donors, supplemented by book and DVD sales. We accomplish a lot with a little. Our modest budget—augmented by the tireless commitments of numerous volunteer supporters—allows us to maintain our current operations. However, as we hope to have communicated here, we are poised to expand our reach and our influence—via online distribution of the documentary, greater promotion of our annual book series, and, most of all, expansion of the campus affiliates program via our new Global Critical Media Literacy Project.

Promoting freedom of the press, highlighting media bias, and opposing news censorship, Project Censored is among the longest-running media watchdog organizations in the United States. Our track record and reputation is well established. Furthermore, we know of no other organization that systematically provides students the kind of direct and hands-on training in media literacy and critical thinking skills that Project Censored does.

We ask you to please support us financially as you are able and to remember us in your estate planning.

Sincerely,

Peter Phillips, PhD
President, Media Freedom Foundation/Project Censored
PO Box 571
Cotati, CA 94931
(707) 874–2695
peter@projectcensored.org

HOW TO SUPPORT PROJECT CENSORED

NOMINATE A STORY

To nominate a Censored story, send us a copy of the article and include the name of the source publication, the date that the article appeared, and page number. For news stories published on the Internet, forward the URL to mickey@projectcensored.org, andy@projectcensored.org, and/or peter@projectcensored.org. The deadline for nominating *Censored* stories is March 15 of each year.

Criteria for Project Censored news story nominations:

A censored news story reports information that the public has a right and need to know, but to which the public has had limited access.

The news story is recent, having been first reported no later than one year ago. For *Censored 2016* the Top 25 list includes stories reported between April 2014 and March 2015. Thus, stories submitted for *Censored 2017*, our fortieth anniversary edition, should be no older than April 2015.

The story has clearly defined concepts and solid, verifiable documentation. The story's claims should be supported by evidence—the more controversial the claims, the stronger the evidence necessary.

The news story has been published, either electronically or in print, in a publicly circulated newspaper, journal, magazine, newsletter, or similar publication from either a domestic or foreign source.

MAKE A TAX-DEDUCTIBLE DONATION

Project Censored is supported by the Media Freedom Foundation, a 501(c)(3) nonprofit organization. We depend on tax-deductible donations to continue our work. To support our efforts on behalf of independent journalism and freedom of information, send checks to the address below or call (707) 874–2695.

Donations can also be made online at www.projectcensored.org.

Your generous donations help us to oppose news censorship and promote media literacy.

Media Freedom Foundation
PO Box 571
Cotati, CA 94931
mickey@projectcensored.org
andy@projectcensored.org
peter@projectcensored.org
Phone: (707) 874-2695

ABOUT THE EDITORS

MICKEY HUFF is director of Project Censored and serves on the board of the Media Freedom Foundation. To date, he has edited or coedited seven volumes of *Censored* and contributed numerous chapters to these works dating back to 2008. Additionally, he has coauthored several chapters on media and propaganda for other scholarly publications. He is currently professor of social science and history at Diablo Valley College in the San Francisco Bay Area, where he is cochair of the history department. Huff is cohost with former Project Censored director Peter Phillips of *The Project Censored Show*, the weekly syndicated public affairs program that originates from KPFA Pacifica Radio in Berkeley CA. For the past several years, Huff has worked with the national planning committee of Banned Books Week, working with the American Library Association and the National Coalition Against Censorship, of which Project Censored is a member. He also represents Project Censored as one of the cohosting and cosponsoring organizations for the National Whistleblowers Summit held annually in Washington DC. He is a longtime musician and composer and lives with his family in Northern California.

ANDY LEE ROTH is the associate director of Project Censored. He coordinates the Project's Validated Independent News program. He has coedited five previous editions of Project Censored's yearbook, in addition to contributing chapters on Iceland and the commons (*Censored 2014*), the Military Commissions Act (*Censored 2009*), and news photographs depicting the human cost of war (*Censored 2008*). His research on topics ranging from ritual to broadcast news interviews and communities organizing for parklands has also appeared in journals including the *International Journal of Press/Politics*; *Social Studies of Science*; *Media, Culture & Society*; *City & Community*; and *Sociological Theory*. He reviews books for *YES! Magazine*. He earned a PhD in sociology at the University of California, Los Angeles, and a BA in sociology and anthropology at Haverford College. He has taught courses in sociology at UCLA, Bard College, Sonoma State University, College of Marin, and most recently, Pomona College. He serves on the boards of the Claremont Wildlands Conservancy and the Media Freedom Foundation.

For more information about the editors, to invite them to speak at your school or in your community, or to conduct interviews, please visit projectcensored.org.

ABOUT THE COVER ART

Hilary Allison

The illustration on the cover was drawn from the concept of media as commons, in light of the 800th anniversary of the Magna Carta and its sister document, the Charter of the Forest. In the shrinking spaces between what is privately owned, and on the lines we cast between our windows—or screens—there is opportunity to air the stories, ideas, and information that would otherwise be torn down.

HILARY ALLISON is a freelance illustrator and cartoonist, and an editor of the political comix anthology *World War 3 Illustrated*. She lives in New York. Her portfolio lives at HilaryAllison.com.

Index

A2-B-C film
  domestic distribution and protection
    for families, 183–84
  Japan Designated Secrets Bill and,
    184–85
  media democracy and, 183–87
  screening cancellations, 185–86
  self-censorship and, 186–87
  unresolved ending, 187
ABC, 12, 40–41, 146, 203
ABC Evening News, 14
ABC News, 137, 203
ABC World News, 61
Abe, Shinzo, 54
Ablow, Keith, 153
Abu Assi, Diaa, 121
Academi, 261, 263
Academy Awards, 135–36
ACLU. *See* American Civil Liberties
  Union
Action Coalition for Media Education
  (ACME), 28, 199
  service learning and, 208
  skills for GCMLP, 209–11
  thinking arenas, 210–11
activism, 27, 315
Aegis Defense Systems, 258–59
African Americans. *See also* justified
    homicides; police killings; Race
    Forward
  black paranoia, 234–37
  crime and, 153
  Fourteenth Amendment and, 191
  police killings, 155
  Tuskegee syphilis experiment,
    235–36, 245
  victims, 154
After Capitalism (Schweickart), 309
Agent Orange, 66
Ahangar, Parveena, 282

Ahmed, Nafeez, 75–76, 103, 107
albedo modification, 80
Albert, Michael, 308, 311
ALEC. *See* American Legislative
  Exchange Council
Alperovitz, Gar, 313
Alsema, Adriaan, 73–74
Alternatives to Violence Project (AVP),
  108–9
American Beverage Association, 71
American Civil Liberties Union (ACLU),
  57, 77, 122–23
American exceptionalism, 58
American Gulag, 313
American Legislative Exchange Council
  (ALEC), 125
American Paradigm Schools (APS),
  108–11
American Public Television (APT),
  178–79
American Sniper, 135–36
Amnesty International, 77
anti-immigrant sentiments, 146–47
AOL, 203
APDP. *See* Association of Parents of
  Disappeared Persons
APS. *See* American Paradigm Schools
APT. *See* American Public Television
Apuzzo, Matt, 47
Arctic Council, 55–56
arctic warming. *See also* global warming
  global effect, 55
  methane and, 54–57
Arquette, Patricia, 191–92
arsenic, 42
Ashcroft, John, 264
Associated Press, 104, 172, 229, 238,
  240
  on black paranoia, 235–36
  Drop the IWord Campaign and, 195

Association of Parents of Disappeared
    Persons (APDP), 282–83, 286
asylum seekers, 70
Atlantic, 80
Atwood, Margaret, 223
AURAGOLD program, 87–88, 91, 93
Ausick, Paul, 112
authoritarian command economy, 311
AVP. *See* Alternatives to Violence Project

backdoor data collection, 81–83, 91
Back to Full Employment (Pollin), 311
Baga Massacre, 150–51
Balderas, Ignacio, 262
Balog, James, 89
Baltimore Sun, 51
Barger, Brian, 229
Bashir, Khansa, 284–85
Bayer, 64–65
BBC, 86
Becker, Richard, 58–59
Beckwith, Paul, 54–55
Benjamin, Medea, 189
Benkler, Yochai, 35
benzene, 42
Berman, Morris, 201
Bernstein, Carl, 242
*Between Democracy and Nation: Gender
    and Militarism in Kashmir* (Kazi),
    283, 287
Bezos, Jeff, 62
Biden, Hunter, 105
Biden, Joe, 105
Big Media, 210
The Big Story, 238
Bilderberger Group, 256
bin Laden, Osama, 249, 260
Bishop, Amy, 154–55
black paranoia, 234–37
Blackwater, 259–61, 273n26
Blair, Dennis, 76
Blandón, Danilo, 230–31, 233
Blitzer, Wolf, 156
Bloods, 246
Bonaire, 63
Booker, Cory, 125
Bosacki, Dean, 264
Boston Marathon bombings, 271

Boyd, John, 181
Brady, Tom, 137
British East India Company, 257
Britt, Donna, 235, 237
broken windows policing, 313
Brown, Ellen, 49, 153
Brown, Michael, 152–54, 299n68
Brown, Taylor Kate, 86–87
Bueerman, Jim, 61
Buffett, Warren, 62
Bureau of Investigative Journalism,
    45–46, 76–77
Burnett, Erin, 156
Bush, George W., 103, 138, 145, 264
Bush, Jeb, 139

Cabezas, Carlos, 239
Caldeira, Ken, 80–81
Caldicott, Helen, 188–89
CALEA. *See* Communications Assistance
    for Law Enforcement Act
Calgary Herald, 83–84
California Easter Airways, 268
capitalism, 306–7, 309
Caplan-Bricker, Nora, 86
carbon dioxide
    deforestation and, 83
    humans releasing, 55
    methane and, 54
    removal, 80
Carlson, Tucker, 142
Carter, Charly, 51
Cascadia bioregion, 170–72
Castillo, Celerino, III, 238–39
CBS, 12, 40, 86, 227, 228
CBS Evening News, 61
censorship
    A2-B-C film self-censorship, 186–87
    centering, 21–24
    consequences, 13
    corporate, 14, 18n9
    direct and indirect, 33–34
    eliminating signal, 17
    Fox News, 142
    Galeano experiencing, 33
    government, 16, 181
    Jensen definition, 22
    Project Censored self-censorship,

15–16, 19n18
sources, 14
Center for Biological Diversity, 42–44
Center for Food Safety, 67
centering censorship, 21–24
Centers for Disease Control, 73
Central Intelligence Agency (CIA)
    Blackwater and, 260
    cooperative media assets, 242–43
    on "Dark Alliance: The Story behind
        the Crack Explosion," 240–41
    denial of plots, 231
    drone strikes and, 47–48
    drug trafficking ties, 227–29, 236,
        238, 239, 246
    ICREACH search engine and, 78
    internal reports, 247
    New York Times on, 242
    spying, 249
    torture of terrorism suspects, 75–77
    on WMDs, 202
Ceppos, Jerry, 228, 243–46
Cerberus Capital Management LP, 269
Chalabi, Ahmed, 264
Chang, Li-Wen, 223
change, 306
Charlie Hebdo, 150
Chasing Ice, 89
Cheney, Dick, 103, 132
China, 68–69
Chipman, John, 105
Chomsky, Noam, 69, 132, 201
Chossudovsky, Michel, 53
Christian Science Monitor, 88
Chrysler, 306
CIA. *See* Central Intelligence Agency
civil liberties
    acknowledging, 93
    ACLU, 57, 77, 122–23
    erosion of, 34, 301
    privacy, 92
Clarridge, Duane, 239
Clear Channel Communications, 264
Cleary, Sean, 265
climate change
    geoengineering and, 81
    reforestation and, 80
    Washington Post denial, 145
Climate News Network, 88

Climate Science Watch, 175
Clinton, Bill, 264
Clinton, Hillary, 188
    announcing candidacy, 132, 139–40
Club of Rome, 308
CML. *See* critical media literacy
CNN, 74, 137, 139, 155
    war on terror and, 147
coca crop dusting, 269
cocaine, 227–29, 238. *See also* "Dark
    Alliance: The Story behind the
    Crack Explosion"
Cochabamba, Bolivia, water protests,
    48–49
Cockburn, Alexander, 48
Coen, Michael, 74
Coffey, Shelby, III, 232
Cohen, Richard, 236–37
Cohn, Cindy, 82, 92–93
Colbert, Stephen, 181
Cold War, 103, 107
Collective Courage (Nembhard), 313
Collier, Victoria, 50
Collins, Suzanne, 223–24
Colombia Reports, 73–74
colonial feminism, 295
Colorlines, 195
Columbia Journalism Review, 242
Comey, James, 81–82
    on FBI role, 92–93
Committee to Protect Journalists, 23
Common Core, 208
Common Dreams, 57
Communications Assistance for Law
    Enforcement Act (CALEA), 82
community-nurturing economy, 306
community organizing, 34
company culture, 16
Congress, 17n3, 82, 94, 105
    act introduction, 125
    contempt of, 171
    investigations, 240
    war resolution, 136
    working through, 174
Constellis Holdings, 261, 263–64
Constitution, U.S., 24–25, 191. *See also*
    specific amendments
Cooper, Anderson, 141
cooperation, 223, 313

cooperative commonwealth, 313
cooperative community, 301, 304
cooperative media assets, 242–43
corporate censorship, 14, 18n9
corporate control, 34
corporate media, 16, 34, 58
  Bush, J., and, 139
  celebrity sideshow and, 143
  on deforestation, 83
  disinformation campaigns, 201–3
  distortions, 29
  fracking debate and, 44
  geoengineering and, 81
  Internet and, 133–34
  on problem-solving, 304
  reporting on Muslims, 151
  on sensationalistic violence, 156
  staged events and, 145
  xenophobia and racism, 147
corporate power, 230, 301
Costa Rica
  renewable energy and, 62–63
  tourism and agriculture, 63
CounterPunch, 172
creative thinking, 305
Crips, 246
Crisis, 33
critical media literacy (CML)
  defining, 203–8
  digital footprints and, 206
  high school courses, 204
  multi-literacy focus, 204–5
  technology for transformational self-
    expression, 205
  virtual playgrounds and, 207
critical thinking, 28, 91, 199, 210
Crone, Jack, 92
Cronkite, Walter, 15
Cumbers, Andrew, 312
Curtis, Denise, 123
CyTerra, 266, 275n57

Daghistani, Faisal, 264
Daily Caller, 142
Daily Kashmir, 287
Daily Mail, 92
Dallas Morning News, 238
Daly, Herman, 308, 312

D'Andrea, Michael, 47
"Dark Alliance: The Story behind the
    Crack Explosion" (Webb), 28
  advancing story, 238–40
  assets in media, 242–43
  attacks against, 230–34
  black paranoia and, 234–37
  CIA on, 240–41
  circumstantial evidence, 248
  disappearance of, 243–46
  legacy of resistance, 246–49
  Los Angeles Times on, 232–33, 236,
    241, 247
  New York Times on, 233–34, 236, 245
  overview, 227–29
  press and productive relations,
    240–42
  significance of series, 229–30
  Washington Post on, 231–32
Darrow, Charles, 190
Darwish, Mahmoud, 277
Davis, Fania, 109–10
DEA. See Drug Enforcement Agency
decision-making, 49, 169, 301, 307, 310
Defense Systems Limited, 265
deflated Super Bowl footballs, 136–37
deforestation
  Canada, 83–84
  carbon dioxide and, 83
  corporate media on, 83
deliberative democracy, 314
Democracy Collaborative, 304
Democracy Now!, 88, 136, 144
Denmark, 63
Department of Defense (DOD), 257, 259
Department of Justice, 86
deregulation, 173, 175
desertification, 120
Deutch, John M., 245–46, 248
Devine, Pat, 311
DeYonker Jason, 264
2,4-Dichlorophenoxyacetic acid, 66–68
digital footprints, 206
digital information overload, 206–7
disinformation campaigns, 201–3
Dissent NewsWire, 171–72
Divergent (Roth), 223–24
Dixon, Bruce A., 237
DOD. See Department of Defense

Donahue, Phil, 146
Dow AgroSciences.64, 66–67
Draitser, Eric, 103
drone strikes
  CIA and, 47–48
  heart of, 46–47
  New York Times on, 47
  Obama on, 47
  over Pakistan, 45–47
  on al-Qaeda, 45–48
Drop the IWord Campaign, 195
Drug Enforcement Agency (DEA), 78
drug trafficking, 227–29, 236, 238, 239,
  246
Du Bois, W. E. B., 313
Dutch East Indies Company, 257
DynCorp, 268–69

Earth First! Journal, 171
Earth Island Journal, 172
earthquakes, 43, 54
East Siberian Arctic Shelf (ESAS), 55
Eastwood, Clint, 135
Ebola outbreak, 130, 146–48
Ecologist, 172
Economic Democracy, 309
economy
  authoritarian command, 311
  community-nurturing economy, 306
  economic inequality, 40
  global human economy, 310
  human scale, 309
  locally oriented economic model, 309
  new, 304–5
  no-growth ("steady-state"), 311
  political economy, 302–4
  restorative economics, 310
  solidarity networks, 314
  World Economic Forum, 41, 256
Electronic Frontier Foundation, 93
Ellsberg, Daniel, 173
Emirates Red Crescent Authority (ERC),
  120
employee-owned firms, 304, 309
employment, 196, 211, 311
Engel, Richard, 144
Enlist Duo, 66–67
environment. *See also* arctic warming;

carbon dioxide; global warming
  environmental collapse, 271
  environmental movement, 307
  environmental protection, 311
  killing of environmentalists, 84–85
  Environmental Protection Agency (EPA),
    44
  on drift, 67–68
  on fracking impact, 44
Epstein, Adam, 63
ERC. *See* Emirates Red Crescent
  Authority
Erinys, 264–65
ESAS. *See* East Siberian Arctic Shelf
European Court of Human Rights, 123
Extreme Ice Survey, 89

Facebook, 203, 217
Facing Race conference, 196
Fairness and Accuracy in Reporting
  (FAIR), 61–62, 144, 151, 181
  on Iraq War, 202
Falklands War, 143–44
Farah, Douglas, 231–32
FARC. *See* Revolutionary Armed Forces
  of Colombia
Farrakhan, Louis, 237
fascism, 255–58, 269, 271
FBI. *See* Federal Bureau of Investigation
FCC. *See* Federal Communications
  Commission
FDA. *See* Food and Drug Administration
Federal Bureau of Investigation (FBI)
  backdoor data collection, 81–83, 91
  Comey on role, 92–93
  harassment in Cascadia, 170–72
  ICREACH search engine and, 78
  on justified homicides, 58–59
Federal Communications Commission
  (FCC), 14, 37
  ISPs regulation, 112, 114
  net neutrality and, 113–15
  Open Internet Order, 114–15
feminism, 219–20
  colonial, 295
  feminist movement, 307
  feminist dystopia, 219, 223, 225n5
Fendt, Lindsay, 63

Fifth Amendment, 171
Fili-Krushel, Patricia, 192
financial crisis, 39, 107, 305
First Amendment, 25, 112, 171, 181
First Look Media, 144
Fischer, Holly, 131
Fletcher, Michael A., 234, 237
Food and Drug Administration (FDA), 174
Forbes, 41, 113
forced displacement, 69–70
Foreign Policy, 84
The Forerunner, 221
Fourteenth Amendment, 191
Fox News, 79, 106, 136, 139, 141
    biased coverage, 156
    on Brown, M., shooting, 153–54
    censorship as News Abuse, 142
fracking, 42–44
Freedom of Information Act, 175
free press, 25, 27, 130
Freeway: Crack in the System, 247
Friends of the Earth, 64–65
Fukushima, Mizuho, 185
Fukushima nuclear disaster, 52–54. *See also A2-B-C* film
Fulwood, Sam, III, 236, 237

G4S, 266–68
G-7, 256
G-20, 256
Gabriel, Larry, 50–51
Galeano, Eduardo, 26, 169
    censorship experienced by, 33
    on direct and indirect censorship, 33–34
    insight, 95
    on solidarity, 34–35
    on writing, 36
Gallagher, Ryan, 78–79, 87, 92
GAP. *See* Government Accountability Project
Garner, Eric, 156
Garrett, Jonathan, 264
gate keeping, 22
gay marriage, 131
Gaza. *See also* Palestine, women resistance

    crippling poverty, 121
    desertification, 120
    disease in, 17
    Israel blockade, 138
    Israel bombing, 120, 127n7
    Israel military control, 119
    movement restrictions, 118–19
    water supply, 26, 117–21
GCMLP. *See* Global Critical Media Literacy Project
GDP. *See* gross domestic product
gender binaries, 219–20
gender equality, 191
General Motors, 306
General Union of Palestinian Women (GUPW), 281
genetically modified organisms (GMOs)
    in Ukraine, 106
    USDA ignoring, 66–68
Geneva Convention, 76
geoengineering, 80–81
GHSDH. *See Global Health Strategies on Diet and Health*
Gibson-Graham, J. K., 308
Gillula, Jeremy, 82, 92–93
Gilman, Charlotte Perkins, 217–25
Giuliani, Rudolph, 152, 153
Global Capitalism and the Crisis of Humanity (Robinson), 269
Global Critical Media Literacy Project (GCMLP)
    ACME skills for, 209–11
    CML identified, 203–8
    conclusion, 212
    launch of, 199
    need for, 199–200
    opportunities, resources, approaches, 211–12
    Project Censored model for, 209
    service learning, 208–9
    truth emergency and, 201–3
Global Health Strategies on Diet and Health (GHSDH), 71
global human economy, 310
global information ecosystem, 90
globalization, 29, 255
Global Justice Ecology Project, 172
Global Muckraking (Schiffrin), 249
global stabilization, 268

Global Trends report, 69–70
global warming
    atmospheric warming, 88–89
    Washington Post on, 89
global wealth, 38–42
Global Witness, 84–85
Globe and Mail, 172
GMOs. *See* genetically modified
    organisms
Golden, Tim, 234
Gómez, Ivan, 239
Goodwin, Herb, 170, 172
Google, 12, 17, 203
Gore, Al, 264
Gough, Myles, 63
Government Accountability Project
    (GAP), 27
    media democracy and, 173–76
government censorship, 16, 181
government surveillance, 16, 18n15,
    57–58, 78. *See also* Central
    Intelligence Agency; Federal
    Bureau of Investigation; National
    Security Agency
    critics, 92–93
Gray, Freddie, 60, 152, 153, 155
gray-water systems, 52
Great Transition, 305
Green Is the New Red, 172
Greenland meltwater, 88–89
Green New Deal, 310
Greenwald, Glenn, 93
gross domestic product (GDP), 302
Group 4 Falck, 267
Guantánamo Bay military prison, 77
Guardian, 60, 63, 82, 92, 123
GUPW. *See* General Union of Palestinian
    Women
Gustin, Felicia, 123
Guterres, António, 70

Hahnel, Robin, 308, 311
half widows, 285–86
Hamas, 119, 127n7, 138
The Handmaid's Tale (Atwood), 223
Hanke, Steve, 107
Hannity, Sean, 136
Harnecker, Marta, 308, 311

Hart, Peter, 144
Harvard Political Review, 150
Hasse, Alma, 170–71
Hauter, Wenonah, 67
Hayden, Michael, 48
Healthy Hunger-Free Kids Act of 2010
    (HHFKA), 71
Hedges, Chris, 201
Heinberg, Richard, 312
Herland (Gilman)
    celebration of motherhood, 221–22
    as censored story, 221–23
    feminist dystopia genre, 219, 223,
        225n5
    gender binaries abolished in, 219–20
    lessons from, 219
    Mother's Day compared to, 218–19
    overview of contemporary relevance,
        217–18
    teaching, 223–24
    utopian society in, 218, 222
Herman, Edward S., 132, 201
Hersh, Seymour M., 249
HHFKA. *See* Healthy Hunger-Free Kids
    Act of 2010
Hickox, Kaci, 147
Hicks, Stephen, 150
hijab, 295
Hildes, Lawrence, 172
Hill, 105
Hirasa, Cheryl, 179, 181
Holmes, James Egan, 154
Holmes, John, 265
Homeland Security, 270
Homrok, Emily, 86
honeybee decline, 64–65
Hooks, Stacy, 147
House Un-American Activities
    Committee (HUAC), 242
Houston Chronicle, 172
Howat, Ian, 89
HUAC. *See* House Un-American
    Activities Committee
human rights movement, 270
Human Rights Watch, 57
Hunger Games (Collins), 223–24
Hunter, Wenonah, 44
Hussein, Saddam, 202
Hutchings, Michael, 265

Iceland, 63
ICREACH search engine, 78–79, 91, 93
ignorance, 12, 17
IIRP. *See* International Institute for Restorative Practices
IMF. *See* International Monetary Fund
income, 302, 315n2
Independent, 238
independent news reporting, 34, 94
Independent Television (ITV), 238–40
India, 278–79
information industry, 22
Ingraham, Laura, 146
Inman, Bobby, 264
Institute for Policy Studies, 308
institutional racism, 313
institution innovation, 303–6
Inter-American Development Bank, 176
Intercept, 78–79, 87, 88, 92
International Atomic Energy Agency, 52
International Institute for Restorative Practices (IIRP), 111
International Monetary Fund (IMF), 106, 255
International Peace Research Association Foundation, 284
International Year of Cooperatives, 304
Internet, 11, 17n4. *See also* net neutrality; social media
    corporate media and, 133–34
    information decline, 203
    Internet Slow Down Day, 113
    Open Internet Order, 114–15
    targeted advertising, 204
    Web pages, 13
Internet Service Providers (ISPs), 112, 114
Inter Press Service, 83
investigative journalism, 13, 19n17
    best in United States, 21
    Bureau of Investigative Journalism, 45–46
Iran, nuclear deal, 132
Iraq
    Green Zone, 263
    ISIS, 151
    Nisour Square killings, 260–61
    U.S. invasion, 103, 145–46
    U.S. sanctions, 149
Iraq War
    FAIR on, 202
    PMCs and, 257–58
Islamic State of Iraq and Syria (ISIS), 151
Islamophobia, 148–51
Israel, 26
    Gaza blockade, 138
    Gaza bombings, 120, 127n7
    Gaza military control, 119
    Palestine occupation, 287–94
ITV. *See* Independent Television

Jackson, Tim, 312
Jamail, Dahr, 54–55
James, LeBron, 138
Japan Designated Secrets Bill, 184–85
Jarvis, Anna, 218
Al Jazeera, 117
Jensen, Carl, 11, 15, 140
    censorship definition, 22
    death of, 23
    free press and, 25, 130
    improving professional journalism, 157
    inspiration from, 129–30
    legacy, 29–30, 158
    on national media research project, 22
    Project Censored launched by, 21
Johnson, Adam, 74
Johnson, Nicholas, 24
journalism. *See also* investigative journalism
    Bureau of Investigative Journalism, 45–46, 76–77
    communication and inspiration, 36
    journalistic balance, 93
    journalist rights and responsibilities, 90–92, 94
    solutions, 34
Journal of Personality and Social Psychology, 200
Junk Food News, 14–15, 26
    American Sniper snubbed, 135–36
    deflated Super Bowl footballs, 136–37
    introduction, 129–31

potential presidential candidates,
138–40
Williams, R., suicide, 137–38
justified homicides. *See also* police
killings
double standards, 153–55
FBI on, 58–59
as News Abuse, 151–57
unequal coverage of riots and
celebrations, 155–57

Kafka, Franz, 182
Kashmir, women resistance, 29
APDP, 282–83, 286
arrests, 279
half widows, 285–86
hijab as pride and identity, 295
Kashmiri Women in Peace and
Disarmament, 283
media portrayal, 294–96
military presence and torture,
278–79
overview, 277–79
protests and demonstrations, 283–84
role of women, 282–84
sexual integrity, 295
sexual violence and, 286–87
women under occupation, 284–87
Katis, Tom, 261, 264
Katz, Jesse, 232–33
Kazi, Seema, 283, 287
Kearns, Cristin, 73
Keim, Brandon, 65
Kennedy, John F., 144
Kerry, John, 46, 102–3, 231
on methane, 55
on Ukraine crisis, 104–5
Kill the Messenger (Schou), 247
King, Angus, 69
King, Martin Luther, Jr., 235
Kingsolver, Barbara, 12, 26
KLA. *See* Kosovo Liberation Army
Koch, Charles, 139
Koch, David, 139, 181
Koehler, Robert, 178
Korten, David, 308, 310
Kosovo Liberation Army (KLA), 266
Kramer, Becky, 172

Kuipers, Robert, 178–79
Kunugi, June, 117
Kurtz, Howard, 231
Kustlin, Mary Ellen, 67
Kyle, Chris, 135–36

L-3 Communications, 266
LaGesse, David, 238
Land-Air Inc., 268
Lartey, Jamiles, 60
Lauer, Matt, 192–93
Laughland, Oliver, 60
laws
CALEA, 82
Freedom of Information Act, 175
HHFKA, 71
Japan Designated Secrets Bill,
184–85
Muslim personal, 285
REDEEM Act, 125–26
Sarbanes-Oxley, 174
Telecommunications Act, 113
three-strikes, 123
USA PATRIOT Act, 94
Lazare, Sarah, 54
lead poisoning, 188
Leahy, Stephen, 83
Lee, Matt, 104
legacy media, 23
LePage, Paul, 147
Letterman, David, 143
Levin, Marc, 247
Lewis, Vernon B., Jr., 265
LGBTQ rights movement, 191, 307
Liberation, 58
life sentences, 26
New York Times on, 126
Proposition 47 and, 124
record highs among inmates, 122–26
three-strikes law and, 123
Limbaugh, Rush, 146
Limits to Growth report, 308
Lippman, Walter, 14
living systems principles, 310
locally oriented economic model, 309
Loory, Stuart H., 242
Los Angeles Times, 44, 55–56, 68, 84, 88
on "Dark Alliance: The Story behind

the Crack Explosion," 232–33,
    236, 241, 247
  Drop the IWord Campaign and, 195
  get Webb team, 232–33
  lynchings, 249

Maddow, Rachel, 141
Magie, Elizabeth, 190
Magna Carta, 24–25
Malaysian passenger airliner downing,
    104
Malcolm X, 235
Malcolm X Grassroots Movement, 313
male gaze theory
  impact studies, 193
  in media, 192–93
  media democracy and, 191–94
  overview, 191–92
Mann, Matt, 261
Manufacturing Consent (Herman and
    Chomsky), 132
Mayer, John, 181
Mazzetti, Mark, 47
McCauley, Lauren, 57
McChesney, Robert W., 23–24, 203
McCombs, Red, 264
McCorry, Kevin, 109–10
McFarlane, Robert, 259
McManus, Doyle, 233
media. See also Action Coalition for
    Media Education; corporate media;
    critical media literacy; Global
    Critical Media Literacy Project;
    social media
  ACME, 28
  assets in, 242–43
  Big Media, 210
  cooperative media assets, 242–43
  freedom on the line, 24–26
  glare, 240
  hegemonic values, 200
  legacy, 23
  literacy, 133–34
  male gaze theory in, 192–93
  objectivity claims, 131
  oppressed women portrayal, 294–96
  silence, 303
  SmartMediaEducation network, 210

Ukraine crisis covering, 102–7
  women in, 27
media democracy
  A2-B-C film cancellations and,
      183–87
  GAP and, 173–76
  halting FBI harassment in Cascadia,
      170–72
  independent media halting FBI
      harassment, 170–72
  male gaze theory and, 191–94
  Nuclear Savage: The Islands of Secret
      Project 4.1 documentary, 177–82
  overview, 169–70
  Race Forward and, 194–97
  From a Woman's Point of View radio
      show and, 187–90
Media Matters, 144
Meet the Press, 131
megaloads, 170–71
Meneses, Norwin, 230–31, 233, 239
methane, 54
  arctic warming and, 54–57
  burp of, 55
  Kerry on, 55
  levels at all-time high, 54
Meyer, Robinson, 80
militarism, 189
military. See also private military
    companies
  harassment of Palestine women,
      293–94
  India in Kashmir, 278–79
  Israel control of Gaza, 119
  sexual violence on Colombian
      children, 73–75, 99n70
Military Professional Resources Inc.
    (MPRI), 265–66, 274n52
Millender-McDonald, Juanita, 248
millennials, 133–34, 200, 207
Miller, Judith, 145–46
Minow, Newton, 134
misinformation, 12, 71, 201, 203
misperceptions, 17
Mitchell, John L., 236, 237
modern monetary theory (MMT), 310
Mohrenschildt, George de, 144
Monopoly game, 190
Monsanto, 64–65

GMOs in Ukraine, 106
Roundup, 67
Montana, Joe, 137
Morrison, Alastair, 265
motherhood, 221–22
Mother Jones, 80, 143
Mother's Day, 218–19
MoveOn.org, 203
Moving the Mountain (Gilman), 219
MPRI. *See* Military Professional
   Resources Inc.
MSNBC, 74, 131, 156
   pro Iraq invasion voices, 145–46
muckraking, 22–23, 25, 28, 249
Muslims
   Baga Massacre, 150–51
   personal law, 285
   reporting on, 150–51
mutualism, 313

Nader, Ralph, 94
National Academy of Science (NAS),
   80–81
National Institute of Dental Research
   (NIDR), 72–73
National Institutes of Health, 72
National Public Radio (NPR), 74–75
National Security Agency (NSA), 48,
   92, 175
   AURAGOLD program, 87–88, 91, 93
   ICREACH search engine, 78–79,
      91, 93
   surveillance, 94
Nation of Islam, 237
NATO. *See* North Atlantic Treaty
   Organization
Nature, 65
NBC Nightly News, 61–62
necessary illusions, 132
Nembhard, Jessica Gordon, 308, 313
neofascism, 269
neonicotinoid pesticides, 64–65
net neutrality, 26
   corporate providers threatening,
      112–15
   FCC and, 113–15
   Obama on, 113
   opponents, 114–15

networked fourth estate, 35
new activism, 315
New Economics Foundation, 309
new economy, 304–5
New Republic, 86
News Abuse
   celebrities and, 141–42
   conclusion, 157–58
   Ebola outbreak, 146–48
   examples, 130–31
   Fox News censorship, 142
   illusions of objectivity, 131–32
   Islamophobia and, 148–51
   justifiable homicides, 151–57
   Miller rewriting history, 145–46
   as propaganda, 140–41
   Williams, B. and O'Reilly
      controversy, 142–45
news perspectives, 205
Newsweek, 48, 81
newsworthiness, 36
New Yorker, 46
New York magazine, 143, 156
New York Times, 74, 88, 132, 249
   on Arctic Council, 55–56
   on Brown, M. shooting, 153
   on CIA, 242
   on Clinton, H., 139
   on "Dark Alliance: The Story behind
      the Crack Explosion," 233–34,
      236, 245
   deceitful news practices and, 144–46
   on drone strikes, 47
   Drop the IWord Campaign and, 195
   on geoengineering, 81
   on life sentences, 126
   on neonicotinoid pesticides, 65
   on PEN America, 58
   on *Verizon v. FCC*, 113
Next System Project, 302–3, 314–15
Nicaraguan drug traffickers, 229–31, 233,
   238–39, 240, 244
NIDR. *See* National Institute of Dental
   Research
Nisour Square killings, 260–61
nitrates, 42
No Apologies (Miller), 145–46
Nobel, Alfred, 189
Nobel Peace Prize, 189

No Child Left Behind, 208
no-fly lists, 270
no-growth ("steady-state") economy, 311
Nohl, Karsten, 88
North Atlantic Treaty Organization
        (NATO), 103
    bases encircling Russia and China,
        68–69
    TCC protected by, 256
    Ukraine crisis and, 106
NPR. *See* National Public Radio
NSA. *See* National Security Agency
nuclear attack plans, 188–89
Nuclear Savage: The Islands of Secret
        Project 4.1 documentary, 177–82
    cancellation, 177, 179
    decline, 182
    funding, 178
    media democracy and, 177–82
    prizes, 179
    reviews, 178–79
    sanitizing and truncating, 180–81
    suppressing, 181

Obama, Barack
    on American exceptionalism, 58
    on drone strikes, 47
    Iran nuclear deal, 132
    misinformation about, 201
    on net neutrality, 113
    Summit on Countering Violent
        Extremism, 149
    tax reform and, 40–41
    on torture, 75–77
    Ukraine crisis and, 103, 105–6
Ocean Conservancy, 56
The Oh Really? Factor (Hart), 144
oil, 148
Oliver, John, 15, 113
Operation Cast Lead, 127n7
Operation Protective Edge, 128n7, 138
order policing, 313
O'Reilly, Bill, 141, 153, 156–57
    false news reporting and, 143–44
    Williams, B., controversy, 142–45
Organic Consumers Association, 67
Orlowski, Jeff, 89
Orr, Kevyn, 50

Orwell, George, 182
Ostrander, Madeline, 51
Oswald, Lee Harvey, 144
Otis, John, 75
Oxfam
    addressing economic inequality, 40
    Even It Up campaign, 39–42
    global wealth study, 39–42

Pakistan, drone strikes, 45–47
Palestine, women resistance, 29
    arrests, 277
    environmental hazards and, 291–93
    fighting forced expulsion, 287–88
    GUPW, 281
    Israeli occupation effects, 287–94
    limited education access, 295–96
    loss of children, 287–91
    media portrayal, 294–96
    overview, 277–79
    role of women, 279–82
    sperm smuggling, 282
    threats and harassment by military,
        293–94
Palestine Liberation Organization (PLO),
    280
Pantsios, Anastasia, 67
Pariser, Eli, 203
Parry, Robert, 102–4, 229, 238
participatory planning, 311
Parvez, Khurram, 278
patriarchy, 219–21
PBS. *See* Public Broadcasting Service
PBS NewsHour, 79
PEN America, 57–58
Pentagon, 178
    bases encircling Russia and China,
        68–69
    Pentagon Papers, 173
Pesci, Joe, 180
PFLP. *See* Popular Front for the
    Liberation of Palestine
Phillips, Peter, 29–30, 130
Physicians for Social Responsibility, 189
Pilkington, Ed, 82–83, 92, 123
Piltz, Rick, 175
Pincus, Walter, 231–32, 241–42
PLO. *See* Palestine Liberation

Organization
pluralist model, 313
plutocracy, 134
PMCs. *See* private military companies
Podugu, Pooja, 150
police brutality, 313
Police Foundation, 61
police killings
    charges for, 60
    increase in, 58–60
    protests, 59–60
    unarmed black Americans, 60
    underreporting, 61
    Washington Post on, 60–61
political economy, 302–4
Pollin, Robert, 311
Popular Front for the Liberation of
    Palestine (PFLP), 280
Postman, Neil, 201
Potter, Will, 84–85
poverty, 271, 302
    call to alleviate, 62
    elimination, 311
    Gaza, 121
    rates of, 316n4
    reporting on, 61–62
Prince, Erik, 259, 261
private military companies (PMCs), 29
    Aegis Defense Systems, 258–59
    agents, 271
    analysis of, 269–72
    Blackwater, 259–61, 273n26
    Constellis Holdings, 261, 263–64
    DynCorp, 268–69
    Erinys, 264–65
    G4S, 266–68
    globalization of, 270
    Iraq War and, 257–58
    MPRI, 265–66, 274n52
    neofascism and, 269
    privatization of war and, 270
    services, 270
    TCC protected by, 256–58
    Triple Canopy, 261–63
privatization
    neo-liberal, 312
    of war, 270
    of water, 50
Project Censored, 199. *See also* Global

Critical Media Literacy Project
    campus affiliates program, 35
    Jensen launching, 21
    Jensen's definition of censorship
        and, 22
    labels rejected by, 23
    model for GCMLP, 209
    review process, 37–38
    service learning and, 208
    student involvement, 22
Project Censored mission
    audience lack of education, time,
        interest and, 12–13
    junk food news, 14–15
    ownership and, 13–14
    resources, 15
    self-censorship, 15–16, 19n18
    time and space, 14
propaganda, 22
    News Abuse as, 140–41
Proposition 47, 124
PR Watch, 65
Psaki, Jen, 104–5
public airwaves, 27
Public Broadcasting Service (PBS), 177,
    179–81
public ownership, 312
public-public partnerships, 312
Putin, Vladimir, 103–5
Pyatt, Geoffrey, 106

al-Qaeda
    drone strikes on, 45–48
    ISIS and, 151
Quayle, Dan, 269
Quinn, Jack, 264

Race Forward
    approach and vision, 194–95
    Drop the IWord Campaign, 195
    Facing Race conference, 196
    media democracy and, 194–97
    racial justice movement
        commitment, 195–96
    systematic approach, 196–97
racial justice movement, 195–96
racism, 59, 152, 237

corporate media and, 147
institutional, 313
structural, 313
Radford, Tim, 88–89
RAINN. *See* Rape, Abuse & Incest
National Network
rainwater harvesting, 49, 51–52
Rand, Paul, 125
Rape, Abuse & Incest National Network
(RAINN), 87
rape kits
ignored, 86
untested, 85–87
Raw Story, 145
Reagan, Ronald, 145, 188, 259
Rebel Girls (Taft), 223
Reclaiming Public Ownership (Cumbers),
312
reclamation of commons, 305
REDEEM Act, 125–26
reforestation, 80
Rendall, Steve, 62
renewable energy
Bonaire, Iceland, Denmark, Hawaii,
63
Costa Rica and, 62–63
Republican Party, 201
research, 12, 72–73
International Peace Research
Association Foundation, 284
Jensen on, 22
restorative economics, 310
restorative justice, 123
in prisons, 109
successes, 109–10
for violent schools, 108–11
Restorative Justice for Oakland Youth
(RJOY), 108–11
Revolutionary Armed Forces of
Colombia (FARC), 73, 75
Ribeiro, John, 114
Ribeiro da Silva, José Cláudio, 84–85
Rice, Jerry, 137
Rich, Frank, 132
rights. *See also* civil liberties
European Court of Human Rights,
123
human rights movement, 270
Human Rights Watch, 57

journalist, 90–92, 94
LGBTQ rights movement, 191, 307
Ripley, Jessica, 86
Rivera, Geraldo, 154, 156
The River Project, 51–52
RJOY. *See* Restorative Justice for Oakland
Youth
Robinson, William, 269
Rodger, Elliot, 154
Rodrigue, George, 238
Rogers, Ed, 145
Romney, Mitt, 139
Ross, Alexander Reid, 171–72
Ross, Freeway Rick, 230–33, 239
Roth, Veronica, 223–24
Rubio, Marco, 140
Ruiz, César, 74
Rundquist, Soren, 67
Russia, 68–69. *See also* Ukraine crisis

Sandline International, 258
San Francisco Chronicle, 195
San Jose Mercury News, 110, 227–30, 235,
238, 240–46
Santo, Maria do Espírito, 84–85
Sarbanes-Oxley, 174
SAS. *See* Special Air Services
Satterthwaite, Meg, 77
Scahill, Jeremy, 46
Schiffrin, Anya, 249
Schoen, Seth, 82, 92–93
Schor, Juliet, 308, 309
Schou, Nick, 238, 247
Schuessler, Jennifer, 58
Schulman, Jeremy, 80
Schumacher Center, 308
Schweickart, David, 308, 309
Science, 64
Scorsese, Martin, 180
sea levels, rising, 88–89
Securicor, 267
self-censorship, 15–16, 19n18, 186–87
self-help, 313
Sentencing Project, 122, 125
September 11, 2001 terrorist attacks,
202, 264
service learning, 28, 208–9
sex trafficking, 269

sexual integrity, 295
sexual violence
    on Colombian children by U.S.
        military, 73–75, 99n70
    Kashmir women, 286–87
Shakhova, Natalia, 55
Shane, Scott, 47
Sharoni, Simona, 296
Sheard, Whit, 56
Shepherd, Chuck, 15
Shultz, Jim, 48
signal to noise ratio, 17
Simon, Joel, 23, 90–91
Simon, Michele, 64
Singh, Rajendra, 52
60 Minutes, 227
SmartMediaEducation network, 210
Smiley, Tavis, 62
Snow, John, 269
Snowden, Edward, 78, 87, 93, 94, 175
socialism, 306–7, 309, 312, 316n9
social media, 11–12, 134, 205–6
    Facebook, 203, 217
solidarity
    economy networks, 314
    Galeano on, 34–35
solutions journalism, 34
sourcing, 132
Sparks, Keith, 75
Special Air Services (SAS), 265
sperm smuggling, 282
Speth, Gus, 313
Spicer, Tim, 258–59
Der Spiegel, 88
Spokesman-Review, 172
Stangler, Cole, 112
Stanton, Elizabeth Cady, 191
Stars and Stripes, 142
Steingraber, Sandra, 188
Stewart, Jon, 15
stop and frisk, 313
structural racism, 313
Sugar Association, 71
sugar consumption
    promoting with tobacco industry
        tactics, 71–73
    tooth decay and, 72–73
    WHO recommendations, 71
Summit on Countering Violent

Extremism, 149
superweeds, 67–68
Swaine, Jon, 60
Syngenta, 64–65
Syria, 151
systemic solutions for systemic crisis
    alternative models and approaches,
        308–13
    limitations, 314
    Next System Project, 314–15
    overview, 301–3
    real alternatives, 306–8
    underreported institutional
        innovation, 303–6

Taft, Jessica, 223
Taliban, 150
Tantaros, Andrea, 147
tax reform, 40–41
TCC. See transnational capital class
Tea Party, 131, 145
TechTimes, 88
Telecommunications Act, 113
Tellus Institute, 308
TEPCO. See Tokyo Electric Power
    Company
thallium, 42
Thiede, Travis, 170
three-legged calves, 14, 18n12
three-strikes law, 123
Time magazine, 74–75, 235
Todd, Chuck, 131
Tokyo Electric Power Company
    (TEPCO), 52–53
torture
    CIA, of terrorism suspects, 75–77
    of Kashmir women, 278–79
    Obama on, 75–77
transnational capital class (TCC)
    financial core, 271
    NATO protecting, 256
    overview of twenty-first-century
        fascism, 255–58
    PMCs protecting, 256–58
    war on terror and, 256
TreePeople, 51
Trilateral Commission, 256
Triple Canopy, 261–63

truth emergency, 201–3
Truthout, 54, 86
truth telling, 26, 27
tsunamis, 54
Turness, Deborah, 192–93
Tuskegee syphilis experiment, 235–36,
    245

UCS. *See* Union of Concerned Scientists
Udry, Sue, 171
Ukraine crisis, 26
    fiscal and humanitarian, 107
    Kerry on, 104–5
    media covering, 102–7
    NATO and, 106
    Obama and, 103, 105–6
    Putin and, 105
    Wall Street Journal on, 104
UN. *See* United Nations
underreporting, 11, 14
    Fukushima nuclear disaster, 54
    institution innovation, 303–6
    Kashmir sexual violence, 286–87
    Palestine limited education access,
        295–96
    police killings, 61
Unger, Roberto Mangabeira, 308
UNHCR. *See* United Nations High
    Commissioner for Refugees
Union of Concerned Scientists (UCS),
    71–72
United Nations (UN)
    International Atomic Energy Agency,
        52
    International Year of Cooperatives,
        304
    Security Council, 265
United Nations High Commissioner for
    Refugees (UNHCR), 69–70
United Nations Reliefs Works Agency
    (UNRWA), 70
USA PATRIOT Act, 94
USA Today, 81, 195
    on Oxfam, 41
US Department of Agriculture (USDA),
    66–68
USS Cole, 259

Validated Independent News stories
    (VINs), 37
Vancouver Province, 84
Vega, Renan, 74–75
Ventura, Jesse, 146
Verizon Communications Inc., 112, 113
Verizon v. FCC, 113
Vice News, 82, 92–93
VINs. *See* Validated Independent News
    stories
violence, 314. *See also* sexual violence
    AVP, 108–9
    corporate media on sensationalistic,
        156
virtual playgrounds, 207
Voices Unheard, 283
von Suttner, Bertha, 189

Wackenhut, 267, 275n59
Wade, Lizzie, 63
wages, 302, 315n1
Wall Street Journal
    circulation, 13
    on employee-owned firms, 304
    on Ukraine crisis, 104
war. *See also* Cold War; Iraq War
    Congress resolution, 136
    Falklands War, 143–44
    privatization of, 270
    water, 49
Ward, Christine, 125
war on terror, 137
    advocates, 264
    CNN and, 147
    TCC and, 256
War Times, 123
Washbourne, Jacob C., 262
Washington Post, 88, 241
    black paranoia tone, 234–35
    climate change denial, 145
    on "Dark Alliance: The Story behind
        the Crack Explosion," 231–32
    Drop the IWord Campaign and, 195
    on geoengineering, 81
    on global warming, 89
    on neonicotinoid pesticides, 65
    on police killings, 60–61

on Triple Canopy, 262
Washington Times, 172, 242
wastewater dumping, 42–44
water
    barons, 49
    contamination, 42–44
    grabbing, 49
    remunicipalization, 50
    shortages, 49–50
    shutoff protests, 50–51
    wars, 49
Watt, Steven, 77
wealth, 302. *See also* poverty;
    transnational capital class
    distribution, 310
    global wealth, 38–42
weapons of mass destruction (WMDs),
    202
Web 2.0, 200
Web 3.0, 200
Webb, Gary, 28, 227–29
    blacklisted, 246
    continued work, 246–47
    death of, 247
    investigation, 238–39, 242–44,
        248–49
    Los Angeles Times team against,
        232–33
    media glare shifted to, 240
    recovering lost history, 248
    reporting, 232, 234
    resignation, 246
    uncovering truths, 237
Wells, Ida B., 249
WHCA. *See* White House
    Correspondents' Association
Wheeler, Tom, 114, 115
whistleblowers, 173–75
White, Jack E., 235, 237
White House Correspondents'
    Association (WHCA), 132
White House Council on Women and
    Girls, 85–86
WHO. *See* World Health Organization
Wilce, Rebekah, 65
Wild Idaho Rising Tide (WIRT), 170
Wilkinson, Frank, 171
Williams, Brian, 62, 141, 192
    false news reporting and, 142–43

O'Reilly controversy, 142–45
Williams, Jodi, 189
Williams, Robin, 137–38
Willis, Michael, 89
Wilson, Darren, 153
Wilson, Woodrow, 218
Wired, 63, 65, 114
WIRT. *See* Wild Idaho Rising Tide
With Her in Ourland (Gilman), 219
WMDs. *See* weapons of mass destruction
Wolff, Richard, 308
Wolfowitz, Paul, 176
Woman's Point of View radio show,
    187–90
women. *See also* Kashmir, women
    resistance; Palestine, women
    resistance
    feminism, 219–20
    feminist dystopia, 219
    in media, 27
    White House Council on Women
        and Girls, 85–86
work-and-spend cycle, 309
World Bank, 52, 106, 176, 255
World Economic Forum, 41, 256
World Health Organization (WHO)
    on sugar consumption, 71
    water standards, 117
World Refugee Day, 69
Worstall, Tim, 41
Wright, Erik Olin, 308

xenophobia, 147, 149

Yanukovich, Viktor, 104
Yeh, Jennifer, 112
Yemen drone strikes, 137
Yes? Magazine, 50–51, 109
Yorio, Joseph, 261
Yost, Helen, 170–72
Yurganov, Leonid, 55

Zenko, Micah, 47
zero tolerance, 313
Zia, Ather, 284, 294
Zinn, Howard, 127